A Great Society?

A Great Society?

BERTRAM M. GROSS, EDITOR

Basic Books, Inc., Publishers · *New York | London*

To Arthur F. and Imogene Bentley

The Authors

DANIEL BELL. Professor of Sociology, Columbia University; formerly editor of "The New Leader" (1941–); labor editor of *Fortune;* author of *History of Marxian Socialism* (1952), *Work and Its Discontents* (1956), *The End of Ideology* (1960); editor of *The New American Right* (1955), revised as *The Radical Right* (1963).

KENNETH E. BOULDING. Professor of Economics and Research Director, Center for Research on Conflict Resolution, University of Michigan; formerly Danforth Visiting Professor, International Christian University, Tokyo, Japan (1963–1964); received American Council of Learned Societies Prize for Distinguished Scholarship in the Humanities (1962) and other awards; author of *The Meaning of the Twentieth Century* (1964), *Disarmament and the Economy* (ed., with Emile Benoit, 1963), *Conflict and Defense* (1962), *Linear Programming and the Theory of the Firm* (ed., with W. A. Spivey, 1960), *Principles of Economic Policy* (1959), *The Skills of the Economist* (1958), *The Image* (1956), *The Organizational Revolution* (1953), *A Reconstruction of Economics* (1950), *There Is a Spirit* (1945), *Economics of Peace* (1945), *Economic Analysis* (1941).

PETER F. DRUCKER. Professor of Management at the Graduate Business School, New York University, and a management consultant; formerly an economist for various international banks, American correspondent for a group of British newspapers, Professor of Politics and Philosophy at Bennington College; author of *The New Society* (1950), *The Practice of Management* (1954), *America's Next Twenty Years* (1957), *The Landmarks of Tomorrow* (1960), *Managing for Results* (1964).

BERTRAM M. GROSS. Professor of Political Science and Director, National Planning Studies Program, Maxwell School of Citizenship and Public

Affairs, Syracuse University; Chairman, Executive Committee, International Group for Studies in National Planning (INTERPLAN); editor of National Planning Series, Syracuse University Press; formerly visiting professor at Harvard Business School, University of California (Berkeley), and the Hebrew University; Fellow of the Center for Advanced Study in the Behaviorial Sciences (1961–1962); Executive Secretary of the President's Council of Economic Advisors; member of Arlington County Planning Commission, Northern Virginia Regional Planning Commission, and First Chairman of the National Capital Regional Planning Council; author of *The State of the Nation: Social Systems Accounting* (1966), editor of *Action Under Planning* (1966), author of *The Managing of Organizations* (2 vols., 1964), *The Legislative Struggle: A Study in Social Combat* (1953).

NORTON E. LONG. Professor of Political Science, Brandeis University; formerly Assistant Administrator, National Housing Administration; Professor of Political Science, Michigan State University (1955–1957) and Northwestern University (1958–1961); author of *The Polity* (1962), *The Corporation in the Modern Society* (1960).

FRANK E. MANUEL. Professor of History, New York University; Fellow of the Center for Advanced Study in the Behavioral Sciences (1962–1963); author of *The New World of Henri Saint-Simon* (1956), *The Eighteenth Century Confronts the Gods* (1959), *The Prophets of Paris* (1962), *Isaac Newton, Historian* (1963), *Shapes of Philosophical History* (1965).

HERBERT MARCUSE. Professor of Philosophy, University of California; formerly Research Fellow at the Russian Research Center, Harvard University and at the Russian Institute, Columbia University, and Professor of Philosophy, Brandeis University; author of *Eros and Civilization: A Philosophical Inquiry into Freud* (1955), *Soviet Marxism: A Critical Analysis* (1958), *Reasons and Revolution: Hegel and the Rise of Social Theory* (1941), *One Dimensional Man: Studies in the Ideology of Advanced Industrial Society* (1964).

MICHAEL MARIEN. Graduate Assistant, Maxwell Graduate School of Citizenship and Public Affairs, Syracuse University; formerly Budget Analyst, University of California; organizational consultant, Unitarian Universalist Association; poverty worker, Appalachian Volunteers (VISTA Associates).

HANS J. MORGENTHAU. Albert A. Michelson Distinguished Service Professor of Political Science and Modern History, and Director, Center for the Study of American Foreign and Military Policy, the University of Chicago; formerly Professor at the Institute of International and Economic Studies, Madrid (1932–1935); member of the Institute for Advanced Study, Princeton; author of *Politics Among Nations* (1946, 1954, 1960, 1966), *The Purpose of American Politics* (1960), *Politics in the Twentieth Century* (3 vols., 1962).

DON K. PRICE. Dean, Graduate School of Public Administration, Harvard

University, formerly Associate Director, Public Administration Clearing House (1946–1953), Deputy Chairman, Research and Development Board, Department of Defense (1952–1953), Vice-President of the Ford Foundation (1954–1958), President, American Association for the Advancement of Science (1965–1966); author of *Government and Science* (1954), *The Scientific Estate* (1965).

SIDNEY RATNER. Professor of History, Rutgers—The State University; member of the Institute for Advanced Study, Princeton (1956–1957), author of *American Taxation: Its History as a Social Force in Democracy* (1942); co-author of *John Dewey: Philosopher of Science and Freedom* (1950), *Vision and Action* (1953), *Life, Language, Law* (1957), *Essays in American Histiography* (1960), editor of *Inquiry into Inquiries* (1954), co-editor of John Dewey and Arthur F. Bentley, *A Philosophical Correspondance, 1931–1951* (1964).

ALVIN TOFFLER. Author; member of the sociology faculty, New School for Social Research; member of the Board of Directors of the Salzburg Seminar in American Studies and the Advisory Board of the American Foundation for Continuing Education; formerly an associate editor of *Fortune;* author of *The Culture Consumers* (1964), *Future Shock* (1968).

ROBIN M. WILLIAMS, JR. Professor of Sociology, Cornell University; Senior Statistical Analyst, European Theater of Operations, U.S. War Department (1943–1946), Director of the Social Science Research Center, Cornell Universtiy (1949–1954); co-author of *The American Soldier* (Vols. I and II, 1949), *American Society: A Sociological Interpretation* (1951, 1960), *Strangers Next Door: Ethnic Relations in American Communities* (1964).

Foreword 🦆 A White House–Academia Dialogue STEPHEN K. BAILEY

This volume is the first serious and concerted effort by members of the American university community to appraise the actual and potential contents behind the political slogan of a "Great Society" in America.

Its origins go back to discussions among a few professors of political science at Syracuse University during the early fall of 1960. We felt that the predominantly economic orientation embodied in the New Deal and the Fair Deal did not provide a broad enough basis for the presentation of significant issues to the American public during the 1960 presidential election. We were more impressed by the spirit than by the content of John F. Kennedy's call to "get America moving again." We felt it more important to indicate *where* and *how* America should move. Accordingly, we suggested that the political campaigning on domestic issues become more adjusted to a "politics of affluence" rather than concentrating so much on full employment, economic growth, and economic security. We made certain specific proposals for attention to the great human needs that would emerge as America made greater progress toward meeting minimum economic needs. Our proposals were turned aside with the firm (albeit flattering) comment by a campaign manager that "such things had not been said before . . ."

During the subsequent three years, we were delighted to note President Kennedy's pioneering efforts on behalf of many things that had not been said or done before at the White House. Through personal action and example, both he and Mrs. Kennedy raised the level and the quality of American aspirations.

In 1964, with the economic growth sparked by the Kennedy administration already moving us in the direction of a new politics of affluence, both President Johnson and Senator Goldwater campaigned on moral and ethical issues. In his May 1964 address at the University of Michigan, President Johnson unveiled an approach to domestic policy that, although built on the Square Deal, the New Freedom, the New Deal, the Fair Deal, and the New Frontier, promised to go far beyond them all:

In your time . . . we have the opportunity to move not only toward the rich society and the powerful society, but upward to the Great Society. The Great Society rests on abundance and liberty for all. It demands an end to poverty and racial injustice, to which we are totally committed in our time. . . . But most of all, the Great Society is not a safe harbor, a resting place, a final objective, a finished work. It is a challenge constantly renewed, beckoning us toward a destiny where the meaning of our lives matches the marvelous products of our labor. . . . I intend to establish working groups to prepare a series of White House conferences and meetings on the cities, on natural beauty, on the quality of education, and on other emerging challenges.

Within a few weeks' time the President and the White House staff organized the largest, most detailed, and most highly differentiated *ad hoc* mobilization of expertise in our country's history. Indeed, the complexity of this operation was so great that, in his *The Making of the President, 1964,* Theodore H. White could merely express the hope that "some day, some historian of ideas in politics should find the time to tell the full story, with all its anecdotes . . ." Specifically, he urged that this history tell the story

of the gathering of task forces of American scholars and experts through the summer of 1964; of their work on their various specialties (education, cities, beauty, taxes, foreign aid, transportation and other areas, to a total of fourteen); of the binding of their reports by November 15th, of their reexamination by governmental task forces in November and December 1964; of the boiling down of their ideas into three fat black books described as an "encyclopedia of American problems, of what has to be done"; of the final rendering down of these encyclopedias by December 25th into one volume of legislative proposals, supervised by Moyers, the thirty-year old thinker who is the chief companion of the conscience of the President; and their final presentation to Congress as bills for enactment in the Spring of 1965 [pp. 396–397].

In the spring of 1965, as the Congress was moving forward rapidly toward the enactment of these many legislative proposals, some of us once again began to ponder the emerging character of domestic policy. At that time, with an abundance of detail on *where* and *how* we were moving, some of us felt it imperative to initiate a broad and general appraisal. With my encouragement, a plan for a faculty seminar on the Great Society was developed by a committee of professors from four departments in Syracuse University's Maxwell Graduate School of Citizenship and Public Affairs: Bertram M. Gross, Professor of Political Science; S. M. Miller, Professor of Sociology: Jerry Miner, Associate Professor of Economics; and Robert J. Shafer, Professor of History. The committee obtained financial support from Mrs. Imogene Bentley, widow of Arthur F. Bentley, one of America's foremost philosophers and political scientists. It then arranged for the preparation and personal presentation of major papers by prominent scholars from other universities: Brandeis, California (San Diego), Chicago, Columbia, Cornell, Harvard, Michigan, the New School, N.Y.U., and Rutgers. This group included some of the Johnson administration's strongest critics as well as "neutrals" and supporters.

In view of the national significance of this effort, I sent the seminar plan to President Johnson. On May 6, 1965, the President responded by suggesting five specific questions for our consideration.

As editor of this volume, Professor Gross—in consultation with his committee—has taken on the task of trying to answer these questions in Chapter 1. In so doing, he has drawn heavily on the views of the authors of the subsequent chapters. He has also profited by an inter-generational dialogue with our graduate students. Four graduate students wrote special essays answering one or another of the questions. The nineteen graduate students in Professor Gross's Fall 1966 seminar on national policy making and planning played an active role in analyzing all the questions. One of the students who both prepared an essay and took part in the seminar has assisted in writing the first chapter.

The discussion in the student seminar inevitably led to the feeling that both students and professors were eager to continue the dialogue by addressing some questions to President Johnson. This led to the unique structure of this book, whereby the eleven "guest" papers are sandwiched between "The President's Questions—And Some Answers" (Chapter 1) and "Some Questions for Presidents" (Chapter 13). As a result, the unprecedented White House–Academia dialogue in this volume, particularly in the first and last chapters, should be unusually rewarding to students, teachers and practitioners of government in America.

Most of "The President's Questions—And Some Answers" center on four eminently practical issues: the administration of federal programs at the local level, public-private collaboration, pilot projects, and individual excellence and creativity. The President's fifth question, "What are the international dimensions of the Great Society?" is at a higher level. I find one of the Gross-Marien answers particularly significant, although deceptively simple: that we should never refer to *the* Great Society, but rather to *a* Great Society. This innocent change from "the" to "a" suggests the importance of a more mature realization of the potentiality of other peoples in a world which is rapidly becoming, to use Peter F. Drucker's phrase, a "global village."

The next eleven chapters apply a wide variety of perspectives to an even wider range of topics. Distinguished scholars from the fields of political science, public and business administration, sociology, economics, history, and philosophy use their knowledge and wisdom in examining system and historical models, social concepts, the individual in society, local and private initiative, changing political alignments, our affluent economy, big science, the arts, and the contributions of Arthur F. Bentley to the study of social processes. Whether the reader is in agreement or not, all should certainly find stimulation in the identification by Robin M. Williams, Jr., of "major institutional rigidities in American life"; the numerous criticisms by Herbert Marcuse of "the existing not so great society"; Norton Long's advocacy of moving from a "poverty of opportunity" to "spiritual full employment"; the warning by Hans J. Morgenthau that we should not assume the roles of missionary, crusader, or world policeman; the penetrating call by Daniel Bell toward rethinking some of our basic approaches to decision-making; Peter F. Drucker's view that the Great Society rhetoric "addresses itself to yesterday" and that "new political alignments" are needed to handle "new realities"; Frank Manuel's noble vision of the end of "The Age of Heroes" and the beginning of "The Age of Man"; the assessment of "the space-military complex" by Kenneth Boulding, and the advocacy of "a modest society" which moves from a "cowboy economy" of exploitation to a "spaceman economy" of extreme conservation; the warning by Don K. Price of new problems of political responsibility created by rapid growth of science; Alvin Toffler's suggestion of "parallel professionalism" to help develop a new renaissance of the arts; and Sidney Ratner's explanation of Arthur F. Bentley's thinking on social relativism and the transactional approach to studying man-in-society. Indeed, the authors and their contributions follow in the great tradition of Arthur F. Bentley by fusing science, values, and social action.

With this very thought of continuity in mind, the final chapter, "Some Questions for Presidents," raises some fundamental issues which will remain of lasting political significance well after the 1968 elections. The major question raised is "What should be the new tests of presidential leadership?" In reply, Professor Gross suggests that the White House should become "a center of creative stability in the midst of turbulent change." He pins this down by a series of highly controversial propositions concerning five new "presidential roles." Liberals may be shocked by his attack on the "pie economics" of economic growth (which he himself had earlier contributed to), the limitations of Welfare State minima, and the idea that poverty can lead to world war. Conservatives may be shocked by his attack on "do-badders," the "illfare lobby," "inhumanists," and "communoids," together with his advocacy of a "newer economics" and "triadic comity" among the United States, Russia, and China. Everyone concerned with public affairs will be interested in his comments on the "intelligence gap," the United States as a "transitional society," the social systems approach to the "City of Man," "synergic statesmanship," and politics as the art not of the possible but of the improbable.

Many of the specific ideas in this volume, of course, are already being seriously considered or acted on by public or private agencies. Perhaps the most dramatic of these is the proposal—first publicly discussed in the course of our Great Society Seminar—for an annual Social Report of the President which, together with the Economic Report, will contribute to an over-all assessment of the state of the nation. By early 1967 it became widely known that work was under way to prepare professional materials that could be used in proposing an initial Social Report. The rationale was expressed in a working memorandum by the two co-chairmen of the project, William Gorham, Assistant Secretary of Health, Education, and Welfare, and Daniel Bell, Professor of Sociology at Columbia University:

No society in history has, as yet, made a coherent and unified effort to assess those elements in the society which facilitate and which bar each individual from realizing to the fullest extent possible his talents and abilities, in order to allow him to find a job, or establish a career commensurate with his talents, to live a full and healthy life equal to his biological potential, to establish the conditions for an adequate standard of living which allows him to live in a civilized fashion, and which provides a physical and social environment which enhances his sense of life. We believe that these are aims implicit in the American purpose. We believe that the means of realizing these are possible. If it is agreed that this is an appropriate and adequate focus, the function of the Social Report would be to provide a continuing assessment of our abilities to realize these aims.[1]

As one who wrote a book on the emergence of the Employment Act of 1946, I am honored at the opportunity twenty-one years later to observe (and indirectly take part in) this new development in democratic institutions: the first effort of any government to provide its people with an annual stock-taking in terms that are not only economic, but which also express the human and cultural values that economic measures are expected to serve.

Although written almost entirely by academicians, this is not a traditional "academic" volume. The authors have taken courageous and controversial stands—well beyond the range of scientific verification—on vital matters of public policy. They have also opened up new vistas for scientific analysis, as already evidenced by the recently published "social indicator" volumes of *The Annals*.[2] Such "fall-out" can only result in a new vitality for the social sciences. Indeed, in the exciting (and conflicting) views expressed in this volume, I sense the same kind of drama which must have pervaded the early days of rail, auto, and air travel and which is presently associated with space travel and investigations into the atom and the secrets of life itself. From this combination of analysis and prescription, I sense the beginning of an era in which the social sciences may contribute as much to our lives as the physical sciences already have and continue to do. This dialogue may hopefully serve as a starting point for an enlarging process of government and academia working together with others to build a truly Great Society in a more peaceful world.

•NOTES

1. Quoted in Bertram M. Gross and Michael Springer, "A New Orientation in American Government," Chapter 1 in *Social Goals and Indicators for American Society: I, The Annals* of The American Academy of Political and Social Science, Vol. 371 (May 1967).

2. Vol. 371 (May 1967) and Vol. 373 (September 1967).

Acknowledgments

On behalf of the contributors and myself, I wish to convey my sincere appreciation to the many individuals who have contributed to the development of this volume. It is fitting to begin by thanking the other members of the Great Society Seminar committee—Professors S. M. Miller, sociology (now at New York University); Jerry Miner, economics; and Robert J. Shafer, history. Through their generous assistance the Seminar series came into being.

Other busy individuals from several major universities and a variety of academic disciplines participated in the Seminar, making significant contributions as commentators. Their carefully prepared rejoinders gave direction both to the course of the Seminar and to the revisions of the papers which make up this volume. We extend our thanks to Max Bloom, business administration; Jesse Burkhead, economics; Alan Campbell, metropolitan studies; Stanley Diamond, anthropology (The New School for Social Research); Faqir Muhammad, political science (Queens College); Julian Friedman, political science; Andrew Hacker, political science (Cornell University); John Honey, political science; Arnold Honig, physics; Max M. Kampelman, lawyer (Treasurer-Counsel to the American Political Science Association); Louis Krasner, music; David R. Krathwohl, Dean, School of Education; Maynard C. Krueger, economics (University of Chicago); Gerard J. Mangone, Associate Dean, Maxwell School; Paul Meadows, sociology; Donald Meiklejohn, public affairs, philosophy; Daniel P. Moynihan, political science (Harvard-M.I.T. Joint Urban Center); David Owen, English; George Stern, psychology; Sidney Sufrin, economics; Thomas S. Szasz, psychiatry (New York Upstate Medical Center); Victor A. Thompson, political science (University of Illinois); Gabriel Vahanian, religion; and George

Wiley, formerly Deputy Director of the Congress of Racial Equality (CORE).

A number of graduate students deserve recognition for actively participating in the sessions, working out responses to the President's questions, and assisting in other capacities. David Curzon labored valiantly in organizing the Great Society Seminar and in consulting with various contributors in editorial matters. Lambert Wenner assisted in the editing of the final manuscript of this volume.

We are especially indebted to President Lyndon B. Johnson for presenting the Great Society Seminar with five challenging public policy questions; to Dean Stephen K. Bailey of the Maxwell School for encouraging us in the search for answers and in the preparation of our "counter-questions"; and to Mrs. Imogene Bentley for providing the necessary funds.

BERTRAM M. GROSS

Syracuse, New York
January 1968

Contents

A Great Society?

Chapter 1

The President's Questions—and Some Answers BERTRAM M. GROSS AND MICHAEL MARIEN

In May 1965, President Lyndon B. Johnson presented the following questions to the Arthur F. Bentley Seminar on The Great Society at Syracuse University:

1. How can Federal programs be administered to permit maximum initiative and control on the local level, yet avoid waste, inefficiency, feuding, and corruption which serve to discredit these programs? (This problem is at the very heart of the War on Poverty, for example, in its emphasis on community development.)

2. What are the best techniques for bringing public and private agencies into collaborative efforts without endangering the independence of the private agencies?

3. How can the Federal Government initiate pilot projects in order to test new types of programs without being obliged to conduct them simultaneously in every state and community?

4. What are the best ways for recognizing individual excellence and individual creativity so that the Great Society does not simply deal with individuals in the mass?

5. What are the international dimensions of the Great Society?

In these questions President Johnson has dealt with certain historic issues in the American system: federalism, relations between government and private enterprise, experimentation in government, excellence and creativity, and our involvement with other nations. Despite their modern phrasing, these are old questions that have been with us since the founding of the Republic. Yet they are questions particularly relevant to today's Politics of Affluence, whether described as Johnson's "Great Society," Rockefeller's "Just Society," Reagan's "Creative Society," or Goldwater's "Free Society."

These are not simply questions confronting President Johnson and other top political leaders. They are foremost among the questions pressing on all the top officials of the government and all members of Congress—and they may well be even more pressing in the future. Answers to some of these questions will loom large in many of the policy statements of candidates for President and Vice President in 1968, 1972, and 1976.

Although time will make many of our tentative answers obsolete, the questions will remain relevant—even beyond the Vietnam tragedy and the bloodshed in our own streets. We can deal only with the present, and we have done so with the suggestions from the authors of the subsequent chapters, students,[1] academic colleagues, and "practical men." Yet, the following can at best only serve as the starting point for a new dialogue. Indeed, we believe that the most significant contribution at this time may be simply to restate the President's questions in more specific and up-to-date form. Operational answers, of course, can only be developed on the firing line of governmental decision-making.

A serious pursuit of the President's five questions inevitably leads back to the two basic questions originally formulated in starting our Great Society inquiry:

1. Just what is—and should become—the content of the Great Society idea?
2. How can we best measure desired and actual change in any society?

The first question, of course, has to do with the most complex and controversial aspects of human values, national purposes, and political leadership. The second question goes to the heart of our ability to understand the complexities of social reality. For the United States is not only in transition, but is probably in the throes of one of the most perplexing transitions in today's world. A Great Society idea—or any other idea about a desired future—can be successful only to the degree that we know what is happening in the present.

These two critical questions will be dealt with in the final chapter of this book. In answer to the first, the author will touch on such basic themes as a "newer" economics, the transeconomic quality of life, the future of Great Society programs, and the coming tests of presidential leadership. The response to the second question will probe the nature of our information (and misinformation) on change in America and the world. In both cases, the "answers" will take the form of questions to the current President—and those interested in succeeding him in the White House.

FEDERAL PROGRAMS AT THE LOCAL LEVEL

The President's first question raises some of the most intractable issues of "creative federalism." The question bluntly acknowledges the dangers of "waste, inefficiency, feuding, and corruption" sometimes associated with control at the local level. The dilemma is that too much federal control leads to conspicuous duplication and lack of initiative and responsibility on the local levels. On the other hand, federal funds often go astray at the hands of "unenlightened" local interests, leading to "waste, feuding, and corruption." Specifically, President Johnson points out that "this problem is at the very heart of the War on Poverty, for example, in its emphasis on community development." In answering this question, we shall use the War on Poverty as our starting point.

PRESIDENTIAL LEADERSHIP ON URBAN BATTLEFRONTS

As Commander-in-Chief, President Johnson has already visited the front lines of our armed forces in Asia. But neither he nor the Vice-President has toured the poverty lines in our own country. Here a new urban battlefront has erupted.

The summer 1967 disorders vividly underlined a situation in which there should be no retreat. The commitment to all American citizens should be at least as great—if not greater—than the commitment to a small Asian government halfway around the world. Backing off from the constructive battlefronts of rebuilding our cities and warring on poverty will invite further eruption on destructive battlefronts, resulting in death, injury, property destruction, lost wages and profits, vast public expenses, anxiety, suspicion, and a further decay of American cities.

But the problem goes even deeper. Disorders in so-called "progressive" cities such as Detroit and New Haven do not mean that helping hands are being bitten. They do show what may happen when the performance of over-advertised programs lags far behind the rising aspirations of American Negroes. And they further show the results from decades of civil disobedience.

If we are seriously concerned about crime in our streets, then it is time to take an honest look at the real criminals: those lawbreakers concealed in the crevices of urban respectability. It is time to take the spotlight off such petty offenders as civil rights demonstrators, whose visable acts are performed with an honest willingness to pay the consequences if necessary. The large-scale, continuing, yet invisable offenders are those slum landlords (including universities) who violate local building codes, the stores (including large department stores) who gouge the poor through illegally high interest rates, the real estate speculators who are still undermining the Supreme Court's rulings on segregation, the corrupt police officials who wink at all such law-breaking, and the high-minded bankers who finance it and profit from it.

Courage on any battlefront is critically linked to the quality of leadership at the top. When a President and Vice-President—after elections as well as before—personally demonstrate their willingness to put the finger on those who have been violating Federal law, the United States Constitution, and the most elementary principles of everyday morality, we might have reason to expect greater initiative by local leaders on behalf of genuine law and order in our cities.

LONG-RANGE GOALS BY COMMUNITY ACTION PROGRAMS

One of the most creative of all recent moves toward creative federalism has been the promotion of Community Action Programs under the Economic Opportunity Act. The CAPs have brought the problems of poverty strongly to the attention of local elites, who, until 1964, ignored them or thought only in terms of traditional palliatives. In the first stage of their activities the CAPs addressed themselves to such immediate and indispensable goals as (1) getting organized and accepted in the local community; (2) obtaining participation by the poor themselves; (3) getting funds from all available sources; and (4) thereby developing and implementing various immediate programs. At their best, however, these specific programs have been preliminary skirmishes. Nowhere have they yet added up to a long-range program of the kind of local action needed to eliminate poverty in America.

In late 1966 the Washington economists in the Office of Economic Opportunity prepared their first projections for a ten-year program to end poverty by 1976. These projections were used in supporting the O.E.O.'s request—under the President's new "systems analysis" budget procedures—to the Bureau of the Budget for its 1967–1968 appropriation. Unfortunately, this was largely an idle statistical exercise. *Little was done by the O.E.O. to consult with the CAPs on such a vital matter.* Little was done to indicate the specific actions—local, state, and federal—that might be needed to translate into reality the beautiful statistical curve of declining poverty. Nothing was done by the Bureau of the Budget, which has not yet learned how to apply its new "Planning-Programing-Budgeting-System" to federal aid for *local* programs, to insist that *local* programs be crystallized more fully.

It is now time for the federal government to ask each local community to develop a *long-range program for combating poverty.* This program should be geared to the broad goals of raising the number of people above minimum levels of (1) personal or family income; (2) fixed and liquid assets (including insurance and savings); (3) basic services and facilities, both public and private; (4) useful employment; and (5) voting opportunity and other forms of democratic participation. It should provide room for private business, local government, public schools, colleges and universities, and welfare agencies. It should include the local research needed to spark a greater measure of local initiative. On this basis, together with improved national programs, it might be possible to "end poverty by 1976."

Some federal assistance will be needed to get such local planning under way. This should be done by a central group which includes people who have already distinguished themselves (albeit receiving more wounds than medals) on the anti-poverty battlefronts.

FEDERAL AID WITH FEWER STRINGS

Considerable confusion has been created in our urban areas by the profusion of new federal aid programs in health, education, housing, urban transportation, pollution, recreation, and the arts. One writer counted 300 such programs operated by 21 departments and independent agencies through 150 major bureaus and offices in Washington and 400 regional and subregional offices in the field.[2]

This multiplicity of special purpose programs has resulted from the practical exigencies of maneuvering new measures through the shoals of congressional opposition. But now that Congress has acted, there are new administrative exigencies calling for the consolidation of many special-purpose financial aids into broader programs. This process of consolidation cannot be properly handled simply by "tax refunds" or "block grants" to the states, as often proposed. Under our typically American form of federalism, the national government is inescapably involved in providing financial aid to local as well as state governments. Through contracts, loans, and grants it channels resources to private business enterprises, universities, and regional bodies which play a major role in local development. This multiplicity of aid recipients must be preserved. But it can be made more fruitful if policy makers are given better information on the direct and indirect impact of federal expenditures (including those of subcontractors) on state and local areas. The ability of the Bureau of the Budget to get this information will provide a test of its capacity to operate the new budgeting system.

Since there can be no single, all-purpose formula for the consolidating of federal aid programs, action is suggested on the following fronts:

1. Provision for a small percentage of federal revenues to be turned over to the states, with only those controls needed to assure non-discriminatory practices and the use of such funds for additional services rather than for tax reductions.

2. Provisions for block grants to local governments for such innovative purposes as comprehensive urban development.

3. The use of these funds as incentives for the modernization of local governments, including the provision of new metropolitan and regional institutions.

There will always be strings to federal aid. But with action along these lines, there could be fewer strings and less red tape.

GREATER DECENTRALIZATION BY FEDERAL AGENCIES

No improvements in the consolidation of federal aid programs, however, will eliminate the need for greater decentralization by federal agencies themselves to regional and subregional offices. Major steps have already been taken by some, such as the Federal Aviation Administration (now in the Department of Transportation) and the Internal Revenue Service. New decentralization efforts are now being planned by the Office of Education and the Department of Housing and Urban Affairs. Yet most departments—especially the older ones—are still run in the old-fashioned, overcentralized way. Many of them include large, powerfully supported bureaus which, while they may provide for intra-bureau decentralization, very efficiently resist efforts of the Department heads to achieve inter-bureau coordination at the local level. This creates even greater confusion in the lives of local citizens and officials of local and state governments, but the mushrooming problems are not so dramatically announced as, for example, an F.A.A. failure in air traffic coordination.

The confusion may be still further increased when a Secretary tries to establish control over these bureaus merely by building up his central planning staff in Washington. This is a necessary step—particularly in such inchoate departments as Transportation, and Housing and Urban Development. But it is not enough. Many problems of intra-departmental conflict and neglect can be properly handled only at the regional or subregional level where decisions can be more in contact with the complexity of real-life problems. To help eliminate "waste, inefficiency, and feuding" in his own family, therefore, we suggest that the President have the Bureau of the Budget arrange for a special study of new approaches to regional and subregional decentralization and coordination. Special consideration should be given to (1) the appointment of regional intra-departmental coordinators with the rank of Assistant Secretary, and (2) the preparation of regional and/or metropolitan inter-departmental budgets as a further improvement to the new federal budget system.

"STATE OF THE METROPOLIS" REPORTING BY MAYORS

Improved local planning is essential to any serious progress in handling our mounting urban problems. Major contributions can be made by long-range goals set up by the local anti-poverty programs and other agencies, the consolidation of federal grants, and more decentralization by federal and state agencies. But there is no substitute for comprehensive planning under the aegis of locally elected officials. Ideally, according to Norton E. Long in Chapter 4, this should be done by metropolitan governments. In practical terms, however, the problems faced by urban areas can hardly wait until metropolitan governments are created. Furthermore, some critics are not convinced of the desirability—apart from the feasibility—of metropolitan governments.

As an immediate measure, mayors of major urban centers should begin *annual public reports on the quality of urban life*. This means going far beyond the typical mayor's report clipped together from the budget justifications of city departments. As President Johnson recommended in his 1967 State of the Union message, each sub-federal unit should examine its capacity for government in today's world. This means reporting on the problems, successes, and failures of an interrelated whole, including health, welfare practices, education, poverty levels, employment and sub-employment,[3] production, investment, minority group enterprises,[4] civil rights and liberties, white attitudes toward Negroes, air and water pollution, cultural activities, and transportation.

But no central city is an island unto itself. Many of its most productive people sleep (and send their children to school) in the suburbs. The periphery often provides the economic sinews for the center. Thus, to know the state of the city, a mayor—and his planning staffs—must know and be concerned with the major developments in the surrounding local jurisdictions.

Accordingly, we suggest that center-city mayors develop annual public reports on the "State of the Metropolis." Federal encouragement and aid will be helpful in such undertakings. It will be equally helpful to enlist the participation of the elected heads of local governments in the area and their planning staffs. A major role might often be played not only by informal cooperation, but also by formally established metropolitan or regional councils or conferences. In either case, genuine progress in implementing plans depends on the power to get action. This means political organization on the metropolitan front, even though it may be in the uniquely American form of nonpartisan or bipartisan politics.

PUBLIC-PRIVATE COLLABORATION

"But in the *new federalism*," writes Peter F. Drucker in Chapter 7, "still other political units [in addition to the states] are directly in relation with the federal government and work directly with it. And, increasingly, institutions that are not governmental but private become the agents of government in the fulfillment of public functions and even in the formulation of public policy."

In dealing with this dimension of the "new federalism," the President's second question is addressed to techniques of improved public and private collaboration. Two decades ago this question would have been largely associated with a concern lest private agencies endanger the independence of government. While this concern cannot be laid aside, the President recognizes the danger that government can harm the independence of private agencies.

We shall not comment directly on the complex problems of contractual relationships, conditions for financial assistance, control methods, and consultation, important though these techniques may be. Interpreting "techniques" in a broader sense, we shall suggest certain critical fields of public-private collaboration.

SEVEN CIVILIAN "RAND CORPORATIONS"

In the complex modern world effective action is impossible without professional research. The development of capacities for such research is one of the explanations for advancing productivity in American agriculture, industry, and transportation.

A historic step in developing advanced research capacity for government was the creation of the RAND Corporation, a private agency, to tackle problems for the United States Air Force. Linked informally with some of the best universities in the country, RAND has operated largely on contracts from the Air Force and other military agencies. RAND personnel developed the systems analysis used by Robert McNamara in the Department of Defense and its personnel and concepts now play a large role in the federal government's new Planning-Programming-Budgeting System.

One of the techniques contributing to RAND's success as a private research contractor is that its professional personnel have always been given large amounts of time to work on a variety of problems *of their own choosing*, rather than being confined entirely to services for the corporation's military clients as in university-related research organizations. Nevertheless, RAND's orientation has been predominantly military. Although it will increase its variety by engaging in more civilian work in the future, it would be impossible (and perhaps undesirable) for one such research organization to give appropriate attention to the huge range of new problems faced by the civilian agencies of government.

It is suggested, therefore, that various federal departments provide the contractual support needed for the formation of perhaps seven RAND-style corporations, covering areas such as (1) low-cost housing; (2) mass transportation; (3) mass-media education; (4) the "white problem" of discrimination against Negroes; (5) crime and narcotics; (6) public agency management; and (7) the arts. Specialization along such lines, if not carried too far, would be greatly preferable to the present practice of channeling civilian research projects into RAND itself. Through the healthy processes of competition, moreover, the new corporations should improve the quality of the expanding work that RAND will unquestionably undertake in the civilian field.

Each new research corporation should continue the RAND policy of providing its professional personnel with free time for *basic* research. In this way it will be better able to attract and develop the high-caliber talent needed for the most productive *applied* research. But there should also be considerable leeway for organizational experimentation. One corporation might be closely associated with a major university—although unlike present university-related research organizations, there will be more free-wheeling activity. Other corporations might easily be linked to private business, trade associations, or labor unions.

BUSINESS AND LABOR IN URBAN DEVELOPMENT

A basic theme running throughout this book is the need for *institutional* change. Although reform movements in America have historically concentrated on the growth of *government* institutions or governmental control over private enterprise, the new federalism requires a new approach to *business* institutions.

Specifically, we need Big Business in the field of housing and urban development. The building industry is still a small-scale, old-fashioned operation. Builders are not able to provide construction workers with the employment security, annual wages, and career opportunities needed as a basis for modern technology, quality control, and low unit costs. Under present institutional arrangements private builders cannot make a profit by building homes for low-income families and individuals. They do not have the research capacity or the perspective required for constructive cooperation with urban planners. As a result, they have tended to develop highly effective political skills in subverting land-use plans or "rigging them" for private profit. Recent urban development programs have not done much more than subsidize central land acquisition for non-housing development by the existing institutions. As a result, they have done little more than "un-house" low-income families (largely Negroes) and re-house banks, department stores, and office buildings.

An encouraging institutional change has been the decision by General Electric to build new towns. Other large corporations are also surveying the possibilities, but many of them still make the timid, rooted-in-the-past assumption that *profitable* operations must be confined to "new towns" (where land costs are lower) or to upper-income housing. As a next step, the Department of Housing and Urban Development should explore with large corporations the profit potentialities of (1) new towns *in town* with (2) *mixed-income* neighborhoods; (3) remodeling of or repair of old structures; (4) the construction of schools, hospitals, and other public facilities; and (5) the consolidated use of government subsidies now available for various aspects of urban development.

Similar developments are also possible through corporations established by the larger and more imaginative trade unions. With trade unions commanding far greater financial resources than in the past, the financial basis exists for a new wave of trade-union pioneering. Attention should especially be given to encouraging Negro enterprises. Many urban equivalents are needed to parallel the Poor People's Corporation recently set up in Mississippi. It should be noted that "soul" enterprises were largely untouched in the 1967 urban turmoil.

MORE MIXED ENTERPRISES

Traditionally, public-private collaboration has been based on contractual, credit, and consultative relations between organizationally *distinct* entities. An important aspect of recent institutional progress, however, is the development of *mixed* or *combined* entities. As pointed out by Norton E. Long in Chapter 4 and Daniel Bell in Chapter 6, the traditional public-private, socialist-capitalist distinctions are becoming increasingly blurred in fact. Both in Western Europe and among the developing nations (often with help from the United States) there has been considerable progress in launching a large variety of mixed enterprises. But the United States itself has been singularly backward in this area. Private business interests have often falsely assumed that mixed enterprises would undermine the more strictly private sectors. Government officials and liberals have often falsely assumed that mixed enterprises would necessarily operate against the public interest. Old-fashioned exponents of neat hierarchical models in public administration based on the classical Weberian bureaucratic ideal often see "quasi-independent" or "semi-autonomous" public corporations as playing havoc with their organization chart simplifications.

Two important breakthroughs suggest some paths toward overcoming our backwardness. The New York-New Jersey Port Authority is a publicly established corporation which obtains its funds by selling bonds to private investment institutions. It is a model of efficient management in the interests of both its bondholders and the public. Yet, it is charged, the Port Authority has not used its resources to develop an adequate transportation plan in the New York metropolitan area. But this is not a sin of omission that can fairly be charged against the Port Authority. The omission is, rather, the failure of the governments involved to establish appropriate mixed enterprises in the field of mass transportation. In this case, the only way to capitalize on the new technological research already under way on transportation problems in this area may well be the creation of a Northeast Mass Transportation Authority covering the entire megalopolis from Boston through New York and Philadelphia to Baltimore and Washington.

The other breakthrough was the formation of COMSAT to control communications satellites and make them internationally available. COMSAT is financed jointly by federal and private capital and includes both government and private representatives on its board of directors.

Much more imagination is needed in the development of authorities and corporations of this type. Unquestionably, the Port Authority and COMSAT models can be improved upon—particularly when adapted to meet the special needs for housing, transportation, water supply, communication facilities, and other important services and facilities. Education itself is a major area for such exploration. Private corporations are already running Job Corps centers and trade unions are training unskilled adults under the Manpower Development and Training Act. But further private effort is needed in training for new sub-professional and professional career ladders, continuing adult education, and developing the curricular "soft goods" to accompany the new "teaching" machines.

USE OF PILOT PROJECTS

In a world of scientific and technological progress, pilot projects are indispensable. They provide the means of testing and improving new ideas before they are put into widespread use. One shivers at the thought of the loss of life and limb if every new improvement in airplane design were not thoroughly tested and evaluated before it is accepted.

But the "soft" sphere of social programs and social institutions has lagged behind the "hard sciences" and the "hard technologies." Here where the need for new ideas is even greater, the need for testing is also great. Unfortunately, there is a vast difference between testing a new educational program and a new airplane. The complexities are much greater. The criteria of success, if obtainable, are usually not only vague but controversial. Unlike the airplane's artificial wind tunnel, the social laboratory is the world of real people who cannot be subjected to the traditional controls of laboratory science.

The President's third question recognizes one of the most baffling difficulties in applying the test approach to social problems. The announcement of pilot projects to be undertaken in a few selected areas usually creates demands of "Spread the money more equitably" from those without project money. This is exactly what happened with the Demonstration Cities Program under the combined pressures of mayors and congressmen. A program for a few large demonstration projects was converted into a scatteration of small projects. These will demonstrate nothing except the inadequacy of small-scale approaches to city rebuilding. The French planners have a word for it: *saupoudrage* (or sprinkling). The American word—and verdict—will be *failure*.

ENOUGH DIFFERENT PROJECTS

A simple answer to President Johnson's third question is "Develop a large enough variety of projects to allow the simultaneous testing of *some* new programs in all areas of the country."

It is now time to have a spectacular demonstration in Detroit—a constructive one. Suppose Detroit is *not* to get a large-scale "school park" under the Department of Health, Education, and Welfare. Could it not have—most appropriately—a huge urban redevelopment demonstration under the auspices of the Department of Housing and Urban Development? Or a major new experiment in modernizing vocational education in collaboration with private companies and the Department of Labor? Better yet, could not such efforts include a massive demonstration of genuine "Black Power"— of what a Negro community (with appropriate encouragement instead of snide interference from the community at large) can do for itself?

In other words, the political problem of scatteration cannot be handled entirely on an *intra*-departmental basis. It requires cooperation and coordination among many departments.

Within any one agency, of course, a certain amount of geographical dispersion is essential, both politically and scientifically. In aeronautics a single wind tunnel can simulate different kinds of climatic conditions, but no pilot project in Detroit can lead to valid conclusions about what may be desirable or feasible in Dallas, Denver, or Dayton.

Whether the focus of experimentation is on schools, job training, demonstration cities, beautification, or health services, there will have to be different applications in each of several regions, perhaps involving ten projects at the same time. This may sound expensive. But it is now time to seek the same quality in the development of our social "software" that we put into our space and military hardware.

BETTER TESTING AND EVALUATION

Some projects are experiments in name only. The words "pilot" and "demonstration," as S. M. Miller has aptly pointed out, are often used as "cover-ups" for lack of political commitment or the absence of proper funding. They may provide a semantic façade for using a five-foot rope to rescue a drowning man a hundred feet off shore.

Proper testing, therefore, first requires careful identification of the problem, followed by some plausible approach to scale. Proper testing also requires such elementary provisions as the following:

1. The development of specific criteria for success and failure;

2. The collection of reliable information;

3. The evaluation of performance both by those handling a project and by more impartial (even if less intimate) observers; and

4. The release for public scrutiny of the evaluations and the supporting information.

We know of no case where these requirements have yet been met. We have no information that the Bureau of the Budget, which is the President's staff aid in appraising major projects, has developed such requirements. In fact, while the new budget system calls for a flood of program evaluations, appraisals under it are often made by biased observers and often kept "administratively confidential," even to officials of concerned agencies.

MORE EXPERIMENTATION IN STATES

One of the great potentials of our federal system is the opportunity for social experimentation by state and local governments. The decay of urban areas in all parts of the country—and the similarity of the Negro revolt against these conditions—indicates the lack of state and local initiative. Federal financial assistance is not always needed: for example, pilot projects could be instituted in the field of social justice. Is there a police department anywhere which is free of bigoted members and is completely representative of the racial and ethnic groups which it serves?

There are certain extremely important areas where breakthroughs can be achieved *only* through state action. For example, local government revenues depend largely upon the property taxes levied by local jurisdictions. These in turn depend on property valuation, or assessment, which is usually handled on a rather non-professional (to put it euphemistically) basis. In a recent study published by the Brookings Institution[5] Professor George Break suggests a more professional and equitable basis for local taxation. He proposes the creation of State Assessment Agencies to take over, or guide, the work now performed by large numbers of small assessment districts. Under Professor Break's plan, the state agencies would certify the result to local governments, which would then apply their own tax rates to assessed values.

Another area for breakthrough involves education. As one scientist imaginatively proposes for a series of pilot schools:

To get out of the rut of our standard educational structure . . . we need to try schools of several different kinds, in different types of communities, in slum areas and rich suburbs, in company towns and scientific laboratory communities, to find out which kind of program under different circumstances produces the most alert and creative citizens.[6]

Let us hope that governors who have *talked* about a "New Deal" for the states as a matter of *national* policy will also consider *acting* along these and related lines. Imaginative projects would be particularly appropriate in Michigan, California, New York, and other states whose governors seem particularly "available" for selection as Pilot-in-Chief of the federal government. The lack of such projects—or their failure—would not speak well for an individual aspiring to a position where such activity takes place on a much grander level.

INDIVIDUAL EXCELLENCE AND CREATIVITY

Almost half a century ago, in *The Great Society,* Graham Wallas recognized the threat of large-scale organization (which is what he meant by "great") to human individuality. This theme has been restated with increasing vigor by William H. Whyte, Jr., in *The Organization Man,* Herbert Marcuse in *One Dimensional Man,* and many other social critics. In his effort to stimulate "creative federalism" and private initiative, President Johnson has seen the danger that large-scale organizations may "simply deal with individuals in the mass."

In his fourth question, the President focuses on a major aspect of this problem, the threat to individual excellence and creativity. The use of both terms is important. Excellence may be achieved in accordance with established modes and criteria. Creativity, in contrast, often departs from present norms and establishes new standards of excellence.

THE "KITCHEN" AS WELL AS THE "SALON"

In Chapter 3 Herbert Marcuse contends that literature and the arts is "the dimension in which the individual is in the most authentic sense 'creative.'" He suggests that "the artistic dimension" is the only real home of individual creativity. Marcuse thereby presents us with an authentic, old-world version of "salon" standards. Salon excellence and salon creativity are those that have traditionally been recognized by the aristocratic patrons of the arts and humanities. This is a great tradition. It has given us the works of Michelangelo, Molière, and Mozart.

Lyndon Johnson's approach is both more modern and more democratic. He would welcome scientists and educators into the salon. He recognizes the unique opportunities for excellence and creativity that individuals may obtain in, and through, large-scale organizations. His political orientations increasingly respond to the interests of the new professional elites discussed by Peter F. Drucker in Chapter 7.

But it is stultifying to maintain the popular idea that creativity is the exclusive possession of artists, literary people, and scientists. Creativity is found at any age, in any occupation, in any place. Simply put, creative responses are new, different, extraordinary. They are sometimes unpalatable to our beliefs, for it is the creative person who discovers that "the emperor has no clothes." In a dynamic society we cannot afford the cruel reaction of bygone days when creative persons were labeled heretics, only to be honored posthumously. We cannot afford to define excellence only in terms of the snob-appeal ranking of "greats" and "near greats" in selected occupations.

It is not enough to build a bigger salon for the glamorous, well-behaved, and fortunate few. Creativity and excellence must be recognized in all lines of work, not merely in high-status occupations. The "kitchen" to be recognized includes housewives, parents, teachers, policemen, auto mechanics, ghetto workers, small businessmen—all of those in the unheralded walks of life who make the salon possible. We must also recognize the individual excellence and creativity that enter into collective performance—whether by a bank that develops cheaper consumer credit for the poor, a company that makes a better light bulb, a neighborhood association that does an outstanding job in organizing the poor, or a union that develops improved forms of collective bargaining.

We will suggest two general directions in which active recognition can avoid dealing "with individuals in the mass." First, in addition to the highest standards used in judging those with the best endowments, we must also learn to use relative standards. For achievement can also be measured in terms of a person's inherent capacities and the external restraints upon him. If, for example, Child A from an impoverished background gets average grades in school, and Child B from a rich cultural background gets higher grades, A has achieved as much as B and perhaps more. A's potential may be even greater, but his achievement too often gets lost in the "massive middle," while B gets a scholarship to the college of his choice. Whether in the federal budget system or in the lowly grade school, output can only be meaningfully evaluated when related to input.

Second, there must be a plurality of acceptable avenues for excellence and creativity. When the normal avenues to self-fulfillment are sealed off by society, the individual will seek excellence in ways that are socially unacceptable to the larger society. In writing of his Harlem childhood, Claude Brown in *Manchild in the Promised Land* tells how a Negro child has little alternative but to be "good with his hands." In later years a man attuned to the street culture of the slums finds excellence by hustling in the narcotics trade or as a "Murphy Man," while women are forced to prostitution.

Many new avenues can now be opened through the New Careers concept,[7] an anti-poverty strategy which relieves professionals in human service occupations from duties which can be performed by less skilled workers. This scheme can quickly involve the old, disabled, and untrained as aides to teachers, welfare workers, police, recreation leaders, family planners, researchers, and anyone in the health professions. Jobs are provided first, with training built in, allowing opportunity for unlimited vertical and horizontal mobility. Thus a position is not just a job. It is truly a career, demanding all the excellence and creativity which the individual has to offer.

Recognition of the New Careers concept has recently been provided by the Scheuer-Nelson Sub-Professional Career Act, which would open the door to new public service jobs in governmental and non-profit agencies. But, although a few jobs have been created, career ladders have not yet been set up. Once established, this concept could also apply to the aged, as recently suggested by Secretary of Labor Wirtz.

BROADER OLYMPICS AND "NOBEL STYLE" AWARDS

A more relativistic approach to excellence and creativity does not necessarily mean less appreciation for the highest standards of human performance. Genius and near-genius must be increasingly encouraged and treasured. At the same time, the standards for genius must not be compromised—a task which becomes increasingly difficult in an age where wealth and satisfaction are to be easily had, without the pains of struggle. And the more severe the critical standards, the better the area of concern will be served.

At the end of the nineteenth century two of the world's most effective methods of recognizing superlative performance were initiated. In 1896 the Olympic Games of the ancient Greeks were revived, and have continued ever since on a four-year basis. In 1901, in Sweden, the annual Nobel awards were initiated for superlative achievement in five fields: physics, chemistry, physiology or medicine, literature, and peace.

The tremendous value of the Olympics and the Nobel prizes is their international character. Their limitation is their narrowness. There are no truly comparable competitions or awards in the performing and fine arts, architecture, the social sciences, or even mathematics. True, international festivals and competitions in music, drama, and film have been established in a number of countries, but just enough to demonstrate the need for doing much more under truly international auspices.

The United States should take the lead in exploring a comprehensive program whereby UNESCO would encourage or even take responsibility for those areas not covered by the Olympics Games and the Nobel prizes. Such a program might include conducting the Olympics themselves more frequently, something that was hardly feasible in 1896. It should include both competitive (as with the Olympics) and non-competitive awards (such as the Nobel prizes). It should also provide for larger opportunities for the people of the world to enjoy the fruits of superlative performance through traveling exhibits and performances, and "Telstar" broadcasting. Jan Peerce, the great Metropolitan Opera tenor, has recently proposed a Culture Corps to share American talent with peoples of other nations. This unilateral action would be valuable. But it would be even better for the United Nations to operate a multilateral program, so that Americans isolated behind their Golden Curtain could share the wealth of talent in the rest of the world.

The federal government should also initiate a critical appraisal of its own awards and medals. At present the great majority of these consists of traditional efforts to recognize valor in military combat. In contrast to this military emphasis on destruction, a haphazard array of civilian awards for constructive activities has developed in recent years. This entire jerry-built "system" should be surveyed by a Special Committee on Awards and Medals, to include psychologists and other social scientists. Proposals should be made for a general system that would reward both "salon" and "kitchen" efforts which help to fulfill the entire array of national purposes.

MORE FUNDS FOR ARTS, HUMANITIES, AND PARTICIPATIVE SPORTS

Despite economic affluence, American artists have long experienced tremendous difficulties in obtaining the support needed for true excellence and creativity. For decades, indeed, the United States has lagged behind both Western and Eastern Europe in its support of the arts. In recent years a major start has been made in overcoming this lag. President Kennedy prepared the way. President Johnson obtained congressional passage of the legislation and appropriations initiating the National Foundation on the Arts and Humanities. This has encouraged similar activities at the state and local level. The National Foundation's work thus far, however, has been based on little more than "symbolic appropriations," for example, $15 million for fiscal 1968. A vast increase beyond the paltry sums now available is necessary if we are truly to move toward a society where everyone will have a chance—in President Johnson's words—"to touch beauty . . ." Federal payments to the public in this area (by all agencies) should be raised to at least half a billion dollars a year, with part going on a matching basis to cities and states. With this amount of encouragement the present cultural expansion (which includes many elements of slack and depression) might be converted into a cultural Renaissance as an integral part of American life.

As Alvin Toffler has suggested in Chapter 11, we must begin to think of "parallel professionalism," a combination of both the market-supported and the state-supported. Underlying both, of course, we need more highly specialized educational institutions to provide high-quality training in the arts and humanities and conduct talent searches to identify the most promising students. We must provide still greater encouragement to more varied and better-informed amateurism, with greater facilities for amateur and sub-professional performances and exhibits. We must greatly expand the opportunities for enjoyment of the arts among lower-income groups and for personal advancement by the poor on the basis of artistic or physical, rather than merely linguistic, excellence.

As a backdrop for all this, we should promote beauty and taste-fulness in everyday life. The highways are a good and perhaps the easiest place to begin. But we should then drive back toward town and concentrate upon the slums and urban blight, upon housing and home furnishings, upon schools and work places. It is not simply the old and dilapidated, but also the vapid, "tacky" structures mushrooming in the name of modern low-cost efficiency. These are tomorrow's slums in a throwaway culture. Yet, it would seem that we have the potential and certainly the affluence to live in a truly beautiful nation.

Among the ancient Greeks the arts, humanities, and sports were interconnected. But in the modern world the vast undertakings of spectator sports have eclipsed athletic activities by individuals and small groups. The difficulty is not the commercialism of professional athletics, but the distorted overemphasis on competitive athletics which has pervaded secondary and higher education. All-City, All-State, and All-American teams, Saturday's Hero, the 3-Letter Man, and the $100,000 musclebound Bonus Baby all form a surrealistic atmosphere where excellence by a few—in a few popular sports—is vastly over-rewarded. As Professor Earle Zeigler of the University of Illinois points out, there is too much emphasis on the semi-professional (presently defined as amateur) at the expense of truly amateur and even dilletante interests.

If the experience from "the playing fields of Eton" is essential to the conduct of the more serious affairs of mankind, then there should be every effort to develop participators rather than spectators. This calls for action along the following lines:

1. Athletic pluralism should be facilitated through opportunities for taking part in a greater variety of sports. Swimming, track, soccer, handball, badminton, tennis, table tennis and wrestling facilities—to name but a few—should be as much available as those for baseball, basketball, and football. If these are provided at all levels of our educational system, students will have a better chance to select those in which they are most interested and cultivate participant skills and attitudes that might carry over into later life. These facilities should be available in the evenings and during vacations to supplement community recreational facilities.

2. Similar to the relative standards needed in the classroom, there should be greater provision for relative standards in the world of sport. Boxing and wrestling permit individuals to compete within their weight class, and in judo and chess competitors are divided into skill classes. Whatever the sport, there should be a level where any individual may have a reasonable chance to be encouraged by the taste of success. With many acceptable and multi-tiered avenues in the world of sport, the amateur should be encouraged to do his very best in whatever he is best at. Given this approach, a taste for excellence can be encouraged among all citizens.

3. Above all, promotional and follow-up activity is needed for the full use of recreational facilities. Some of the vast energies now channeled into whooping it up for spectator sports could well be redirected toward the organized participant sports required for the better health of an increasingly sedentary, over-fed and under-exercised population.

Once we decide to leave the aristocratic salon and look elsewhere for excellence and creativity, we must above all turn to the government office. Otherwise, the "dead hand of bureaucracy" could—in a society where the functions of government are inevitably growing—undermine efforts at progress in all fields.

In the true spirit of President Johnson's question, therefore, we must ask the question in this fashion: "What are the best ways to develop an atmosphere of excellence and creativity in public service?" At this level there can be no answer more fundamental than that provided by the two words: "Personal example."

The President himself must recognize his *own* responsibility for "setting the tone" by recognizing excellence and creativity in all forms. This includes the more unpalatable forms embodied in opposing the President's own ideas or actions and in formulating proposals that might not be immediately acceptable to him. The President must recognize his own responsibility in expecting the heads of departments and agencies to establish a similar tone in their own organizations. An operational consensus after formal decisions are taken can be truly effective only if there are genuine opportunities for dissent as decisions are being formulated. Even the first Great Society programs, limited though they may be, cannot be effectively administered by a group of trained conformists.

President Johnson has often talked of his "dreams" for America's future. If these are to come true, we shall need more "dreamers" in the public service, in contrast to the great bulk of "practical men" concerned with today's flow of paper from "In box" to "Out box." Dreamers embody the freshness that is increasingly necessary to deal with changing realities.

"Perhaps our labels are used inversely," as Professor Louis Krasner suggests. "The dreamers may have sound, realistic and practical visions, while the practical minded gentlemen who shake their heads and say that such visions are too complicated, unnecessary, and unrealistic, are the real dreamers . . . dreaming that the status quo can be maintained." [8] Some of the most practical dreamers today are the idealistic young Americans who have gone to distant villages of Asia, Africa, and Latin America with the Peace Corps, or to the poverty-stricken areas of this country with VISTA.

But the need for dreamers in every government agency is acute—

to overcome the nightmares of routinization and sterility created by inordinately long tenure. One of the greatest devices for freshening both individuals and organizations is a system of job rotation. The Constitution now limits presidential tenure to two terms, and former President Eisenhower has recommended a limited tenure for members of Congress. But for every member of Congress who holds unmerited position through seniority alone there are scores of high bureau officials presiding over petrified organizations which deny any semblance of excellence and creativity. By staying in the same position decade after decade, these officials cut off all ambition on the part of younger people with new ideas. On the other hand, these same officials may have valuable skills which could be profitably used elsewhere if rotation were encouraged. Could not J. Edgar Hoover, for example, have been more useful in the last ten years as an American representative on international agencies dealing with narcotics smuggling? Would we not have a more modern, vital, and up-to-date F.B.I. if this opportunity for upward mobility had been given to the people that Hoover himself brought into the organization?

ACTION AGAINST THREATS TO INDIVIDUAL LIBERTIES

To the extent that basic personal liberties are impaired, all opportunities for excellence and creativity, whether in kitchen or salon, are undermined.

In a recent period McCarthyism represented a clear danger to personal liberty in America. Ostensibly originating as protection against foreign espionage, it quickly developed into a broadside attack upon the federal service. The hysteria of that period—in which both President Eisenhower and entire departments of government were irresponsibly smeared—is over. But, as shown by Robin M. Williams, Jr., in Chapter 2, we still suffer from an "enormous growth of investigatory and punitive powers, ostensibly centered on questions of loyalty and security, but sometimes threatening long-established civil and political rights and liberties." It is now high time for a calm and judicious review of the federal government's elaborate procedures for security and loyalty clearance.

Surveillance has been greatly aided by new electronic listening devices which have immeasurably expanded the already existing invasions of privacy through wiretapping. Computers will soon make possible a national data bank where government agencies may have immediate access to the most intimate details of each citizen's private life. Our growing concern with mental health can also work against individual liberties. Professor Thomas Szasz has pointed out [9] the forcible incarceration of individuals in mental hospitals without due process of law and the unjust stigma attached to those who have suffered real or imagined mental "illness." These and other dangers should be carefully sifted by a new Joint Commission on Civil Liberties set up by the Congress and the President.

But legal protection of our constitutional liberties does not guarantee that people are willing and able to use them. The well-adjusted, well-oiled, one-dimensional man has little concern with civil liberties. His thoughts are not his own and, when expressed, offend no one.

We may well wonder whether our public schools may not be developing more "total conformists." After closely studying a number of high schools, one observer writes that "Adolescents are among the last social groups in the world to be given the full nineteenth-century colonial treatment." [10] He notes that, by emphasizing control of students, they have failed to encourage frank and honest expression. With the rapidly increasing federal interest in public education, it would be wise to inquire as to whether the outpouring of funds to the schools is reinforcing or breaking up this pattern which works against the use of our constitutional rights.

INTERNATIONAL DIMENSIONS

The President's first four questions are instrumental. They merely ask "How to?"

"What are the international dimensions of the Great Society?" is more complex. In one sense, it seems purely descriptive. In this spirit an answer might analyze the complex interrelations that have been developing between foreign and domestic policies. In another sense, "are" really means "should be." This could lead into a direct discussion of the major issues of foreign policy and particularly our global strategy or lack of strategy.

We shall accept the question in both senses, but mainly by identifying certain underlying factors that have been too long ignored. If this leads to the charge that we are really only restating the question and are not providing full answers, we plead guilty. In defense, we can merely point to the limitations imposed both by this chapter (as contrasted with the concluding chapter, where these matters will be somewhat expanded upon) and by the conscience of scholars committed to groping for the truth in a world of complex and changing uncertainties.

"GREAT SOCIETY" PROGRAMS AND FOREIGN POLICY

We shall not try even to identify, let alone analyze, all the major relations between domestic and foreign policies. We shall merely touch descriptively on a number of highly strategic relations, some rather obvious, others that have been ignored or underestimated.

First, the expanding dimensions of the Vietnam war have dimmed the enthusiasm felt for Great Society goals and programs at home. They have diverted the attention and energies of the President, his staff, and the heads of departments from the political and administrative tangles involved in the new programs for education, health, housing, urban development, and transportation. They have diminished the support of an academic community that would otherwise be much more energetically involved both in helping handle these tangles and in charting new paths into the future. Let it be noted that none of the distinguished critics in the following chapters, despite their occasional "sound and fury," objected to the fundamental thrust of the Great Society programs at home. The profound disenchantment of Herbert Marcuse, Hans Morgenthau, and Kenneth Boulding—as well as the lesser reservations of others—is based almost entirely on foreign action, much less on domestic action or inaction.

Second, it must be pointed out that in strictly economic terms the expanding war in Asia has become increasingly competitive with Great Society programs. Several years ago one heard a "guns vs. butter" debate. Despite stringencies, many domestic programs continued to grow—but not fast enough. With a deepening domestic crisis, many responsible leaders have begun to ask whether our highest priorities are not at home, and to flatly state that we must choose between wars.

Third, in terms of grand politics, there has been a terrifying reciprocity between the parallel efforts to become a great power in the Pacific and Asia and to pioneer in new forms of social progress at home. The former tends to placate—in part—powerful interests opposed to domestic progress. The latter tends to placate—in part—

important groups that have been deeply divided on, if not opposed to, the expansion of unilateral military operations abroad. This is one of the many reasons for the relative "consensus" achieved by President Johnson during the early years of his administration. But with little visible success on either battlefront, dissensus has firmly gained the upper hand. The graceful balancing act of limited commitment on all fronts has been submerged under the cries for decisive action on one front at the exclusion of the other.

Fourth, all the old distinctions between "domestic" and "foreign" policies are rapidly blurring. Programs that are purely "domestic" have international implications. Foreign programs not only depend upon domestic support and domestic politics, as Peter F. Drucker points out in Chapter 7, but they have major second order effects on domestic programs. Thus a full examination of the international dimensions of the Great Society vision—or even the bundle of Great Society programs—requires a comprehensive viewing of the changing American system in the changing world environment. This important question as to appraising the changing "state of the nation," will be dealt with in the final chapter.

"A" NOT "THE" GREAT SOCIETY

Any slogan has its dangers.

The major danger in the term "great society" lies in some of the ambiguities lurking behind the word "great." This word suggests the grandeur not only of size but of wealth and power. It carries with it some of the overtones of military dominance associated with the phrase "the great powers."

These associations cannot readily be overcome. The United States is one of the largest countries of the world. It *is* the richest country, and steadily growing richer. Despite conspicuous failure against unconventional, small-scale methods in a small "weak" country in Asia, it *has* achieved an awesome level of nuclear and conventional military power. In explaining the Great Society philosophy President Johnson and his major spokesman have gone far to emphasize that the "greatness" they seek is something different from (albeit based on) size, wealth, and power. A major thrust has been the emphasis upon the human, non-material values that can emerge more fully once man's basic needs for material security have been met. They have shifted the emphasis from the economy as the central concern of public policy to the conditions of Society as a whole. In this sense "great" unquestionably means "good," as Hans J. Morgenthau points out in Chapter 5. But not "good" in a vague, abstract way! Rather, "good" in a sense that is indeed better than merely reducing the threats of poverty, ignorance, and disease. "Good" in the more positive sense of providing a fuller life for those to whom—in President Johnson's words—"prosperity alone is just not enough . . ." It is in this sense that the Great Society vision has emerged as the first by-product of the politics of affluence. This is why it is already being imitated (and may yet be improved upon) not only by Republican presidential contenders at home but by political leaders in other highly industrial countries.

In the initial presentation of this vision, unfortunately, President Johnson repeatedly used the article "the." It is idle to speculate whether this usage was a grammatical accident or a reflection of implicit faith in American superiority over the rest of the world. The point is that the continued use of *"The* Great Society" by both the press and the administration has served to give an impression of self-proclaimed superiority. At home it has probably reinforced historic tendencies toward seeing America as a model for the world, as a missionary in the world, or even as a holy crusader committed to spreading "Americanism" or "the American way of life." It is reinforced by the parallel notion that we are obligated to serve as "world police-man." Abroad, by exaggerating the image of America as self-chosen model, missionary or crusader, it has strengthened the latent resentment that people always feel against anyone who is larger, richer, and more militarily powerful. It has probably accentuated the perceptions of Americans as arrogant, immodest, and insensitive. It has probably thickened the "Golden Curtain" of incomprehension and misunderstanding that some observers have found between the United States and the rest of the world. The immodesty and arrogance of those Americans who really see us as *The* Great Society of the world has scarcely contributed to the better understanding in other countries (many with their own strongly felt claims to greatness) of the genuinely human thrust behind American efforts to become *A* Great Society.

Considerable effort may be needed to undo the damage. Whether we choose to call it "Great" (with Johnson), "Just" (with Rockefeller), "Creative" (with Reagan), or "Free" (with Goldwater), we should make it perfectly clear that we do not have and are not aspiring to a world monopoly on any of these aspects of "goodness." We must truly recognize—by acts as well as words—that there are many styles and forms of goodness and that many other nations deeply believe that *they* have reason to be proud of themselves as "Great," "Just," "Creative," and "Free." This was seen long ago by Arthur F. Bentley. As indicated by Sidney Ratner in Chapter 12, he realized that the estimated values of his own group were not necessarily the best for that group and that the intensity of his belief in his set of values does not justify imposing these values on others, especially in foreign cultures.

TOWARD GREATNESS IN THE WORLD SOCIETY

To achieve our own form of greatness, it might be helpful to do somewhat better in perceiving world-wide reality. In Chapter 7 Peter F. Drucker puts it this way:

> The central reality which is likely to generate or at least to shape the issues in American international politics is the fading away of the two axioms on which American foreign policy has been based since World War II. These are the axiom that the international economy was dependent on the United States economy rather than that there was interdependnce; and the much more important axiom that "communism" and "Russia" were synonymous with "the enemy."
>
> As the result of the erosion of these axioms it is no longer possible to assume that any action taken by the United States in its capacity as the leader of the free-world community is automatically in the interest of the United States as a nation, and vice versa.

In a nutshell, Drucker advocates a cure for the ingrained myopia that seems to have pervaded many parts of the Congress and the State Department, distorting the premises of some foreign policy decisions by the White House.

But curing myopia, desirable though it may be, will not provide long-range vision. The new generation of men and women born after the Depression have something of this vision—although some of them, old before their time, seem better suited for a simpler, less complicated world. But many are more oriented toward a world of high technology, lifelong education and learning, and space exploration. Above all, as Drucker suggests, they "take for granted the 'global village'—that is, the integration of the entire earth through communications into one locus of experience."

The central fact in the world today is the emergence of a world society, a society in which people all over the planet are bound together by increasingly interdependent interests while also divided by deep conflicts and suspicions aggravated by the myths we believe about each other. In addition to its size, this tenuous world society has other claims of greatness, particularly if it can develop institutions better able to help its downtrodden and channel inevitable conflicts into non-military forms of settlement. What better form of greatness and world-wide respect could America seek than to help remedy the weaknesses and build the greatness of the emerging world society and its fragile institutions?

•NOTES

1. Papers specifically addressed to President Johnson's questions were prepared in the spring of 1966 by Eugene Lewis, Walter Mahler, Michael Marien, and Stephen Sywulka. The following students considered the President's questions during a fall 1966 seminar conducted by Professor Gross: José Alcalde, Obi Anyasinti, Thomas Brown, Joseph Farrell, Stephen Giddings, Marilyn Hastings, Paul Kerz, Virginia Koehler, Michael Marien, Reginald Mascarenhas, Douglas Montgomery, Edward Nemeth, Somchai Poonakasem, Chong-Sur Pyen, Michael Springer, Mary Stephano, Ann West, Nancy Westcott, and Allan Wulff. Comments by Bert Wenner have also been very helpful.

2. Richard Harwood, *The Washington Post*, January 18, 1967.

3. Sub-employment is a new concept developed in the Labor Department after many years of dissatisfaction with traditional unemployment measures. In addition to the "officially" unemployed, the sub-employment calculation adds (1) half of the able-bodied males not looking for work and thus not in the "official" labor force, (2) half of the estimated male "undercount," (3) all employed part-time and looking for full-time work, and (4) all employed full-time at sub-poverty-level wages. The application of this concept, however, has proceeded at a snail's pace. Measurements have only been made in selected areas of eight cities (Detroit and Newark not among them), and the shocking findings of rates averaging over 33 per cent sub-employed in the ghettoes have yet to be widely disseminated and acted on.

4. Although Negroes represent more than 10 per cent of the population, they constituted less than 2.5 per cent of all "Self-employed Managers, Officials, and Proprietors" in both 1950 and 1960. During this decade, the absolute number fell (at the same rate as the total) from 58,865 to 45,464 (*1950 Census*, Vol. II, pt. 1, Table 128; *1960 Census*, PC (1)-1D, Table 205).

5. George F. Break, *Intergovernmental Fiscal Relations in the United States* (Washington, D.C.: Brookings Institution, 1967).

6. John R. Platt, "Diversity," *Science*, CLIV, No. 3753 (December 2, 1966), 1132–1139.

7. Arthur Pearl and Frank Riessman, *New Careers for the Poor* (New York: The Free Press of Glencoe, 1965).

8. Statement at Great Society Seminar, Syracuse University, October 15, 1965.

9. Statement at Great Society Seminar, Syracuse University, November 12, 1965.

10. Edgar Z. Friedenberg, *Coming of Age in America: Growth and Acquiescence* (New York: Random House, 1963), p. 4.

Chapter 2

A Model of Society—The American Case ROBIN M. WILLIAMS, JR.

In this essay, we examine American society as a social system, and we ask what conceptions of that system might be most useful in analyzing and understanding it as it begins to search out new pathways to the Great Society. Accordingly, first, we have to find out what it means to talk of "systems" and "models."

WHAT ARE SYSTEMS?

A system is a bounded set of units or elements standing in specifiable relations among themselves and operating in some sense as a unit.[1] There is an "inside" and an "outside." The system endures for some important period (this may be a few millionths of a second or billions of years). Relations of elements within the system differ from relations outside the system. To *some* extent a system acts and is acted upon as a unit; the degree of unity may be very high or rather low. Systems vary greatly also in the degree to which they are "open" or "closed." Closed systems (e.g., the solar system) are those in which many of the relationships of chief interest to us can be ascertained and predicted from data bearing only on intrasystem structures and processes; data on external variables can be ignored. In the case of open systems, such as organisms and personalities, boundary exchanges are numerous and are crucial for internal states of the system. Clearly, social systems are highly open systems.

Social systems consist of streams of communications or "transactions" between and among social actors. In these communications, expectations are established (and changed), meanings are transmitted, values are expressed, coercion is applied, approval and love or disapproval and hostility are expressed, deference and respect are given. Recurrence (pattern stability) in systems of shared symbols makes possible the extension of order in social action through time and space. To note the existence of such patterning is a way of saying "structure." Social systems are continually changing; as Professor Bentley noted in vivid analogy, they also always have some structure through time.[2] This structure is always made up of activities, of social acts, and relationships among them. To describe a social system, consistently with Bentley's conceptions, one has to show how, down through the flow of time, each set of activities connects with (affects, is interdependent with, is affected by) other activities. To say "system" is thus to say "connexity"[3] of item with item throughout the alleged system.

The major alternative to a conception of social behavior as that of atomistic responses of separate individual units interacting "directly" one-to-the-other is "to see acting units as parts of organized systems, which have properties other than those attributable to isolated units and the most general conditions of interaction between 'men as men.' They have languages, cultural values, legal systems, various kinds of institutional norms and generalized media [money, social approval, political power, influence]. Concrete behavior is not a function simply of elementary properties, but of the kinds of systems, their various structures and the processes taking place within them."[4]

A social system is not the same as a *total* system of *human action*. A total system of human action is composed of social, cultural, psychological, and organismic elements. The units of social systems are not concrete human individuals but *social actors,* analyzed as the authors of the role performances emitted from social statuses (positions). In the analysis of social systems one must be fully aware of how cultural, psychological and organismic factors affect the functioning of institutions and collectivities. But clarity cannot be maintained if we mix all these elements together into the amorphous conceptual muddle represented by the usual common-sense notions of "individual" and "society."

To be sure, the human units of concrete societies are obdurate organisms and complex personalities that resist being *only* "units." Unlike any respectable machine, they keep making outrageous attempts to redesign their own circuitry.[5] From the standpoint of centralized control, as exemplified in George Orwell's *1984*, they are highly unreliable. On the other hand, the "needs" and "interests" of social actors are, to a perhaps surprising extent, incited and shaped by the very same social system that at first glance seems to exist only as a means to "the individual's gratifications." Social organizations, for instance, are not mere expressions of fixed, given, "individual" needs, but constitute, rather, *closed circuits,* operating back upon individuals to reconstitute them, and so on in endless succession.[6]

It is clear in any case that one cannot generalize directly from "traits" or "personality characteristics" of individuals to macro-social processes of larger-scale systems. Nor is it legitimate to generalize from the findings of research on interpersonal behavior in small groups to these macrosopic processes of collectivities without a specific empirical demonstration that the transfer is valid.

Actually, it is often the case that complex systems may be analyzed statistically as developing sets of relations and trends without attempting to make exact individual predictions concerning the units that make up the collectivities. One need not know particular individual personalities directly in order to predict, for instance, when organized militancy is most likely on the part of a disadvantaged ethnic or racial minority, or where structural unemployment will have its greatest incidence.

A social system, then, consists of an energized web of overlapping interactions among social actors, sufficiently stabilized to permit us to discern recurrent relationships and institutionalized patterns. How may such a complex entity be conceptually represented? In choosing our approach, we have to decide what place and weight to give in social analysis to "rationality" in human affairs—an ancient and still empirically moot question.[7] It is now generally accepted that classical economics posited a type and degree of economic rationality that only poorly fits much actual behavior. The pure power maximizers that are assumed in some "gaming" theories today likewise represent an abstraction that may be dangerously misleading in many cases. In criticizing such overly rational models, much work in modern sociology and social psychology has developed an image of a "social" man who has internalized the norms of his mentors and reference groups as constitutive of his ego ideal and superego. At the extreme, this "oversocialized" man always "does his duty" and that "as a matter of con-science," even when so doing sacrifices his self-interests as an economic and political man. This exaggerated model likewise only crudely represents social reality.

Now, amiable eclecticism is no adequate answer to the crucial problem of choosing among these divergent assumptions and the adduced contradictory evidence supporting each of them. We must find the means to a more specific and orderly set of answers. Yet it is, indeed, a fact that all of the "models" cited do fit a certain important portion of social reality. Men often do act in an economically rational manner on the stock exchange, in the commodity market, in the administration of a manufacturing corporation (or of a university), and in the allocation of household income. Similarly, one may observe a certain amount of systematic rationality in the acquisition and use of political power, in military strategy, in diplomatic negotiations, and in the organization of authority. At the same time, one observes that such "rationality" often is at the service of *collectivities* and not merely of narrow short-range *individual "self-interest"* (the latter being a concept that always needs close inspection in its context). Furthermore, it is easily seen that at least some men, some of the time, do act in terms of values and norms that they honor and express even at great sacrifice of conventional rewards and securities. (Beyond this, we have been increasingly aware of the substantial frequency of psychotic conditions in ordinary populations and of the ubiquity of neurotic mechanisms in so-called "normal" people.)

Without belaboring the point, then, it has become evident that whenever we use a "rational man" model, we must, at the least, be prepared to supplement it at every point at which evidence and theory suggest qualification, and to be cautiously alert for missing data.

The problem may be illustrated by a brief consideration of social conflict and integration. Our model must include provision for data bearing on the sources and consequences of opposition of interests and of social conflicts of varied kinds. Formidable as this task undoubtedly is, it is by no means impossible. The main outlines of conflict and opposition, after all, are well known, even if imprecisely: economic interest-blocs, labor-management, ethnic, racial, religious, regional and sectional groupings, and so on. At all levels of American society, there are oppositions of interests, rivalries, competition, conflict, and the processes of conflict resolution. The relatively high frequency of successful bargaining and compromise in this society is in part an outcome of the rich texture of multiple and overlapping economic and political interdependencies.

It has often been said that a society riven by many crisscrossing lines of divergent interests is in less danger of massive social upheaval than is a society polarized around only a few cleavages. Recently James Coleman has pointed out that in situations of opposition of interests, given rational self-interested actors and more than one issue to be resolved, a collective decision can be made; but, if there is only one issue to be acted on, external power is likely to be used with the consequence of escalation of conflict. If there are several issues of varying importance to different social actors, then "so long as an actor can exchange power over actions that have little or no effects on his interests, in return for power over actions which interest him, this is the best way of gaining his interests." [8] *Under these conditions, and over a succession of bargains, actors learn to keep agreements since they learn that their long-run interests require the belief of others in one's reliability.* Coleman predicts on the basis of this analysis that disruptive conflict is most likely when there are only a few interests at stake and little possibility of bargaining exchanges. He concludes that "if a collective decision is to be reached without the use of external power, there must not be one action which interests each actor more than all the other actions in which they are collectively engaged." [9]

The conflicts internal to societies are much better understood today than when Marx postulated a monolithic system of economic interests, polarizing capitalistic societies into two massive divisions. As Parsons says: "The view is rather that of a complex set of interdependent components in which economic and . . . political interests play their part, but at the same time, normative and cultural factors are independently operative." [10] The integration of large-scale and complex social systems, however, does not arise so directly from detailed normative consensus as is the case in small "primary group" systems. Nevertheless some agreement upon a minimal set of values and norms is a defining property of social systems, even those of national scope. Such a consensus emerges out of and reinforces and stabilizes economic and political interdependence. [11]

Whatever our model of the society is to be, then, it must allow for both rational and non-rational conduct and for conflict as well as consensus.

WHAT ARE MODELS?

First, "models" may be ideal states or conditions toward which we strive. Second, models may be replicas on a different scale of the thing modeled, as a model airplane in a wind tunnel, a table model of an urban development, a model of the solar system, and so on. More generally, models are representational: they are means of representing or simulating the variables and interrelations that make up the thing, situation, event, or process that is the object of our attention. In many instances, by manipulating the model we are enabled to make predictions about the future behavior of the "real thing," the system to which the model refers. Models represent an attempt to go beyond the sheer labeling of definitions and the cumbersome inefficiency of propositional inventories.[12] Models are particularly likely to be found useful when the thing we wish to represent is made up of a large number of empirically separable elements that are interacting in many relationships, according to different and varying functions. Under these conditions—which obviously are typical of social systems —it often is nearly impossible to imagine all the effects of different states of the system, short of being able to actually use a veridical model.

Every model is a pattern of symbols, rules, and processes regarded as matching, in part or in totality, an existing perceptual complex. Each model stipulates, thus, some correspondence with reality, some relevance of items in the model to the reality, and some verifiability between model and reality.[13]

For complex entities (and others are not of present interest), a model may permit simulations of interdependencies that otherwise might entirely escape our imagination.

Through any important stretch of time—say, five years—a national society is always changing through numerous interrelated processes.[14] People are leaving the system through emigration, tourism, overseas service, and death. New personnel are added as tourists, visitors, immigrants, and births. The people going out and those coming in are never identical genetically or socially; hence, the "social mix," as Everett K. Wilson calls it,[15] is continually changing. These changes, in turn, affect the age and sex composition of the population; changes in age and sex composition, then, affect marriage and birth rates, participation in the labor force, demands for goods and services (e.g.,

education, hospital care), and possibly changes in savings and investments.

Meanwhile, interrelations among institutions will be generating
numerous pressures for change and resistances to change. Industrial
research, for example, undertaken in the interests of lowering costs of
production may introduce an automated system that displaces large
numbers of unskilled and semiskilled workers, who cannot find new
jobs. Under the impact of unemployment, their already tension-laden
family units may further disintegrate. Youths growing up in such situations, and themselves without prospects of employment, frequently
become delinquent. Ensuing increases in group hostility may lead to
disorder and to increase in intergroup stereotyping. Through such
hypothesized processes, an adequate model ought to make it possible
for us to go by definite steps in analysis from new developments in
technology to riots in the streets of New York, Chicago, Los Angeles,
or Detroit.

Meanwhile, other processes will be going on. Suppose the average
level of material living is rising rapidly, but very unevenly in different portions of the society. Suppose that as real income rises, persons
who expect a continuing increase will increase their spending to a
level resulting in a constant proportion saved. Suppose that those who
fear a future recession save at an increased rate. If so, we must have
data on economic expectations in order to understand saving behavior. Further, if some elements of the population are falling—in income—relative to other socially visible elements during a time of
generally increasing affluence, the relatively deprived are especially
likely to manifest militant discontent. To predict the form and exten-
siveness of such discontent (including its potentiality in political
movements) requires data on the size of the affected population; its
regional and rural-urban distribution; its racial, ethnic, and religious
composition; its objective social-class position and its subjective class
identification.

Meanwhile, other changes will be taking place. After a certain
critical level of production in manufacturing has been reached, "the
tendency in an industrialized economy is for an increasing proportion
of the national product to be composed of services." [16] In turn, this
means changes in occupational opportunities, involving shifts in the
abilities, skills, disciplines, and knowledges demanded. Demand for a
general educational upgrading is one result, having complex consequences upon the educational system.

Meanwhile—but enough surely has been said to illustrate both the complexity and the specificity needed for adequate modeling. In addition, a really refined analysis would demand that we take into account the fact that some elements are associated in a linear, others in a curvilinear fashion,[17] that a change in one variable may have an immediate or a much delayed impact upon another, and that antecedent-consequent relations are sometimes direct—and sometimes highly indirect—through a series of intermediate impacts and feedback loops.

As a matter of practical strategy, it is therefore apparent that our initial models will have to be highly selective—which means that they are and will be highly simplified. It is accordingly the first rule for wisdom in the use of models to be especially alert to possible distortions of reality occasioned by elements and relationships that are missing from the model but very much present (even if sometimes hidden) in the real societal world.

Many of the classical questions of macroscopic analysis of large-scale social systems are now outmoded, and their restatement can serve no viable purpose, save to expose critical errors. How naïve it now seems, for instance, to oppose "technological" to "nontechnological" factors in efforts to account for social change. The question is not whether one or the other broad class of "factors" is more or less important than some other. The question always is, what specific antecedent states of what variables reliably predict specified outcomes of the consequent variables of primary interest in a particular problem. Only when the general-classificatory approach is abandoned can we expect any real movement toward explanation of systematic recurrence of events. For posing questions of societal policy in a practically meaningful way, a social-system model is of great and increasing usefulness.

WHAT ARE NATIONAL SOCIAL SYSTEMS?

A national social system includes all subordinate social systems ultimately subjected to regulation by a central state, i.e., an associational structure successfully claiming a final monopoly of political authority in the legitimate use of coercion and of organized physical violence.[18] Nation-states, of course, have not always existed, and it is not necessary to assume that they will always continue to exist in the same way or with the same importance as has been the case since the eighteenth century. Even in the modern totalitarian nations, the state is not co-extensive or identical with the total society. The "control" or "dominance" of the state is a relative thing—relative to the other basic social structures and processes coexisting within the state's claimed physical territory and relative to the powers of other nation-states. Once more, we are here indebted to the early insight expressed in Bentley's insistence that dominance always is the control of one *activity* or *set of activities* over another or others and that "control" is always two-directional:

It is not merely government that dominates underlying activities but underlying activities that dominate government. It is not merely opinions that dominate underlying activities but underlying activities that dominate opinions. The values and meanings must be worked out in both ways before they can hope to be understood in either.[19]

The basic notion here is that the activities of men always connect with the activities of other men, and, even more fundamentally, that the specification of any activity can only be made in terms of other activities. A "system" in human society is always to some extent open-ended, it always exists in some degree, rather than as an either-or matter. This is eminently true in the arena of power and authority— of politics and governing.[20]

A model of a national society has to incorporate not only its internal units and relations, but also the involvement, and characteristic modes of behaving, of the nation and its subunits in relationships with other specific nations and with international organizations. An especially important item to be included is the extent to which the nation and its subunits are inwardly or outwardly oriented.[21]

A national society, taken in its full concreteness, involves a *human population* inhabiting a *bio-physical environment,* using numerous *artifacts* that are produced, maintained, and used by means of *knowledges* and *skills.* The society's members relate themselves to members of other societies, and some relations are representative for the entire society as a collective unit. At any point in time, the society's members carry a describable culture, including language, concepts, science, law, beliefs, values, goals, symbols, and numerous norms providing definitions of behavior, thoughts and feelings. The major normative structures in all societies are the *institutions,* i.e., interconnected subsystems of important obligatory norms guiding conduct in sets of status roles that cohere around major foci of interests. The main institutions include:

1. Kinship and family, centering upon sexual interests, reproduction and socialization of children, a wide variety of affective interests, and status ascription.

2. Social stratification, centering upon distributive interests in the allocation to individuals, kinship units, and other social units of the scarce values of prestige, authority, power, safety, wealth, and income.

3. Economy, centering upon production, exchange, and redistribution of scarce and transferable values ("utilities").

4. Polity, focused upon the acquisition and use of power and authority to control the basic relational system among individuals and other social units.

5. Education, focused upon the production and distribution of knowledge, in the widest sense, and upon the transformation of social persons through inculcation of all aspects of culture, including both the sciences and the arts.

6. Religion, focused upon ultimate meanings and values and involving ultimate commitments and assurances.

7. Recreation, diffusely concerned with a great variety of expressive interests that serve to release tensions, reinforce affective social bonds, and model conduct for other institutions.

As an energized structuring of activities that endures through time, a society will be found to contain many activities that are not highly patterned or guided by firm normative structures. Many of these activities are newly emerging; some are the flotsam and jetsam of disintegrating older patterns. Some of the "open spaces" in normative patterning represent diffuse agreement to permit latitude for individual uniqueness, especially in expressive or tension-releasing behavior.

Only when all the institutions have been described in their full connexity, both internally and among themselves, and when overarching value orientations also are described, can we begin to understand the cross-sectional normative texture as a whole. And only when we add to this essentially *cultural* description a specification of the concurrent, cross-sectional *social organization* are we in a position to say, "here is a reasonably complete representation of the total society." This means that we must be able to describe as concrete structures: (1) all main forms of existing collective behavior—audiences, crowds, mobs, panics, riots, crazes, fads, fashions, manias, and social movements; (2) basic primary groups—families, play groups, cliques, factions, friendships, congeniality groupings; (3) voluntary special-interest associations; (4) complex formal organizations (e.g., corporations, government departments, churches, universities); (5) "total institutions" (involuntary closed organizations, such as prisons and mental hospitals).

Actually we have not yet completed the task of specification of the cultural and social structure unless we have understood as an implication of what has just been said that the *interrelations* among institutions and social organizations be described. It is apparent that each major institutional sector is connected with all the others. The connections are of several different kinds: (1) through direct representative roles, e.g., clergyman to educator to political leader; (2) through indirect social linkages, e.g., unemployment affects family life, which affects achievement of children in school, which affects later position in social stratification; (3) through mediating and adjudicating mechanisms, e.g., the Supreme Court; (4) through diffuse field structures, especially mass communications and the fiscal and market systems. Through such channels and mechanisms each more or less well-defined institutional complex articulates with all the others. It is useful just to make the possible connections explicit, even in the excessively crude way depicted in Table 2-1.

TABLE 2-1. INTERCONNECTIONS OF INSTITUTIONS

	Kinship & Family System	Social Stratification	Economy	Polity	Education	Religion	Recreation
Kinship & Family	—						
Social Stratification	1	—					
Economy	2	7	—				
Polity	3	8	12	—			
Education	4	9	13	16	—		
Religion	5	10	14	17	19	—	
Recreation	6	11	15	18	20	21	—

NOTE: Each of the 21 cells in the matrix represents the intersection of many status-roles, composed of very large numbers of specific norms.

Finally, our account of the operation of the national social system has to include indicators of the physical and mental health of the population and indicators of social stress and tension.

With such an inventory and analysis in hand, one would at long last literally be in a position to speak of "the State of the Nation."

WHAT IS OUR MODEL OF AMERICAN SOCIETY?

Now, a large number of partial conceptual schemes, implying very different "models," have been applied to American society.

There is the model of historical drama in which conspicuous events are seen as the expression of great men who have shaped the course of national destiny.

There is the economic model, which sometimes tends either to ignore or to take as "given" all factors not capable of immediate expression as economic magnitudes.

There is the power model, which focuses on political factors and often tends to define politics and government as predominant elements in the total historical process.

There are many varieties of psychological models. Some social psychological formulations are congruent with the approach we will use here. Others represent an extreme psychological reductionism, which attempts an individual-aggregative explanation of large-scale social structures and processes.

As partial formulations of aspects of reality, all these approaches may yield valuable knowledge and raise interesting questions. However, it is very clear that none is adequate alone to represent the actual national society, nor can all combined carry out the needed task.

To accomplish the urgently required job of building a "national system of social accounts" or a "model of the national society," three great initial steps must be taken. First, we must add a detailed model of the *social* system. Next, we must fill this model with strategic sets of data, many of which do not now exist but must be developed. Third, we must begin to assemble into one integrated model the economic, political, psychological, and sociological models.

The question has been asked: Was there a coherent model underlying the writer's book, *American Society: A Sociological Interpretation*? Originally, the organizing and informing conceptual entity behind the work was not so much a model as a set of concepts plus an "image" or "vision" of the workings of a large and complex societal aggregate. There was present the basic idea that behavior shows lawful regularities that are to an important degree potentially predictable. There were the central concepts of *structure* and *system*, and the more particularized concepts of culture, norm, institution, status, role, value, belief, social organization, group, association, bureaucracy, and so on. The "vision" was a particular kind of morphological image of the dynamic interactions of millions of people being guided by and reacting back upon the institutional norms that partly defined their life problems and the thinkable solutions to these.

There was, then, *this* kind of a set of constructs. The set initially lacked any very exact formulation of the connections among the various elements and units making up the conceptual complex. Certainly it was very far indeed from the capability of being formulated as a mathematical model. Nevertheless, there was a guiding sense of systematic interconnections of structures and processes, and as this approach was followed, more and more of the empirical materials were seen to "fall into place." *Within* major institutional sectors particular norms and statuses and social processes proved to be causally or functionally interrelated, e.g., free mate choice and neolocal residence, nuclear family autonomy, high social mobility, omnilineal kinship, rapid social change, discontinuity of generations, and prolonged adolescence. Connections *among* institutions, similarly, were perceived: kinship ties affect labor mobility, bureaucratic employment reacts upon parents' ways of socializing children, and religious-group identities affect political behavior.

It soon became apparent that institutions (defined as interconnected sets of obligatory social norms that specify systems of statuses) vary in structure from highly *diffuse* to highly *nucleated*.

The institutions of social stratification are highly diffuse, i.e., generalized prestige rank is the result of numerous convergent and conflicting evaluations of individuals and other social units. The complex correlates of occupation, education, income, wealth, place of residence, authority, power, and "style of life" are partly determined by ascription at birth, partly assigned, and partly achieved. *Within* specific social organizations, e.g., a business firm, the segmental stratification may be determined by a central authority. But inclusive stratification in the total community and society is quite diffuse in the American case.[22]

Kinship and family institutions are also diffuse, with nearly fifty million primary families, each a unit of solidarity and decision making. Education and religion represent intermediate degrees of nucleation and centralization. Economic and political institutions are, of course, highly nucleated and increasingly centralized with regard to decision making and coordination.

Following these leads a detailed picture of the society was presented: highly complex, interconnected, dynamic, and often conflicting. The problem of societal integration seemed crucial in a society of this kind, and we attempted to analyze the sources of conflict and of integration. The eventual formulation was that all societies are held together by these processes:

1. *Interdependence:* mutual advantages in satisfying interests in safety, income, wealth, power, authority, prestige, and other scarce, distributive values.

2. *Authority and Power:* the legitimate or *de facto* exercise of an ultimate monopoly of coercion to maintain order and to enforce a settlement of claims to advantage.

3. *Consensus:* agreements on beliefs, norms, and values.

4. *Cathexis:* the ongoing networks of interpersonal attachments and repulsions at the level of primary interaction.

Inventories of the specific ways in which these complexes of variables operate is an essential part of practical politics and administration. It seems that the time has come to start this vital kind of societal bookkeeping.

In the effort to build an empirically valid model of the national society, we cannot rest content short of the most sophisticated data and statistical procedures. Thus, in the present example, we would not want an index of "consensus" that simply reflected the proportion of the population agreeing with a certain position on a public issue. At the least we should seek an indicator that would take into account, for example, the presence of essentially noncommitted persons, as well as the existence of factions or blocs, at various levels of salience and intensity of commitment.

One of the pointed questions raised by the topic under discussion is whether or not social science has now reached a point at which it is possible to prepare a general model for American society—or an even more ambitious goal—for any society. The answer hinges upon how comprehensive and exact our requirements are for a "general model." If we require exact measurements of thousands of variables, in a form suitable for complete mathematical statement in equations subject to determinate solutions—then clearly we are not ready, nor is it likely that we will be for a long time to come. But if we are willing to descend to current realities, it is reasonable to say that partial and approximate models—partly quantitative, partly qualitative—already are within reach. To reach them, however, requires major effort. Provision must be made, on a large scale, to develop basic data not now collected on cultural and social structures and social and psychological processes. Whole families of indicators need to be developed and data collected routinely and systematically on such matters as: upward and downward social mobility, family stability and instability, physical and mental health, crime, community conflict and conflict resolution,[23] social segregation and discrimination, scientific and technological creativity, religious commitments and religious innovations, group formation and dissolution in various types of communities, and changes in values.

Suppose that within five years we have developed the social accounting now called for as an urgent necessity by Professor Bertram Gross, and that a greatly improved general model of American society is generating new predictions and steadily helping us to create new data. How should such a model change as we move toward the Great Society? In one view, it should be moved in the directions of (1) more complete coverage of variables; (2) greater exactness in the indicators used; (3) greater capability of quantitative expression; (4) improved analysis of the complex interaction effects among the elements making up the model; (5) greater sophistication in qualitative mapping of unmeasured factors and variables; (6) greater sophistication in allowing for possible effects of unmeasured factors; (7) improvement in the procedures and technology of computer simulation. These are stern aspirations, but nothing less will answer to the needs ahead.

A final requirement is of the utmost importance: The model should respect the fact that *a society that honors the freedom of individual persons must alter its own goals as its members change theirs. A person-centered society can never bind the future irrevocably.*[24]

IN WHAT WAYS IS AMERICAN SOCIETY CHANGING?

The question has been posed for this essay: "What are the major changes in the United States since *American Society* appeared? In structure, processes and performance?" The book in question first appeared in 1951. During the subsequent fourteen years—from Korea to Vietnam, if you will—most of the main trends identified by the book's analysis have continued. There have been few major surprises, but the scope and tempo of change have lent excitement and challenge to later analysis.

It is not a myth that the "tempo" of life has been increasing.

This is not only a matter of increases in the speed of transport on land and water, in the air, and in outer space. It is also reflected in increases in per capita telephone calls, telegrams, letters, books, magazines, electronic messages, chemical stimulants and tranquilizers, scientific and technological innovations ("the information explosion"), and foreign travel.[25] Increasingly, planned technical innovation occurs. We have institutionalized many important sources of change, as exemplified by the great industrial research laboratories, the university research installations, the medical institutes, and the massive military research and development programs.

A prosperous society with a highly developed monetary system, with free choice of consumer goods, and with high geographic mobility is a highly permeable society, in which individuals have great freedom in making and unmaking social relationships. There is a fine-grained flexibility in the structure that combines considerable homogeneity in norms of public behavior with much variability in many details of private behavior. Quick, responsible, and often intense experiences develop in a rapidly shifting series. Such relations, for instance, occur in business and professional conferences, negotiations, changes of jobs, political bargains, recreational gatherings, and the transient contacts of travel. Complications of role-sets, more and more, are coming to be accepted as normal, tolerable, or even desirable.

In contrast, in the public area there is the enormous growth of investigatory and punitive powers, ostensibly centered on questions of loyalty and security, but sometimes threatening long-established civil and political rights and liberties.

Major long-term trends in social structure include: increased objective interdependence on the national scale (economically, technologically, politically); decreased local isolation and autonomy; increased depersonalization of social organization; and greater occupational specialization, but lessened differentiation of classes, ethnic groupings, regions, and racial categories. Increased socio-cultural homogeneity facilitates society-wide organizations and centralized decision making. Along with the growth of large-scale formal organizations and the multiplication of special-interest associations has gone a reduction in the importance of ascriptive social positions. In a setting of rapid social change and of much geographic and social mobility, these trends create a basis for much crowd behavior, formation of publics, and collective movements. Networks of personal acquaintance and friendship often become fluid, widely dispersed, and of low intensity.

A society with these characteristics is highly adaptable to technological and economic changes. The extent to which the adaptations are stressful to individual personalities is largely unknown.

The long-term increases in the scale of our society and in its complexity have created increased urgency for improved societal knowledge—and for its fast delivery to crucial points of decision making. In the interdependent world of the future, disaster may not be avoidable. But it is certain that disaster will be fostered by any inadequacy in fast and accurate feedback concerning the consequences of centralized decisions in the polity and the economy.

In common with much of the rest of the world, American society and culture have participated at an accelerating rate in the cognitive revolution of the last few centuries. Increasingly we have a "civilization" in the basic sense developed by Robert Bierstedt: a way of life that is sophisticated about itself. As he explains, a noncivilized society has art without esthetics, tools without technology, religion without theology, techniques without science, trade without economics, knowledge without philosophy, personalities without psychology—and society without sociology.[26] A civilization has procedures, concepts, and institutions for reflective self-examination. It is knowledgeable both about the external physical world and the human-social world. Barring the massive catastrophe that we all know hangs by a thread above us, the trend toward sophistication appears to be essentially irreversible. Beginning with the grossly external features of physical nature, it has moved progressively toward the disciplined understanding of man and society.

An essential implication, if this thesis is true, is that our model of American society must include careful specification of its resources and arrangements for self-analysis and for the heightening of the generalized cognitive capacities of its individual and collective actors.[27]

One of the striking changes of the last decade has been the emergence into sharp public awareness of the chronic poverty beneath our obvious affluence. Poverty has been with us before, but during the late 1940's and early 1950's it was the poverty of an inarticulate population, largely hidden from public view and ignored whenever possible. We are becoming aware that we may be developing a stratum that will be permanently unable to improve its lot unaided. Many of those in the lowest income strata are aged persons, the chronically ill and handicapped, and mothers in broken homes.[28] Others are located in stranded areas of low economic opportunity. Others are non-whites who represent what Bayard Rustin has called "the disastrous convergence of class and color." Finally, many are unskilled or uneducated workers for whom there simply is not an "adequate" demand in our present economic structure.

Increasingly, however, we have *one* society: local and regional differences within the nation are gradually being reduced. Political affairs and governmental actions are increasingly centralized. The same is true of crucial decisions in the economy. Trends toward national centralization are evident in the mass media, in the educational system, and in virtually every other sector of the society. Nowhere is the pressure toward national uniformity more striking than in what we might call the new Science Establishment.

As Donald R. Fleming has pointed out, our society has been engaged in a long process of "continentalizing American science and culture." [29] The projected "equalization" of regions of the United States in federal science grants is the expectable outcome of the political processes in an equalitarian democracy in which centralized redistribution of wealth and power has come to involve control of scientific and technological research and development. The enormously increased importance of scientific research and development since World War II and especially since Sputnik I is no longer just "educational," nor merely "economic," nor just "military." It has come to be seen as an avenue to wealth and power for individuals, firms, industries, metropolitan areas, regions, and nations. The federal science budget in 1940 was about $74 million; it is now approximately $15.5 billion. Big science has become big business—and big politics. In the new political awareness, "the distribution of university science was seen as affecting the ultimate distribution of wealth and power in American society." [30]

The main net thrust of all developments here reviewed, and of others we have no space to consider, is in the direction of what I have called an "integrated mass society." [31] It may be suspected that this concept is close to the idea of the Great Society. The dominant trends are toward affluence; consensus; centralization; advanced technology; high levels of formal education; equalization of rights, privileges, and substantive conditions of regions, races, ethnic groupings, and religious groupings; security—and enjoyment values; low tension; and increased expressiveness. The main movements are from particularism to universalism, from ascription to achievement, from affectivity to affective neutrality (with important counter-trends *re* expressivity in recreation), from diffuseness to specificity, and from self-interest to collectivity-interest (with complex redefinitions of both).

These developments relate to another question posed for this essay: "Would it be correct to say that American society is now moving from the 'industrial' to a 'post-industrial' stage?" The answer, we believe, is a qualified "yes," The following facts sum up the case:

1. White-collar occupations now account for more than one-half of the labor force, and the proportion continues to increase.

2. Industrial workers are a constant rather than a growing component of the work force.

3. Services rather than manufactured goods account for the most rapid growth in the economy.

4. The basic problem of the economy is no longer production but rather how to certify the needed consumption.

5. Increased governmental facilitation, regulation, and direct production are here to stay for the foreseeable future.

6. A large and increasing proportion of investment in corporations is derived from nonindividual, nonprofit agencies, including pension funds.

7. The problems created as side effects of industrialism are not capable of solution within the framework of the older industrial system.

8. All of the above, however, do not imply that industrial output is not crucially important, nor do they imply that the economic power concentrated in large-scale industry is not highly consequential for both government and the total way of life of the American people.

It is apparent, I believe, that the loosely articulated social and cultural pluralism of nineteenth-century America has greatly changed. A central question for the future is: Can the valued liberties and flexibilities of the national tradition be preserved and extended in the massive, powerful, technologically advanced, and centralized society we now have?

ARE THERE MAJOR INSTITUTIONAL RIGIDITIES IN AMERICAN LIFE?

In attempting to answer this question, it would be misleading to draw an analogy between social rigidity and neurotic personality processes. Yet it may be interesting and productive to compare the two (quite different) processes. Here is a research psychiatrist's account of the nature of a computer program designed to simulate basic neurotic processes:[32]

> The essentials of this neurotic process are conflict producing a danger signal which in turn produces a transformation of belief until the danger is eliminated. The safety-first postulate of avoiding danger takes precedence over the discharge through expression postulate. The transforms are adjustive mechanisms, but they are maladaptive since they result in loss of information, misrepresentations of beliefs, and insufficient discharge leading to increasing repetitive preoccupation with conflictual areas. If the program attempts to interrogate itself about its own information, it cannot express directly some of its most highly charged beliefs and it receives as answers distorted derivatives of these beliefs.

If one had been told in advance that this paragraph describes the social processes by which white Americans deal with discrimination and segregation directed toward Negro Americans, one might well have accepted it as such. The parallel lies in loss of information and distortion of reality through defenses against anxiety generated by conflict of values or interests.

It seems quite clear that predominant among conspicuous rigidities in American society is the enormous failure to accept Negro Americans as human beings. I put the matter in this blunt and non-academic style to emphasize the massive simplicity of the value conflict that lies at the heart of the matter.

It is often said that our social institutions have not kept up with the pace of technological change. W. F. Ogburn's notion of "culture lag" has become part of the popular sociology of the literate public. The notion that social and cultural "adaptations" lag behind the need for change brought on by technical innovation suggests different rates of change in different parts of the society. If this is true, where are the disparities most obvious and where are they most hidden?

It is plain that the attribution of "lag" or "disparity" is a value judgment. It is a *judgment* because we have no exact way of measuring and comparing rates of change in different parts of the system. How does one compare rates of industrial innovation with changes in family structure, unionization, popular music, religious ritual, and political ideology? We do not say it cannot be done; we do say that as of today it generally is not done. It is a *value* judgment because "fast enough" or "not fast enough" means that we are weighing one or more value(s) against others. With this understanding, we can go on to make a few provisional diagnoses.

First, the most obvious disparities. Any serious observer of our current American scene will have his own favorite list. First on mine is the disparity between the high technology of mass destruction and the limited knowledge and socio-political technology of managing and resolving opposition and conflict. Second is the rigidity of economic and political arrangements that perpetuate racial discrimination and segregation—with enormous economic and social costs. Third, is the (I believe) losing battle against the spoliation of our physical environment, as witnessed by gigantic metropolitan slums, urban sprawl and blight, rural slums, highways defaced by signs and by automobile junkyards, and by every variety of building clutter— and as witnessed by pollution of streams and lakes, destruction of plant and animal life, and well-nigh criminal pollution of the air we breathe. Fourth, the disparity between our national emphasis on instrumental activism and our potential capacities for gratifying interpersonal relations, on the one hand, and for esthetic creation and appreciation, on the other. There is evidence of sacrifices in mental health, social gratification, and esthetic experience in our race to "get things done."

Among the less obvious disparities, one may be allowed to suspect that the American people have not adequately reaped the rewards of self-insight and full acceptance of the emotional life. By the same token, second, it is likely that the virtues of contemplation have been underestimated, relative to activism. Third, there is not yet a clear public appreciation of the disparity between the rich potential contribution of the social sciences for our civilization and the actual limited support and understanding they currently are accorded. A closely related disparity, fourth, is the gap between what we already know about personality, society, and culture and the application of that knowledge in policy and action, at all levels of the national life. Fifth, although a highly controversial point, I believe that much of American "popular religion" represents a historically anachronistic misunderstanding of genuine religious insights and of intellectually acceptable theology. (For example, it often confuses means and ends, mistakenly equates social conformity with goodness, and thinks that neurotic guilt is the same as conscience.) A sixth perhaps non-obvious gap exists between the objective conditions that, for the first time in history, could permit creative living for the bulk of the population, and the actual preoccupations of white Suburbia today.[33] And this thought leads finally to a seventh disparity—the gap between the new potentials for relations between persons, men to men, women to women, men to women, in relation to the actual frustrations and alienations reflected in much current behavior.

A further question raised for this essay is: "Are there significant ideologies or doctrines that interfere with adaptive change?" It is clear that such a question encourages the present writer to "live dangerously." For what is "ideology" to someone else may be "sound doctrine" or "simply the truth" to me. Nevertheless, recognizing the inevitable value-laden and controversial nature of any answers that one can give, we do have a few suggestions.

By "adaptive changes" I understand, at the minimum, changes that would improve the society's chances for survival, or increase its technical and economic efficiency, or reduce disabling conflict, or reduce personal suffering. By "ideology" or "doctrine" we mean here a set of beliefs and values purporting to furnish guidelines for empirical social arrangements. In these terms, I would regard the following doctrines as retarding adaptive changes:

1. *Irresponsible localism:* those doctrines (sometimes including certain so-called "states' rights") that assert or imply that any community, state, or region is free to set itself up as the arbitrary judge of its own conduct, even when the conduct is clearly unethical and dangerous.

2. *Racial superiority:* a pervasive set of assumptions and evaluations, not accurate or well supported by scientific evidence, that block reasonable approaches to solving massive social problems and conflicts.

3. *Monolithic and rigid anti-communism:* a stereotyped conception of communism and a rigid commitment to policies established under conditions very different from those of today that hinder needed rational statecraft.

4. *Unrealistic laissez-faire ideology of economic affairs* sometimes hampers understanding of organizational and financial procedures needed for optimum functioning of the American economy.

5. *Doctrines of individual responsibility and culpability carried to self-defeating extremes* in dealing with alcoholism, drug addiction, sexual deviations, delinquency, mental illnesses, and criminal recidivism. Rigid notions inherited from pre-scientific thinking hamper efforts to treat and cure those behavior disorders for which traditional sanctions serve neither to deter, nor to correct, nor to rehabilitate.

TOWARD THE GREAT SOCIETY?

Finally let us turn to the dimensions along which we may judge a society to be great. It may be supposed that the term "greatness" literally may be applied to any characteristic that is positively valued by someone. What we consider great, in short, depends upon our values. We may judge a society as great in military power but lacking in ethical greatness, or great in the creative arts but poor in civic virtue, and so on. Looking at American society against the background of the main historically received value themes, I suspect that the conception of the Great Society most likely to be accepted and supported here includes these elements:

1. Economic growth and a high level of consumption.

2. Protection of the disadvantaged by a minimal level of support in adversity.

3. Widespread equality of opportunity for high-quality education.

4. International security.

5. Freedom of choice in occupation, residence, marriage, politics, religion, and a wide range of values and tastes.

6. Development and conservation of natural assets.

7. Growing appreciation of expressive culture, and support for creative work in the arts and sciences.

8. Increased understanding and ethical sensitivity in everyday life.

To state even these highly general objectives is enough to suggest the formidable difficulties of attaining them. At the same time, the statement of goals is the first essential step in moving toward realistic attainment of them.

James K. Feibleman has introduced the concept of *transparent facilitation* to refer to the operation of established organizations in such a way that they unobtrusively serve their functions, purely as means and never as ends in themselves.[34] When transparent facilitation is being maximized, the organization does not intrude itself between the individual and his attainment of his goals and gratification of his needs. To secure such facilitation requires another kind of transparency, namely, the openness of the society to examination and analysis. In Bentley's terms, one of the tasks of socio-analysis—indeed, he said it was "almost the sole hope" of a better society—was to bring out "fully and continuously and systematically, the meanings and values and weights of all the opinionative phases in terms of all the activities that are at play. It is a process of socio-analysis that we need, not unworthy perhaps of being contrasted in that phrase with the work of psychoanalysis."[35] Many persons and groups in our society favor nothing less than transparency; they are endangered by clarity. Yet clarity will be our society's salvation, or nothing will.

Homeostasis in organisms is *not* infallible, but it does not require purpose or intelligence. In social systems, homeostasis is not infallible or automatic; it often does require both purpose and intelligence. No "automatic" process is now checking delinquency or dissolving urban slums or producing acceptable solutions to involvement in local wars around the world.

Social intelligence requires knowledge and analysis. The main intent of this essay has been to help in some small measure to prepare the way for actions in the near future, for the beginning of necessary reporting and analysis at the highest political levels. I believe this to be an essential development for the maintenance and growth of freedom and responsibility in the American society of the future.

•NOTES

1. See Floyd Allport's designation of "system" as a "recognizably delimited aggregate of dynamic elements that are in some way interconnected and interdependent and that continue to operate together according to certain laws and in such a way as to produce some characteristic total effect." *Theories of Perception and the Concept of Structure* (New York: Wiley, 1955), p. 469.

2. See Arthur F. Bentley, *Relativity in Man and Society* (New York: Putnam's, 1926), p. 182: "Man-society is not a fluid process, its activities freely functioning, each for itself, out to a tenuous gaseous analogy. The activities cohere, they are clotted."

3. *Ibid.*, pp. 205–206.

4. Talcott Parsons, "Levels of Organization and the Mediation of Social Interaction," *Sociological Inquiry*, XXXIV, No. 2 (Spring 1964), 219.

5. See Robert Boguslaw, *The New Utopians: A Study of System Design and Social Change* (Englewood Cliffs, N.J.: Prentice-Hall, 1965), Ch. 5.

6. See James K. Feibleman, *The Institutions of Society* (London: Allen & Unwin, 1956), p. 193: "Institutions, in short, begin as means to ends that lie beyond them, but they have a tendency to turn into ends in themselves, and thus to continue their own existence at the cost of whatever it was they had originally served."

7. See Bertram M. Gross, "The State of the Nation: Social Systems Accounting," in Raymond A. Bauer (ed.), *Social Indicators* (Cambridge: M.I.T. Press, 1966).

8. James S. Coleman, "Collective Decisions," *Sociological Inquiry*, XXXIV, No. 2 (Spring 1964), 169: "Thus we will assume to begin with a set of actors (wholly self-interested, as indicated before), whose actions have some effects for

one another." A difference between utilities of outcomes constitutes the *interest* of the actor.

9. *Ibid.*

10. Talcott Parsons, "Marx's Sociological Theory," *Abstracts of Papers* (American Sociological Association, 1965), p. 9.

11. Peter M. Blau, "Justice in Social Exchange," *Sociological Inquiry,* XXXIV, No. 2 (Spring 1964), 205: "Social values and norms can be considered mediating links of social transactions, which serve as a basis for indirect exchange, and through which the range of transactions become expanded beyond the limits of direct social contacts."

12. See Conrad Arensberg, "American Communities," *American Anthropologist,* LVII, No. 6 (December 1955), 1143–1162.

13. Paul Meadows, "Models, Systems and Science," *American Sociological Review,* XXII, No. 1 (February 1957), 4. See in the same issue James M. Beshers, "Models and Theory Construction," pp. 32–38.

14. See Guy H. Orcutt *et al., Microanalysis of Socioeconomic Systems: A Simulation Study* (New York: Harper, 1961).

15. *Sociology: Rules, Roles and Relationships* (Homewood, Ill.: The Dorsey Press, 1966), Ch. 8.

16. Gross, *op. cit.,* p. 58.

17. If relationships are nonlinear, it will be difficult to predict from data on processes of change what will be the steady-state performance of the system.

18. See Bentley, *op. cit.,* p. 119: "We may perhaps say that the term state indicates a great complex of closely coinciding activities, which hold together and get enough representative process for stability. The state is fundamental not as a mystic being but only in the sense of this stability, this durational extent, this relative permanence."

19. *Ibid.,* p. 180.

20. David Easton, *A Systems Analysis of Political Life* (New York: Wiley, 1965).

21. See J. David Singer, "The Political Science of Human Conflict," in Elton B. McNeil (ed.), *The Nature of Human Conflict* (Englewood Cliffs, N.J.: Prentice Hall, 1965), p. 143; Chadwick F. Alger, "Comparison of Intranational and International Politics," *American Political Science Review,* LVII, No. 2 (June 1963), 406–419.

22. Stratification is much more nucleated in some societies, as illustrated by the caste organization in India and the organization of the estates in medieval Europe.

23. Recall Bently's formulation, *op. cit.,* p. 199: "Because we stand at a time of great conflicts we have no right to say that those conflicts are irresolvable. All social life is a resolution of conflicts, provisional always, with new conflicts arising, with the intolerable activities being driven out, with new methods being secured, with destructions at times and places, but with new creations succeeding.

"Knowledge of our group attachments and their relativities—that, and that alone, can give us the greater approximations to virile peace which is what we all most crave, and of what we all most despair in the hidden part of our lives, while our values are given us in darkness."

24. See Boguslaw, *op. cit.,* p. 124: "System designs with fixed, unalterable goals inevitably assign second-level or lower priorities to such things as operating unit integrity or operating unit values."

25. During the last decade the permeability of national systems has rapidly increased—as indicated by frequency of visiting friends and relatives abroad, foreign sojourns on business, study abroad, technical assistance, international non-governmental organizations, and membership in United Nations secretariats. See Robert C. Angell, "The Growth of Transnational Participation," *Abstracts of Papers* (American Sociological Association, 1965), p. 131.

26. Robert Bierstedt, *The Social Order* (New York: McGraw-Hill, 1957), pp. 53–54.

27. It is easy to show that cognitive errors about basic social conditions exist on a large scale in today's United States of America. Thus, most white people have no real understanding of recent riots among Negro Americans in our large cities. In Rochester, New York: "Only 12 percent of the whites cited grievances as a cause of the riots or indicated sympathy with the situation of the Negro." See Dean Harper, "Aftermath of a Long, Hot Summer," *Trans-action*, II, No. 5 (July–August 1965), 9.

28. There are now about 4.5 million recipients of A.D.C. (aid to dependent children); one-half of these are non-whites. The proportion of husbandless married women of child-bearing age among non-whites is over one-fifth and rising; in 1960 of all nonwhite women ever married, 30 per cent were without a husband.

29. "The Big Money and High Politics of Science," *The Atlantic*, CCXVI, No. 2 (August 1965), 41.

30. Fleming, *op. cit.*, p. 43.

31. "Social Change and Social Conflict: Race Relations in the United States, 1944–1964," *Sociological Inquiry*, XXXV, No. 1 (Winter 1965), 8–25.

32. Kenneth Mark Colby, "Computer Simulation of a Neurotic Process," in Silvan S. Tompkins and Samuel Messick (eds.), *Computer Simulation of Personality* (New York: Wiley, 1963), p. 173.

33. See the special issue of *Ebony:* "The White Problem in America," August 1965.

34. Feibleman, *op. cit.*, p. 179.

35. Bentley, *op. cit.*, p. 196.

Chapter 3

The Individual in the Great Society

HERBERT MARCUSE

Prior to exploring the presumed function of the "individual" in the "great society," a brief definition (or rather redefinition) of these terms is required. For I propose to proceed by placing the official and semi-official ideas and speeches about the Great Society in the context of their prospective realization, and in the context of the prevailing conditions (political, economic, intellectual) which determine their (possible or impossible) realization. Unless these factors are brought to bear on the idea, it remains mere speech, publicity, or propaganda —at best a statement of intentions. It is the responsibility of the scholar to take them seriously, that is to say, to go beyond the words or rather to stay this side of the words, in the given universe of powers, capabilities, and tendencies which defines their content.

I start with the notion of the Great Society as presented by President Johnson. I think its essentials can be summed up as follows: it is (1) a society of "unbridled growth," resting on "abundance and liberty for all," which demands an "end to poverty and racial injustice"; (2) a society in which progress is the "servant of our needs"; (3) a society in which leisure is a "welcome chance to build and reflect," and which serves "not only the needs of the body and the demands of commerce, but the desire for beauty and the hunger for community."

This picture is preceded by the statement that our society can be a place where "we will raise our families, free from the dark shadow of war and suspicion among nations." And it is followed by an enumeration of the areas where the construction of the Great Society can begin, namely: (1) the rebuilding of our cities, and of the transportation between them, in accord with the needs of the constantly growing population; (2) the reconstruction of the polluted and destroyed countryside, in order to regain "contact with nature" and to protect "America the beautiful"; (3) the improvement and enlargement of education and educational facilities. And when all this is done, we will not have reached the end of the struggle, for "most of all, the Great Society is not a safe harbor, a resting place, a final objective, a finished work. It is a challenge constantly renewed, beckoning us toward a destiny where the meaning of our lives matches the marvelous products of our labor."

GREAT SOCIETY VS. CAPITALIST ENTERPRISE

Let me pause here and register my first dissent. I began intentionally with the most speculative, most "utopian" aspect because it is here that the basic direction of the program (and its innermost limitations) is most visible. First a slight matter of style: the meaning of our lives should "match" the "products of our labor"—shouldn't it be the other way around? In a free society, the meaning of life is determined by the free individuals, who determine the products of their labor accordingly. By itself, the phrasing may not preclude this interpretation, but in the context of the whole section it assumes special significance. Why should the Great (and Free) Society *not* be a resting place, a safe harbor? Why should it be a challenge constantly renewed? The dynamic of endlessly propelled productivity is not that of a peaceful, humane society in which the individuals have come into their own and develop their own humanity; the challenge they meet may be precisely that of protecting and preserving a "safe harbor," a "resting place" where life is no longer spent in the struggle for existence. And such a society may well reject the notion (and practice) of "unbridled growth"; it may well (I shall come back to this) restrict its technical capabilities where they threaten to increase the dependence of man on his instruments and products.

Even today, long before the start on the road to a free society, the war on poverty might be waged far more effectively by a redirection rather than by an increase of production, by the elimination of productivity from the areas of socially necessary waste, planned obsolescence, armament, publicity, manipulation. A society which couples abundance and liberty in the dynamic of unbridled growth and perpetual challenge is the ideal of a system based on the perpetuation of scarcity—more and more artificially created scarcity, namely, the need for ever more and ever new goods of abundance. For in such a system, the individuals must spend their lives in the competitive struggle for existence in order to satisfy the need for the increasing products of labor, and the products of labor must be increased because they must be sold at a profit, and the rate of profit depends on the growing productivity of labor. In less ideological language, this was called the law of the enlarged accumulation of capital. Under this aspect, the Great Society appears as the streamlined and improved continuation of the existing not-so-great society—after the latter has succeeded in cleansing itself of its sore spots and blemishes. Its ability to do so is assumed. But the scholar cannot grant the assumption without examination: we leave the speculation on the Great Society and return to the program for its construction, or rather for its preparation within the existing society.

Foremost is the war on poverty. The critical literature on it already is so large that I can be brief in my references. This war is supposed to be waged by the "affluent society" against poverty *in* the "affluent society"; thus it may turn out to be a war of this society against itself, taken of its internal contradiction. The real conquest of poverty would mean either full employment as the normal, long-range condition of the system, or unemployment and a dole sufficiently large to live the good life—also the normal, long-range condition of the system. Both achievements are within the (technical) capabilities of an advanced industrial society (paradoxically, the second may be the historical consequence of the first!). But the concept "advanced industrial society" has to be broken down into its actual main forms: capitalist and socialist. Here, we are concerned with the former only. In it, the real conquest of poverty is counteracted and "contained" by the prevailing social institutions. Full employment, as constant condition, implies a constantly high (and, with rising productivity, a constantly rising) level of real wages, not canceled by rising prices. This would be equivalent to a decline in the rate of profit below the limit tolerable to private enterprise. It is perhaps conceivable that something like full employment can be attained by an expanding war (or defense) economy, plus an expanding production of waste, status symbols, planned obsolescence, and parasitic services. But even disregarding the clear and present danger

of an international explosion, such a system would produce and reproduce human beings who could by no stretch of the imagination be
expected to build a free, humane society. For the construction of a
Great Society depends on a "human factor" which hardly appears in
the program, namely, the existence of individuals who, in their attitudes, goals, and needs, are qualitatively different from those who are
educated, trained, and rewarded today: the aggression mobilized
(and repressed) in the maintenance of a society geared to permanent
defense militates against progress toward higher forms of freedom and
rationality. To be sure, non-destructive full employment remains a
real possibility: it requires nothing more, and nothing less, than the
actual reconstruction outlined in the President's program—that is,
the rebuilding of the cities, of the countryside, and of education. But
this very program requires the elimination of the particular interests
which stand in the way of its fulfillment. Today, they include capital
and labor, city and countryside politics, Republicans and Democrats,
and they are the powerful interests on which this Administration
largely relies.

The truism must be repeated: not only the magnitude but the
economic basis of the program is incompatible with these interests.
The transformation of the cities into a human universe involves far
more than slum clearings: it involves the literal dissolution of the
cities and rebuilding according to rigidly enforced architectural
plans. If undertaken for the population as a whole rather than for
those who can pay, the reconstruction would be plainly unprofitable,
and its public financing would mean the abrogation of some of the
most powerful lobbies in the country. It would, for example, imply
the establishment of a wide and efficient network of public transportation, replacing the private automobile as the main vehicle of business and leisure—the end of the motor industry as now organized.
The "beautification" of the countryside would imply the (rigidly enforced) elimination of all billboards, neon signs, the reduction of the
innumerable service stations, roadside stands, noise makers, and so on
which have rendered impossible the desired "contact with nature."
Generally, and perhaps most important, reconstruction would require the elimination of all planned obsolescence, which has become
an essential prop for the system inasmuch as it ensures the necessary
turnover and the competitive rat race. In all these aspects, the realization of the program seems irreconcilable with the spirit of capitalist
enterprise, and this contradiction becomes perhaps most strikingly

apparent in the program's insistence on beauty. Here, the words assume a false ring, the language becomes that of commercial poetry, and it comes almost as a relief when Mrs. Johnson, dropping the ideological language, goes out to proclaim beauty as an economic asset: according to the Los Angeles *Times* (September 8, 1965): "Preserving the attractiveness of a city is a primary economic asset, a way to get payrolls. The city that is beautiful brings a high return on the dollar."

ADVANCED INDUSTRIALISM'S EFFECT ON PEOPLE

I now come to the "human factor" and I shall take up education, the third area of reconstruction, in the course of my discussion. Who are the human beings, the individuals who are supposed to build the Great Society?

They live in a society where they are (for good or bad) subjected to an apparatus which, comprising production, distribution, and consumption, material and intellectual, work and leisure, politics and fun, determines their daily existence, their needs and aspirations. And this life, private, social, and rational, is enclosed in a very specific historical universe. The individuals who make up the bulk of the population in the "affluent societies" live in a universe of permanent defense and aggression. It manifests itself in the war against the Vietcong and in the struggle against the Negroes, in the huge network of industries and services which work for the military establishment and its accessories, but it also manifests itself in the violence released and made productive by science and technology, in the terror of publicity and fun inflicted on captive audiences. Against the age-old argument that violence and aggression have always been a normal factor in all societies, I must insist on the qualitative difference. It is not only the magnitude of the destructive potential and the scope of its realization that distinguish a chariot race from an automobile race, a canon from a missile, hydraulic from nuclear energy. Similarly, it is not only the speed and range that distinguish the means of mass communication from their predecessors. The new quality is introduced by the progressing transfer of power from the human individual to the technical or bureaucratic apparatus, from living to dead labor, from personal to remote control, from a machine (or group of machines) to a whole mechanized system. I should like to reiterate that I do not (yet) evaluate this development: it may be progressive or regressive, humanizing or dehumanizing. But what actually occurs in this transfer of power is also a transfer of guilt-feeling responsibility—it releases the individual from being an autonomous person: in work and in leisure, in his needs and satisfactions, in his thought and emotions.

At the same time, however, the release is not liberation from alienated labor: the individuals must go on spending physical and mental energy in the struggle for existence, status, advantage; they must suffer, service, and enjoy the apparatus which imposes on them this necessity. The new heteronomy in the work world is not compensated by a new autonomy over the work world: alienation is intensified as it becomes transparently irrational, and it becomes unproductive as it sustains repressive productivity. And where the established society delivers the goods that raise the standard of living, alienation reaches the point at which even the consciousness of alienation is largely repressed: individuals identify themselves with their being-for-others.

In such circumstances, society calls for an Enemy against whom the prevailing conditions are to be defended and against whom the aggressive energy which cannot be channeled into the normal, daily struggle for existence can be released. The individuals who are called upon to develop the Great Society live in a society which wages war or is prepared to wage war all over the world. Any discussion which does not put the program of the Great Society into the international framework must remain ideological, propaganda. The Enemy is not one factor among others, not a contingency which an evaluation of the chances of the Great Society can ignore or to which it can refer to in passing—his existence is a determining factor at home and abroad, in business and education, in science and relaxation.

We are here concerned only with the Enemy in relation to the program of the Great Society, more specifically, with the way in which the Enemy (or rather the presentation of the Enemy and of the struggle against him) affects the individuals, the people who are supposed to change the "affluent society" into the Great Society. Thus the question is not to what degree the armament industry and its "multipliers" have become an indispensable part of the "affluent society," nor whether the present dominance and policy of the military establishment are in the "national interest" (once the national interest is defined in terms other than those of these policymakers themselves). Rather the question I want to raise is: Does the existence of the

Enemy prejudge—and prejudge negatively—the capability and the capacity to build the Great Society? Before I enter into a brief discussion of the question, I must define, and redefine, "the Enemy." And I shall do so by submitting a precarious hypothesis.

Is the Enemy still communism *per se?* I think not. First, communism today exists in many forms, some in conflict and contradiction with the others. And this country does not combat all of these forms, and not only for tactical reasons. Second, capitalist trade with communist countries is constantly increasing, and precisely with those countries where communism seems to be most stable. Moreover, communism is most firmly and solidly constituted in the Soviet Union, but for quite some time the U.S.A. and the U.S.S.R. have not really treated each other as Enemies (capitalized!)—in fact one even hears talk of cooperation and collusion, while the Enemy against whom the system is mobilized is presented as precluding cooperation and collusion. Third, it is difficult to regard communism as threatening this country—even on the campuses and among the Negroes. Looking at the facts, geographical and otherwise, I would say that mobilization is carried out and war is actually waged against (and among) semi-colonial and formerly colonial peoples, backward peoples, and have-nots, communist or not. This is not the old colonialism and imperialism (although in some aspects the contrast has been overdrawn: there is little essential difference between a direct government by the metropolitan power and a native government that functions only by grace of a metropolitan power). The (objective) rationale for the global struggle is, not the need for immediate capital export, resources, surplus exploitation; it is rather the danger of a subversion of the established hierarchy of master and servant, top and bottom, a hierarchy that has created and sustained the have-nations, capitalist *and* communist. There is a very primitive, very elemental threat of subversion—a slave revolt rather than a revolution, and precisely for this reason more dangerous to societies that are capable of containing or defeating revolutions. For the slaves are everywhere and countless, and they indeed have nothing to lose but their chains. To be sure, the established societies have faced the subversion of their hierarchy before: from within, by one of their own classes. This time, the threat comes from without, and precisely for this reason it threatens the system as a whole; the threat appears as a total one and those who represent it have not even a potential vested interest in the established societies. They may have no blueprint for positive reconstruction, or they may have one which would not work, but they simply do not want to be slaves any longer, and they are driven by the vital need to change intolerable conditions—and to do it differently from the old powers. This primitive rebellion, this revolt indeed implies a social program, namely, the awareness that their society cannot be constructed along the line of the have-nations which perpetuate servitude and domination. Their struggle for liberation is *objectively* anti-capitalist even if they reject socialism and want the benefits of capitalism, and their struggle is *objectively* anti-communist even if they are communists, for it aims beyond (or this side of) the established communist systems.

I used the term "objectively rational" in order to emphasize that I do not imply that the factors or tendencies just outlined are those intentionally pursued by the policy makers. I rather suggest that they are operative "behind the back" of the policy makers, and perhaps even assert themselves against the will of the policy makers—as historical tendencies which can be extrapolated from the prevailing social and political conditions. At the surface there is another, far more obvious rationale for permanent mobilization and defense, that which is expressed in the "domino theory" and the notion of the communist drive for world revolution. The notion as presented by the makers of policy and information does not correspond to the facts, but there is a kernel of truth in the domino theory. Any spectacular victory of the rebellious have-nots in any one place would activate their consciousness and their rebellion in other places as well—perhaps even at home. Moreover, for capitalism, such a victory would mean a further dangerous narrowing of the world market—a rather remote danger, which would materialize only if and when the backward countries have reached real independence, but a danger serious enough, for example, with respect to Latin America. For the Soviet Union, the economic danger does not prevail, but the threat to the established regime seems real enough. One can safely say that the attitude of the Soviet leaders toward revolution and rebellion is at best ambivalent if not hostile, as is clear in the conflict with China.

It is the most advanced industrial society which feels most directly threatened by the rebellion, because it is here that the social necessity of repression and alienation, of servitude and heteronomy is most transparently unnecessary, and unproductive in terms of human progress. This is the hidden rationale behind the cruelty and violence mobilized in the struggle against the threat, behind the monotonous regularity with which the people are made familiar with, and accustomed to, inhuman attitudes and behavior—to wholesale killing as patriotic act. What the free press achieves in this respect will perhaps later be remembered as one of the most shameful acts of civilization. Hardly a day passes when the headlines do not celebrate a victory by announcing "136 Vietcong Killed," "Marines Kill at least 156 Vietcong," "More than 240 Reds Slain." I have lived through two world wars, but I cannot recall any such brazen advertisement of slaughter. Nor can I remember—even in the Nazi press—a headline such as that which announces: "U. S. Pleased over Lack of Protests on Tear Gas" (Los Angeles *Times,* September 9, 1965). This sort of reporting, consumed daily by millions, appeals to killers and the need for killers. And a New York judge has epitomized the situation when, in paroling two youths "who were arraigned on a charge of murdering an East Side derelict and then rearrested on a charge of killing one of their companions," he remarked, according to *The New York Times* (September 8, 1965): "They should go to Vietnam, where we need soldiers to kill Vietcong."

I have suggested that the international situation of the affluent society is in a very specific sense an expression of its internal dynamic: of the conflict between the (social, political) need to preserve the established power structure within the nation and abroad on the one hand, and the historical obsolescence of this need on the other, as dramatized in the rebellion of the backward peoples. In this conflict, society mobilizes its individuals' aggressive energy to such an extent that they seem hardly capable of becoming the builders of a *peaceful* and free society. It seems that such an undertaking, which would aim at a qualitatively different society, would mean a break, a rupture with the established one, and thus would require the emergence of "new" individuals, with qualitatively different needs and aspirations. I now propose to go one step farther and to raise the question whether the advanced industrial society has not negated the traditional notion (and possibility) of the individual in reality, while at the same time perpetuating and extolling it ideologically. In other words, does the individual still have a progressive and productive social function, or is individuality being surpassed by new advanced forms of productivity and their organization? Have individuality, personal autonomy, individual enterprise become obsolete, brakes rather than vehicles of (technical) progress? Again, I emphasize that I propose to discuss this question without prejudice in favor of transmitted "values": it may well be that the passing of the individual can be called "positive" in terms of human as well as technical progress. I begin with a brief re-examination of the notion of the individual as it has become representative of the modern period. Only a rough sketch will be attempted.

THE EVOLVING CONCEPT OF INDIVIDUALISM

In its new historical function, the notion of the individual originates in the Protestant Reformation. The religious and the secular, the internal and external manifestations develop simultaneously. In this dual function, the individual becomes the unit of the new society: in spirit, as the responsible subject of faith, thought, and conscience; and in the spirit of capitalism, as the responsible subject of free enterprise. The two manifestations remain interrelated, but two trends may be distinguished which increasingly conflict with each other as the new society advances: on the one hand there is the development of the free moral and intellectual subject, on the other hand the development of the subject of free enterprise in free competition. We may also say: the individual in the struggle for himself, for moral and intellectual autonomy, and the individual in the struggle for existence are separated. They are still at harmony in Descartes's *ego cogito:* the individual is the subject of science which comprehends and conquers nature in the service of the new society, and he is the subject of methodical doubt, of critical reason against all established prejudices. But the harmony is fallacious: the unity of the two spheres is dissolved. The individual as subject of the capitalist struggle for existence, economic competition, and politics takes shape in the philosophy of Hobbes, Locke, Adam Smith, Bentham, while the subject of individual autonomy, moral and intellectual, is epitomized in the Enlightenment, in Leibnitz and Kant.

The conflict between the philosophical traditions reflects the unfolding conflict in the social reality. Freedom was supposed to be the individual's essential quality in theory and practice, thought and action; quality of the inner and the outer man. In this sense, the individual was the corollary of private enterprise: moral responsibility and the autonomous personality were to have their actual basis in economic and political freedom. The individual is *proprietor:* not merely in the sense of possessing material resources, goods, and services necessary for the realization (demonstration, validation) of his freedom in his society, but in the sense of having acquired these things by virtue of his own labor or control over another's labor (already in Locke!) and having made them his own—the material expression of his productive, creative personality. This notion, of the individual as proprietor which dominates the philosophical theory of the individual from Hobbes to Hegel, was hardly applicable, in any general sense, to the acquisitive society, in which the majority of the population remained deprived of such autonomy. But there was one class, and for a long time the ruling class, that of the agrarian and industrial entrepreneurs, of whom it could be said that they were the masters of their own enterprise: individually responsible for their decisions, choices, risks—rewarded if their decision was a good one, punished if it was bad, according to the verdict of the free, competitive market. Through the freedom of private enterprise, this class (roughly, "the bourgeoisie") developed the productive forces on an individualistic foundation—under the conditions of free capitalism which prevailed in the industrial countries until the end of the nineteenth century. And the same economic masters were autonomous individuals in their own house: determining the education of the children, the level of the household, the pattern of behavior—they enforced the Reality Principle in a rather authoritarian manner. "Masters in their house," in their business, and in their home, they could do without the government, without "public relations," without standardized mass media; thus they could be considered the living representatives of individualistic culture.

Today, no long discussion is necessary to show that the conditions under which this form of individual enterprise could flourish have disappeared. Contemporary American society has surpassed the stage of productivity where individual units of production engage in free competition with each other; with the transformation of liberalistic into organized capitalism, "individuality" in the economic sphere (and not only there!) has become obsolete, dwarfed by the rapid and overwhelming growth in the productivity of labor, and by the growth of the means and instruments for utilizing this productivity. In view of this historical development, the question arises where and how, in the advancing industrial society of our type, we can envisage the development and expression of creative individuality. But before entering into this discussion, I want to trace the vicissitudes of individuality in the dimension in which the individual is in the most authentic sense "creative": that of *literature and the arts.*

Indeed, the artistic dimension seems to have been the only real home of the individual, the only place where man could be an individual in his material as well as in his intelligible existence—not only as inner but also as outer man. In contrast to the economic individual, the artist realizes his individuality in a form of creative work which modern culture has extolled as a manifestation of higher freedom and higher value. And unlike the inner moral and spiritual autonomy attributed to the individual ("person") by the idealistic philosophy, the freedom of the artist is of more substantial stuff; it expresses itself in his *oeuvre* and in his life. The great personalities of the Renaissance could combine artistic, political, and economic individualism: Jakob Burckhardt's phrase "the state as work of art" expressed this unity. The phrase may convey a highly idealized picture, but it indicates the gap which separates the origins of individualism from its late stages. In the fully developed bourgeois society, the market value supersedes the value of individual creativity; when the latter serves to increase the former, it is the market rather than the individual which asserts itself. The individual in the full "classical" sense, as a true self, now appears possible only as *against* his society, in essential conflict with the established norms and values: he is an alien, outsider, or a member of the "inner emigration." In this society, the individual cannot fulfill himself, cannot come into his own: this is the message of the representative literature at least from the *Sturm und Drang* to Ibsen. In the inevitable struggle with society, the individual (always in the emphatic sense of the term) either perishes, or resigns —renounces that uncompromised freedom and happiness which was first the promise and goal of "development." The creative individual starts as a nonconformist; in the established society, he cannot be a "realist" without betraying himself; his autonomy is that of his imagination, which has its own rationality and truth (perhaps more valid, more rational than that of the Establishment). But as he sets out to live and to work in accordance with himself and his faculties, he recognizes that he must resign himself and find his autonomy in reason rather than imagination. In other words, the individual finds himself to the degree to which he learns to limit himself and to reconcile his happiness with being unhappy: autonomy means resignation. This is the story of the great development as illustrated by these novels: *Wilhelm Meister, Education Sentimentale, Grüne Heinrich, Récherche du Temps Perdu.*

EDUCATION FOR DISSENT

There is, however, another form in which the individual appears in bourgeois society and which perhaps most fully actualizes individuality, namely, the *poète maudit*. He indeed lives his own life: on the margin and against his society. The individual becomes authentic as outcast, drug addict, sick, or genius. Some of this authenticity is still preserved in the "bohemian," even in the beatnik; both groups represent vaguely protected and permitted manifestations of individual freedom and happiness not enjoyed by the citizen who defines freedom and happiness in terms of his government and society rather than on his own terms.

This long digression from the Great Society seemed to me necessary in order to separate the ideology of the individual from his realization, and to point out how the creative individual has been largely localized in the "artistic dimension," that is, in the sphere which was until now far removed from the daily business of life—a sort of immaterial, more spiritual reality. Something of this is still reflected in President Johnson's emphasis on beauty, imagination (which, however, coupled with "innovation," has a technical-commercial ring), and creativity. And some observers of the contemporary scene raise explicitly the problem of the place and function of the "creative" individual in the advanced industrial society. In fact, with the growth of this society, and with the spread of automation, mass production, and standardization in the daily business of life, "individuality" is being increasingly reserved for any remaining areas of "creative" acitivity or receptivity—whatever "creative" may mean. In the context of the authoritative statements on the Great Society, "creative" seems to refer to the production of things, services, works, and spaces which are not only useful but also beautiful, satisfying not only material but also spiritual needs, enhancing the liberty, joy, and richness of the human existence. We must stress at the outset that this quest for the creative individual in advanced industrial society directly involves the social organization of labor. For if creativity is to be more than an individual privilege confined to an elite, then it must be a possible mode of existence for all members of the Great Society, without any discrimination other than that suggested by the different individual capacities themselves. Moreover, the embodiments of creativity either have to be produced in the material process of production (such as

houses, parks, furniture, *objets d'art*), or the material process of production must provide the material basis and environment for the creation and reception of such goods. How and where can individual
creativity, on a social scale, develop in a society in which material
production is being increasingly mechanized, automated, standardized? The following alternatives present themselves: (1) either the
material production itself changes its character fundamentally and is
transformed from "alienated" to non-alienated work; (2) or material
production is completely divorced from creative individuality (except for the technological intelligence and imagination brought to
bear on the productive apparatus), and the individuals are creative
outside the process of material production.

I shall start with the first alternative. Further progress of industrial society is tantamount to progress in mechanization and mass
production. The reduction of individual energy in the production of
the necessities is also progress also in human terms; the elimination of
individual labor power from this production would be the greatest
triumph of industry and science. Any attempt to reverse the trend on
a social scale by a reintroduction of modes of work closer to handi-
craft and artisanship, or by reducing the mechanized apparatus while
leaving intact the established social control of the productive and distributive process, would be regressive in terms of efficiency as well as
human development.[1]

Thus, the emergence of the autonomous and creative individual
cannot be envisaged as a gradual transformation of existing alienated
into non-alienated labor. In other words, the individual will not
come to life as worker, technician, engineer, or scientist who expresses
his creativity in producing or attending to the established apparatus
of production. The latter is and remains a technical apparatus which,
in its very structure, militates against autonomy in the work process.
Autonomy rather presupposes a basic change in the relations of the
producers and consumers to the apparatus itself. In its prevailing
form, the latter controls the individuals whom it serves: it fosters and
satisfies the aggressive and, at the same time, conformist needs which
reproduce the controls. Nor would a mere transfer of controls mean
qualitative change unless and until the new administrators (and the
people at large) experience the vital need for changing the very direction of technical progress toward the pacification of the struggle for
existence. Then, the "realm of freedom" may perhaps appear in the
work process itself, in the performance of socially necessary labor. The

technical apparatus could then serve to create a new social and natural environment: human beings could then have their own cities,
their own houses, their own space of tranquillity and joy: they could
become free and learn how to live in freedom with the others. Only
with the creation of such an entirely different environment (which is
well within the capabilities of technology and well beyond the capabilities of the vested interests which control technology), would the
words "beauty," "creativity," and "community" designate meaningful goals; the creation of such an environment would indeed be non-
alienated labor.

The other alternative for the emergence of the "individual" in
the advancing industrial society is expressed in the notion that the
individual, as an autonomous and creative person, *develops outside*
and *beyond* the material work process, outside and beyond the time
and space required for "earning a living" or producing the socially
necessary foods and services. Under this general notion are subsumed
two very different and even contradictory concepts: the Marxian distinction between the realm of freedom and the realm of necessity, and
the modern idea of creative leisure.

Marx's "realm of freedom" presupposes a social organization of
labor guided by the standards of utmost rationality in the satisfaction
of individual needs for the society as a whole. Thus, it presupposes
collective control of the production process by the producers themselves. But for Marx, the production process remains a "realm of necessity," that is, heteronomy, imposed on man by the continued struggle with nature, scarcity, and weakness. The time spent in this
struggle would be greatly reduced, but it would still take up much of
the individual's existence. The remaining time would be free time in
the literal sense that it would be under the autonomy of the individual: he would be free to satisfy his own needs, to develop his own
faculties, his own pleasures. Now it seems to me that contemporary
industrial society has all but closed this realm of freedom, and closed
it not only by virtue of its ingression into all spheres of the individual
existence (thus preconditioning the free time) but also by virtue of
technical progress and mass democracy. What is left to individual creativity outside the technical work process is in the way of hobbies, do-
it-yourself stuff, games. There is, of course, the authentic creative expression in art, literature, music, philosophy, science—but it is hardly
imaginable that this authentic creativity will, even in the best of all
societies, become a general capability. The rest is sport, fun, fad.

These conditions of advanced industrial society, then, seem to invalidate Marx's idea of free time. Freedom is also a matter of quantity, number, space: it demands solitude, distance, dissociation—the unoccupied, quiet space, nature not destroyed by commerce and brutality. Where these conditions do not prevail, the realm of freedom becomes a most expensive privilege. Not only the reduction of the working day and the restoration of nature but also the reduction of the birth rate would be the prerequisite.

In contradistinction to the Marxian concept, the notion of "creative leisure" is realistic and conforms to the contemporary conditions. Marx's "free time" is not "leisure time," for the realization of the all-around individual is not a matter of leisure. Free time pertains to a free society, leisure time to a repressive society. When, in the latter type of society, the working day must be greatly reduced, leisure time must be organized, even administered. For the laborer, employee, or executive enters into his leisure time equipped with the qualities, attitudes, values, behavior belonging to his station in his society; he has his being-for-others as his own; his leisure activity or passivity will simply be a prolongation or recreation of his social performance; he will not be an "individual." In the Marxian concept, man is free also in the realm of necessity to the extent to which he has organized it in accordance with his human needs, in transparent rationality; freedom thus links the two realms: the subject of the working day is also the subject of free time. In the contemporary industrial society, man is not the subject of his working day; consequently if he is to become the subject of his free time, he has to be made into such. And until the repressive organization of the working day is abolished, he will be made into a subject of leisure by exactly the same powers which govern the working day. Creativity can be learned, culture can be learned, but as long as learning and teaching do not transcend the established conditions, the result will be the enrichment, beautification, adornment of an unfree society. Instead of invoking the image of human freedom, creative culture will contribute to the absorption of this image into the status quo, which it will make more palatable.

But does not the evolution of technological civilization in its own course promote and require the development of new mental energies, of new intellectual faculties which, in turn, tend to transcend the prevailing conditions and to create liberating needs and aspirations? There is an increasing need for scientific and technological intelligence in the process of material production which will have to be satisfied; and there is also no doubt that this intelligence is creative. However, the mathematical character of modern science determines the range and direction of its creativity, and leaves the non-quantifiable qualities of *humanitas* outside the domain of exact science. The mathematical propositions about nature are held to be *the* truth about nature, and the mathematical conception and project of science are held to be the only "scientific" ones. This notion amounts to claiming universal validity for a specific historical theory and practice of science and other modes of knowledge appear as less scientific and therefore less exactly true. Or, to put it more bluntly: after having removed the non-quantifiable qualities of man and nature from scientific method, science feels the need for redemption by coming to terms with the "humanities."

The dichotomy between science and humanities (a treacherous designation: as if science did not partake of humanity!) cannot be overcome by mutual recognition and respect; its resolution would involve the ingression of humanistic goals into the formation of scientific concepts, and, vice versa, the development of humanistic goals under the guidance of such scientific concepts. Prior to this internal unification, science and the humanities will hardly be equipped to play a major role in the emergence of a free society. The humanities will be condemned to remain essentially abstract, academic, "cultural"—quite divorced from the daily work process. Science, on the other hand, will continue to shape the work process and, with it, the daily universe of work and leisure; but it will not bring about, by virtue of its own process, the new human freedom. The scientist may well be moved by supra-scientific goals, humane goals, but they will remain external to his science, and they will limit and even define his creativity from outside. Thus, the scientist or the technician, occupied in the designing and construction of a bridge and road net, of facilities for work and leisure, and in the planning of towns may (and indeed often does) calculate and construct something beautiful, peaceful, and humane. However, his creation will be functional in terms of the functioning of his society, and his transcending goals and values will be defined by this society. In this sense, his creativity will remain heteronomous.

The individuals who are supposed to live in the Great Society must be the individuals who build it—they must be free *for* it before they can be free in it. No other power can impose or force their society on them—not because a "despotism of freedom" *per se* contradicts liberation, but because no power, no government, no party exists which is free for such dictatorship. So it must still be in the process of material production, of socially necessary labor and its division that the new society would have to take shape. And since individual autonomy is being eliminated from this process, the emergence of freedom and the redirection of efforts would be a matter of changing the *control* over the productive process. Moreover, the construction of the Great Society as a free society would involve more than a change in the controlling powers: it would involve the emergence of new needs and aspirations in the individuals themselves—needs and aspirations essentially different from, and even contradictory to, those sustained, satisfied, and reproduced by the established social process.

But is it not the very essence of a democratic society to allow the emergence of new needs and aspirations, even if their development threatens to demand new social institutions? Here is the fundamental task of education, the third area of reconstruction designated in the program for the Great Society. It calls for an extension and growth of education, "in quality as well as in size." Let us consider first the question of quantitative growth. Not too long ago, many voices spoke out against general education: it was considered dangerous to law and order, to culture, if the people (the lower classes) would learn how to read and write. Of course, it was the *established* law and order, the *established* culture which was to be protected from more education. Today, the situation is very different, and education is considered a desideratum for the established law and order, and for the established culture. No cultural and intellectual expression—no matter how subversive—is to be excluded from the curriculum. Marx is taught alongside Hitler; drugs are part of the equipment of existential psychology; and even the philosophy of the Marquis de Sade is sometimes respectfully treated in the classroom. Fortunately, I do not have to discuss here the question whether this achievement indicates progress in freedom and critical thought, or rather progress in the immunity and cohesion of the existing society and its values.

In any case, this cultural affluence is still better than further restriction and repression of knowledge, but it cannot *per se* be taken as progress toward a better society. Indeed, this coordination of the negative and the positive, the subversive and the conservative, reduces the qualitative difference between them; it accomplishes the flattening out of opposites, of contradiction. A change in the prevailing pattern—that is to say, a liberation of free, critical, radical thought, and of new intellectual and instinctual needs—would necessitate a break with the benevolent neutrality which embraces Marx and Hitler, Freud and Heidegger, Samuel Beckett and Mary McCarthy; it would necessitate partisanship—education to partisanship—as against a tolerance and an objectivity which in any case operate only in the realm of ideology and in areas which do not threaten the whole. However, precisely this tolerance and objectivity are the shibboleth of the democratic process in its prevailing institutions. Progressive education which could create the intellectual climate for the emergence of new individual needs, would come into conflict with many of the powers, private and public, which finance education today. Qualitative change in education is qualitative social change, and there is little chance that such a change could be organized and administered; education remains its prerequisite. The contradiction is real: the existing society must offer the possibility of education for a better society, and such education may be a threat to the existing society. Thus we cannot expect popular demand for such education, nor endorsement and support from above.

Kant stated as the goal of education that children should be educated, not in accordance with the present but with that of a future, better condition of the human race, namely, in accordance with the idea of *humanitas*. This goal still implies the subversion of the present condition of man. I wonder whether the spokesmen for education toward the Great Society are aware of this implication. To the degree to which the technical, material, and scientific resources for the development of a free society are available, the chance of its realization depends on the human, social forces who would *need* such a society—need it not only objectively (*an sich*) but also subjectively, for themselves, consciously. Today, this need is active only among a minority of the population of the "have" societies, and among the fighting people in the "have-not" areas of the world. In the technically advanced countries, education can indeed help to activate the need which "objectively" is universal, but it would be a strange, most unpopular, and unprofitable education. For example, it would include immunization of children and adults against the mass media; unhampered access to information suppressed or distorted by these media; methodical distrust of politicians and leaders, and abstention from their performances; and organization of effective protest and refusal which do not inevitably end with the martyrdom of those who protest and refuse. Such education would also aim at a basic transvaluation of values: it would require the debunking of all heroism in the service of inhumanity, of sport and fun in the service of brutality and stupidity, of the faith in the necessity of the struggle for existence and in the necessity of business. To be sure, these educational aims are negative, but the negation is the work and appearance of the positive, which first has to create the physical and mental space where it can come to life—and thus requires removal of the devastating and suffocating equipment which now occupies this space. This destruction would be the first manifestation of the new autonomy and creativity: the appearance of the free individual in the new society.

THE INTERNAL CONTRADICTIONS OF THE GREAT SOCIETY PROGRAM

In the course of my analysis, I have tried to limit myself to topics I feel qualified to discuss. This means excluding specific administrative problems, such as the relation between federal and local authority, public and private agencies, and so on. These questions presuppose existing institutions as implementing the program for the Great Society, whereas I assume that this program would lead beyond their framework and authority.

Another problem area is that of "organization," that is, whether the ubiquitous organization characteristic of, and indispensable for, the functioning of advanced industrial society does not militate against "individual" creativity and initiative. The opposition of organization to freedom is ideological: while it is true that freedom cannot be organized, the material, technical (and perhaps even the intellectual) preconditions of freedom require organization. Not the growth of organization is to blame, but the growth of bad, exploitative organization. Against it, counter-organization is called for. For example, if the civil rights movement had an organization more powerful and more militant than the force of its opponents, it would be far more effective. A similar response could terminate the now endless debate as to the right balance between federal and local government, jurisdiction, initiative, and so forth. If the composition of the federal government indicates progressive policies, its power and authority should be made to prevail rigorously, and vice versa; otherwise, the issue is simply one of power politics, local or national.

One might also point up the international, global content of the Great Society. I note frequent acceptance of the national framework of the program: the Great Society will be an American society. But if one thing is clear, it is that the Great Society, if it should ever come about, will *not* be an American society, although this country may conceivably and initially be the leading power. Not only are some of the values which have come to be associated with the American way of life (such as the commercialization of the soul, togetherness, the sanctity of business, the science of human relations) incompatible with a free society, the warlike coexistence of the affluent society with the have-not part of the world, neo-colonialism in any form, conflicts with the very idea of a Great Society. Similarly, some of the values associated with Eastern civilization (especially its traditional aversion to "business," its emphasis on contemplation) could be revived in the new society, while other Eastern values would be incompatible with it.

To sum up: the program of the Great Society is of a substantial ambiguity which reflects the alternative prospects of the affluent society whose program it is supposed to be.

1. It can be read as a program for the extension and amelioration of the status quo: a higher standard of living for the underprivileged part of the population, abolition of discrimination and unemployment, beautification of cities and countryside, improvement of transportation, better education for all, and cultivation of leisure. Unless a policy to the contrary is proposed, it must be assumed that this development is to take place within the institutional, cultural, and mental framework of the competitive struggle for economic existence. Such a program, translated into reality, would indeed mean a vast improvement in the prevailing conditions. However, even within the given framework, the realization of the Great Society would require a permanent and considerable reduction of the military establishment and its physical and mental manifestations throughout the society—and that is to say, it would require major political and economic changes, foremost of foreign policy. Short of such change, the Great Society would be like a welfare state prepared to turn into a warfare state.

2. The program can be read as envisaging the essential transformation of the existing society which is suggested by its technological capabilities, namely, a transformation into a society where not full but marginal employment (or even unemployment) in necessarily alienated labor is the basis of growth. This would mean subversion of the prevailing organization of the economic process and subversion of

the prevailing process of education: in short, it would mean a fundamental transvaluation of values and the emergence of new individual
and social needs. This would also mean a radical change in the relation between the have and have-not societies—the rise of an international society beyond capitalism and communism.

Under both aspects, the traditional concept of the individual, in
its classic-liberal as well as Marxist form seems to be untenable—canceled (*aufgehoben*) by the historical development of productivity. Individuality, the "person" as autonomous agent, would find increasingly less place in the work process. In the first alternative (extension
and amelioration of the status quo), individuality could be (and perhaps would have to be "artificially" maintained and fostered: some
sort of organized, administered individuality expressed in external
paraphernalia, gadgets, fads, hobbies, and, outside the work process,
in cultivated leisure, decoration, and decor. Authentic individuality
would remain the distinction of the creative artist, writer, or musi-
cian. The idea of making this creative potential general among the
population at large militates against the very function and truth of
the artistic creation as a form of expression—not because it must necessarily remain the privilege of a creative few, but because it implies
dissociation from, and negation of, common sense and common
values: ingression of a qualitatively different reality into the established one. In the case of the second alternative (fundamental transformation of the society), individuality would refer to an entirely new
existential dimension: to a domain of play, experiment, and imagination which is outside the reaches of any policy and program today.

I wish to conclude on a less utopian note. Perhaps my most serious doubt concerning the Great Society is caused by the fact that
American foreign policy all but invalidates the domestic program for
the Great Society. The issues of coexistence, of the relations with the
have-not countries, of neo-colonialism, and the military establishment
are not contingent external factors—rather they determine the prospects of growth, improvement, and even the continued existence of a
society, great or not so great. Declarations as to the need for extending the American program to other nations are contradicted by the
brutal and dirty war in Vietnam, by the direct or indirect intervention against social change wherever it threatens vested interests, by
the flowering of military bases all over the globe. For these conditions
testify to the dominance of powers which are incompatible with the
grand design for peace, freedom, and justice. It is the presence of

these powers rather than the absence of capabilities and intentions which gives the program its ideological character. The Great Society will be a society that can exist and grow in peace, without the built-in need for defense and aggression—or it will not be at all.

•NOTE

1. The situation is entirely different in the backward countries where the improvement and humanization of existing pre-industrial modes of work could conceivably counteract the trend toward exploitative control of industrialization by foreign or native capital—provided real national independence has been attained.

Chapter 4

🐛 *Local and Private Initiative in the Great Society* NORTON E. LONG

The "Great Society" is an aspiration, not a blueprint. It is an invitation to a collective search for the ways and means by which renewed and vital meanings can be given to the enduring and emergent values of our civilization in the context of the human predicament that now confronts us. Government is an expediential thing of shifts and contrivances—politics is the art of the possible. But this is not the whole story, or even most of it. Government is a fountain of honor. It creates the table round and lifts us to noble quests. In the sense of classic political philosophy, it makes not life, but a good life possible. The separation of church and state has obscured the spiritual function of government.

When Roosevelt spoke of the presidency as the best pulpit in the land, he expressed his realization of his job as high priest of the norms. Our well-warranted fears of the tyranny of a church-state and our equally warranted fears that a pseudo-spiritual mobilization has created and can create a hell on earth, prudentially counsel the avoidance of "enthusiasms." The eighteenth-century good sense of human materialistic skepticism—some less vulgar version of our consumership—might seem far safer than risking becoming a society of "true believers." Yet this option is scarcely open to us. Given our material power, we will either harness it to the discipline and satisfaction of humane and civilized goals or like bored and sadistic children we will find our appropriate *Lord of the Flies.*

The search for a Great Society is in its way as urgent and in all probability its achievement is a condition prerequisite to the defusing of an explosive world.

The aging Mao desperately seeks a way to assure the continuance of his faith and works from the apostasy of a new and less zealous generation. The agnostic technicians of the Kremlin doubtless feel that communism is good for the people and in any event it is the creed that legitimizes their own claim to power. They too have their own version of consumership in the goulash communism of Khrushchev. The disintegration of Marxism as a secular religion confronts its leaders in a far shorter time span than Christianity with the problems of national churches, doctrinal revision, and ecumenicalism.

THE SPIRITUAL FUNCTION OF GOVERNMENT

The human predicament that man cannot live by bread alone is the curse of the affluent and even of the more than subsistent society. The production of meanings for the sustenance of man becomes more urgent than bread. Life requires purpose, and when the past elaborations of purpose have grown stale and incapable of informing a role structure, the moral architecture of the human habitation must be rebuilt.

It is natural, given our heritage, that when we seek to give our national enterprise renewed meaning, we turn to the current version of Roosevelt's submerged third, ill-housed, ill-fed, ill-educated, and only marginally a part of the larger society. The relief of avoidable human misery seems a unifying goal well-nigh universally acceptable in the culture. As many students of ethics have pointed out, it has the merit of insisting on no concrete definition of the good life, confining itself to the removal of generally agreed-on evils.

Bathing the feet of the poor has a deep symbolism in the Christian tradition. But there is enduring wisdom in St. Thomas à Kempis's saying that charity is for the sake of him who commanded it rather than for him who asks it. There is nothing lovely about the results of involuntary poverty, though some may live nobly despite it. The war on poverty can involve a false spirituality in much the same way as the civil rights movement. Meaningless members of the middle class seek meanings for themselves through serving the poor and even through contact with a putatively unspoiled segment of a decadent society. Much as the Norodniki of Czarist Russia went to the peasants, young Americans go to Negro hipsters who still can "burn." Reformist Marxists of the Peking persuasion abandoning the corrupt proletariats of the United States and Soviet Russia, the cities of our world, tell university audiences that health and a better future lie with the primitive innocents of the villages of Africa, Latin America, and Asia. Thus the cult of the noble savage, whether of the city slum or the underdeveloped countryside, is offered as a nostrum for the *tedium vitae* of the affluent society and its spiritually unemployed. Lenin knew better; he said of the working class that by themselves they would never rise higher than to trade union consciousness. Of the peasants his prognosis would have been even dimmer. The cult of the noble savage in any of its current guises is, as it always has been, a piece of sentimental attitudinizing. As ersatz spirituality, it is destined to the ash can, though like many another bit of shoddy ethical goods it may for a time take in decent, generous, naïve people.

The removal of the avoidable misery in our society, and for that matter on the planet, is a perfectly respectable and reasonable purpose for men of good will to entertain. It certainly should be one of the purposes of a great and hence generous and humane society. However, as a society, we cannot structure our lives and pattern our culture to the relief of poverty as if we were so many little sisters of the poor.

Indeed we are not. Our war on poverty figures out at some $30 a head per year to those defined as poor by the Council of Economic Advisers. Even if administrative costs were nil and barring magic, this is but a very small earnest of, hopefully, seriously good intentions. If we regard the greatness of budgetary magnitudes as indicative of the areas in which our society wishes to be great, defense, space, agriculture, and roads are the areas in which as a nation we seem to aspire.

Fortunately, our expenditures on education have made that undertaking in the awed language of the press our largest industry. Perhaps a nation whose combined budgetary expenditure at all levels of government is as great as ours may claim with some justice to be seeking educational greatness. While some may carp at a crassly quantitative dollar standard, there seems at least a certain persuasiveness in the view that America's educational aspirations are characteristic of what may be best in its aspiration to be a Great Society. In fact it can be seriously contended that the congeries of values associated with American education are front and center in the civic conscience. The school has been our secular church and our chosen instrument for inducting the alien to American ways.

Plato was not far wrong in regarding education as the single most important activity of the state. The *Republic* has been held by some to be a treatise on education, by others as a treatise on justice. The two are intimately connected. Education for Plato performed the role of a central casting department, assigning to the individual his appropriate social role after a careful process of selection and conditioning. The educational decision makers of our own society do a fairly definitive job of determining who are to be judged men of gold, silver, or brass. As our main sorting device for assigning differential access to the opportunity structure, our educational system does Platonic justice even when it consciously would avoid this grave responsibility.

OUR OUTWORN CALVINISM

American education embodies two main and conflicting values, achievement and equality. They clash and are uneasily reconciled in a series of unstable, shifting compromises. Equality of opportunity, a fair field with no favorites in which the individual is the architect of his own fate, his achievement, is the commonly expressed educational ideal. It was and to some extent still is the ideal of a society that would like to believe success or failure to be the reward of individual moral worth. Such a view either denies the existence of the impediments of class and circumstance, minimizes their importance, or, recognizing them, seeks their removal or mitigation.

Since the Great Depression, the belief in the individual's sole responsibility for achievement or failure has become pretty well eroded. So much so that an un-innerdirected generation can cry "sick, sick" in mockery of concerned elders fussing over its adolescent deviance. Genuine attempts to remove arbitrary handicaps become confounded with a denial of all individual responsibility. One can be sick or maladjusted, but one cannot, with foreknowledge and full consent of the will, fail. Mortal psychiatric sin is inadmissible. The gift of "freedom now" in civil rights or the gift of educational opportunity is only very partially in the power of anybody to bestow, be it willingly or in response to effective protest. The balance between what people must do for themselves and what society can do for them is real. Much, however, can be done to ensure more adequate realization of the ideal of a fair field. We may even wish to change the age-old metaphor and structure, our model of meaningful achievement in some other form than a race.

Education as the central mechanism of role assignment in our society, the doer of Platonic justice, has been by and large content to accept the roles society has offered and the current social valuation of them. The apostle of juvenile revolt, Paul Goodman, has pointed with some exaggeration to the growing absurdity of many of the roles that the society provides. The Calvinist ethic of work in which the service of God and the economy can be identical is losing its grip in an affluent society. The hierarchy of snobbery, both social and corporate, that makes the college degree a minor order of nobility and a necessary condition for upward mobility and social acceptability provides the schools with whatever orientation and validation they possess. The human emptiness and educational superficiality of this arbitrary standard are the basis of the justified attack on the "rat race."

The assumption behind American education has been that the society was providing an adequate array of roles to give full play to the talent and imagination of the oncoming generations. A society engaged in opening a new continent, living, at least until 1929, on the bare margin of subsistence, might be forgiven for assuming that the pursuit of bread could adequately absorb its energies. Beyond this overriding necessity, other activities of the spirit were only frosting on the cake, nice to have, but really a frill. The term "frill" is a key one in education. It expresses not only the critical view of publics with respect to nonessential educational activities but, concomitantly, what educators have induced the public to regard as essential. Essentiality in education comprises the traditional matters that are thought to socialize to the received value system and that create the invidious honorificence of stratification. In fact, because middle-class aspirations to maintain or win social acceptability for their offspring through college have dominated school administration, such logic as the school curriculum has, derived from the collegiate gatekeepers' examining system. Vocational education has been the orphan without effective sponsorship save for a hopelessly outdated agriculturally oriented vested interest and a narrow craft concern with a limited field of apprenticeship. In the absence of realistic vocational education and given the largely social and snobbish ends of middle-class educational concern, it is scarcely surprising that the educational pattern for the poor is taken from the school of Henry Higgins. The *My Fair Lady* school of education sees its job as enabling the poor like Eliza to pass. Passing is indeed functional for upward mobility and the putatively worthless speech patterns of the poor deserve to be thankfully replaced with an acceptable standard patter.

But this is not the whole story of American education. Even if snobbery and a crude job orientation have been its dominant themes, these have been accompanied with a broad appreciation of a wide array of other interests—the frills that dismay educational fundamentalists and sensitive taxpayers. The American school in its mass mission has done at least as much as that of any other country to introduce its millions to art, music, literature, science, and the avenues of imaginative growth. It may have failed to make the honorific embellishments of Western civilization more than honorific embellishments as snobbery sees them, but it has given many the opportunity to take off from the drawing room accomplishment to genuine meanings of their own.

What the school has thinly portrayed is the rich array of roles that Western civilization has elaborated, through which the individual may seek to have meaning for himself and society. The array of meanings that our schools present to our youth are, however, unevenly and weakly conceived, our cultural inheritance of values with which we build unendingly our version of a Great Society. These are our materials and our aspiration, the youth and its future. The Great Society is the lives its people live. It is great to the extent and only to the extent it permits and encourages its members to live greatly. Both in its diversity and in the architectured mutual support of its diversities, it provides a cathedral of meanings and a habitation of warmth.

After World War II the Full Employment Act became a national commitment of sorts to ensure that the ordinary operations of the market were not left to take their course when that course meant substantial hardship. Our present new commitment to the war on poverty is an extension of that earlier pledge whose redemption has scarcely been achieved. In the course of our development from the goal of full employment to the goal of the abolition of poverty we have begun to appreciate that what we have in mind transcends the older conceptions of a society almost totally engaged in and directed by the economy and its automatic forces. While we have considerable and justified faith in the efficacy of the world of work as socializer to the culture and provider of significant occupational and social roles, that faith can no longer be blind. Its justification requires a sufficiency of works and these are no longer adequately forthcoming if indeed they ever were. Waging the war on poverty is opening the society's eyes not only to the malfunctioning of the economy for the hard-core unemployed and to the inadequacies of our provision for the aged, the crippled families, and the all too numerous exceptions to our effective opportunities, but equally we are beginning to see that a kind of spiritual poverty more desolating than the economic may be the unintended product of our outworn Calvinism. Serving the economy may no longer produce as a by-product in any humanly adequate sense the significant service of any humanly adequate god.

The full employment that we are coming to dimly appreciate as our emerging goal is a full employment of our human resources to the fullest of their spiritual capacities. We have, to be sure, first to be able to live before we can learn to live well. But having mastered the material basis of existence, we can no longer rely on the discipline of that age-old task to structure the life of a society that has transcended the discipline of economic necessity. As a society, like a rich individual, we can no longer look to the discipline of earning our daily bread by the sweat of our brow to give form and structure to a life that must now be determined by will and character rather than by the externally imposed order of economic coercion. Our conception of poverty will have to include the merely materially rich. We have learned since 1929 that any absolute standard of material poverty obsolesces. Our standards constantly alter the measuring rod. While this is no reason to limit our concern with material privation, however elastically defined, it indicates that an increasing dimension of the poverty with which we must be concerned is the poverty of opportunity for living lives of humanly significant action. It is with this dimension of full employment and impoverishment that the would-be Great Society must concern itself.

Our emancipation from the whip of economic scarcity carries with it the difficult obligation of freely determining what we propose to do with our lives. Quite simply, this is what the Great Society is all about. It is about the political philosophy that should inform our purposes and legitimize not only our government but our conception among the various conceptions of mankind of a good social order. We are ill at ease with the task. When in metropolitan area after metropolitan area business and civic leaders spend large Ford Foundation grants to collect Sears Roebuck catalogues full of facts, they are dismayed to be told by academic and other experts that the facts will not free them from the painful obligation of choosing what version of the good life they want to embody in the choices they must make. There is no scientific escape hatch from the problem of valuation and choice. Necessity provides limits on the realistic range of alternatives but no easy out from confronting one's values, making up one's mind, and persuading one's fellows.

LOCAL DISTRIBUTION OF PUBLIC GOODS

Our society is increasingly characterized by the production and distribution of public goods. Some 43 per cent of the new jobs created in the past three years have been in the public sector. Our economy is managed by guidelines for the hortatory control of prices and wages, a hortatory control that may be backed up by sanctions such as the dumping of stored aluminum to thwart an industry price hike in defiance of the guidelines. We move into a mixed and managed economy greatly fearing the epithet socialist, vigorously proclaiming our faith in free enterprise and a free market economy, while equally determined not to commit ourselves to the tender mercies of their unfettered operation. The Great Society that we grope toward must be one that embodies our conviction that private and public enterprise, market and planning can be combined in such fashion as to emphasize their respective virtues and restrain their respective vices.

If the content of the Great Society is the full employment of its human resources in a rich and satisfying array of roles that elaborate the traditional and emerging values of Western civilization and the world civilization of which we are increasingly a part, our concern with national, state, and local government, with local and private initiative, must be dictated by their relevance to our purposes. Insofar as the institutions we now possess have a going-concern value, they are worthy of the respect Edmund Burke recommended for the hard-won capital of any society. That admitted, they must be judged not with any obscurantist reverence, but in terms of their capacity to further or to hinder the enterprises we presently cherish. In some sense the institutions and techniques do have value for their own sake, but only to a limited degree compared to the objects for whose attainment they serve. While calculations of expediency counsel the folly of any wholesale attempt at immediate institutional change, the Great Society can scarcely be more than a public relations slogan if it purports no change from the institutional status quo.

The country has evolved from a confederation of colonies to a nation and from a congeries of local nationalisms to an increasingly national society. Its governmental structure imperfectly reflects the evolution. An agrarian, federal past is still strong in our institutions and in the still current ideology. State loyalties have sharply receded since the Civil War, but they still form redoubts for vested interests who find them useful and for regionalized dissent from the national consensus. As the experimental laboratories of Justice Holmes, the states may have more to be said for them than hostile critics will admit. Though afflicted in many cases with a palsied penuriousness, this has been by no means a universal story. The federal carrot and stick do indeed account for much state innovation but by no means all of it. The states as bulwarks against a mindless and overmastering centralization are neither as valuable as their apologists claim nor as worthless as their detractors assert. They need to be thought about in their capacity to make positive contributions to the realization of a Great Society and equally in their capacity and likelihood to seriously stand in the way.

The two most critical events for the future of the states are the implementation of the Supreme Court's one-man, one-vote doctrine and the Heller Plan to transfer to the states without strings some part of the nationally collected revenues. The implementation of the Supreme Court's decision is important both because of its likely alternation of the range, weight, and mix of values involved in the states' decision making process and in the caliber of the states as significant theaters of public action. The latter is not unrelated to the former. The quality of people attracted to the public business and the quality and standards of the civic audience they can command are vital to the states' decision making process. Actors and audiences are bearers, supporters, and critics of values and their practical implementation.

Consideration of our attitude toward the role of the states in a Great Society is particularly relevant to the Heller Plan. Fiscal anemia, stemming in some cases from actual lack of adequate resources and in others from the supposed constraints of interstate competition for the location of wealth and industry, has resulted in a growing tendency for initiatives and power to move to the federal government as the most efficient and politically competent source of tax collection. Any substantial increase in the fiscal blood stream, especially if the transfusion carried no strings, would have the likely effect of increasing the vitality of the states. In the view of some, this would be a tragic mistake. In their eyes, the states, far from constituting a valued asset in the effort to create a Great Society, are a serious obstacle in its path. There is certainly a crying need to take a careful look at what kind of local government structure would be most appropriate to realizing a Great Society. Our past commitment to what may be an outworn and jerry-built federalism is not necessarily irrevocable. The gradual obsolescence of the states through fiscal anemia may not be the worst way to bring about institutional change.

This view is shared especially by liberals who see the federal bargain as essentially one that allows Southern whites more or less free rein to exploit Negroes. In addition, the gross population and resource differences among the states seem to render them radically incompetent to fulfill their formal potentialities in a Great Society. The pattern of interstate competition between the weak and the strong seems more likely to inhibit the strong than to energize the weak. If the weak are incapable of meeting minimal national standards for the market basket of state public goods, national transfer payments similar to intrastate or intracity transfer payments become in order. With things as they are, despite promising changes in federal need formulas for some education programs, the strong states as well as the weak will insist on proportionate shares in the national largesse. To assist the schools of Maine and Mississippi, California, Illinois, and New York have to make transfer payments via the federal government to one another as well as to those genuinely in need. The overhead costs of pumping the local taxpayers' money up to Washington and back down the bureaucratic conduits reduce the marginal efficiency of the California, Illinois, and New York federally collected, locally spent tax dollar by a very sizable fraction. Of course, there are those who doubt whether the tax dollars would be collected in comparable magnitudes for education even in California, Illinois, and New York if the more efficient and politically painless federal tax machinery were not invoked. Politically from this point of view the large overhead transfer cost may have its justification.

But the foregoing are relatively unimportant questions compared to the major ones. These seem to be with respect to our internal governmental structure: first, is the Great Society we have in mind building to all intents a unified nation rather than a federation of states; and second, if the Great Society we wish to build is a unified nation, do we still want it characterized by important degrees of regional self-government? The answer to the first question seems to have been clearly given by our political and economic history. The Civil War and the growth of the national market have so ensured the unity of the country that this rather than its diversity is the major political fact. The process leading in this direction seems now irreversible. Any Great Society we build will be that of a nation. However, our tradition is one of local self-government and we are certainly going to want something more than mere administrative decentralization. A major concern for us must be to discover, within the context of our traditions and aspirations, the feasible pattern of local self-government that best fits the moral structure we are working toward.

THE POLITICS OF METROPOLITAN DISTRIBUTION

In the Great Depression there was a general feeling that the states failed and verged on bankruptcy. The national government was the only institution capable of meeting the crisis and moving us through it. Major efforts were made to find new and more effective units of regional government than the states. The search for natural regions resulted in a large stock of overlay maps produced in the hope of finding some fit between federal field areas, population, resources, geography, and common problems. The upshot, however, was the sad conclusion that no more greatly compelling arrangement than the existing states shone forth from the data of research. With the waning of the depression, the hunt for new regions of government to replace the states was largely abandoned. Lush war-produced revenues, postwar prosperity, and major new state efforts in the production of education, mental health facilities, and other public goods have given the states renewed vitality. Both those they serve and those interested in the conduct of state government are now powerfully motivated to preserve the going system. It has come a long way since the depths of the depression.

If we think the Great Society needs regionally decentralized self-government, we are not likely to find, despite their seeming incongruity, other areas more obviously satisfactory than the present states. However, this does not mean that because one accepts the states as having continuing roles in the Great Society one either accepts their present functioning or is precluded from seeking additional structures of local self-government. The major fact that confronts us on the domestic scene is the rise of the metropolitan area to preponderance, and soon perhaps to overwhelming preponderance, in our pattern of settlement. Most of us now live in some two hundred metro-

politan areas. Shortly, perhaps the great bulk of the American people
will be living in a fraction of these areas. The quality of American
life as it is lived will be the quality of the life of these areas, good, bad,
or indifferent. The Great Society in the United States can only be
great in a meaningful human sense if these areas are capable of greatness. Here, if anywhere, President Johnson's concern that we ask not
how big but how good is in order.

In a sense our attitude toward the future role of the states is to a
degree predicated on our attitude toward the governmental future, if
any, of our metropolitan areas. If we conclude that giving meaning to
our conception of the Great Society requires the creation of appro-
propriate governmental institutions to mobilize leadership and resources and to share resources in these areas, this will have profound
consequences for the future of the states and their comparative importance in our system of government. Successful governmental structuring of metropolitan areas not only would mobilize leadership and
resources not now mobilized in these areas, it would profoundly alter
the balance of political power. In doing so, it could not help altering
the mix of values, perspectives, and group influences that determines
public policy. In realistically thinking about the implementation of
our conception of the Great Society, we need to think about the values and influences that will determine decisions at any level of
government and the capabilities of the level to mobilize resources commensurate with the requisites of effectively implementing the decisions taken. Clearly, when we think about the existing state governments and potential metropolitan governments, we need to bear in
mind how we evaluate them as decision-making agencies and resource-
mobilizing agencies in the Great Society we hope to build. The likely
and now somewhat determinable effects of the Supreme Court's rulings affecting legislative apportionment are highly in order. Beyond
this we need to ask whether strengthening the states through some
variant of the Heller Plan would hinder or could be made to help the
development of metropolitan-area governments. Those most firmly
opposed to strengthening the states see them as narrowly unrepresentative and hopelessly resistant to meeting the needs of urban populations. Reapportioned state legislatures may make the prospects of desired state action less bleak.

It does, however, seem likely that a decision to strengthen the
states would strengthen bodies which, even if made more representative by the Supreme Court decision, would inevitably be reluctant to

see competing metropolitan governments arise. The importance of this probable reluctance needs to be weighed. It is also worth thinking about whether an either/or policy is all that is available to us. In some cases the state government may well make the most sense as the vehicle for metropolitan government. This would obviously be the case in Rhode Island. In other cases, the still large populations outside of metropolitan areas require more than existing local governments and may offer no usefully possible intermediate layer of government between themselves and the states. We may well be condemned to working our way pragmatically to piecemeal solutions using the governmental institutions and habits we now possess while adding to and altering them wherever possible to further our purposes. Burke's wisdom cautions us to respect the social capital in political institutions and habits that has been painfully accumulated in the course of our history. Society can only be treated as so much formless clay for utopian modeling by those whose vision of the ideal takes no account of the possible and remains untempered by humility or respect for the existing human achievement.

Evaluation of what is desirable and possible governmentally requires us to keep clearly in mind our purposes and the relevant institutions for their attainment. Governments, national, state, and local, are so many devices for mobilizing and allocating resources. Markets, likewise, are devices for mobilizing and allocating resources. Viewed as devices, although these are in reality historically developed institutions, we can look at them objectively in terms of their fitness to achieve the ends in view. National, state, and local governments are obviously quite different in their capacities to mobilize resources and are also different, given effective constituencies, in their allocation of resources mobilized. Equally, if we look at the private sector as opposed to the public, there are significant differences in the kinds of goods produced and the ways in which the goods are allocated. Our policy choices as to how resource mobilization and allocation in the society is to be structured between levels of government and between public and private initiatives depend on the outcomes we value and the most effective mix of governmental and/or private initiatives for producing the desired outcomes.

As noted earlier, the two major values in American society—achievement and equality—are in tension. In the past, the tension has been solved by giving the citizens formal equality in government and accepting actual inequality in the economy as the inevitable and indeed desirable result of differential achievement. This division between the formal equality of government and the actual inequality of the economy led Marxists and many others to characterize bourgeois democracy as a fraud. The seeming emptiness of a political democracy divorced from the workings of the economy has been radically altered by the rapid increase in the production and importance of public goods. Indeed, one of the main problems of a society committed both to an equality norm among citizens and to unequal incomes is how to give effect to this income inequality in the consumption of public goods. As long as the private sector was the overwhelmingly important producer of goods, rationing by price gave full effect to inequalities in income, as it largely does now in the Soviet Union, where the public sector and the private are merged. In addition, differential political power did, and to an important degree still does, serve to differentiate the consumption of public goods in our cities even among formally equal citizens. Variations in quality of schools, garbage collection, police protection, and the like, are still notorious. Nonetheless, the equality norm among citizens coupled with the political activation of submerged groups is bringing about the homogenization of public goods.

To give effect to unequal incomes in the consumption of public goods, the preferred strategy is to achieve territorial segregation of their consumption through suburbanization. The metropolitan area, with its congeries of local governments, provides many competing residential hotels with different qualities of service and different classes of paying guests. It is not surprising that the politics of many local politicians resembles that of hotelkeepers concerned with competing for desired clientele and avoiding undesirable or nonpaying guests. Where local politicians rise a notch above this, property-tax considerations—among others—make their model that of a real estate operator seeking to maximize his revenue from a given tract of land with its inescapable encumbrances. The metropolitan area has become an ecology of governments offering a wide range of public goods and permissible land uses. To some, this seems a perfectly sensible way to reflect the pluralism of the society and to rescue some measure of quality from the menace of homogenized equality. To others, it represents the fragmentation of the community, political absenteeism, social irresponsibility, tax dodging, and the ghettoization of the less fortunate. Both views have their measure of truth and both need some degree of reconciliation if equality, quality, and achievement are to be given appropriate meaning in a Great Society.

At the national level of government, a mix of values and influences has been at work that has made it politically possible and expedient to pass civil rights legislation, utilize national leverage on behalf of equal employment opportunity and open occupancy, and to inaugurate the war on poverty. In its general tendency, this is a politics of role reallocation and equality of opportunity. It means a national purpose to open up improved avenues to housing, education, jobs, and status for deprived minorities. The politics that has made this national purpose achieve both legislative and executive enunciation and some limited degree of realization is supported in many cases by the same people who locally, in practice, support the territorial segregation of public-goods consumption. In effect the local territorial segregation of public-goods consumption powerfully limits any attainment of a national policy of redistribution. Housing has become a key to education, education a key to jobs, and jobs are the key to income, which is the key to housing—at least where the minimal democracy of the dollar is allowed to prevail. For minorities this democracy of the dollar, the free competitive market of the capitalist ideal, is nullified by that other capitalist ideal, the right to discriminate. The existence of fragmented local governments responding to highly unrepresentative samples of populations and problems has reacted back on the federal government to blunt, in the reality of administration, its legislatively expressed goals. Working through local governments, and in some cases through private enterprise as required by law, has meant the accommodation of the expressed federal purpose to the political realities of the status quo of local and private enterprise.

Nowhere has this been more tragically the case than in urban renewal, where the poor have been unhoused with the aid of federal subsidies and banks have been rehoused with the aid of federal subsidies. Given the self-definition of mayors as municipal realtors, it is scarcely surprising that they should, to the extent feasible, use federal aid to maximize the tax yield of their real estate and even on occasion to rid themselves of nonpaying guests. Federal bureaucrats, responding to the survival needs of their agencies, become accomplices in this redirection of national policy. In this they are given support and coercion by congressmen who react to the effectively expressed wishes of those who represent the governments and electorates of the fragmented metropolitan areas. What is frequently viewed with cynicism as the moral failure of politicians and bureaucrats is simply the predictable result of the governmental way interests and values are structured and represented. Given the game and players desiring to win, the effective rules and strategies allow the players no other option unless indeed they decide to change the structure of the game.

This last is what concerns those, who would change the metropolitan area from an ecology of jealous Balkanized principalities surrounding an eviscerated central city fast becoming a ghetto of the Negro, the aged, the poor, and the very rich into a community politically structured to organize its fiscal and leadership resources in a balanced response to the whole range of problems that confront the people of the metropolitan area. Governments can be organized to reflect narrow and selfish interests or they can be set up in such a way as to be able, and even be compelled, to aspire to greatness. Presently, stricken with fiscal anemia, plagued by social absenteeism and the triviality of the country club suburb with its toy government, the nation's metropolises are organized on a necessarily dog-eat-dog, devil-take-the-hindmost basis. Despite the fact that the country's metropolitan areas contain the overwhelming bulk of the nation's financial assets and human talent, they are neither structured, legally empowered, nor possessed of a political and social theory with which to mobilize their spiritual and material wealth behind a meaningful and challenging conception of a common life. A Great Society in an urban age is inconceivable on the basis of the present divisive disorganization of our metropolitan areas which has substituted the competition of municipal realtors for the conduct of responsible politics.

THE POTENTIAL OF METROPOLITAN GOVERNMENT

Creating the political organization (to mobilize the resources) of our two-hundred-odd metropolitan areas is an essential first step toward freeing and powering local initiative to build a Great Society. No smaller areas possess the means and the potential leadership talents to address themselves to the full array of problems that can only be meaningfully tackled at the local level. The redistributive task that means opening up the avenues to housing, education, and jobs requires local leaders who are in a position to have to face the problem, who have the requisite legal and financial means to effectively work at the problem, and who are of stature and command a following sufficient to carry local publics with them. The federal government cannot by fiat achieve redistributive goals that require major restructuring of local roles. The paratroops of Little Rock or the marshals of "Ol' Miss" momentarily coerce but do not persuade. Without local leaders responding to the same array of problems and groups as the national government, the nation is almost in the position of an army of occupation in hostile territory. We begin to realize that to achieve for its citizens nationally valued goals, the nation requires a truly national system of local self-government responsive to the forces and values that move the capital. Lacking local governments adequate in leadership, territory, finances, and power to face major tasks, the future of self-government where the people live, and perhaps in the nation itself, becomes seriously doubtful. A national system of local governments, complementing the nation's response to national needs, is a prime necessity for the achievement of a Great Society. The fragmented metropolis is a broken mirror which is utterly incapable of reflecting a great or unified national purpose.

Putting a governmental structure over the local ecology of divided governments is scarcely enough. Metropolitan Toronto has achieved a public-works success worthy of Robert Moses but has failed to move beyond brick and mortar to human problems of greater importance and is now faltering before the need to redistribute fiscal resources. New York City, which would seem big enough for greatness, is said to verge on bankruptcy and suffers from apparent lack of purpose and firm direction. Governments without adequate financial power become as contemptible as government under the Articles of Confederation. Metropolitan governments without access to the ample fiscal resources within them would be hardly more than outsized special districts. Such governments, unless capable of attracting human talent of stature, would be as stunted as their leadership. To attract the leadership capable of the vision of greatness, the problems of the government and the powers available to meet the problems must be such as to realistically permit the aspiration to greatness to be more than an empty piece of Chamber of Commerce rhetoric. The United States has settlements of untold richness in human talent and material resources. These could be significant theaters of action providing the stage for the highest forms of human excellence and lifting their audiences to a noble sense of human worth. Thus far, they are no more than census statistics with traffic problems, crime rates, slums, and central business districts—conglomerates without sense of purpose or capacity for self-direction.

While the metropolitan areas are the only ones below the

states embracing enough territory and a typical enough sample of the nation's population to undertake the necessary politics of role redistribution and to transcend the suburban politics of public-goods segregation, there is a real danger that they could become so many shambling New Yorks in which all quality was lost in a sodden, equalized mediocrity. Our commitment to equality of opportunity does not have to, but it can have such a result. We can level down as well as up. We can homogenize our diversity in the name of equality, and in rejecting the undesirable consequences of economic inequality deny the relevance of any qualitative standards. We need to look at our principles. Our major rationing device in a private economy has been price, which gave primary effect to inequality of incomes. While the public sector was small and much of its product, such as military security, only collectively consumable, the equality norm among citizens was accepted. Now that public goods, especially schools, have become a major item of consumption, there is a powerful drive to maintain the same consequences of unequal income in the public sector that now occur in the private. Running counter to this is the pressure to ensure that all citizens be assured equal access to public goods of like quality. Thus the dilemma arises between the claim for equality among citizens and the claim of those with greater incomes to reflect those greater incomes in superior public goods. Where these superior public goods are schools which serve as the gatekeepers to jobs and the opportunity structure, this amounts to the demand to provide one's offspring with differentially superior opportunities, and this is the crux of the matter.

Our society is as clearly committed to unequal incomes as is the Soviet Union, and for the same reason. Along with equality, we accept the conflicting goal of achievement, and for this goal we as well as the Russians require an incentive system. For most, the incentive system consists of monetary rewards that can be cashed in for an array of goods. We, like the English, have been attempting to move from a plutocracy to a meritocracy. In practice, this means giving scholarships to bright poor boys to go to Oxford or Harvard. The modification that this device makes in the total opportunity structure and the increases in the chances of upward mobility are less than spectacular. They may, however, serve to take some of the curse off a crass plutocracy and despite the anguish of the old grads, it has placed some limitation on the capacity of the achievers of one generation to buy the way for the non-achievers of another.

The possibilities and problems of education in metropolitan areas are critical for the building of a Great Society. They are so because the Great Society, to be great, must make full use of its human resources; and to do so, it must educate and motivate these resources to their highest capacity. How to achieve a truly meaningful equality of opportunity in the schools without succumbing to a homogenized mediocrity is the essential difficulty posed by the central city. The case of the central city, however, is radically different from that of an entire metropolitan area. Neither in resources nor in range of population is there any real comparability. Barring segregation by flight from a whole metropolitan area—an utterly unlikely possibility —what has occurred in the one cannot occur in the other. The interesting possibility, and indeed the hope for a truly Great Society, lies in the possibility of some other device for achieving quality education than discrimination based on parental income and skin color. It would seem that a school system based on the resources of an entire metropolitan area might, like a great state university, achieve quality without depending upon the present methods and diversity as well.

If one conceives of the task of the school as the development of the human resources in its territory, it is clear that this task is rendered meaningless unless there will be employment for these resources. The mockery and the tragedy of education in music, the arts, and all too many other fields is the lack of opportunity for adult careers in the subject studied. Avocational interests are of the greatest value, but they cannot substitute for the serious pursuit of a vocation. Our educational systems provide the unused means for developing an inventory of our human talent and a forecast of the job outlook for its useful and creative employment. The occupational outlook needs to be expanded beyond its present narrowly private sector horizons. Private and public sectors alike require careful study to determine whether the present prospect both bids fair to clear the labor market and—hopefully of well-nigh equal importance—provides adequate outlet for the meaningful use of talent. We need spiritual full employment as well as physical. Such a conception of full employment will require a new system of national, state, and local accounts. It will also require the development of target goals designed to make full employment more than a slogan.

In the search for the meaning of a fully employed society providing the greatest possible outlet for the individual talents of its members, we will need to avail ourselves of a wide range of institutions.

Socially desired goals may often prove to be most effectively advanced by private means or by mixed private and public means. The Iron Curtain countries have begun to recognize the extraordinary advantages of individual and institutional initiatives and the danger of the deadening routines of a hidebound bureaucracy. The yardstick competition of the T.V.A. is likely to need fruitful reversal in the yardstick competition of private colleges and universities with their state-run counterparts. The possibility that the state university system of California, one of the country's outstanding achievements, might degenerate into a paper-shuffling civil service as lacking in morale and creativity as the New York City school system, is built into the dynamics of centralized administration. N.A.S.A. and A.R.P.A. have found that both space and the military can get much of their work, and even more important their needed new thinking, done for them by enlisting the unfettered energies of independent organizations.

The old, hard, socialist-capitalist division of institutions into public and private enterprise is giving way before a gradual realization that what we are concerned with is a variety of instruments and interacting instrumentalities for achieving socially desired ends. The profit system becomes one of the best cueing systems ever designed for producing uninstructed cooperation among people in a net of non-verbal communications, and an essential device for determining costs and opportunity costs even in socialist systems. The public responsibility becomes one of creating a generalized system of goals and goal supports that will permit the fullest use of individual and institutional initiatives for their attainment. The exploration of space with its complex of private, public, and academic cooperation is a useful model for the creative development of a fully employed society.

While N.A.S.A. can fruitfully treat the country as a regionalized whole for supplying its needs, it seems likely that the fully employed society will have far wider arrays of roles in the regions appropriate to its attainment. The metropolitan area may well need to have nearly the full gamut of nationally available roles to provide its inhabitants with an adequate range of employment opportunities to meet their human potential. Not least important among needed roles are those of vital neighborhood actors who can transform the poorer districts of the large city from lifeless administrative areas into living subcommunities. The participant democracy envisaged by the poverty program is attuned to the reduction of a pervasive sense of powerlessness and alienation. While the idyll of Greek democracy is probably even more a figment of the romantic imagination in the case of the poor than in that of the suburban middle class, organized pressure and even effective machine politics have been historic devices, both for socialization and upward mobility. Most promising for the development of the urban frontier is the ancient national policy of giving a farm to those who will prove out the property. In the urban frontier, we need a similar device to turn those who have no stake in the community into propertyholders interested in maintaining their equities and with a concern for their neighborhoods. The V.A. program pioneered giving veterans housing with zero equities and long-term mortgages. We can do the same in our slums for those who will maintain their own housing and do neighborhood work, whether in single houses or what can be treated as cooperative apartments.

For those of low income the role of propertyowner is one of the most powerful socializers. We need to use it to convert the rootless and the hopeless into people with at least some equity in the society and a visible chance of increasing it. The costs to government, city, state, and nation of excess maintenance in public housing could be reduced tremendously if tenants were converted into owners and the ownership were earned in a fashion similar to that of the farms in the national domain. Enough propertyowners with a stake in neighborhood maintenance and improvement could provide the human means for transforming gray areas. These are the potential leadership cadres through whom nonphysical planning can come to have meaning and human renewal become more than an empty phrase to accompany the brick and mortar of urban renewal.

In the next twenty years, it is projected that the city of Chicago will add to its population a new city the size of Detroit. Almost one hundred per cent of this population will be added outside of the present city limits. Something like this will be occurring all over the country. A new urban America is being developed outside of the old. Most of our attention and funds are being devoted to a belated attempt to patch up and refurbish our central cities. Little effective attention and only minor resources are going into making the most out of the new urban America that is spawning in the tracts of suburban developers and in the tangle of new and old jurisdictions that our demand for public-goods segregation has created and still is creating. We are showing small concern with how the metropolitan jungle proliferates or how its growth might be controlled and even made to assist significantly in solving the problems of the central city and the older suburb. A few imaginative approaches, such as the projected Oakland East and the already building Reston (near Washington D.C.), show how planned communities can be developed. In the case of Oakland East, the new community will not only be internally balanced but will provide needed space to relieve ghettoization in the older Oakland.

If housing, schools, jobs, income are related in a vicious circle which the poor and the minorities can hardly break, the Great Society must be prepared to help them. It is generally agreed that education is the key to jobs and housing is the key to education. Where we can most effectively break the circle is by planning and developing new towns in which the segregation of public goods from those of low income will be prevented. Federal funds and federal insurance can dominate and encourage large-scale new town and tract development. Instead of piecemeal support for class and racially segregated political entities, the full weight of the federal government could and should be placed behind what we think the Great Society should mean in the patterns of human settlement. At the very least this should mean a fight to de-ghettoize the minorities and the poor. We know that segregation promotes the perpetuation of the culture of poverty. We are interested in creating a leveling-up and preventing a leveling-down process. This means at the very least that we must be interested in creating opportunities for disadvantaged groups to live in such numbers with the advantaged that desirable neighborhoods will be maintained and that the poor will be enriched and nobody impoverished.

This is a program which many will approve in theory. It cannot succeed if every man is left to seek security for himself. This produces only segregation by flight and lopsided neighborhoods. Planned and controlled population proportions produce conditions compatible with the maintenance of quality and with equal access to it. Without planning and control, the equality norm among citizens leads to the search by higher income recipients of means to give effect to their higher incomes through the territorial segregation of public-goods consumption. We need to work out in our new towns the pattern by which the middle class will not need to segregate itself politically from the poor in order to have quality neighborhoods and quality schools. Access by the poor and the minorities to these goods depends upon their being spread around in such a fashion as nowhere to seriously jeopardize quality standards. This result cannot be achieved by reliance either on the workings of the real estate market or on the piecemeal development of local political jurisdictions. From a territorial point of view, nothing much less than a metropolitan area would be sufficient to relate total population in such a way as to maintain varying but reasonably high standards of public goods. But beyond this backing up by federal funds and support, a Great Society ideal of what the local community needs to become would be necessary to help create the conditions for effective metropolitan action. Only in well-organized metropolitan areas can a Great Society fully employ the human resources of an urban civilization.

The Great Society we hope to build is not on a planet to itself. Its greatness cannot be that of the ancient Chinese behind their wall. Gunnar Myrdal has likened the world to what the United States would be if all the rich and the middle class were on Long Island, defended from the rest of the country by army, navy, and air force. This he thinks is the condition of the Northern Hemisphere. The United States, Canada, Europe, and Russia vis-à-vis the rest of the world. Whether he believes Mao's uprising of the villages against the cities of the world to be a serious threat—at least in Mao's sense—is not clear. Certainly, the threat is militarily and probably even economically empty. But whether or not the starving majority of the world constitutes a physical threat, it must constitute, like our own poor, a challenge to our humanity. We cannot, except at peril to our own souls, harden our hearts and close our ears and eyes to the human disaster that confronts us. A Great Society could scarcely deserve the name were it to fail to respond to the major problem of mankind.

The war on world poverty is a war which, like World War II, if waged with equal vigor, would fully employ all our population. Unlike that other and present wars, it would not be man the wolf of man, but might be William James's moral equivalent for war. In the prosecution of this war, roles of dignity and meaning should be available to our whole society. In a great and necessary task needing all our energies, the Great Society might come to be.

Chapter 5

❦ *The International Aspects of the Great Society* HANS J. MORGENTHAU

THE GREAT SOCIETY

THE NATURE OF THE GREAT SOCIETY

The Great Society is the latest in a series of characterizations of American policies of reform, which was preceded by Theodore Roosevelt's Square Deal, Woodrow Wilson's New Freedom, Franklin D. Roosevelt's New Deal, Harry Truman's Fair Deal, and John F. Kennedy's New Frontier. In these historic predecessors of the Great Society the adjective at least hints at the political reality to which the term refers. "New" is the opposite of "old,"of the status quo—social, economic, or political—which the new policy sets out to change; in Wilson's New Freedom, the "new" refers in particular to the renewal of the promises of America.[1] "Fair" and "square" are synonyms for "just," and the proponents of the programs so characterized pointed emphatically to the injustices which they proposed to remedy (e.g., Theodore Roosevelt's "malefactors of great wealth" and Harry Truman's "special privilege").

Yet what does "great" refer to in the real world? The term has both a quantitative and a qualitative connotation. The Great Society can mean the big society, as it does in Graham Wallas's book which addresses itself to the problems raised by large-scale political organization, in analogy to big industry and big labor.[2] It can also mean the good society, that is, a society that conforms to a philosophic ideal, striving to translate the values of that philosophy into reality. Walter Lippmann uses the term in this sense.[3]

No clear-cut authoritative statement illuminates the meaning of Lyndon B. Johnson's Great Society. The President's statements, especially his Ann Arbor speech of May 22, 1964, after distinguishing between the rich and powerful society, on the one hand, and the Great Society, on the other, present a catalogue of general objectives, either quantitatively extending established measures of social welfare so as to embrace all potential recipients, or extending the responsibilities of the federal government to the qualitative and intangible aspects of American life. The quantitative elements of the Great Society are perfectly intelligible. They continue and endeavor to consummate the American tradition of social and economic reform. A direct line of development connects Theodore Roosevelt's war against the monopolies, Franklin Roosevelt's regulatory interventions into the economic life of the nation, Truman's assumption of responsibility for full employment with Johnson's attempt at stamping out poverty altogether. In its quantitative goals, the Great Society is oriented toward an intelligible and generally accepted set of values.

The Great Society lacks such a set of values to orient itself by when it contemplates the qualitative elements of American life. It seeks the enhancement and ultimate consummation of the individual's dignity and self-sufficiency. Richard N. Goodwin, then special assistant to the President, defined that ultimate qualitative goal of the Great Society most eloquently in the address he gave on July 20, 1965, before visiting foreign students at the D.C. Armory:

> The Great Society looks beyond the prospects of abundance to the problems of abundance. It is aimed, not simply at the disinherited, but at the large majority of Americans who have conquered material want, who do look forward to a better life, who live with a wealth unmatched by any nation in any time. . . . Yet instead [of happiness] we find discontent with what we have, dissatisfaction with the life we created, unhappiness and restlessness. . . . For America is the first post-industrial society. And in that post-industrial age the old assumptions—the moving ideologies of social progress— are dissolving. And we must find a new framework of thought, if we are not to lose the old values too. That is the shaping purpose of the Great Society. For there is one central cause for our condition. It is the fear of the individual that he has become meaningless in the great human enterprise. . . . Everywhere there is growth and movement, activity and change. But where is the place for man? . . . The task of the Great Society is to ensure our people the environment, the capacities, and the social structures which will

give them a meaningful chance to pursue their individual happiness. . . . Thus the Great Society is concerned not with how much, but how good—not with the quantity of our goods but the quality of our lives.

Yet when the Great Society approaches the specific implementation of this general goal, it appears to founder. It proposes to improve the quality of American education. But where is the philosophy of education which could guide it? It assumes responsibility for the beautification of our cities and countryside and for the advancement of the arts. Yet by what esthetic standards does it intend to distinguish between what is beautiful and what is ugly? The government has three alternatives to choose from. It can impose an official set of values upon the cultural life of the nation, to the exclusion of all others. The official esthetics of Nazi Germany and Stalinist Russia provide the latest, particularly repulsive examples of this type of cultural policy. The government can also take over the functions of a Maecenas or a Medici prince and support the outstanding representatives of diverse schools in their competition for recognition. Finally, the government can apply the standards of majoritarian democracy as a substitute for a set of substantive cultural values. That is to say, it can do what appears to be popular or, to use Oliver Wendell Holmes's trenchant phrase, it can accept as the cultural standards of the Great Society what the crowd wants. Or, to put it still another way, it can make "consensus" the ultimate standard for its policies, cultural and otherwise, seeking to achieve the Great Society. Here is indeed one of the foundation stones and the Achilles' heel of the Great Society.

CONSENSUS AS FOUNDATION OF THE GREAT SOCIETY

President Johnson has consistently referred to the consensus of the American people as the ultimate source of the legitimacy and of the rightness of his policies. He likes to cite public opinion polls for the purpose of disarming his critics and proving that his policies are right. Thus the will of the government supported by popular consensus is called upon to fill in the substantive lacunae in the scheme of the Great Society. The Great Society, then, is whatever the government wants it to be, provided that popular consensus supports it. This consensus delineates the outer limits of the Great Society's substance. What the consensus refuses to support, therefore, gives rise to political conflict, which is by definition excluded from the Great Society. At this point the requirement of consensus is at war with even the quantitative requirements of the Great Society.

American society has indeed reached a consensus on the general principles of the Great Society, such as equality of rights and opportunities, the abolition of poverty, the restoration and beautification of our cities, the qualitative improvement of American life. The consensus on the first two of these principles is at bottom nothing more than the reaffirmation of the principles upon which this nation was founded; the first of these principles was reaffirmed once before, a century ago, in the legislation of the Reconstruction period, which has in good measure remained a dead letter. What is new is an apparently vigorous attempt at putting these hallowed and neglected principles into practice. Yet in the measure that these principles are being put into practice, they are bound to challenge the very reality of consensus. For it is impossible to create the Great Society in the image of these principles without radically transforming the political, economic, and social status quo.

The Great Society, in the measure that it is "great," is bound to be a society radically different from that in which we live today. Now submerged social forces will rise, competing with the forces of the status quo. In the measure that they enjoy the vigorous support of a powerful government, they have an edge in that competition. The realization of equal opportunities for all and a successful war against poverty are tantamount to the creation of a large new labor force, competing in a shrinking labor market on equal if not favored terms with those at present gainfully employed. The restoration of our cities under government auspices implies radical change in the control and the values of real estate. Public mass transportation can only be established at the expense of the private motor industry and its subsidiary industries. The systematic shift of an economy of scarcity to one of abundance, in which the government will provide all with the necessities of life, will shift the gravity of economic power from the private to the public sector.

It is utopian to expect that such a radical transformation of the power structure of American society will be supported by a consensus. It can only be achieved as the result of a series of strenuous and violent social conflicts. These conflicts are likely to produce novel political alignments which will render meaningless the traditional juxtapositions between capital and labor, right and left, conservative and

liberal. More likely than not, the united front of capital and labor
will defend the status quo against domination by an all-powerful government from above and disintegration through the infiltration of a
large new labor force from below.[4]

Thus it must soon become obvious that the Great Society and
consensus cannot be had at the same time. The price to be paid for
the Great Society is social conflict, and those who prize consensus
above all else cannot help but sacrifice the Great Society on the altar
of consensus. President Johnson, verbally committed both to the
Great Society and to consensus, must choose, and that choice will become the more imperative as he approaches the threshold of the Great
Society. However, President Johnson seems to believe that he can escape that choice, that he can have the Great Society and consensus,
too. He is led to this belief by a basic misconception of what consensus means for a democratic society. This misconception results from
the confusion between two concepts vital to democratic government:
consensus and the consent of the governed.

All politically civilized societies owe their continuing existence to
a consensus concerning the foundations of society. The possible objectives of that consensus range from the general character of that society
and government, its personnel and procedures, to the concrete objectives of policy; typically, the consensus emerges out of a struggle between antagonistic and frequently incompatible conceptions of what
the consensus should be. Thus the citizens of a democratic society
conclude among themselves, as it were, a social contract in which they
agree upon their common purposes, the procedures by which these
purposes are to be effectuated, the institutions which are intended to
serve them.

It is on the common foundation of this consensus that the political controversies between parties and interest groups are fought out,
and it is only by virtue of this consensus, in which all partake, that
the disputants can afford to submit to the arbitrament of the vote and
the decision of the courts. For what separates them concerns not the
foundations of society, the ultimate interests and values for which
men will kill and die, but only issues, which, while important, do not
decisively affect those ultimate interests and values. Consensus provides a setting, restraining and relativizing, within which political
conflicts can be fought out without endangering the existence of political society itself.

Consensus may arise from conflict, such as international or civil war, but once it has been achieved, it is not subject to change by the democratic processes. Quite to the contrary, the democratic processes are predicated upon its continuing and unchanging existence. It follows that dissent from the consensus is tantamount to opting-out of the political society which has been built upon it, and that active opposition to the consensus is tantamount to treason. A republic, for instance, can afford to tolerate some adherents of monarchy as marginal eccentrics, but it cannot afford to tolerate a political movement seeking to replace the republic with a monarchy.

Consensus must be sharply distinguished from the consent of the governed. Consensus is the general precondition for any civilized government; the consent of the governed is the precondition for a particular democratic government. The consent of the governed does not concern itself with the fundamentals of the democratic polity, which it takes for granted as vouchsafed by the consensus, but with the specifics of a particular democratic government at a particular point in time. Without consensus no civilized political society can survive; without the consent of the governed a democratic government cannot survive in power. The dissent of the governed, in turn, far from being tainted with the stigma of disloyalty since it rises from the common foundation of consensus, is a prerequisite of democratic vitality. The vitality of democratic competition is predicated upon the chance, in principle open to all, that the dissenters of today may carry the day tomorrow. Thus competition for the consent of the governed is the very lifeblood of democratic politics. A democratic government from whose policies or personnel the governed withhold their consent must either change its policies and personnel or make way for another government enjoying that consent. A democratic government, in order to pursue its policies and to govern at all, must be ever solicitous of the consent of the governed.

The philosophy of the Great Society confuses consensus and the consent of the governed. The Johnson administration seeks for its policies a consensus while it is entitled only to the consent of the governed. It is forced into this confusion through its commitment to two mutually exclusive goals: the Great Society and the avoidance of political conflict. These goals can indeed be pursued simultaneously only if the consent of the governed is equated with consensus and, in consequence, dissent with disloyalty. From these illicit equations two policies follow with logical necessity: the elimination of dissent by bringing the full powers of persuasion and intimidation of the government and of the mass media supporting it to bear upon the dissenters, and the ostracism of the recalcitrant dissenters.

The domestic opposition to the Vietnam war has provided the opportunity for putting this mechanism for the creation of consensus into practice. Large numbers of members of Congress have been silenced by actual threats or the fear anticipating such threats. The labor unions have been brought into line by similar methods. Newspapers have been pressured into supporting, or at least toning down their criticism of, official policy. To mention but another example of which I have personal knowledge: a former prominent member of the administration and then a private citizen was reprimanded on the express orders of the President after he had testified before a congressional committee expressing some reservations about our policy in Vietnam. The attacks upon my competence as a scholar, appearing simultaneously in the most diverse places, point to a central inspiration aiming at silencing or at least discrediting me. More effective in creating a mass consensus than these individual instances, which could be multiplied many times, is a general climate of opinion which, while paying lip service to the virtue of democratic dissent, treats dissenters from the consent of the governed as though they were dissenters from the American society.

These attempts at transforming the consent of the governed into a consensus will not be successful. For the survival of freedom in totalitarian societies, most strikingly revealed in the Hungarian Revolution of 1956, has taught us that the desire to be free is as fundamental a human aspiration as the desire to live, to love, and to have power. More particularly, the desire to be free, as a counterpoise to the pull toward conformity, is built into the very foundations of American society. Thus dissent, as an expression of freedom of thought and action, will survive in this country. But if the present trend continues, it is bound to change the position of dissent within the political spectrum and the function it fulfills for American society. For in the measure that the government closes the legitimate channels of democratic dissent and equates legitimate dissent with disloyalty and treason, dissent will tend to become what the government supposes it to be. Despairing of competing on an equal footing for the determination of American policy, denigrated by the government and its eager volunteer servants, driven by the general public to the fringes of American society, what began as dissent from the consent of the governed will tend to end as dissent from the American consensus. The burners of draft cards, the wavers of Vietcong flags, the advocates of Vietcong victory have already taken that step; others are likely to follow by taking the place outside the American consensus the government has assigned to them. Their position toward the American consensus from which these and similar individual acts of alienation from American society spring is that of Abraham Lincoln when he wrote to Joshua Speed on August 24, 1855, with reference to a possible victory of the Know-Nothings: "When it comes to this, I shall prefer emigrating to some country where they make no pretence at loving liberty—to Russia, for instance, where despotism can be taken pure, and without the base alloy of hypocrisy." [5]

Once the policies seeking to realize the Great Society clash head-on with the measures aiming at transforming the consent of the governed into a consensus, the government will face an insoluble dilemma. If it persists in building the Great Society, it will have to cope with defections on the part of substantial segments of the population whose values and interests will be adversely affected by the new policies. The large bloc of citizens for whom consensus and the consent of the governed have become identical and who support whatever the government proposes, will be opposed by another large bloc which, unable to defend and promote its values and interests from within the American consensus, will oppose the consensus from without. What should have been a civilized political conflict within a consensus shared by all will then threaten to become a civil war between two incompatible conceptions of what the consensus ought to be. Thus a false conception of the functions consensus ought to perform for democratic society will rend the Great Society asunder.

If, on the other hand, the government desists from building the Great Society beyond the point at which it commands consensus, it will not build it at all. For it will not be able, as we have seen, to attack the roots of the evils it seeks to remedy without giving battle to the powerful groups whose interests and values block the road to the Great Society. Thus regardless of what we shall do, we cannot have the Great Society and consensus at the same time. And even if we choose consensus over the Great Society, we are likely to see consensus dissolve in social conflict, if not civic disorder. For those segments of the population whose hopes and expectations have been aroused by the promises of the Great Society may not passively reconcile themselves to the continuation of a status quo which they have learned to consider intolerable. Thus, regardless of what we shall do, we are not likely to have consensus even if we forgo the Great Society in order to have it.

This inner contradiction between the aims of the Great Society and consensus as the instrument for their achievement is but a special instance of an even more fundamental inner contradiction between the aims of the Great Society and the means by which they must be accomplished. For even if the Johnson administration were to be willing to accept the dissent of the governed as legitimate, it would still be faced with the necessity of expanding drastically the powers of the federal government in order to make the Great Society a reality. The Great Society requires a massive commitment of federal power, of which the enforcement of consensus is only a peculiar and, in a sense, an accidental manifestation. That commitment is of necessity at war with the Great Society's ultimate goal: the use of the productive forces of modern technology for the enhancement and ultimate consummation of the individual's dignity and self-sufficiency.

The unprecedented productive forces of modern technology, in order to be marshaled on behalf of the individual, require a central direction and management, which in turn threatens the freedom of the individual. The glaring contrast between the Marxist utopia of individual self-fulfillment and the communist practice of totalitarian direction and control is a case in point. It is an idle exercise in intellectual futility and political romanticism to rail against this contradiction between means and ends, as the "New Left" tends to do. The contradiction is existential. It cannot be exorcised by arguments against the "curse of bigness" and by indulgence in Rousseauist dreams. It has to be faced and lived with.

The crucial issue is not how to get rid of "big government" but how to maintain and restore the integrity of the individual in the face of "big government." To be insouciant about the dangers of "big government" is as intellectually untenable and politically pernicious as is the romantic expectation that somehow the individual's position vis-à-vis the government can be restored by dismantling the latter. The "big government" of the Great Society is an inescapable fact of contemporary life. The pregnant question before us is, how can the benevolent intentions of the Great Society on behalf of the individual be accomplished? The answer to that question, only to be adumbrated here, is to be found in the original wisdom and the accumulated experience of the American system of government, which is a system of checks and balances, subject to the rule of law.

AMERICA AND THE WORLD

AMERICA AS MODEL FOR THE WORLD

From the very beginning of American history, there has existed an organic relationship between the character of American society and its relations to other nations. It was as an example for other nations to emulate that America offered itself to the world. The very creation of the United States was regarded both by the founders and foreign observers as an experiment which had a meaning not only for the United States but for all the world. America, wrote Thomas Paine, "made a stand not for herself, only, but for the world, and looked beyond the advantages which herself could receive. Even the Hessian, though hired to fight against her, may live to bless his defeat; and England, condemning the viciousness of its government, rejoice in its miscarriage." [6] "A just and solid republican government maintained here," Thomas Jefferson wrote to John Dickinson on March 6, 1801, "will be a standing monument and example for the aim and imitation of the people of other countries; and I join with you in the hope and belief that they will see from our example that a free government is of all others the most energetic, and that the inquiry which has been excited among the mass of mankind by our revolution and its consequences will ameliorate the condition of man over a great portion of the globe." [7] And in the words of Lincoln: "the Declaration of Independence . . . [gave] liberty, not alone to the people of this country, but hope to the world for all future time. It was that which gave promise that in due time the weights should be lifted from the shoulders of all men. . . ." [8] Responding to these American expectations, the French statesman Turgot wrote to Dr. Price on March 22, 1778, as follows:

All right-thinking men must pray that this people may arrive at all the prosperity of which they are capable. They are the hope of the human race. They should be the model. They must prove to the world, as a fact, that men can be both free and peaceful and can dispense with the trammels of all sorts which tyrants and charlatans of every costume have presumed to impose under the pretext of public safety. They must give the example of political liberty, of religious liberty, of commercial and industrial liberty. The asylum which America affords to the oppressed of all nations will console the world. The facility of profiting by it, in making escape from the consequences of bad governments, will compel the European powers to be just, and to see things as they are. The rest of the world will, by degrees, have its eyes opened to the dispersion of the illusions amidst which politicians have been cradled. But, for that end, America herself must guarantee that she will never become (as so many of your ministerial writers have preached) an image of our Europe, a mass of divided powers disputing about territories or the profits of commerce, and continually cementing the slavery of peoples by their own blood.[9]

This conception of America's being a model to be emulated by other nations did at first not affect the foreign policy of the United States. It only imposed upon America the obligation to arrange its domestic affairs in such a way as to serve as an example for mankind. At the turn of the century, in consequence of the territorial acquisitions following the Spanish-American War, an activist conception of America's mission in the world was added to the passive one of serving as an example.

AMERICA AS MISSIONARY FOR THE WORLD

The promise of universal happiness, implicit in the American experiment, obviously did not mean that all men could achieve it by simple imitation, but it did mean that no group of men was *a priori* excluded from achieving it and that, as a matter of principle, given favorable circumstances, all men could achieve it. Such circumstances were of two kinds: the objective conditions of existence—that is, empty spaces and natural wealth such as had favored the Americans —and the ability of a people ingenious and partial to innovation to make use of these objective conditions.

From this conception of the American experiment's relation to the world at large it was only a step to the acceptance, on the part of America, of the positive obligation to assist less favored peoples, subject to American influence, to achieve the happiness enjoyed by Americans. Thus the territorial expansion of America, hesitating and embarrassed, beyond the boundaries of the continent at the turn of the century goes hand in hand with the self-confident and vigorous expansion of the American principles and practices of government. In that fashion territorial expansion could be justified as serving the American mission, and so could its liquidation after that mission seemed to have been achieved. It then appeared that America had not just stumbled upon the Philippines, Cuba, and Puerto Rico without knowing what it was doing, but that these historic accidents became, if they were not from the beginning, instruments through which America used its power for the benefit of other peoples. The hyperbolic moralisms with which American expansion has been traditionally justified, then, contain elements not only of subjective sincerity but also of objective truth. The idea of the American mission to the less fortunate peoples of the world is certainly a political ideology, a rationalization and justification of policies that were undertaken for other and primarily selfish reasons. But that idea expresses also a serious commitment to a mission that is merely the American mission projected beyond the territorial limits of America and circumscribed only by the reach of American influence.

Senator Albert J. Beveridge of Indiana summarized this missionary philosophy when he said in the Senate on January 9, 1900, that

self-government and internal development of other lands will be the dominant notes of our second century. And administration is as high and holy a function as self-government, just as the care of a trust estate is as sacred an obligation as the management of our own concerns. Cain was the first to violate the divine law of human society which makes of us our brother's keeper. . . .

The Declaration of Independence does not forbid us to do our part in the regeneration of the world. If it did, the Declaration would be wrong. . . .

He [God] has given us the spirit of progress to overwhelm the forces of reaction throughout the earth. He has made us adept in government that we may administer government among savage and senile peoples. Were it not for such a force as this the world would relapse into barbarism and night. And of all our race He has marked the American people as His chosen nation to finally lead in the regeneration of the world. This is the divine mission of America, and it holds for us all the profit, all the glory, all the happiness possible to man. We are trustees of the world's progress, guardians of its righteous peace.[10]

AMERICA AS CRUSADER

The missionary conception of the relationship between our domestic situation and our foreign policy here blends into the third, the crusading one. As missionaries of the American experiment we would offer our assistance to others who were free to accept or reject it. As crusaders we would impose it on the rest of the world, with fire and sword if necessary. The actual limits of such a crusade would be the limits of American power, its potential limits would be the limits of the globe. The American example is transformed into a formula of universal salvation by which right-thinking nations would voluntarily abide and to which the others must be compelled to submit. The classic example of this new relationship between America's domestic purpose and its foreign policy is Woodrow Wilson's crusade for universal democracy.[11]

Had Wilson's United States conceived of itself as just a power among others, it would, like other powers, have looked to its own advantage and competed with its allies for the spoils of victory. For Wilson, World War I was the instrument through which America would achieve the purpose for which it was created: to bring the blessings of its own political system to all the world. America would free all the world, as it had freed itself, from the scourge of authoritarian government, power politics, the balance of power, the armaments race, alliances, spheres of influence, and the rest. The purpose of the war was not only to end war but to end power politics as well.

Thus American participation in World War I revealed itself as the very consummation of the American experiment. America would remain faithful to its purpose in a negative way by not seeking any advantage, territorial or otherwise, for itself; and it would remain faithful to its purpose in a positive way by not only offering its own equality in freedom as a model to be emulated but also by spilling its blood and spending its treasure to make the world safe for democracy —that is, to enable the world to emulate America. In Wilson's thought and action the democratic crusade was thus a logical extension of the American experiment, adapted to the circumstances of the twentieth century.

Toward the close of World War II and in its immediate aftermath, the United States took upon itself the task of the reconstruction of the world by reviving the Wilsonian conception. Emerging from the war as the most powerful nation on earth, without whose global involvement the political world could not be reconstructed nor its national interests be safeguarded, the United States now faced the Wilsonian problem without the benefit of the isolationist escape. With only two power centers left in the world, of which the other happened to be the Soviet Union, the choice of 1920 was no longer open to the United States; that choice would now have meant anarchy in Europe and Asia to be followed by the establishment of order under the auspices of communism.

If the United States could no longer isolate itself from a world

infected with what it chose to call power politics, it had to decontami-
nate the world from that infection in order that it might be safe for
the United States to become permanently involved with it. Our leaders therefore anticipated and prepared for a postwar world where, in
the words of Secretary of State Cordell Hull, "there will no longer be
need for spheres of influence, for alliances, for balance of power, or
any other of the special arrangements through which, in the unhappy
past, the nations strove to safeguard their security or promote their
interests." [12] These expectations, voiced in 1943 after Great Britain,
the Soviet Union, and the United States had agreed upon the establishment of the United Nations, moved President Roosevelt, to declare in his March 1, 1945 report to Congress on the Yalta Conference:

> The Crimean Conference . . . spells the end of the system of unilat-
> eral action and exclusive alliances and spheres of influence and balances of
> power and all the other expedients which have been tried for centuries—and
> have failed.
> We propose to substitute for all these a universal organization in which
> all peace-loving nations will finally have a chance to join in.[13]

When Wilson prepared for the postwar world with similar expectations, his contemporaries could still try to restore the traditional
hemispheric limitations of the American purpose by returning to isolationism. They simply disavowed him by turning their backs on
America's involvement in the affairs of the world. No such disavowal
of Roosevelt's and Hull's expectations was necessary, and no such return to isolationism was possible at the end of World War II. The
Soviet Union's interpretation of the Yalta agreements in terms of the
expansion of Russian power and not of international cooperation revealed the utopian character of Roosevelt's and Hull's expectations
and threatened the European balance of power and, through it, the
vital interests of the United States. This made it obvious that for the
United States the fruit of victory was to be neither a minimal nor-
malcy without power politics nor the safety of hemispheric isolation.
The expansion of Russian power, threatening the security of the
United States, ushered in a new and formidable crisis of the American purpose abroad.

That crisis proceeded in two distinct stages. The first was a period of adaptation, of restoration, of re-creation culminating in the
"fifteen weeks" of 1947 during which a whole new system of American

foreign policy was devised, derived from a radically new conception of the American purpose abroad. That first stage came to an end with the conclusion of the armistice in the Korean War in 1953. The second stage of the postwar crisis of the American purpose abroad, in which we find ourselves at the moment of this writing, differs sharply from the first stage. Rather than being a crisis of restoration and of achievement, as was the first stage of the postwar crisis, it is a crisis of perplexity, of seeming inability to continue the process of adaptation, restoration, and re-creation so auspiciously begun. The novel problems of the postwar world were at first successfully met in one great creative effort, and now the nation settled down to meeting the novel problems of today with the remedies of yesterday, transforming yesterday's creative effort into today's routines.

THE GREAT SOCIETY AND THE WORLD

THE GREAT SOCIETY AND THE AMERICAN MISSION ABROAD

The projection of the Great Society onto the international scene is clearly in line of succession to Wilson's and Roosevelt's conception of America's mission abroad. It is missionary in theory and crusading in practice. The theory was formulated in general terms by Ambassador Arthur Goldberg's speech to the United Nations General Assembly of September 23, 1965:

> In my own country we are embarked under the leadership of President Lyndon B. Johnson in a search for a "Great Society."
>
> This vision of a just democratic order is based on consent of the governed and due process of law, on individual dignity, on economic diversity and on the just satisfaction of political, economic and social aspirations.
>
> We in the United States reject reactionary philosophies of all extremes. We seek to build instead on what we regard the most enlightened and progressive philosophy in human history, that the aim of government is the maximum self-fulfillment of its citizens and that the good life should be within the reach of all, rather than a monopoly of the few. Both domestically and in international affairs there can be no island of poverty in seas of affluence.
>
> We espouse equality not only as a principle. We seek equal opportunity for all as an accomplished reality. And we are resolved to enrich the life of our society by developing human, as well as natural, resources. And we are determined not merely to increase material production but to assure such

equality to guarantee genuine social and economic justice, to eliminate poverty and also to realize qualitative improvements in the life of our citizens—in more attractive and functional cities, in a more beautiful countryside and through learning and the arts.

And this is not the program of any one group or one class or one political party in our country. Nor is the vision it proclaims exclusively American. It is a vision common to all mankind. It fell to my lot for twenty-five years to represent the great labor movement of our country. And one of the great labor leaders with whom I was long associated, Philip Murray, when I asked, what was the aim of the labor movement, to which he dedicated his life, paused and thought and said the aim of the labor movement is a society in which each man shall have a rug on the floor, a picture on the wall, and music in the home. And I think that is a good goal for all of mankind.

So what we seek for our own people in a Great Society at home, we seek for all mankind.

This statement of principles was outlined in President Johnson's speech of September 16, 1965, at the Smithsonian Institution. In this speech, the President declared that "we mean to show that this nation's dream of a Great Society does not stop at the water's edge. It is not just an American dream. All are welcome to share in it. All are invited to contribute to it." He committed the United States to "a broad and long-range plan of world-wide educational endeavor" and announced the appointment of a task force for that purpose, headed by the Secretary of State and with the Secretary of Health, Education, and Welfare as a member. The President enumerated the five components of this plan: assistance to developing countries in their educational efforts; help to American schools and universities to "increase their knowledge of the world and the people who inhabit it"; international exchange of students and teachers; increase of "the free flow of books and ideas and art, works of science and imagination"; the organization of "meetings of men and women from every discipline and every culture to ponder the common problems of mankind."

In his State of the Union message of January 12, 1966, the President expanded his program for the global Great Society by declaring:

This year I propose major new directions in our program of foreign assistance to help those countries who will help themselves.

We will conduct a worldwide attack on the problems of hunger and disease and ignorance.

We will place the matchless skill and the resources of our own great America, in farming and in fertilizers, at the service of those countries committed to develop a modern agriculture.

We will aid those who educate the young in other lands, and we will give children in other continents the same head start that we are trying to give our own children. To advance these ends I will propose the International Education Act of 1966.

I will also propose the International Health Act of 1966 to strike at disease by a new effort to bring modern skills and knowledge to the uncared-for, those suffering in the world, and by trying to wipe out smallpox and malaria and control yellow fever over most of the world during this next decade; to help countries trying to control population growth, by increasing our research—and we will earmark funds to help their efforts.

In the next year, from our foreign aid sources, we propose to dedicate one billion dollars to these efforts, and we call on all who have the means to join us in this work in the world.

The philosophic roots of this program for the global Great Society were discussed in a report of *Time* magazine of September 3, 1965, concerning the influence of Barbara Ward's *The Rich Nations and the Poor Nations*[14] upon the President's thinking. *Time* refers to this book as "the LBJ selection of the century" and "Baedecker to the great Global Society." It quotes the President as having said that "I read it like I do the Bible," and that the book "excites and inspires me." Miss Ward is quoted as returning the compliment by saying: "His profound and compassionate understanding of the roots of poverty gives a unique dimension to the leadership he offers the world." *Time* characterizes the book as "messianic materialism" and finds its influence in the President's speeches.

Reading Miss Ward's book with one's expectations thus aroused, one is bound to be disappointed. The book is a journalistic exposition of facts generally known, of dubious assumptions held by our political folklore to be true, of simple remedies simplistically proposed. What the book has to say about the psychological conditions prevailing in the new nations and their special susceptibility to communism is correct and well put; but it has been said before more succinctly and more profoundly. Especially the first chapter, dealing with the nations of the West, is full of sweeping historic and philosophic generalizations which either are not true at all or could be accepted only with equally sweeping qualifications. The explanation of modern nationalism as springing primarily from the desire for equality is certainly open to doubt. So is the assumption that "the revolution of rising expectations" is a universal phenomenon from which no nation is exempt. And so is the remedy of increased foreign aid as the instrument with which to satisfy these rising expectations.

Most of the concepts with which the book operates are defined with extreme vagueness. "Bearing these differences in mind, we must nevertheless try to define communism and one way would be to say that it is an attempt to put all the revolutions of our day into one coherent system" (p. 63). Much of the book is trivial. "Yet dreams are dreams and men cannot live without them" (p. 66). But the book is written in an animated style and sometimes with a clever turn of phrase, which signifies little or nothing of substance but conveys the appearance of originality or even profundity. Its dominant mood is one of dynamic moralism and sentimentality, sympathizing with the poor nations, good-naturedly chiding the rich nations and calling them to action, however vaguely defined.

Yet the decisive fault of the book is its philosophic naïveté and intellectual superficiality. None of the great moral and intellectual issues, to which the relations between the rich and poor nations give rise, is explicitly posed and validly discussed. The moral and intellectual foundation of the book's thesis—that the rich nations must help the poor nations to overcome their poverty—is taken for granted. Thus the very conception of the relations between rich and poor nations as being nothing more than a quantitative extension of the relations between rich and poor individuals within the same society is posited as self-evident. So is the moral conclusion that the rich nations are obligated to help the poor nations. So is the practical expectation that the quantitative extension of foreign aid is actually capable of eliminating poverty on a world scale. There is no awareness at all of the political conditions from which stems the persistent poverty of many new nations, nor is there any awareness of the political issues to be settled before foreign aid can become effective in countries whose governments have a political stake in the status quo of poverty and backwardness. This and similar problems have been widely discussed since the beginning of the Sixties. Yet so far as this book is concerned, the discussions might as well never have taken place.

This is, then, on all accounts a second-rate book. It would not have occurred to me to compare it with the Bible. On reflection, the only point of comparison I can detect is the requirement, applicable to both books, to accept their basic assumptions on faith. Yet what is inevitable in theology is intolerable in the social sciences. To call this book a Baedecker for the global Great Society is to completely misjudge the functions that admirable guide has performed for generations of travelers. Given your point of departure and your destination, it would tell you accurately which road to travel, the conditions of the road, the different modes of travel, the time of travel for each mode, the expenses to be incurred, and what to expect at the destination. Miss Ward's does nothing of the kind for the trip to the global Great Society. It envelops the landscape in an impenetrable fog, no less blinding for smelling sweetly of benevolence. We do not learn from Miss Ward how to achieve the global Great Society, except that we have to give more foreign aid. We do not learn what the global Great Society would be like except that the gap between rich and poor nations would have disappeared. And we learn from President Johnson and Ambassador Goldberg only that the global Great Society would be a replica on a world scale of the Great Society to the realization of which we are domestically committed.

THE GLOBAL GREAT SOCIETY AND ITS ENEMIES

What are the chances that this vision of a global Great Society can be achieved in practice? Four factors stand in the way of its achievement. Each one of them would suffice to make the achievement unlikely, the four combined make it well-nigh impossible.

We have seen that the Great Society cannot be realized without serious political conflicts and that the refusal to recognize the inevitability of political conflict will doom the Great Society. Yet what is true for the United States is true in particular for those nations to which the global Great Society addresses itself primarily—that is, the developing ones. Their poverty and general backwardness are in good measure not the result of injustices imposed from without or deficiencies of the natural environment, both to be remedied by foreign aid. To a great extent, they are caused by factors that are impervious to such aid. On the one hand, they result from, if not ethnic, at least cultural deficiencies which can be overcome, if at all, only through slow transformation from within. On the other hand, they result from the distribution of political power in backward societies, whose ruling groups have a particular stake in the continuation of backwardness. Their political power is the function of the poverty and illiteracy of the majority of the people. The attempt at remedying these deficiencies from the outside is tantamount to an attack upon the political status quo, to be resisted by the powers that be. The frustrations of the Alliance for Progress and of much of foreign aid in general may be traced to this political factor. The cultural and political receptivity of the nation to be made great sets a limit to the American mission.

Second, the achievements of America as an example to the world were rendered possible by a natural environment—a politically empty, rich, and fertile continent isolated from the centers of international strife—singularly conducive to the development of an open, horizontally and vertically mobile society. Furthermore, these gifts of nature required a people endowed with the moral and rational qualities to take advantage of them. Few nations throughout history have been so favored by nature, and few nations have been morally and rationally equipped for the task nature presented to them. It has been the besetting weakness of America's conception of its global mission from Wilson to Johnson that it has endeavored to separate the American achievement from its uniquely American roots and to erect it into a principle of universal applicability. Wilson and his epigones lifted the American purpose up to the skies, divorced from the concrete conditions of American existence. Yet while they could divorce the American experiment from the American experience, they could not divorce it from the experience of the world. From the former they took it, to the latter they sought to apply it. And in this Wilson failed, as his successors are bound to fail.

Third, the very universalization of the Great Society impairs its plausibility as an example to the world. The plausibility of the America experiment and the possibility of its achievement were from the beginning dependent upon the objective conditions of American existence which drew out certain qualities of the Americans and rewarded them with success. This unique concatenation of objective and subjective conditions, bringing forth unique results, could plausibly be held up as a model for others to emulate only if conditions elsewhere were not totally different from those prevailing in the United States. Even in conditions not completely dissimilar, American principles could apply only as ideal guideposts, not as blueprints to be imitated to the letter. The attempt to demonstrate in action that what had been proven possible in America was possible elsewhere, given good will and material resources, through its very failure cast doubt upon the suitability of the American experiment to serve as a model under any conditions.

This impairment of the plausibility of the American experiment through its universalization is aggravated when the experiment itself lacks intrinsic plausibility. This is, as we have seen, the case of the

Great Society. Its qualitative substance remains undefined and its realization dubious, even within the American context. How can so vague and uncertain an experiment serve as a model for other nations to emulate, let alone as a vehicle for a universal mission?

Finally, the plausibility of the Great Society for other nations is altogether destroyed by its involvement in wars on the soil of developing nations. The conception of a national experiment as a model for the world to emulate has the tendency to transform itself into a missionary endeavor to persuade and help other nations to emulate the example, and such a missionary enterprise tends to transform itself into a crusade which will force laggard and benighted nations for their own good to emulate the example. Thus the New Freedom issued in the Fourteen Points, giving meaning to World War I; the New Deal issued in the Four Freedoms and the United Nations, giving purpose to World War II. Thus the Great Society issues in the anti-communist crusade, seeking to preserve the freedom of nations threatened by communism to choose the Great Society if they so wish, thereby giving meaning to the intervention in the Dominican Republic and the war in Vietnam.

However, the contemporary crusade differs significantly from those that preceded it. The latter were carried forward by a victorious army whose victory seemed to provide empirical proof for the validity of the crusading principles in whose name it was fought. The former must compete, and fight against, a rival conception of the Great Society, more relevant to the experiences and needs of many developing nations than ours. For the anti-communist crusade on behalf of the Great Society, war is not the ultimate manifestation of its victory or of the validity of its principles. Rather it is the instrument with which the Great Society tries to defend its global scope against the onslaught and subversion of its rival.

The very need of a political philosophy claiming universal validity to defend itself against a rival by force of arms leaves at the very least the validity of the universal claim in abeyance. Furthermore, the peoples to be preserved for the global Great Society are likely to be more impressed with the potency of American arms than with the promises of the Great Society. For the voice of the arms is clear and its power is not open to doubt, while the message of the Great Society is faint and inarticulate. What is true of the nations immediately concerned is likely to be true also of the world at large: the clatter of arms drowns out the message of the Great Society.

The connection between the Great Society and war is bound to have also a deleterious effect upon the Great Society at home. No nation, however rich and powerful, can simultaneously create the Great Society at home, spread it abroad, and wage war in order to defend its opportunity to spread. Governments must distinguish between goals that are desirable and those that are necessary, and they must give priority to the latter. The successful waging of war of necessity takes precedence over the achievement of the Great Society at home and abroad. Thus, in the end, war fought to make the world safe for the Great Society makes the achievement of the Great Society impossible.

The waging of war by a government dedicated to the Great Society is also bound to give a powerful impulse to the confusion between consensus and the consent of the governed, upon which, as we have seen, the Great Society is based. In this respect, war psychosis and the Great Society support each other. Both seek national unity in support of the government, that is, a consensus which expels dissent to, if not beyond, the fringes of American society. The opponents of war and the critics of the Great Society, then, keep each other company in that unenviable marginal position. The Great Society waging war can have only one achievement to its credit: it will have weakened the vitality and the creative function of dissent, without which the democratic process is but a sham.

It must also be noted in conclusion that the conscious effort to become great, in a man as in a nation, is not necessarily a sign of strength but may well bespeak an unacknowledged inner weakness. Greatness is a quality inherent in men and nations, not something to be acquired like power and riches. It is not like a woman to be conquered by conscious effort; it is a gift of heaven which is given to those who deserve it, not to those who seek it. Those who seek greatness for themselves and for their nations with frenzied effort may reveal through the very frenzy of their efforts that they are lacking what it takes to be great.

•NOTES

1. See, for instance, Wilson's speech starting the campaign of 1912: "Have we, inheritors of this continent and of the ideals to which the fathers consecrated it,— have we maintained them, realizing them, as each generation must, anew? Are we, in the consciousness that the life of man is pledged to higher levels here than elsewhere, striving still to bear aloft the standards of liberty and hope, or, disillusioned and defeated, are we feeling the disgrace of having had a free field in which

to do new things and of not having done them? The answer must be, I am sure, that we have been in a fair way of failure,—tragic failure. And we stand in danger of utter failure."

2. Graham Wallas, *The Great Society* (New York: Macmillan, 1920), pp. 3 ff.

3. Walter Lippmann, *The Good Society* (Boston: Little Brown, 1937), pp. 362 ff.

4. See my "The Coming Test of American Democracy," *Commentary*, XXXVII, No. 1 (January 1964), 61 ff.

5. Roy P. Basler (ed.), *Collected Works of Abraham Lincoln* (New Brunswick, N.J.: Rutgers University Press, 1959), II, 323.

6. Thomas Paine, *The Rights of Man* (New York: Dutton, 1951), p. 151.

7. A. Lipscomb (ed.), *The Writings of Thomas Jefferson* (Washington, D.C.: Thomas Jefferson Memorial Association, 1905), X, p. 217.

8. Speech in Philadelphia, February 22, 1861, in *The Collected Works of Abraham Lincoln*, IV, p. 240.

9. W. Walker Stephens (ed.), *The Life and Writings of Turgot* (New York: Longmans, Green, 1895), p. 303.

10. Quoted after Ruhl J. Bartlett, *The Record of American Diplomacy* (New York: Knopf, 1947), pp. 386 ff.

11. Before the conflict among these conceptions came to a head in this century, Calhoun saw clearly the dynamic relationship that exists between these three conceptions of America's role in the world, on the one hand, and the American experiment at home, on the other. "It has been lately urged in a very respectable quarter that it is the mission of this country to spread civil and religious liberty over all the globe, and especially over this continent—even by force, if necessary. It is a sad delusion. . . . To preserve it [liberty], it is indispensable to adopt a course of moderation and justice toward all other countries; to avoid war whenever it can be avoided; to let those great causes which are now at work, and which by the mere operation of time, will raise our country to an elevation and influence which no country has ever heretofore attained, continue to work. By pursuing such a course, we may succeed in combining greatness and liberty . . . and do more to extend liberty by our example over this continent and the world generally, than would be done by a thousand victories." Richard K. Crallé (ed.), *The Works of John C. Calhoun* (New York: Appleton, 1854), IV, pp. 416, 420.

12. Report to Congress on Moscow Conference, *The New York Times*, November 19, 1943, p. 4.

13. *Nothing to Fear: The Selected Addresses of Franklin Delano Roosevelt 1932–1945* (Boston: Houghton Mifflin, 1946), p. 453.

14. New York: Norton, 1962.

Chapter 6

🐛 *The Adequacy of Our Concepts*

DANIEL BELL

Why is it, as someone has said, that whenever you ask an intellectual a question, he replies with another question? Why not? It may be that the original question is not the right one. Some other question may be more pertinent to the issue. He may prefer a different question. A question usually implies a problem. Something is ambiguous and requires a resolution. But a problem arises out of an observation, and the observation itself, in the effort to establish its meaning or significance, is embedded in some concept. "The intellectual life of man," William James once remarked, "consists almost wholly in his substitution of a conceptual order for the perceptual order in which his experience originally comes." [1] A concept is a term which groups together diverse attributes or properties of an object or experience, in a higher order of abstraction, in order to relate them or distinguish them from other objects or experiences. (The term "mammal" groups together a whale and an elephant, though one swims in the sea and the other walks on land, to identify common structural principles.)

The first order of questions, therefore, is the adequacy of concepts as related to the purposes at hand. In dealing with the changes in American life or the nature of the Great Society, I intend to set forth some propositions which question the older formulations and, in part, propose some new ones which may be more adequate in understanding some perplexities about American life.

These "questions," some of them rhetorical, some of them ambiguous (as are all true questions), are presented here in the guise of "notes." Notes are often a difficult form for a reader. He wants a tidy exposition which makes its points in some linear fashion (hopefully with some elegance of expression) and which comes to a specific conclusion. In a curious sense, this is a peculiarly "American" demand. The presumption is usually made that every problem has a solution, and one can march toward it in direct, linear fashion. Indirection irritates. It suggests ambiguity or complexity, which, in the American vernacular, becomes translated as evasiveness or hesitation. American life is based on experience, not sensibility; and this, too, is an aspect of the "national style."

The origin of the term *sensibilité*, it might be recalled, derives from the "irritation" of the receptor organs, a tickling of the sensations. The intention of this form, however, is not to irritate the reader (though this may be a consequence), but to suggest the incompleteness of the thoughts and the tentativeness of the formulations. Given the empirical fact that it is written for a deadline, rather than emerging as a product of extended reflection, it necessarily is presented in the form of "notes." This is my apology for being "un-American" in this instance.

SOCIAL CHOICE AND SOCIAL VALUES: THE NEED FOR A NEW CALCULUS[2]

"The great society"—at least in the occurrence of the phrase—has many forebears, but none, perhaps, as startling as Adam Smith. In *The Wealth of Nations,* he wrote:

According to the system of natural liberty, the sovereign has only three duties to attend to; three duties of great importance, indeed, but plain and intelligible to common understandings: first, the duty of protecting the society from the violence and invasion of other independent societies; secondly, the duty of protecting, as far as possible, every member of the society from the injustice or oppression of every other member of it, or the duty of establishing an exact administration of justice; and thirdly, the duty of erecting and maintaining certain public works and certain public institutions, which it can never be for the interest of any individual, or small number of individuals, to erect and maintain; because the profit could never repay the expense to any individual or small number of individuals, though it may frequently do much more than repay it to a great society.[3]

The occurrence of the phrase "a great society" in the context of what are, for Adam Smith, the legitimate functions—and indeed the limitations—of government is striking in the light of the problems of the Great Society today. For Adam Smith was one of the men— the other was John Locke—who "planned" the United States of America. I use the word "planned"—awkward in this context—quite deliberately. For both Smith and Locke laid down the conditions— derived from some specific philosophical assumptions—for the operation of the society that was to emerge in the United States.

The key proposition for Smith, of course, was that every individual, by pursuing his own ends, helps society as a whole. Said Adam Smith:

As every individual, therefore, endeavours as much as he can . . . to direct that industry that its produce may be of the greatest value; every individual necessarily labours to render the annual revenue of the society as great as he can. He generally, indeed, neither intends to promote the public interest, nor knows how much he is promoting it . . . by directing that industry in such a manner as its produce may be of the greatest value, he intends only his own gain, and he is in this, as in many other cases, led by an invisible hand to promote an end which was no part of his intention. Nor is it always the worse for the society that it was no part of it. By pursuing his own interest he frequently promotes that of the society more effectually than when he really intends to promote it.[4]

To put the case briefly and baldly in the modern jargon, Smith's conditions for a free and productive society are: individualism, rationality, perfect information, and rational choice; the good of the society is the aggregate of individual utilities. In fact, Smith laid down, here, a proposition that was almost entirely new in the history of civil society: that in a free exchange, both parties to a transaction could gain. In previous times, it was well understood that the acquisition of wealth in some way was largely through exploitation: conquest, tax farming, tolls, tithes, and so on. Economic life thus, was, in the useful shorthand of modern economics a zero-sum game; one could only win at the expense of a loser. Under the conditions laid down by Smith, economic life could be a non-zero-sum game.[5]

We come to the problem raised by the two quotations from Adam Smith, for economic goods are not of one type, but two: individual goods and social goods. Individual goods are divisible and each person or household buys particular objects and individual service on the basis of free consumer choice. Social goods are not divisible into individual items of possession but are part of a communal service (e.g., national defense, education, beautification of landscape, flood control and so on). These goods and services are not sold to individual consumers nor adjusted to individual tastes. The nature and amount of goods must be set by a single decision, applicable jointly to all persons. Social goods, therefore, are subject to communal or political, rather than individual demand.[6]

The singular point is that in "The Great Society" more and more goods necessarily have to be purchased communally. Defense apart, the planning of cities and the rationalization of transit, the maintenance of open spaces and the extension of recreational areas, the elimination of air pollution and the cleaning up of the rivers, the underwriting of education and the organization of adequate medical care, all are now "public institutions" which cannot be undertaken by individuals, though its creation would "more than repay it to a great society."

Now individuals have their own scale of values, which allow them to assess relative satisfactions against costs, and to make their purchases accordingly. Public life lacks such ready measures. We cannot ask for and individually buy in the marketplace our share of unpolluted air, even if one was willing to pay an extra portion of one's income for it (unless one moved to Arizona; and if all moved, the problem of smog would arise anew). The availability of higher education in the marketplace alone would deny many families the possibility of such learning, and also deny the society some of the social benefits which a more educated, and therefore more productive citizenry might create. We have no effective social calculus which gives us a true sense of the entire costs and benefits of individual and social purchases. (Few individuals think of taxes as the purchase of public services, and even when they do there is little sense of the concrete value—in the dollars-and-cents meaning of goods and services—which they have obtained.) Thus, there is no mechanism which allows us to consider, in terms of costs and benefits, the varying combinations of private consumption and public purchases of goods.

These are practical, political problems. But at this point a theoretical thorn intrudes. For in recent years economists and mathematicians have been able to supply a "rational proof" of the individual utility preference model, but not that of the group welfare function model. Let us turn to what might be called Adam Smith I. In the famous beginning of *The Wealth of Nations* Smith remarks that only human beings engage in truck or barter. An animal who wants attention fawns or seeks to be engaging, and while human beings are sometimes equally servile, they do better by seeking to strike a bargain. (". . . it is in vain for him to expect [help of his brethren] from their benevolence only. He will be more likely to prevail if he can interest their self-love in his favour, and shew them that it is for their own advantage to do for him what he requires of them.")

In effect, one offers another man a rationally calculable advantage. But how does one make such calculations? What is the value of an object or a service to a person, and how compare one object to another? For a man to choose rationally, there must be some underlying standard of value against which he can rate all alternatives. Money is a rough and ready measure. But the "value" of money diminishes as one's hoard of it increases. Ten dollars means much less to a millionaire than to a pauper. (This is one of the difficulties, as well, in applying a theory of "equality" to punishments. Two men may be fined $100 for speeding, but for the millionaire the $100 means much less than for a worker who pays the same fine. Is equality then the "same" punishment, or an equal ability to bear punishments?) Jeremy Bentham proposed the concept of "utility" as the unit for a model of rational choice, in which individuals would rank their preferences in an orderly way. But there was little way of comparing utilities (i.e., how much more one wanted one preference rather than another, its intensity quotient, so to speak) or of working out optimal combinations when one wants different proportions of different things. Utility, like value, came to be regarded as a metaphysical concept, and price alone was taken as the indicator of exchange and comparability.

The publication of *The Theory of Games and Economic Behavior* by von Neumann and Morgenstern, in 1944, rehabilitated the concept of utility by dealing with the conditions of choice, or decision making under risk. One does not know for certain the consequences of a given choice, but one does know the alternatives, and a certain gamble can be built into the choices in which the value of the probability of winning is put over against the probability of losing. (A simple game: under conditions of a gamble you can win a Cadillac, but if you lose you get a bicycle; if you decide not to play you get a Volkswagen. Thus, if the chances are 50-50, will you take the gamble or take the "consolation" prize? What if the chances are 40-60, 30-70, 20-80, 10-90? At what point will you stop taking the risk?) Under such conditions it is possible to assign numerical values to utility which allow you to "scale" (like a temperature gauge, rather than just rank), the preferences individuals may have.[7] It is equally possible, using the various techniques of linear programming, to work out "optimal" solutions in the combination of resources, the maximizing of utilities, and the like.

But when one turns from individual decision making to that of groups, when one considers the problem, quoting Luce and Raiffa, "of how best to amalgamate the discordant preference patterns of the members of a society to arrive at a compromise preference pattern for society as a whole," we seem to be at an impasse. In the first major effort to formulate the problem, Arrow demonstrated, in his *Social Choice and Individual Values,* written in 1951, that the five requirements of "fairness" for social welfare functions are inconsistent (i.e., no welfare function exists which satisfies all of them.)[8] Even the principle of majority rule, which satisfies three and possibly four of the conditions, is subject to the logical contradiction, first formulated by Condorcet, of the paradox of the cyclical majority.

What is paradoxical, however, is that while one can now, for the first time perhaps, set up a rational "model" of the Smith-Bentham world, in real life the basic conditions for rationality—perfect in formation—becomes less and less a possibility for the "players" in the Great Society.

The proof can be demonstrated simply. Supposing there are three voters, A, B, and C, whose preferences on issues x, y, and z are ordered in the following pattern, we find:

	Voters		
Preferences	A	B	C
First	x	z	y
Second	y	x	z
Third	z	y	x

Clearly, x is preferred to y by a majority (voters A and B); y is preferred to z by a majority (voters A and C); from the principle of transitivity (i.e., if an individual prefers x to y, and y to z, we assume he would also prefer x to z) we should predict that x is also preferred to z, and that x, therefore, is the choice of the majority of the voters: but in fact, z is preferred to x by voters B and C, so that no single majority can be formulated on these three issues.[9]

There have been numerous attempts both to modify the original conditions which Arrow put forth as necessary to organize a group welfare function and to resolve the voting paradox (by conceptions of log-rolling, bargains, or the creation of what Anthony Downs has called "passionate majorities"). But so far, at least to the extent that I can follow the technical literature, no satisfactory "solutions" have been forthcoming.[10]

This problem—of seeking to produce a single social ordering of alternative social choices which would correspond to individual orderings—is academic, in the best sense of the word. In the "real" world the problem of social priorities, of what social utilities are to be maximized, of what communal enterprises are to be furthered will be settled in the political arena, by "political criteria"—i.e., the relative weights and pressures of different interest groups, balanced against some vague sense of the national need and the public interest. But it is precisely at this point that the theoretical thorn may begin to prick. For increasingly, one of the "issues" of a Great Society—one which can be defined as a society that seeks to become conscious of its goals —is the relationship, if not the "clash," between "rationality" and "politics." Much of contemporary social theory has been addressed to the rigorous formulation of rational models of man, in which optimizing, maximizing, and minimizing provide models of behavior that are rationally normative. But we seem to be unable to formulate a "group theory" of economic choice. The impasse of social theory, in regard to social welfare, is a disturbing prospect at this stage of the transition to a communal society.

I have raised a problem—the lack of an ordering mechanism to make social choices—and quickly taken it to a level of abstraction which is meaningless to practical men.[11] For theorists, the implications are quite drastic, for these logical conundrums strike at the assumptions of those who think that the general will will emerge out of necessity in democratic debate, and those rationalists—as we all may be —who assume that the public interest is discoverable simply by a summation of preferences. Practical men can take heart, for in all this an intuitive idea is reinforced, namely, that differences between persons are best settled, as so many differences are in the American system, by bargaining. As Robert Dahl has observed:

Many Americans are frequently dismayed by its paradoxes; indeed, few Americans who look upon our political process attentively can fail, at times, to feel deep frustration and angry resentment with a system that on the surface has so little order and so much chaos.

For it is a markedly decentralized system. Decisions are made by endless bargaining; perhaps in no other national political system in the world is bargaining so basic a component of the political process. . . . [Yet] with all its defects, it does nonetheless provide a high probability that any active and legitimate group will make itself heard effectively at some stage in the process of decision. This is no mean thing in a political system.[12]

And this is, perhaps, as it should be. But if we are to rest our case on the legitimacy of the group interest process—and this was the contribution, initially, of Arthur F. Bentley—some other (less rarefied, but still theoretical) questions arise.[13]

GROUP POLITICS AND INDIVIDUAL LEADERSHIP

If rationality and individual choice operating through the market were the theoretical contributions of eighteenth-century economics, the idea of representation and interests was the addition of nineteenth-century politics; and the fusion of the two resulted in a social theory of the free society. The most comprehensive formulation of the political idea was offered, perhaps, by John Stuart Mill, in his essay on "Representative Government." In it, Mill wrote:

The meaning of representative government is, that the whole people, or some numerous portion of them, exercise through deputies periodically elected by themselves the ultimate controlling power, which, in every constitution, must reside somewhere . . .

A place where every interest and shade of opinion in the country can have its cause even passionately pleaded, in the face of the government and of all other interests and opinions, can compel them to listen, and either comply, or state clearly why they do not, is in itself, if it answered no other purpose, one of the most important political institutions that can exist anywhere, and one of the foremost benefits of free government.[13]

The theory of representative government reflected a picture of society as a "balance of forces." The legislature, in this conception, was supposed to contain representatives of the various social divisions and all the class interests in the country, for, as Mill noted in appealing for the right of the working class to be represented in Parliament, "in the absence of its natural defenders, the interest of the excluded is always in danger of being overlooked." Mill, in fact, was so intent on the idea of the representation of minorities that he gave enthusiastic endorsement to the proposal of Thomas Hare for proportional representation, "a scheme which has the almost unparalled merit of carrying out a great principle of government in a manner approaching to ideal perfection as regards the special object in view. . . ." [14]

This normative theory was refined by what might be called the "realist" school of political thought, from Arthur F. Bentley on (or one should say, of course, that Bentley's original formulations in 1908, ignored for many years, were restated three decades later by V. O. Key, David Truman, and Earl Latham), to describe the empirical nature of political reality. If a "group theory" was lacking in economics, it certainly made its appearance, in full flower, in American political thought in the twentieth century. As V. O. Key put it most succinctly:

At bottom, group interests are the animating forces in the political process. . . . Whatever the bases of group interest may be, the study of politics must rest on an analysis of the objectives and composition of the interest groups within a society. . . . The chief vehicles for the expression of group interest are political parties and pressure groups. Through these formal mechanisms groups of people with like interests make themselves felt in the balancing of political forces.[15]

And, in this conception, the role of the politician was to be a broker:

The problem of the politician or the statesman in a democracy is to maintain a working balance between the demands of competing interests and values. . . . Within limits . . . special interests in a democracy are free to express their demands and their disagreements. . . . The politician in a democracy . . . must be able to hold together enough of these special interests to retain power; he must yield here, stand firm there, delay at the next point, and again act vigorously in a confusing complex of competing forces and interests. . . . The politician . . . must play the part of arbitrator and mediator, subject to the criticism of all. To avoid or mitigate conflict, he compromises.[16]

Whatever the truth of this "model" as a description of the "nineteenth century inheritance" [17] (or even as a superficial description of Lyndon Johnson), it is astonishingly out of date for an understanding of politics in the second half of the twentieth century, for it fails to take into account the three most decisive characteristics, or shaping elements, of national policy today: the influence of foreign policy, the "future-orientation" of society, and the increasing role of "technical" decision making.

Foreign policy is not formulated in reaction to the needs and pressures of domestic pressure groups (though once decisions are taken, some modifications may by made in response to their demands—e.g., to build airplanes in the southwest rather than in the northwest). Foreign policy is shaped in accordance with great power and ideological interests, and as responses to perceived threats from other great powers or ideological forces. But its consequence, under conditions of a cold war, is to force a "mobilized posture" on the society as a whole, to create some sense of national unity, and to centralize decision making and enormous resources in the hands of a national administration. (Of the $15 billion spent by the federal government for research and development, 90 per cent goes into three areas: defense, space and atomic energy.) In the past twenty years the social and economic map of the United States has been redrawn more by the influence of defense spending than by any other single factor in the society.

The commitment to economic growth and the new dimensions of social change—its more rapid shock effects on larger and larger sections of the society and the consequent need to anticipate social change and to a considerable extent to direct it—have brought with it a renewed emphasis on planning, on the need to become more conscious of national goals and with the "alternative futures" which a society with a steady productivity (a constant 3 per cent rate of productivity will *double* national output in twenty-four years) can provide. "The process of innovation," write Dahl and Lindblom, "is both scientific and political. It is not enough that new social techniques be discovered; they must also be put to use. Invention and discovery are only the beginning of a process, the next step in which is innovation, a matter of politics. What we are suggesting is that this process taken as a whole is proceeding with astonishing rapidity—it is perhaps the greatest political revolution of our times." [18]

The combination of these two elements brings into play the increasing role of technical decision making. The shaping of conscious policy, be it in foreign policy, defense, or economics, calls to the fore the men with the skills necessary to outline the constraints ahead, to work out in detail the management and policy procedures, and to assess the consequences of choices. The revolutions in military technology (the introduction of nuclear power, the replacement of manned aircraft by missiles) were initiated by scientists. The development of systems-analysis and cost-effectiveness techniques, which have revolutionized both the strategy process as well as the management structure of the Pentagon, was brought about by mathematicians and economists.[19] The management of the national economy, with its close watch on the effects of government spending, requires the services of men skilled in the arts, and such crucial policy questions as when to have tax cuts or tax increases, how much to have and where to apply it, and what the wage-price guidepost should be, increasingly become technical decisions.[20]

But the most important political consequence of all this is the passing of effective power in almost all political systems, from the legislative and parliamentary bodies to the executive, and the re-emergence of what Bertrand de Jouvenal has called, in his elegant fashion, *The Principate*. How could it be otherwise when, in the nature of modern politics, foreign policy is no longer "diplomacy" but an unceasing round of strategic maneuver in which crucial decisions have to be taken speedily, and when, because of the new patterns of social change, the very need to plan policies, rather than lay down laws, gives the initiative to the executive?

In the United States we have seen, in the past twenty-five years, the enormous transformation of the Presidency to the Executive Office of the President with the addition of new staff functions, such as the Bureau of the Budget, the Council of Economic Advisers, and the Office of the Science Adviser, directly within that office. For the long run, it is not the growth of the personal powers and prestige of the President that is important, but the *institutionalization* of such crucial control and directing functions—such as are now carried out by the Budget Bureau and the Council of Economic Advisers—in the executive which reinforces the structural shifts of power.

Although these essential changes—the new role of the executive (or the charismatic leader), the conflict between technocratic rationality with political bargaining, and the orientation to the future—have been variously described, political theory has not yet absorbed these new circumstances into a new conceptual structure. Although the interest-group model has less and less relevance in allowing us to understand the transformation of America into a mobilized polity, even the later, sophisticated versions of this model—cast in terms of systems, and inputs and outputs[21]—repeat the same assumptions, using equilibrium rather than "balance of forces" as the "flywheel" of the model. Instead of models depicting government as a kind of umpire, mediating the inputs provided by conflicting interest groups and allowing them to issue forth in the output of decisions, a more adequate picture would have to see government as a system capable of free action, choosing even which interests to allow to become inputs, and government itself bargaining—on the basis of technocratic decisions—with various interest groups in the society.[22]

Beyond the question of a more adequate empirical model there is the more difficult problem of formulating a normative theory, which —taking into account the ineluctable elements of centralized decision making, the extension of social or communal choices, and the need for conscious social planning (not to "direct" the society, but to facilitate desired social changes)—can set forth rational criteria consonant with the values of a free society. In the construction of such a theory, other elements of re-conceptualization may have to be taken into account. Such re-conceptualizations, by regrouping familiar facts in a new way, may help us identify new problems that will be arising in the Great Society.

NUMBER, INTERACTION, DENSITY

A mass society is one which is not characterized by large numbers, or rather by numbers alone, but by concentration and density. Large land-mass societies may have large numbers of population, but in the past they were spread out over immense areas of land and were largely segmental rather than integral in social organization. It is when segmentation breaks down and peoples come into increasing contact and interaction with each other—in large urban concentrations in the past, or through mass communication today—that the features of mass society appear.[23] Such features are (in the social structure), the divorce of the family from the occupational system, increased specialization, differentiation of function, multiplication of collectivities, hierarchies, formalization of rules, extension of universalism, and (in the culture) the secularization of beliefs, the emphasis on individual experience, the search for novelty and sensation, the syncretism of creeds and forms.[24]

The mass society, in short, reflects what I have called in another context, "the eclipse of distance." While the initial changes are created by the new forms of transportation and communication which bring people into ready contact with each other in innumerable ways, the "eclipse of distance" is not only the foreshortening of time and space in flying across continents, or in being in instant communication with any part of the globe by television or radio, it is also, as

regards the *experienced* time of the person, an eclipse of social, esthetic and psychic distance as well.[25]

The United States, with all its historical particularity, in many
ways has taken over these features of a mass society. Regionalism as a
form of cultural segmentation has largely broken down, though some
political influences remain. The family-based enterprise (farms, retail
establishments, small manufacturing businesses) is of minor importance in the economy. The mobility of individuals, social and spatial,
unprecedented in history, is stupendous.[26]

The effects of the increase in number, interaction, and density of
population are enormous. Here, taking the communication pattern as
a single variable, I shall seek to illustrate it, with three problems.

1. *The loss of insulating space.* If one looks at American history,
what strikes one immediately is the tremendous amount of violence,
particularly labor violence, which took place over a period of sixty-
five years (from 1877, beginning with the railroad strikes and ending
with the outbreak of war at the end of 1941). From any rough set of
indicators that one chooses—the number of times troops were called
out, the number of riots, the number of individuals killed, the
amount of sabotage, the number of man-days of work lost, the
amounts of money spent by corporations in fighting trade unions—it
is highly likely that there was more violence than any country in Europe. Yet the United States did escape the political holocausts that
wracked European society, and some basic accommodation (formal-
ized in the labor representation in the War Production Board and
institutionalized later in the union security clauses established by the
War Labor Board) was reached.

One can identify many factors which account for this difference
between American and European society but surely one of the important ones, particularly before World War I, was what one can call the
factor of "insulated space." One of the distinguishing features of political violence in Europe is that most of it took place close to or at a
political center. (What would have happened in France, for example,
if the Constituent Assembly had met at Dijon rather than at Versailles, twenty miles from Paris and subject to the pressures of the
Paris crowds? Clearly all such *if* questions are unanswerable, but their
formulation allows one to see the possibility of alternative variables.)
In the United States, that early violence took place largely at the
"perimeters" of the society (in isolated coal-mining communities, in
the Chicago and Rocky Mountain areas) and the "shock effects" had
small radial range.

The introduction of modern mass communication allows us, in many cases forces us, to respond directly and immediately to social issues. There is little question that the presence of the television cameras in Selma, Alabama, showing the use of crude violence (snarling police dogs, electrified cattle prods) against the Negro marchers, aroused an immediate national response which was reflected in the presence of thousands of persons who poured into Selma the following week from all over the country. Without television, it is likely that the shock effect, even if transmitted through news photos and newsreels, would have been dissipated (and that before the rise of the mass media this incident would have never had a national impact).

One can see this by a crude comparison of two incidents. In the winter of 1893–1894, the growing economic distress and mass unemployment brought the formation of scattered groups of jobless into "armies" who declared for a "march on Washington" to demand relief. The best known of these was "Coxey's Army," led by the populist "general" Jacob S. Coxey. Although detachments of the armies started out from various parts of the country, and Coxey led his contingent from Massillon, Ohio, only 400 persons reached the national capital, and the "armies" were easily dispersed.[27]

In the summer of 1963, Negro civil rights leaders called for a March on Washington to bring pressure upon the Administration for the passage of a civil rights bill, and by plane, bus, rail, and car, 250,000 persons descended on the capital in an extraordinary demonstration of political purpose. Differences of issue apart, it is clear that the one incident is a product of a regional society, the other of a mass society.

One may applaud the fact that the nature of the mass media increases the likelihood of a spectacular rise in "participatory" democracy, but these instances are also more likely to be on emotional issues (and drawing therefore from the extremes), so that the loss of "insulating space" itself may permit the setting off of chain reactions which may be disruptive of civil politics and reasoned debate.

2. *Communications overload.* Whatever else may be said about the twentieth century, it has produced the greatest bombardment of aural and visual materials that man has ever experienced in his history. To the linotype, camera, typewriter, telephone, and telegraph, the twentieth century has added radio (and radio telephone), teletype, television, microwaves, communication satellites, computers, xerography, and the like. Transistors and miniaturization not only facilitate an incredible packaging of communication senders, receiv-

ers, and recorders in the confines of a space ship, they also allow automobile telephony, walkie-talkies, portable radio and television sets,
and finally, on the agenda, person-to-person communication by
"wristwatch" radio anywhere in the country (and soon the world?).
Radar and loran have taken over most of the air-sea guidance of
transport, while an incredibly deployed watching system like SAGE
(already, in part, obsolete) permits a national command-control system, using real-time computers, to patrol the continental defense
from the distant-early-warning lines.

George Miller, the Harvard psychologist, once demonstrated, in
a marvelous article, "The Magical Number Seven Plus or Minus
Two," the finite limits in the number of different "bits" (or signals)
that a human channel could encompass at one time.[28] But the problem is not the single instant, but the total number of sensations that
an individual is subject to. Some random sampling of the communication media illustrates, in a cursory way, the growth of the networks
of interaction. In 1899, there were one million telephones in the
United States, or 13.3 per 1000 population; in 1963, there were
84,440,000 telephones, or 442.5 per 1000 population. (Over 350
million local calls are made daily.) In 1899, 6,576,000 pieces of mail
were moved in the United States; in 1963, 67,853,000,000 pieces of
mail were sent (more than half of them first-class). In 1924, 1,250,000
families had radio sets, and 530 stations were on the air; in 1964, more
than 90 per cent of families had radio sets and 5,607 stations (AM
and FM) were on the air. In 1949, 940,000 families had television sets
and 17 stations were sending pictures; in 1964, more than 90 per cent
of all families had television sets and 564 television stations were
broadcasting regularly.[29]

The extension of the range of communication has brought the
entire world into instant attention to any listener. Consider only the
multiple geography lessons that each of us has had to learn in the last
twenty-five years, from a knowledge of the strategic value of the
Chagos archipelago as an equatorial staging area halfway between
Aden and Singapore, to the distinction between the Congo Republic
(Leopoldville), formerly Belgian, and the Republic of the Congo
(Brazzaville), formerly French. And consider, too, the number of
different political figures and the bewildering number of political
parties that we have to learn about to keep abreast of the news. (No
wonder the nominee to the American ambassadorship to Ceylon
could not pronounce the name Bandaranike.)

For the society and the political process there are enormous problems which arise from this communications overload. At a time when, in our psychological values, we place a greater emphasis on individuation, where is the possibility of privacy, a "psycho-social moratorium" (a term used by Erik Erikson to describe the need of sensitive adolescents to escape the pressures of schools, career choice, and the like), the finding of open spaces (consider the desecration of Lake Tahoe), and a relief from the stresses created by these incessant "messages" out of the blue? Certainly for the year 2000 this may be one of the most urgent of all social problems.

And for the political process, consider only one image: the problems, terrifying in number, which automatically flew today to Washington as a political center, and the multifarious issues which the President therefore has to confront, and often decide upon, in "real time." Can such a system continue, without breakdown?

Numbers alone, of course, are not the problem. But thinking about them leads us to our next topic.

DIFFUSION AND CHANGE OF SCALE

We have all become accustomed to the idea of the exponential growth of knowledge. Derek Price, in his *Science since Babylon*,[30] has argued that the increase in the total research effort in Great Britain has been approximately exponential since the time of Newton, or a doubling of the scientific effort every ten or fifteen years (or about three times in the course of the working life of a scientist). The holdings of every major research library in the United States have, since the turn of the century, been doubling almost every fifteen years. The late Louis Ridenour, who was one of the first to call attention to this phenomenon, argued that "the most widely various human activities are found, when they can be measured quantitatively, to be changing according to an exponential law." [31]

While we hear much of the *acceleration* of social change today—is the introduction of the computer and the jet engine more of an *acceleration* of social change than the steam engine and the railroad in the nineteenth-century world? The idea clearly is a difficult one to define—there is some evidence that the rate of diffusion of social products, from the shortening of time between a technical discovery and the application of its commercial potential to the marketability of new items, such as television, has stepped up considerably.[32]

The point about diffusion is the critical one for any consideration of social change—and prediction about the future. For it is not
the spectacular innovations (crucial as they may be as turning points)
which are the important elements in changing the social map of a
country, but the diffusion of products—and privileges—and the rate
of such diffusion in a country. For diffusion is not automatic. In the
case of products, it rests upon certain entrepreneurial talents and the
ability to break through the cake of custom or the barriers of en-
trenched interests. In the case of privileges, it rests upon the ability of
disadvantaged groups to mobilize political pressures. And both of
these are operative only within the framework of the value system of a
society.

One of the reasons why the predictions of Tocqueville, made
more than 130 years ago, are still so cogent, is that he had hit upon
the great "master key" to American society—the desire for equality.[33]
In effect, what has been the property or privilege of the few can be
demanded, legitimately, by the many. The enormous change, for example, in the character of higher education, which affects us all, is
not due to any sweeping technological innovation (though there is a
greater need for more professionally and technically trained manpower) or even the bulge of numbers because of the post-World War
II baby boom, but because of the extension of higher education from
the few to the many. In 1935, for example, 12.2 per cent of the (9.2
million) 18–21 age group attended college, while in 1964, more than
40 per cent of the (11.2 million) 18–21 age group was in college.

Out of the same impulses, there is a constant set of rising expectations about what the society can produce. It has been estimated, for
example, that about 20 per cent of our people live in poverty. But
this is a definition of poverty by 1964 standards. If we applied, say,
1947 standards, only about 15 per cent of the people, perhaps, would
be considered poor today.[34] It is the nature of the American experience to "upgrade" constantly the notion of what constitutes a decent
minimum, and correspondingly of poverty. As Herman Miller, the
assistant to the director of the Census, points out in his book *Rich
Man, Poor Man*,[35] according to the Bureau of Labor Statistics, a
"modest but adequate living standard" in New York City in 1947 (as
distinct from poverty) required a family income (in 1961 dollars) of
$4,000 a year. This criterion rose in 1961 to $5,200, a 28 per cent
increase. At this rate, by 1975, the new "decent minimum" for a
family will be (in 1961 dollars) $7,000. As Mr. Miller concludes: our

standards will be lifted a little higher, our belts will be opened another notch, and there will still be a large block of families living under new and higher substandard conditions.

It is this aspect of social change which gives rise to a curious discrepancy of social perception. The national output will double, or individuals will find that their own incomes have doubled over a period of time, yet there will be complaints that people are not living *twice* as well as before. The entry of more and more disadvantaged persons *into* the society, as claimants for goods and privileges, clearly changes the nature of privileges and services themselves.[36] In seeking for clues to social change, therefore, the important task is to be able to identify which aspects of privilege or advantage today will be demanded by the many tomorrow. (More travel, travel to more distant places, winter vacations, summer houses?) And it is the diffusion of these privileges, in terms of increasing number, that provides the clue to the kinds of social and political demands of the coming years.

But changes in number also mean a change in scale. If relationships were linear, there would be no problem; but increased size changes the nature of organizations, results in multiple hierarchies, introduces new problems of coordination, and poses new questions of order and planning. Students at Berkeley, for example, complain of de-personalization because of the size of the university, yet decentralization or the creation of more universities is not a complete answer because of the scarcity of talent relative to immediate demands. The spread of medical care has prompted the introduction of more technological devices (e.g., multi-phase diagnostic screens) which mechanize the doctor-patient relationship, yet this is, in part, a concomitant of a mass society. (The answer: increase the number of doctors, is easy rhetorically yet difficult because of the problems of recruiting more doctors and the long time-lags in the training period— a factor which has given rise in recent years to a demand for the shortening of the college period in order to accelerate entry into graduate school.) The increase in leisure and travel has brought more crowding in the resorts and the museums. The French Riviera, for example, is already a shambles because of the insistence of French workers and bourgeoisie on all taking their *fermeture annuelle* in August.

The question of the size and scope of the social unit—the appropriate size of governmental units, the optimal size of organizations, the decentralization of function, and the creation of a "human scale" in a mass society—is the most crucial sociological problem that arises out of a consideration of the two conceptual frameworks that have been sketched out above: the influence of number, density, and interaction, and the consequences of diffusion and change of scale.

THE APPROPRIATE SIZE AND SCOPE OF THE SOCIAL UNIT

The United States today, for the first time, is genuinely a "national society." In fact, many of the domestic problems we confront do not arise out of such hoary formulations as "capitalism" and "socialism," but from the fact that a multiplicity of problems—education, transportation, welfare, urban renewal, air and water pollution, medical care and the like—no longer are manageable on the state and local level but are now passed on to the national society for solution. In the last twenty-five years we have become: 1) *an intertwined national economy,* in which government has become an active regulator of economic activity as well as a partner in many enterprises; 2) *a national polity,* in which (as demonstrated in the example of civil rights) the government has become an active force for social change and, in consequence of World War II, the Korean War, and now the war in Vietnam, in which there is a permanently mobilized military posture; 3) *a welfare society,* in which medical care, education, and, in increasing ways, income maintenance for the disadvantaged, have become a responsibility of the central government; and, 4) *a national culture,* not only through the diffusion of the popular arts through the mass media, but symbolically (if not quite tangibly) through the creation of a National Humanities and Arts Foundation which will organize government support for the scholarly, creative, and performing arts.

This development, in its own way, dramatizes more than any other single question the problem of the appropriate size of the social unit, in the political as well as the sociological sense. This question can be looked at along four dimensions: the adequacy of the political structure; the question of centralization and decentralization; the distinction as to what is "public" and what is "private"; and the optimal size of bureaucratic structures, private and public. The first two questions are discussed in this section, the other two in the one following.

1. *The adequacy of political structures.* It should strike anyone, on momentary reflection, that in a society confronting the kind of

problems we have, the existing organization of fifty states makes no economic, political, or social sense. What is the rationale for the boundaries of New Jersey, Delaware, Rhode Island, or Maryland? (In his recent inaugural speech Governor Hughes said that New Jersey was undergoing an "identity crisis." Well it might.) Under the Constitution, such concerns as education, welfare, local services, and the like are powers reserved to the states and municipalities. But these entities are no longer able to perform such services. Their tax bases are inadequate; their administrative structures archaic and inefficient.

Our problems are confounded when we go to a lower-level unit of government. In the past, advances in transportation technology served as the strategic variable in determining the scale of urbanization. The limits to urban growth in the nineteenth century were set, at first, by natural waterways and canals, later by railroads and steamships. Since World War I the automobile and the truck have advanced the pace of urbanization and changed its nature. With them have come the central city, the suburb, and the metropolis. Today half of our people live in urban areas. By 1975, it is estimated that three-fourths of all Americans will be living an urban life. As suburbs spread farther away from the central city, the expanding metropolitan areas merge to form a new social and economic unit—the Megalopolis. The skeletal outlines of a northeast Megalopolis from Boston to Washington are already visible. The large crescent around Lake Michigan forms another. The stretches from San Francisco to San Jose and from Los Angeles to San Diego already form ribbon cities. The development of Megalopolis intensifies the need to organize the common use of water, land, recreational resources, and transportation systems for large areas that cut across the boundaries of existing state and local governments.

Yet the situation at the local level is chaotic. There is no decentralization but disarray. The proliferation of government at the local level gives rise to serious problems in the coordination of public programs, in reducing public accountability, in making decisions affecting multi-unit areas, and in contributing to the wide disparities between available financial resources and community and human needs. The complexity of the problem can be seen from the fact that in 1962 the San Diego metropolitan area had 11 municipalities; Phoenix, 17; Houston, 25; Cleveland, 75; St. Louis, 163; Chicago, 246; and the New York metropolitan region, 1,400 local governments—small villages, school districts, sewerage districts, health districts, park districts, police districts, each with its own restrictive powers. These boundaries, historic growths, once adaptive to local needs, are no longer meaningful.[37] Air pollution, waste disposal, and mass transportation are at least metropolitan in scope. Adequate housing can only be obtained if mass-production techniques are introduced into the industry, but the research and development of new materials and methods of construction, or the creation of markets large enough to warrant mass production, are not possible so long as there are thousands of different local building codes—often as many as fifty in a single metropolitan area—in the United States.

2. *Centralization and decentralization.* Clearly what is necessary in the next several decades is a comprehensive overhaul and modernization of governmental structures to find the appropriate size and scope of units which can handle the appropriate tasks. No one expects, of course, that the existing state boundaries will be abolished—for historic, traditional, or political reasons they are likely to be retained. But all sorts of functions can be "detached" and lodged in multi-state or regional "compacts" which can take over such functions. Clearly there are no pat answers. Even the favorite theme of regionalism is not an easy solution, for the definition of what is a region varies not on the basis of geography but on the function to be performed: a water region, a transport region, an educational region, and even an economic region have different "overlays" on the map. One has to define first what it is that one wants to centralize, and what to decentralize.

If a single principle can be established it would be this: that the function of the federal government should be primarily in the areas of policy and funding, and that operative functions be in the hands of regions, metropolises, and non-profit corporations whose size and scope would be appropriate to the function that had to be performed. It is a principle that leads us to the next distinction we seek to make.

THE PUBLIC AND THE PRIVATE

The conventional model of the economy concentrates on the private, profit-seeking center. Yet what is public and what is private, and what is profit and what is not-for-profit is no longer an easy distinction. The aerospace companies are private, yet the federal government purchases 94 per cent of their entire output. Instead of retaining as profits their revenues above costs, all profits above a negotiated sum are returned to the government; the government, rather than the competitive market, determines their profitability, and even their survival. The New York Port Authority and the Triborough Bridge Authority are nonprofit public corporations, yet they make enormous profits which, though they do not go to stockholders, are reinvested in new enterprises far beyond the original charter of these corporations. In practical effect, they differ little from private utilities which pay off a fixed sum of their indebtedness and use profits for reinvestment. The Battelle Institute is a not-for-profit research foundation, the Arthur D. Little is profit-seeking, yet the activities of the two are quite similar and they are competitive. (Battelle did the development work on xerography and now reaps large royalties; Arthur D. Little does a considerable amount of public service work at no fee.) Mutual insurance companies and mutual savings banks are not-for-profit, yet their rates, salaries, and practices are virtually identical with capital stock insurance companies and savings banks. The University of California at Berkeley is a state university yet it receives large amounts in corporate gifts and other private giving. Columbia University is a private school yet more than half of its annual $85 million budget comes from federal contracts and grants. The medical and health service field, the largest "growth industry" in the country, is a commingling of private, profit, non-profit, and government activities. Most physicians are self-employed and operate within the private sector, yet are connected with hospitals most of which are not-for-private, while the federal government increasingly underwrites a large share of hospital construction, medical care for the aged, and the overwhelming portion of research funds in medicine.

It is, in the main, the distinctive role of government as the "funder," but not the operator, of activities that makes for these confusions. One can take as a specific instance the emergence in the ten years after World War II of the not-for-profit "systems research and development" corporations as a paradigm. The archaic civil service rules and the rigid bureaucratic structure made it almost impossible for the government to develop quickly a necessary "in-house" capacity in a number of scientific and defense fields. The creation of RAND (an acronym for Research and Development), housed originally in the Douglas Aircraft Corporation, as a "think factory" for the Air Force provided a model which was quickly used by the Defense Department and other government agencies to create what is, essentially, a new social form. In some instances, these new groupings are independent corporations, in other instances they are housed in universities or are managed by a consortium of universities. The Lincoln Laboratory of M.I.T., under contract with the Defense Department, worked out the feasibility of a distant-early-warning signal system for continental defense, and then set up MITRE (M.I.T. Research and Engineering) to do some of the necessary design work on the system. Since MITRE did not involve any fundamental research, and was not intrinsic to the purposes of the university, it was "spun off" as an independent not-for-profit corporation. The need to train thousands of persons quickly to manage new computer systems involved in continental defense led the Air Force to create the Systems Development Corporation (a spin-off from RAND), and this organization, having pioneered new systems of programmed learning and of computer capabilities, has extended its effort into the educational field, seeking contracts from many organizations far outside the Defense Department. It would take one too far afield to trace out here the complicated pattern of relationships that emerged between the government —principally through the Defense Department, the Atomic Energy Commission, the National Science Foundation, the National Aeronautical and Space Administration, and the National Institutes of Health—and the different kinds of research and development organizations, public and private. But in these instances one has seen a creative adaptivity which itself speaks well for the flexibility of the American administrative system.

If one looks at the not-for-profit sector as a whole, taking into account the wide range of government, educational and health services, the striking fact is that about one-fourth of G.N.P. and "not less than one-third and possibly almost two-fifths of all employment *is accounted for by the activities* of that sector.[38] In the 1950–1960 decade, in fact, nine out of every ten *new* jobs added to the economy were generated in the not-for-profit sector—i.e., by the vastly enlarged role of the federal government in connection with the cold war, the expanded activities of state and local governments in providing community services, and the growth of the education and health and welfare fields. A comparison of the figures over time reveals a marked change of scale. In 1929 the not-for-profit sector accounted for about 12.5 per cent of all goods and services purchases; in 1963 it was slightly above 27 per cent. In 1929 about 4,465,000 individuals, constituting 9.7 per cent of the labor force, were employed in the not-for-profit sector; in 1960 the figure has risen to 13,583,000, or more than one in five of all employed.

The growth of the not-for-profit sector brings into focus as employers of significant amounts of manpower a whole array of organizations whose structure and form differ to a considerable extent from the usual model of "bureaucracy." These are universities, research laboratories, hospitals, community welfare organizations, and the like. The "received" doctrine, as drawn from Max Weber and accepted by most students of stratification theory, posits a bureaucracy as having a division of labor based on functional specialization, a well-defined hierarchy of authority, recruitment, selection, and promotion based on technical criteria, impersonal, "bureaucratic" rules of behavior, and so on. This is the "ideal type" model which is often best exemplified in business corporate structure. Yet the variety of new kinds of organizations that are emerging (particularly ones with a high component of technical and research personnel) indicates that the older models, patterned on pyramidical structures, may no longer be applicable, and that in the coming decades the "traditional" bureaucratic form will have given way to organizational modes more adaptive to the needs for initiative, free time, joint consultation, and the like.[39] The emergence of new structural forms of non-bureaucratic organization is one more item on the long agenda of new problems for the post-industrial society.

A SYSTEM OF SOCIAL ACCOUNTS

We have learned in recent years how to chart economic growth and thus to identify at various points the kinds of policies which may be necessary to stimulate growth. We have begun to perfect an economic reporting system and to establish economic indicators which give us a measure of national performance. But as yet we do not have a continuous charting of social changes and we have been ill-prepared (in such matters as housing, education, or the status of the Negro) to determine our needs, establish some goals, and measure our performance. We have had no coherent accounting of our results, no assessment of gaps or short-falls, no reckoning of social costs and social gains. Lacking any systematic assessment, we have few criteria which allow us to test the effectiveness of present policies or weigh alternatives regarding future programs.

The development of national economic accounting provides us with an instructive picture of the workings of a modern economy. There are at present, for example, four types of accounting systems which allow us to measure different kinds of economic phenomena and transactions: National Income and Product Accounts sums up the total value of goods and services transacted in the economy and the allocation of net income among households, government, business, and foreign units; National Moneyflow Accounts traces the flow of funds between financial and non-financial units, including households and government; National Inter-Industry Accounts sets forth the value of purchases and sales of goods and services among variously "disaggregated" units of business, government, household and foreign sectors; and National Wealth Accounting, in effect a national assets inventory, evaluates the reproducible assets and resources of the nation.

Yet these economic instruments, particularly the G.N.P., are limited in their use, and sometimes—more by popular opinion than by professional economists—give us a distorted picture of the social economy. The G.N.P. measures the sum total of goods and services transacted in the *market* economy. It is immediately apparent that services performed within a household, by a wife, for example, are not "valued." (The British economist A. C. Pigou, a pioneer of welfare economics, once remarked that if a widowed vicar paid his housekeeper a weekly wage, this was an addition to the national income; if he married her, it became a subtraction.) The point at issue is that "income" in rural areas (where a substantial amount of food may be produced at home) is often "undervalued" as against urban income— a fact neglected not only in some discussions about poverty in the United States, but in the international comparisons between the United States and some well-to-do agrarian countries (e.g., Denmark, New Zealand), which on the scale of G.N.P. rank lower than their real income would put them.

Moreover, if national income is understated by considering the G.N.P. alone, the sense of progress can be exaggerated by the "additive" nature of G.N.P. accounting. Thus, when a factory is built, the new construction and the new payrolls are an addition to the G.N.P. If, at the same time, the factory pollutes a stream and builds a filtration plant to divert the wastes, these expenditures, too, become an addition to the G.N.P. In the financial sense, more money has been spent in the economy; but the gross addition simply masks an "offset cost," not a contribution to economic progress. The definition as to what is a genuine addition and what is an offset clearly is a difficult one, but one insufficiently recognized in the popular discussion of national economic accounting. More generally, if the G.N.P. is to be considered a "welfare" or "growth" measuring device, the existence of unemployment or depressed areas raises the question of what is a *per capita real income* as against the measuring rod which now exists. Some way of establishing new measuring devices and levels of performance remains to be established.[40]

One can have a meaningful sense of progress only by knowing its costs, direct and indirect.[41] A difficulty in national economic accounting today is that of directly assigning the costs generated by one group which often are borne by others (e.g., the costs to the community of strip mining, gouging out a countryside). But the problem is not only one of social costs, unfairly generated and widely borne, but the broader cost matrix which would allow us to balance gains against costs.[42]

What we need, in effect, is a System of Social Accounts which would broaden our concept of costs and benefits, and put economic accounting into a broader framework. The eventual purpose would be to create a "balance sheet" that would be useful in clarifying policy choices.

What would a system of social accounts allow us to do? The word "accounts," as it stands now, is perhaps a misnomer. Sociologists have been able to establish few completely consistent sets of relationships (such as the relationship, say, between unemployment and delinquency). Even where sophisticated social analysis can establish relationships it is difficult to establish these in measurable terms. But we can begin by seeking to establish a conceptual framework.

A System of Social Accounts would begin with a series of social indicators that would give us a broader and more balanced reckoning of the meaning of economic progress as we know it. This effort to set up a System of Social Accounts would move us toward measurement of the utilization of human resources in our society in four areas: 1) the measurement of social costs and net returns of innovations; 2) the measurement of social ills (e.g., crime, family disruption); 3) the creation of "performance budgets" in areas of defined social needs (e.g., housing, education); and 4) indicators of economic opportunity and social mobility.

The following elaborations of the four areas referred to above are meant to be illustrative rather than prescriptive. They are intended to suggest the range of problems and the scope of application.

1. *Social Costs and Net Return.* Technological advances create new investment opportunities. These investments are expected to be paid out of the enhanced earnings they produce. But clearly there are losses as well. The major loss is the unemployment created by technological change, particularly in those instances where the advanced age of the worker of the particular skill that is displaced makes it difficult for such persons to find new employment. Or a new plant in an area may create new employment opportunities, yet its by-products—water pollution and air pollution—may create additional costs for the community. Long ago, Professor Pigou demonstrated, in his *The Economics of Welfare,* that there is frequently a divergence between the private cost borne by an entrepreneur and the social cost of production. Into the cost account of the private entrepreneur goes only those items for which he has to pay, while such items as maintenance of the unemployed, provisions for the victims of industrial accidents or of occupational diseases, costs of access roads are borne, in the old phrase of J. M. Clark, as "social overhead costs."

The question of which costs should be borne by the firm and which by the community is clearly a matter of public policy. Increasingly, for example, firms responsible for polluting the waters of a river are asked to bear the costs of filtration. The Ruhr, flowing through West Germany's most dense industrial region, is at present less polluted than it was twenty years ago. Swimming and boating are commonplace. This happy circumstance is the result of a cooperative arrangement between 259 municipalities and 2,200 industries along the river which have developed a system of effluent fees calculated to encourage the construction of waste disposal systems. In this case the entire cost of pollution is assigned to the source. On the other hand, certain costs of severance pay or maintenance of an older labor force on a firm's payroll may be so huge as to inhibit the introduction of useful technological devices and such costs might be borne better by the community than by a firm itself. But these questions of public policy can only be decided when we have a clearer picture of the actual social costs and returns of innovations.[43]

2. *The Measurement of Social Ills.* Every society pays a huge price for crime, juvenile delinquency, and disruption of the family. The costs of child care and mental health are also high. There are no simple causes, such as unemployment, of such social ills. Yet such ills and social tensions have measurable effects on the economy (from the loss of able-bodied workers because of mental illness, to direct losses of property because of thefts and riots). Although data on crime, on

health, dependent children and the like are collected by government agencies, there is rarely any effort to link these problems to underlying conditions; nor is there a full measure of the cost of these ills. Systematic analysis of such data might suggest possible courses of remedial action.

3. *Performance Budgets.* The American commitment is not only to raise the standard of living but to improve the quality of life. But we have few yardsticks to tell us how we are doing. A system of social accounts would contain "performance budgets" in various areas to serve as such yardsticks. A national housing budget, for example, would indicate where we stand in regard to the goal of a "decent home for every American family." It would also enable us to locate, by city and region, the areas of greatest needs and so provide the basis for effective public policy. A series of community health indices would tell us how well we are meeting the needs of our people in regard to adequate medical care.

4. *Indicators of Economic Opportunity and Social Mobility.* More than twenty-five years ago, in *An American Dilemma,* Gunnar Myrdal wrote: "We should . . . have liked to present in our study a general index, year by year or at least decade by decade, as a quantitative expression of the movement of the entire system we are studying: the status of the Negro in America. . . . But the work of constructing and analyzing a general index of Negro status in America amounts to a major investigation in itself, and we must leave the matter as a proposal for later research." [44]

Two decades later, we still have no "general index" of the status of the Negro in America. In a strict methodological sense, no "comprehensive indexes" are perhaps possible, but we can assemble specific indicators. Thus where once it seemed impossible to conceive of a "value" figure for "human assets," the creation in recent years of a "lifetime-earning-power index" gives us a measure to reflect the improvements in income associated with increased education, improvement in health, and reduction of discrimination. Data on social mobility, developed by sociologists, can tell us whether there is a genuine equality of opportunity in the United States and can identify the barriers (e.g., inadequate school opportunities) to that equality. Economists have a term, "opportunity costs," which allows us not only to calculate direct costs but the gains forgone from the use of those resources if they had been employed elsewhere. "Social opportunity" costs may allow us to reckon the possible gains by the utilization of hitherto unused human resources and to weigh, in terms of social costs and social benefits, alternative social policies.

These proposals have an underlying assumption: that the society would be in a better position to appraise its achievements, its needs, and its shortcomings by being able to specify broad national goals. President Eisenhower created a Commission on National Goals, an important step in this direction. The work of President Johnson's task force is a further effort to specify national needs and steps to meet them. All of this suggests, however, that the definition of national goals in major areas has to be a continuing process in which a system of social accounts would serve as a tool to identify the greatest areas of needs.

THE PERSPECTIVE OF TIME

Americans, more than other peoples (as a *national style* not on individual comparison), are an impatient lot. A problem emerges and people want answers—quickly. There are, in fact, two simplistic notions in the American temper: one that all problems are soluble, the second that the way to solve a problem is to pour men and money into it. (Do you want to go the moon? Build a NASA. Do you want to raze the slums? Mount a huge housing program. The fact that problems are not wholly congruent, that in the one case the problem is a "game against nature," and in the other a "game between people," rarely enters into such considerations.)

The extraordinary fact, in relation to the huge range of social problems that confront us, is the recency of the simple tools we have to deal with them. The measurement of our G.N.P., which is the chief indicator of economic performance and growth, was first established as an official government task in 1944, when it was proposed in President Roosevelt's budget message of the year. (National income figures, as a government function, were initially collected in 1942.) The Council of Economic Advisers, as a research, analysis, and policy body for the nation, was created only twenty years ago, and not until six years ago did it begin to function in the way it was intended. Just recently were the techniques of input-output analysis and that of linear programming developed so that only now are we able to lay out an adequate *tableau economique* and plot the varying combinations of resources and requirements in accordance with different values assumptions. And only with these techniques is a model of economic planning actually possible. We still lack any adequate forecasting models of the economy, either for short-run or long-run purposes. Efforts now, as at Brookings, to test econometric models for quarterly economic forecasts, or the Tobin-Solow model for a mathematical model for longer-range forecasting, have only just begun.

In the areas of social planning we are woefully behind. The economic data collected and disseminated by the federal government, and the economic models based on it, are highly relevant to economic policy. Unfortunately they are less applicable to the new problems of social change. National economic and census statistics, aggregated as they are, tell us little about pockets of poverty, depressed communities, sick industries, or disadvantaged social groups. The national data, averaged out, provide few clues to, or relevant information about, regional or local problems. In respect to the integration crises and anti-poverty programs of the 1960's, the federal government finds itself lacking the necessary information for making effective policy decisions in response to these new social problems. The need for this kind of data is urgent. The socio-economic crisis in the 1930's led the government to establish national income and product accounts and thus facilitated macro-economic analysis and economic models on an aggregate national basis. In effect, the government's decision of several decades ago about the type of data to be collected, made on the basis of its own need for information, shaped in considerable measure the direction of economic theory and practice. The new type of social data collection, which is so urgently needed now, undoubtedly will influence the development of social science for the next generation.

If one looks at the development of new intellectual tools—regard alone the promise of the computer and the extraordinary usages possible, from "data banks" to be used in systems analysis to "heuristic programming" for decision theory—government effort in the organized support of science and research, the expansion of the universities, the beginnings of the organized effort to "transfer technology" from military and space programs to civilian use, one's feeling about the future, so far as intellectual possibilities for intelligent planning are concerned, is considerably heartened.

•NOTES

1. See "Percept and Concept," in William James, *Some Problems of Philosophy* (Longmans, Green: New York, 1916), p. 51.

2. In this and in some of the succeeding sections I have drawn from memoranda that I have prepared for the National Commission on Technology, Automation and Economic Progress and for the Commission on the Year 2000 of the American Academy of Arts and Sciences.

3. Adam Smith, *The Wealth of Nations* (New York: Modern Library 1937), p. 651. The phrase, "the great society" appears in three places in *The Wealth of Nations* by my count (pp. 651, 681, and 747), but its meaning is to be found at the conclusion of Book V, Ch. 1—which deals with the revenues of the Sovereign or Commonwealth—and, in context, the phrase, "great society," means here the "whole society" (see p. 767). It is a point of considerable relevance for the discussion above. The capitalized phrase, "The Great Society," occurs, of course, as the title of the book by Graham Wallas. That book (published in 1914) grew out of a course that Wallas gave at Harvard in 1910, which was joined by Walter Lippmann, and though the initial theme is the growing interdependence of peoples, and an ensuing change of social scale, the book itself is not an effort to assess the sources or consequences of this change, but an effort to utilize the findings of the newer social psychology for the rational pursuit of social affairs.

4. *The Wealth of Nations, op. cit.,* Book IV, Ch. 11, p. 423.

5. In actual fact, it was not the existence of free exchange but the existence of technology, with its promise of rising productivity, that created the possibility of economic life remaining a non-zero-sum gain. For an instructive book on the means whereby technology has been the chief means of promoting social equality, see Jean Fourastie, *The Causes of Wealth* (Glencoe, Ill.: The Free Press, 1960).

6. See Howard Bowne, "The Interpretation of Voting in the Allocation of Economic Resources," *Quarterly Journal of Economics,* LVIII (November 1943), 27–48.

7. John von Neumann and Oskar Morganstern (Princeton: Princeton University Press, 1953). For a simple mathematical proof of the possibility of scaling utilities, see Jacob Marschak, "Scaling of Utilities and Probabilities," in Martin Shubik (ed.), *Game Theory and Related Approaches to Social Behavior* (New York: Wiley, 1964). For a more general discussion of utility theory, and decision making under certainty, risk, and uncertainty, see Duncan Luce and Howard Raiffa, *Games and Decisions* (New York: John Wiley, 1958), Ch. 2.

8. Kenneth J. Arrow (New York: Wiley, 1963). The listing of these conditions would be too extensive and carry us too far afield.

9. The most comprehensive effort to deal with the problem is that of Duncan Black, *The Theory of Committees and Elections* (Cambridge, Eng.: Cambridge University Press, 1958). Further discussion can be found in James M. Buchanan and Gordon Tullock, *The Calculus of Consent* (Ann Arbor: University of Michigan Press, 1962). Some earlier discussions are in Robert A. Dahl and Charles E. Lindblom, *Politics, Economics and Welfare* (New York: Harper and Row, 1953), and Anthony Downs, *An Economic Theory of Democracy* (New York: Harper, 1957).

10. See Arrow, *op. cit.* In an appendix to a new edition of his book (New Haven: Yale University Press, 1963) Arrow has sought to counter some discoveries of errors in his proofs by reformulating the conditions to show that the inconsistencies in the conditions still remain and that no logical foundations for a complete social welfare function are possible.

11. But theory does have a way sometimes of confounding practical men. William H. Riker has illustrated the relevance of hidden voting paradoxes through an analysis of the rules for amending bills in the committees of the House of Representatives. He has shown that under a number of rules amendments might be adopted which are not favored by a majority—without this fact ever being known!

Thus, for example, when a paragraph of an amendment and an amendment to an amendment are before a committee, the first vote is on the amendments. If the amendment to a paragraph is passed, it replaces the original paragraph without further vote. Because it votes only twice on three issues, the House does not discover any intransitivity, and a choice may become law which was favored only by a minority. Riker concludes that various situations of this sort may be expected to occur, *in practice,* slightly more than 10 per cent of the time—which should make some practical men uneasy.

This is not to say that "majority voting" is impossible. If one returns to the original example of the cyclical majority it will be seen that the intransitivity of preferences is evident only on a third vote. Thus, to uncover intransitivities, one has to initiate a complete "round robin" matching each proposal with every other, but as Riker notes no legislatures require such matching procedure for groups of more than three proposals. Once the intransitivities are uncovered, one can, as Duncan Black has demonstrated, proceed to a system of "exhaustive voting," which matches candidate against candidate, or issue against issue, to obtain the majority decision in each instance. And, in a more theoretical vein, as Arrow and Black have demonstrated, by ranking preferences on a graph, one can obtain "single-peaked" profiles of each voter; and when all of the profiles for a given group are represented as single-peaked preference curves on one set of axes, a single majority choice can be obtained—if the group is odd in number, or if the chairman votes in case of a tie.

But practical men can take heart from the fact that, in practice, where such disparities of preferences or intensities do occur, some form of log-rolling or bargaining takes place, and, as Tullock and Buchanan have shown, one can fit such procedures into the theoretical resolutions of the voting paradoxes. This still leaves open, again it should be noted, the larger theoretical question of finding a rational solution to a social welfare function. Majority voting is preferred because it satisfies three or possibly four of the five conditions which Arrow has established as necessary for validation, and therefore is the most sensible of "compromises." On some occasions, however, fearing a "tyranny of the majority," one might want to consider some of the more complicated means which have been suggested by Black and Arrow to arrive at a social welfare function. And, finally, there is the point that any solution—at least those suggested so far—does not fulfill the complete logical conditions of arriving at a true social choice.

For further discussion see William H. Riker, *The Theory of Political Coalitions* (New Haven: Yale University Press, 1962).

12. Robert A. Dahl, *A Preface to Democratic Theory* (Chicago: University of Chicago Press, 1956), p. 150.

13. Nag that I am, I would still like, at the conclusion of this section, to return to the justification of the theoretical problem; for even a pragmatist like myself has to recognize the necessity for some rational system (if only as yardstick), of what social choices *could* be. One can carry the argument forward, perhaps, with this consideration: one might, today, with mathematical models and high-speed computers, write a single economic plan for a country that would show, through input-output matrices, the optimal distribution of economic resources, with products valued at full economic costs. But the administrative difficulties in implementing such a plan might be so enormous that, in practice, one would have to resort to the market or some quasi-bargaining system for the actual operation of the economy. Yet the value of such a theoretical construction is that it could serve as a yardstick, establishing "shallow allocations" and "shadow prices" for the system and allowing us to intervene at those points where discrepancies show up. In an analogous sense, one would want a theoretical social choice model in order to have an optimal social welfare function.

13. John Stuart Mill, *Utilitarianism, Liberty and Representative Government* (New York: Dutton., 1936), pp. 228, 240.

The theory of representation and interests, it should be noted, is normative. It is part of Mill's concern to define the "best form of government." Practice, of course, might be entirely different. As Mill notes: "Politically speaking, a great part of all power consists in will . . . opinion is itself one of the greatest active social forces. One person with a belief is a social power equal to ninety-nine who have only interests." *Ibid.*, p. 183.

14. *Ibid.*, pp. 209, 261.

15. V. O. Key, *Politics, Parties and Pressure Groups* (New York: Knopf, 1942), pp. 23–24.

16. *Ibid.*, pp. 10–11.

17. The "group theory of politics," it should be noted, has been challenged on theoretical grounds by Mancur Olson, Jr., who, applying an "economic analysis" to the nature of aggregate choice, argues that interest groups do not represent best the interests of their members. See Mancur Olson, Jr., *The Logic of Collective Action: Public Goods and The Theory of Groups* (Cambridge: Harvard University Press, 1965).

18. *Op. cit.*, p. 8.

19. See Charles J. Hitch and Roland N. McKean, *The Economics of Defense in the Nuclear Age* (Cambridge: Harvard University Press, 1960), and Edward S. Quade (ed.), *Analysis for Military Decisions: The Rand Lectures on Systems Analysis* (Chicago: Rand, McNally, 1964).

20. As one quondam bureaucrat has earnestly argued, "the development of public policy and of the methods of its administration owe less in the long run to processes of conflict among political parties and social or economic pressure groups than to the more objective processes of research and discussion among professional groups." Don K. Price, *Government and Science* (New York: Oxford University Press, 1962)—a statement written little more than ten years after V. O. Key, and reflecting the differences, perhaps, of the pre-war and post-war experiences of political analysts.

21. See, for example, David Easton, "An Approach to the Analysis of Political Systems," *World Politics* (April 1957), 383–400, and *A Systems Analysis of Political Life* (New York: Wiley, 1965). A more mechanical model is presented by William Mitchell, *The American Polity* (New York: The Free Press of Glencoe, 1962).

22. An extreme version of this, perhaps, would be Gaullist France where, for a period of time, almost the entire political system (concentrated in the administrative structure) had become "independent" of the society, initiating the changes (demands, inputs) and making decisions on the basis of technocratic criteria.

23. For the classic statement of the problem, see Emile Durkheim, *On The Division of Labor in Society* (New York: Macmillan, 1933), Book II, Ch. 2.

24. Though the changes in both dimensions derive from a common source, the contrasting demands or impulses in each realm clearly impose an agonizing tension between the two whose consequences, important as I believe they are in locating crucial strains in the society, are beyond the purview of this essay. I have discussed this, to some extent, in "The Disjunction of Culture and Social Structure," *Daedalus*, XCIV (Winter 1965), 208–222. reprinted in Gerald Holton (ed.) *Science and Culture* (Boston: Houghton, Mifflin, 1965).

25. The problems of the loss of esthetic and psychic distance, especially in relation to art, are discussed in the previously cited essay, and in a variant version in *Encounter* (London), XX (May 1963), 54–56.

26. The continuous movement of persons into, out of, between, and within labor markets in any one year is one index of such mobility. Thus, in 1964, the average number of persons in the labor force was 74 million, with about 70 million employed and 3.9 million unemployed. But hidden beneath these national averages, one finds that: 87 million people were in the labor force at some time during the year; 85 million different people held jobs, 43 million entered or re-entered the labor force; 42 million left the labor force for temporary periods or permanently, and 14.1 million different persons experienced some period of unemployment. (Figures from the Bureau of Labor Statistics for the National Commission on Technology, Automation and Economic Progress.)

Between 1955 and 1960, slightly more than *half* of the population (about 80 million persons) changed residences, about 47 million to different homes in the same county, the remainder to different counties or states. In a single year (1962) more than 34 million persons changed homes, about a third of these out of the original counties. See the *Statistical Abstract* of the United States, 1964, pp. 32–33.

The most recent comprehensive study of social mobility, based on inter-generational moves of occupation, shows a continuing movement of upward class mobility into salaried, technical, and professional employments. See Otis Dudley Duncan, "The Trend of Occupational Mobility in the United States," *American Sociological Review*, XXX (August 1965), 491–498.

27. Longevity, it should be pointed out, is a different variable from distance. Coxey, who was born in 1854, ran for President in 1932 on a Farmer-Labor ticket, and died in 1951.

28. See George A. Miller, "The Magical Number Seven, Plus or Minus Two: Some Limits on Our Capacity for Processing Information," *The Psychology of Communication: Seven Essays* (New York: Basic Books, 1967), Ch. 2.

29. These data are taken from the *Historical Statistics of the United States* Chapter R) and the *Statistical Abstract* of the United States, Section 18.

30. New Haven: Yale University Press, 1962.

31. As examples, Ridenour cited the fact that the total assets of life insurance companies in the United States have doubled every decade; the number of long-distance telephone calls, in the forty years between 1910 and 1950, doubled every seven and a half years; the time for circumventing the globe decreased exponentially every quarter century between the time Nellie Bly went around the world, in 1889, to 1928 by a factor of two, and so on. Ridenour sought to work out a law of social change which, in its mathematical formulation, was remarkably similar to the so-called "autocatalytic processes of chemistry and biology." See Louis Ridenour, *Bibliography in an Age of Science* (Urbana: The University of Illinois Press, 1951).

32. A study by Frank Lynn, of a limited sample of 20 major technological innovations during the last 60 to 70 years, indicates that the typical time between a discovery and its commercial recognition had fallen from about 30 years before World War I to 16 years between the wars and 9 years after World War II. The additional time required to convert these basic technical discoveries to actual commercial application had decreased from about 7 or 8 to about 5 years. The rate at which new technologies were diffused throughout the economy after their first introduction had speeded up considerably between the early part of the century and the inter-war period, with only slight further acceleration after 1945. Technological innovations with consumer applications were applied and diffused nearly twice as fast as those with industrial application. See Frank Lynn, *An Investigation of the Rate of Development and Diffusion of Technology in Our Modern Industrial Society*, a study prepared for the National Commission on Technology, Automation and Economic Progress. (INTEC, Inc., October 1965.)

33. Tocqueville had a penchant, as many great theorists have, for seeking such "prime movers." Thus, he also predicted an eventual clash between the United States and Russia on the basis that large land-mass societies with great natural resources would inevitably expand their living space. For a discussion of this, as well as other modes of prediction, see my essay, "Twelve Modes of Prediction," *Daedalus*, XCIII (Summer 1964), 845–880.

34. See Robert J. Lampman, *The Low Income Population and Economic Growth* (Washington, D.C.: Joint Committee on the Economic Report, U.S. Congress, 1961).

35. New York: Thomas Y. Crowell, 1964.

36. A noted British novelist in a recent travel book complained bitterly of the lack of amenities in New York, as evidenced by her inability to get someone to carry her groceries from a supermarket, whereas in Mexico City there were dozens of little boys who, for a few pesos, would be clamoring to help her. By the same logic, it is easier for a person in India, with a smaller income, to hire servants than it is for a person in New York.

37. For an excellent discussion of the problems see John C. Bollens and Henry J. Schmandt, *The Metropolis: Its People, Politics, and Economic Life* (New York: Harper and Row, 1965).

38. These and subsequent figures are taken from Eli Ginzberg, Dale L. Hiestand, and Beatrice G. Reubens, *The Pluralistic Economy* (New York: McGraw-Hill, 1965).

39. For a comprehensive source on the vast literature on the problem see James G. March, *Handbook of Organizations* (Chicago: Rand, McNally, 1965).

40. One can point to other "methodological" problems which limit the use of the G.N.P. as an accounting measure. Professor Fritz Machlup, in *The Production and Distribution of Knowledge in the U. S.* (Princeton, N.J.: Princeton University Press, 1962), writes: "The fact that the production of knowledge of several types is paid for by others than the users of the knowledge and that these types of knowledge have no market prices, raises questions of the valuation for national income accounting as well as for welfare-economic considerations." The question of what the G.N.P. can measure thus becomes an important one.

In a similar vein, Victor Fuchs of the National Bureau of Economic Research, in writing of the expansion of the service sector of the economy, remarks: "There has been a presumption [among economists] that [the real GNP] becomes more useful as a measure the more highly developed the economy is . . . But the trend may be in the other direction because at high levels of GNP per capita a large fraction of productivity effort will be devoted to service [where output is very difficult to measure] and to other activities that are presently not measured at all." One of the activities that is not measured today, in fact, is many government services, since these cannot be valued at market prices.

41. One of the telling indictments most of us have leveled against the communist system is that its headlong drive for economic growth has been accompanied by an appalling indifference to human costs.

42. A "far-out" but still telling example is that of New York City, which in order to reduce the "costs" of snow removal no longer hired additional private trucks to cart away the snow but had its Sanitation Department push the snow into the middle of the busy streets, where passing taxis, buses, and cars would grind it into slush that was then hosed down the sewers. The city reduced its costs, but the amount of slush which splattered on the trousers, coats, and dresses of the passers-by increased the cleaning and dyeing bills in the city by a substantial amount. From the point of view of the city and the cleaning industry there was a distinct gain; but this surely was an "irrational" way of distributing the extra costs involved.

43. Andrew Shonfield, in *Modern Capitalism* (London, Eng: Oxford University Press, 1965), pp. 227–229, points out that the construction of a new subway line in London was held up for over a decade on the premise that it couldn't pay its way until someone demonstrated that the secondary benefits resulting for people *not* using the line—in speeding vehicular flow and the like—would result in a true return on investment which was 10 per cent over the capital cost of the prospect.

44. Gunnar Myrdal, *An American Dilemma* (New York: Harper, 1942), p. 1,068.

Chapter 7

New Political Alignments in the Great Society PETER F. DRUCKER

NEW REALITIES AND ISSUES

THE GREAT SOCIETY AS A TRANSITIONAL PHASE

The objective realities to which American politics must address themselves have been changing drastically in the last fifteen years or so—(1) in population structure; (2) in social and political structure; (3) in respect to the power centers in American society; (4) and in the international environment. As a result, fundamental assumptions accepted as near axioms in both our domestic and our foreign policies are becoming increasingly untenable. The issues around which American politics organize themselves will increasingly be both new and different from those of the last half-century. Long-accepted issues—or at least their traditional formulations—will increasingly come to appear unreal if not meaningless. Above all, the new realities are rapidly making traditional political alignments obsolete.

Alignments that have molded the American political process for most of the last hundred years—the "bridge" role of the "Solid South" and its political power, the strategic role of economic blocs, and so on—are likely to cease functioning. This impact is just beginning to be visible—particularly in the turmoil and agony of the Republican party. It is likely to change significantly both parties, however, if not to alter the accepted polarization of American politics around non-ideological interests and around domestic affairs. It is also quite unlikely that foreign policies can continue to be bipartisan; they are more likely to become the center of major political issues and realignments.

President Johnson's Great Society represents a first response to some of the new issues, both at home and abroad. But it approaches these new issues largely within the old alignments. It appeals primarily to the old values and it employs mostly the traditional rhetoric. The voice is Jacob's but the hands are the hands of Esau.

It is thus essentially a transitional phase—and one would guess that the President is highly conscious of this. The emphasis on "consensus" is above all an attempt, both highly constructive and politically very dangerous, to accomplish some of the most important of the new tasks *before* they have become political issues. Even at its most successful, the Era of Consensus, like any earlier Era of Good Feeling, can therefore only be a prelude to a—probably prolonged—period of vocal dissent, violent political ferment, and sudden political landslides. Tomorrow the basic alignments in American politics as well as the basic issues, and the ways in which we will come to grips with them, are almost certain to be different, not only from those of today but also from those now taken for granted by public and politician alike in this country.

NEW DOMESTIC REALITIES

The recent past—the two decades since the end of World War II, or the fifteen years since the Korean War—has produced clearly visible shifts in the political, social, and economic realities at home and abroad.

In bald statement the changes that appear most significant to me are:

1. Within the last fifteen to twenty years the United States has become a *metropolitan society* in which the great majority of the people live in a fairly small number of large, densely populated metropolitan areas, dependent upon common services, each an intricate system of great technical and political complexity.

2. The center of gravity of the American work force has been shifting from the manual worker—skilled or unskilled, on the farm or in workshop or factory—to *the knowledge worker* who, with a very high degree of formal schooling, puts to work knowledge, theory, and concepts rather than manual skill or muscular brawn. For the knowl-

edge worker, and for an economy based on knowledge work, poverty
ceases to be the general condition of mankind. Not that the knowledge worker is rich, but his income tends to be so high as to remove
the constant anxiety about the next meal with which mankind as a
whole has always lived. Above all, the knowledge worker enjoys a job
security unknown to history.

As a further result of this shift to knowledge work there is in
process a radical change in the position of the manual worker. He
tends to become "non-productive" and socially "marginal." The employed middle class is increasingly the *new majority*.

3. Within these last fifteen years the United States has become a
society of big, semi-autonomous, and tightly organized institutions.
There is not only "big government"—federal as well as state and municipal. Within government the civil services and the armed forces
present large, tightly organized power centers of their own, semi-
autonomous with their own rules and their own leaders. There are
the big university, the big hospital, the big labor union, and many
others.

Business was only the first sphere in American society in which
the large organization appeared, which explains in part why we tend
to think of business whenever we say bigness. American society, as
indeed every modern industrial society, has thus become a *pluralist
society* of big organizations, each serving one, but only one, of the
purposes and needs of society.

The decisive interactions in American society today—and increasingly in American politics—are therefore interactions between
highly organized, large, powerful, and professionalized institutions,
each concerned with its own specific task.

4. Traditional federalism sees relationships of coexistence and
competition between the federal government and the various states.
But in the *new federalism* still other political units are directly in
relation with the federal government and work directly with it. And,
increasingly, institutions that are not governmental but private become the agents of government in the fulfillment of public functions
and even in the formulation of public policy.

5. There is an emergence of new power centers in our society,
rivaling if not already overshadowing the traditional power centers of
American politics such as the traditional economic interests. These
new power centers are: *the military, education, and big science. Education,* while rapidly becoming the largest single employer in this

country and the largest single investor of capital, is not organized as a power center. Yet surely the emphasis on the diploma as a condition of employment represents a tremendous social victory for the educator and puts him in a position of social control such as this country never before granted to any single group.

Military strength and educational strength are now seen as the twin pillars of national strength in the modern world, and as the two attributes of great power status. These two power centers come together in the commitment of government to the promotion of *scientific and technological thrust* as a major new national responsibility and a major new national purpose.

NEW DOMESTIC ISSUES

1. In domestic politics we have already shifted from economically centered issues to issues that are basically political: constitutional, moral, and esthetic. The outstanding example is of course civil rights. Indeed, civil rights is a major issue only because it became apparent that economics alone cannot provide citizenship to the American Negro.

But the war on poverty, though it uses economic terminology, is also a shift away from the economic and toward the political. It was imposed by the affluent society on itself by its own bad conscience— and in large measure by an esthetic concern with the squalor and ugliness in which so many live in an economy of abundance.

The educated professional employee, on the other hand, is prone to alienation rather than to poverty, and beset by the fear of futility rather than by lack of income. What he lacks is not a job but the satisfaction of achievement and a sense of function.

Economic measures are seen now as tools and economic policy as a technology rather than a philosophy dealing with fundamental values.

2. Congress and its function may well become an issue in itself. The developments of the last two decades—big government, big military, big science, and so on—have largely pushed Congress out of being a partner in political decisions. Instead, in a good many areas, it is being reduced to being a critic and commentator. The complex arrangements of the new federalism are largely beyond the power of Congress if not altogether beyond its purview.

American domestic politics, then, seems likely to shift to a concern with the basically political—that is, with constitutional, moral, and esthetic issues. As a result we can expect a new concern with power, its nature, purpose, and control.

ISSUES IN INTERNATIONAL POLITICS

The central reality which is likely to generate or at least to shape the issues in American international politics is the fading away of the two axioms on which American foreign policy has been based since World War II. These are the axiom that the international economy was dependent on the United States economy rather than that there was interdependence; and the much more important axiom that "communism" and "Russia" were synonymous with "the enemy."

As the result of the erosion of these axioms it is no longer possible to assume that any action taken by the United States in its capacity as the leader of the free-world community is automatically in the interest of the United States as a nation, and vice versa. For example, the national-interest approach might dictate a "soft" policy in respect to China but the world leadership approach might lead to a very "hard" one, containing Chinese aggression wherever it occurs.

Bipartisanship in foreign affairs cannot last. "Pragmatism" has had its day; we now need policy again.

POLITICAL ALIGNMENTS

THE OLD ORDER PASSES

The traditional alignments of American politics have by and large proven themselves incapable of carrying the American political process. The most important decisions of the last fifteen years in American politics were made essentially outside of the political process proper. They could hardly have been made within it, for they concerned issues on which no decision is possible within the traditional alignments.

The two crucial decisions in domestic politics during the last decade or so were probably school segregation and reapportionment. Both were reached—without any political discussion to speak of—by the Supreme Court, an extra-political organ.

Similarly in foreign affairs the most important decision was surely the one that committed us to a major war in Vietnam. This decision was reached without any "decision" whatever, and certainly without any public debate. I happen to believe the Vietnam decision to have been the right one, but it is still surprising how little national interest was evident in the early stages of our involvement.

Indeed, the most important among the traditional alignments of American policy are in the process of disappearing altogether.

: *The South Loses Its Casting Vote*

During the last few years one of the two main bases of the traditional alignments—the "Compromise of 1876"—has, in effect, been repealed.

The history books tell us little of this compromise other than that it seated a Republican presidential candidate (Rutherford Hayes), who had actually been outpolled by his Democratic opponent, in exchange for which the federal government withdrew the troops that had kept the "carpetbagger" administrations in power in the states of the former Confederacy. But implicit in this deal—as was clearly understood by all concerned—was a far-reaching compact between North and South. It guaranteed the South non-interference in its "domestic institution"—that is, the unchallenged maintenance of white supremacy. In exchange the South promised tacitly to accept and not to challenge the leadership of the North in all areas except race relations. This was expressed in the common saying that no Southerner could become President.

It was on this compact that the "Solid South" rested. The compromise gave the South power in American politics, and especially in Congress, far beyond its population strength, far beyond even the quality of Southern leadership. One reason for this was the control by the Southerners of the chairmanship of important congressional committees as a combined result of the congressional seniority system and the unchallenged one-party structure of the South.

More important perhaps, though much less visible, was the function of the South as the bridge between the major parties and major factions which guaranteed almost every President a workable majority in Congress but also made the South indispensable. It was obviously to the interest of the South not to have any one party predominate in Congress: the compromise could not be expected to be maintained unless the North depended on it as much as the South did. The Southerners in Congress therefore always tended to make common cause with the minority—except in times of great emergency such as the outbreak of war or the first hundred days of Roosevelt's New Deal.

For ninety years practically every administration has faced a coalition in Congress in which the South, though the junior partner, essentially dictated the terms.

The proximate cause for the "repeal" of the Compromise of 1876 was the northward migration of the Negro which began after World War I. With the Negro in the North having formal political equality —the vote, desegregated schools, and so on—the Negro's deprivation of the same rights in the South could no longer be considered a domestic affair. When the federal government, following the Supreme Court school decision of 1954, attacked white supremacy in the South, the Southerners ceased to honor their part of the bargain. This in large part explains the frustration of President Kennedy's domestic policies.

But the ultimate cause of the sharp change in the position of the South in American politics is the growing shift of the white population to industrial centers. Because the Old South has tended to stay heavily rural and small-town, it no longer has the numbers to support a bridge role and to cast the deciding vote. Or rather, a South that stays rural and small-town cannot have enough population to matter. And a South that becomes metropolitan ceases to be the Solid South, as Atlanta and Miami have demonstrated.

That neither Mr. Truman nor Mr. Johnson was supported by the South amounted to a renunciation of the traditional alliance. But that both could be elected without the votes of the South was much more serious: it proved that the South no longer held the balance of power. Even Mr. Kennedy would still have been elected despite the hair-line margin in his popular vote if most of the states of the Old Confederacy had given their electoral votes to a states' rights Southerner. That, as a by-product, a Southerner has been shown to be capable of winning both nomination and election to the presidency is a rather meager consolation.

The price in civil rights paid for the bridge role of the South was of course exorbitant—and we have hardly begun to pay it. But in terms of contemporary American politics during these ninety years the peculiar role of the South has on the whole been healthy and productive.

There is a belief abroad that the Southerners in Congress tended to be "reactionaries." But this holds true only for their position on race relations, which did not become an issue in American politics until the Depression or perhaps not until World War II. Otherwise the Southerner in Congress was more often than not a radical. Indeed the South was the very center of extreme rabble-rousing populism. Above all, to preserve the power position of his region, the Southerner in Congress had no choice but to seek a consensus. National policy did not shift to the left or to the right because the South shifted; the South shifted because the national center shifted first. In effect the Southerners always had to make it possible for "liberals" and "conservatives" to agree at least sufficiently to permit the business of government to go on.

The long-serving committee chairmen, while often autocratic and immovable, also usually did their homework and thoroughly knew their area. They endowed Congress with a solid backbone of expertise such as no other parliamentary body in the world possesses. One would be hard-pressed to find men who worked harder or who knew their local problems better than the two men from Georgia, Senator Russell and Representative Vinson, who for so many years headed the Armed Services Committees in their respective houses of Congress. It is this expert knowledge that makes Congress still capable of dealing with the federal bureaucracy and gives us a degree of political and policy control over the Civil Service such as is unknown in any other modern nation.

In foreign affairs the absence of major manufacturing and labor union interests in the South enabled the Southerner often to consider the national interest and to take a much bigger view than the Middle-Westerner or the New Englander, swayed as he so often has been by the immediate, short-sighted interests of this or that company or industry.

Finally, "that no Southerner could become President" meant that the senior Southerners in Congress had no further ambition and knew that they had to make their mark in history through their performance as legislators.

For better or worse, the position of the South is gone.

It is no accident that for the first time in the history of the Senate a civil rights filibuster could be broken so decisively (in the fight over President Kennedy's civil rights bill) and that, two years later, the South did not even try to filibuster against Mr. Johnson's much more sweeping bill of 1965. It is no accident either that for the first time since the present system of committee chairmen was introduced around the turn of the century, committee members have successfully revolted against their chairman (against Representative Smith of Virginia, chairman of the House Rules Committee, and Representative Patman of Texas of the House Banking Committee).

I am by no means convinced that the South will abandon the one-party system. It is conceivable that for many years to come the pressures for conformity and for resistance to an alien and unsympathetic outside world may enforce strict voting discipline, to the point where opposition candidates have no chance at all in large areas. But this would create such tremendous tension that no elected representative of the South could expect to have long, unchallenged tenure, and with seniority would go a great deal of the influence and power of the South.

But even if nothing changes in the South, it would not greatly matter one way or the other. For almost a century the arrival of a two-party system in the South has been looked forward to by liberals, inside and outside the South, as the hour of deliverance if not as the panacea for all the ills of the region. It is ironical that just when the two-party system has a real chance to establish itself in the South it has also become quite unimportant. In national affairs the South must increasingly cease to be something separate, indeed something unique. It is rapidly becoming just another sparsely settled and poor region of the country—and as such a fairly unimportant one.

: *The Erosion of the Economic Blocs*

The second major shift in the structure of alignments on which American politics has been resting is the steady erosion of the traditional economic blocs. These blocs—whether labor or farmer or business—can no longer be carriers of policies. They can only, increasingly, become obstacles to any policy whatever, for any change is in effect a threat to them.

The three agencies of the federal government which reached cabinet status between the Civil War and World War II were Agriculture, Commerce, and Labor. Each was created to represent a major economic estate of the realm, and to make sure that its interests were protected. The particular interest group which any one of these bureaucracies represented had a virtual veto power over the appointment of the Secretary. Indeed the secretaries often behaved like ambassadors of a powerful foreign sovereign rather than as members of the President's Cabinet.

By sharp contrast the two new cabinet posts created since World War II (leaving out Defense as a special case in which formerly separate agencies of cabinet rank were consolidated) were Health, Education, and Welfare, and Housing and Urban Affairs—both established not to represent economic interests but to remove major areas of policy from the control of, and domination by, economic interests. (That President Johnson seriously considered naming his most powerful cabinet member, Robert McNamara, as the first Secretary of Housing and Urban Affairs, is an indication that the new agencies are expected to become more powerful and more important than the old economic-interest agencies are.)

Of all the traditional groups only one has an opportunity to remain influential and a carrier of policy: the "managers." For managing is a function that is essential in all the new big organizations; indeed managing is the specific function of big, complex organizations—whether business or armed services, university or government agency or hospital. But of course the only reason why this group might survive as a distinct and organized power center is that the "capitalist" of yesterday has been replaced by the "professional manager" of today, who is not confined to one economic interest but pervades the entire society and who is not exclusively economically oriented. The extent to which managers have succeeded in the much publicized attempt to make themselves trustees for all the interests in the organization—employees, investors, customers, and so on—is a moot point. That they are trying is the important point. This explains why President Johnson has been wooing them: they are a bridge between yesterday's alignments and tomorrow's alignments and as such essential to Mr. Johnson's "consensus."

Labor by contrast has not even begun such a transformation. And except in the event of a major economic crisis it seems rather unlikely that a sufficiently large part of the "employed professional middle class" will unionize itself to restore labor's vitality and growth potential—but also to change the characteristics of labor even more drastically than the change from capitalist to manager has been changing the characteristics of the business interests. The aims of a unionized employed professional middle class are likely to be social rather than economic. And insofar as they are economic they are likely to be in direct conflict with the economic aims of the rank-and-file, blue-collar worker of the traditional unions.

The traditional economic blocs no longer represent the dynamics of American society, if only because the big tasks and the big problems are not economic but political, social, moral, or esthetic. This does not mean that the economic blocs will become unimportant or powerless. The farmer, for instance, has long ceased to have the key position he had up until World War I. But the farm lobby is losing its importance only very slowly.

What does happen, however, is that such groups become purely negative. Any change is a threat to them. The aims of policy are not their aims. They therefore become increasingly vested interests, concerned with the maintenance of a privileged status. Extortion, rather than policy, becomes their business. A handful of "Silver Senators" were able for decades to hold up the American Treasury and the American public. They never were able, however, to make monetary policy; they could only prevent others from making effective policy. This means that we need new groupings and new alignments which can effectively formulate and advocate policies.

: *The Changing Role of Ethnic Blocs*

The most confusing area is that of the ethnic-origin and religious blocs such as the Irish Catholics, the Jews, the Italians, and so on. In different parts of the metropolis their importance will change in different directions.

In the core city, the old "downtown"—the five boroughs of New York, for instance—such blocs should become much more important. The Negro clearly is just now emerging as an organized and powerful ethnic bloc in the core city. His tendency to act as a bloc in city politics must increase. For the individual Negro can achieve advancement and access to opportunities only through organized use of his political power, that is as a bloc and through patronage. The same applies to the Puerto Rican and to the Mexican American.

This in turn is likely to force the other groups—especially relatively poor groups—in the core city to organize themselves and act as blocs. The way in which the Irish Catholics in Boston, for instance, have again coalesced as a bloc to beat off a Negro attack on the "neighborhood school"—that is, on effective segregation—is only one example. And the same holds true of other groups largely composed of industrial workers or lower-grade service employees such as the Czechs in Chicago, the Poles in Cleveland, and the Hungarians in Pittsburgh.

Outside the core city, however, in the suburban areas of the metropolis, ethnic blocs are likely to become very much less important.

Regardless of his origin (unless he should be a Negro), the suburban-ite sees himself characterized by his education—which tends to be advanced—and by his cultural level, rather than by his origin. In fact, he is likely to resent too blatant an appeal to his origin as questioning his status in the American community.

Most of the suburbanites today are young—and third generation. This means that they have overcome their resentment of their parents' culture, which characterizes the second generation and which is of course as close a tie to one's origin as is devotion to one's original language and culture. At the same time, the third generation suburbanite can accept the fact that his grandparents came from elsewhere and can even consider it a distinction, without, at the same time, feeling any great attachment or allegiance to the ethnic group whence they came. And in any case, by the third generation in this country there are not very many white people of pure ethnic origin left.

Ethnic or religious blocs are therefore likely to become complicated—with both appeal and non-appeal to them equally unpredictable. Inside the core city the blocs can be expected to become far more important—and with this would come the strong "boss" and the appeal to "solidarity" instead of issues, ideas, or men. Outside the core city ethnic origin is likely to mean less and less, though religious affiliation may still play an important role in a number of areas.

: Core City and Suburb

The different appeal of ethnic and religious blocs in core city and suburb respectively is only one of the differences that will probably characterize these two elements of the metropolis and that eventually might divide them sharply in national politics.

Altogether, the core city is increasingly likely to present yesterday's politics, yesterday's issues and yesterday's alignment. The very fact that bloc voting is apt to be such a factor will make the core city look to the past rather than to the future—plus the fact, of course, that the core city will probably be the least affluent part of the affluent society. The suburbs, representing the young people and therefore the more highly educated and more prosperous ones, are likely to be paying more attention to tomorrow's problems, especially to the problems of the metropolitan area.

Also the core city will have to bear a greater burden of the metropolitan services, but also increasingly not have the tax resources.

These will be in the suburbs—indeed it is conceivable that the deterioration of the core city will bring a mass exodus of business headquarters to the suburbs. Some of the biggest companies have already moved out. This will create increasing demands on the part of the core city that the suburbs become part of its tax domain—and growing resistance to the core city on the part of the suburbanites.

But probably more important than these tangible factors are the intangible ones. Gradually these two parts of the metropolis are developing two facets of metropolitan culture. It is not only the man from Iowa who says, "New York is a nice place to visit but I wouldn't want to live there." The man from Westchester County feels this even more strongly.

It is therefore conceivable that the geographic alignments in this country—between North and South; between country and town; between agrarian and industrial society—may increasingly be replaced by a split between the core city and the suburbs throughout all regions and all areas of the country. It is conceivable that tomorrow the job of building a national party will in effect mean bringing enough groups from those two constituent parts of the metropolis together behind one program and one candidate. It is also conceivable that tomorrow's political parties will primarily be characterized by having a core-city or a suburban temperament.

This is of course pure speculation, though there are signs of such a development everywhere. But it is also possible that tomorrow's basic alignments, the successors to the economic blocs of yesterday, will be such groups as educators, scientists, and so on—that is, the "interests" of an educated, science-oriented society in which economics is not the preoccupation of the majority.

THE IMPACT ON THE PARTIES

The changes in alignments which are already in full swing are likely to present serious problems to both parties, Republican as well as Democratic.

: *The Struggle for a Republican Future*

In terms of its traditional vote base, the Republican party has become the permanent minority party—and becoming the majority in the Old South would not in any way change this; rather, it would accentuate the isolation of the Republican party. The reason for this is

that the Republican party today is "white Protestant" by temperament, no matter how many Jews, Catholics, or Negroes vote the Republican ticket. And the white Protestant is no longer the political
majority.

Statistically, of course, white Protestants constitute two-thirds of
the population. Culturally also this is and will continue to be a white
Protestant country (despite the prevalence of Jewish jokes and Italian pizza). But politically, a white Protestant party is no longer capable of organizing majority support. Almost half of the white Protestants in the country are rural and small-town and as such no longer
an adequate foundation for national power. And in the metropolis
the white Protestant group represents just about half of the population, or less. For it is in the metropolis that the non-Protestant whites,
Catholics, Jews, and Greek Orthodox are concentrated. It is also in
the metropolis that the Negro increasingly concentrates. More important, however, is the fact that the white Protestant majority does not
see itself as a coherent group in the metropolis and does not vote as
such—precisely because it does not see itself as the minority. And minorities—that is, groups that otherwise would have little influence
and little voice, are the ones that see the need for organizing themselves for the fight for power.

What the strategies are that are available to the permanent minority party we know. For this was the position of the Democrats for
sixty long years, from the Civil War until Franklin D. Roosevelt's
election in 1932. In fact there are only two strategies available—and
the party is likely to be torn internally by the fight between the adherents of either.

There is first the "moderate" strategy—the strategy of those who
essentially say "me too." They expect to come to power precisely because it is not easy to tell them apart from the majority party—except
that they are "out" and therefore not responsible for a catastrophe, a
scandal, or whatever accident befalls the party in power. In such a
situation the moderates hope to be able to attract enough protest
votes from the majority party to get into power and to start working
on making themselves in turn the permanent majority.

All three successful presidential candidates of the Democrats between 1865 and 1932 were moderates: Cleveland, Wilson, and Franklin D. Roosevelt. (In fact, Roosevelt was the most conservative of the
three to begin with and almost the purest embodiment of what used
to be known as a "Gold Democrat." It took him a long time to gain

the confidence of such fairly moderate liberals as Al Smith and Frances Perkins when he first started out in New York State politics.)

The second strategy is the radical one which aims to re-create a new party "dedicated to principles." In line with the ancestor worship that characterizes the rhetoric of American politics, this strategy is likely to present itself as aiming at the restoration of the ideals of the past. Bryan was a "Fundamentalist" and Goldwater a "Conservative." Actually the strategy aims at creating a major crisis and hopes to capitalize on it.

Historians tend to be kind to yesterday's radicals. They have a very good press with posterity—in striking contrast to the bad press they have with their contemporaries. For while the radicals rarely write the nation's songs, they write the nation's pamphlets. Also their measures—which usually are not so very radical after all—tend to be enacted into law long after their paranoid mood has faded away. One then remembers, for instance, that the Populists were in favor of an income tax and forgets that they believed in the conspiracy of bankers, Jews, and Catholics to destroy the Republic and to enthrone the Pope in Washington.

Both strategies have rather stringent prerequisites, none of which is likely to be satisfied for the Republicans in the present situation. The moderates can operate only if they control some important power centers, such as the Democrats' control of the Solid South and of the big cities of the North in the long years of their exile after the Civil War. Specifically the Republican moderates would have to gain control of major metropolitan areas. This would probably require the consolidation of core city and suburbs into one political unit. The voting strength of the Republicans in the suburbs, however, rests squarely on their promise not to let the core city "gobble up" the suburbs and their promise to keep the two separate politically as well as fiscally.

For the radical strategy to work—short of a catastrophe such as this country has so far been spared—requires a candidate who has shown ability for political leadership and enough maturity not to frighten off potential recruits from the moderate ranks of his own party as well as from the opposition. If all he does is to attract the radicals of the other party (as Bryan and Goldwater did), he almost ensures defeat through distrust on the part of the great majority which fears (and rightly) political adventurers.

This, however, only means that the Republican party is unlikely to make up its mind for either strategy—just as the Democrats did not decide on either before the New Deal. This would guarantee long years of internal turmoil for the Republican party in the course of which the first aim of each Republican politician is likely to be to prevent the victory of another Republican rather than to defeat a Democrat. As John Lindsay's campaign in New York City showed, the only way for a Republican to win in such a situation is to be as little of a Republican as possible and to try to be accepted as a genuine "independent."

The Republicans will therefore be forced to look for issues that can unite them and to shun issues that must divide them. Because of the shift in alignments within the country, domestic issues are almost certain to divide the Republicans—save only in the event of a serious depression or a really sensational scandal. The Republicans may therefore attempt to make foreign policy into the platform that unites them.

It is possible therefore that, for the first time since the very early days of the Republic, a major party will organize itself on a foreign affairs platform rather than on a domestic platform. (This is particularly likely to happen if the Democrats manage to solve their internal problem of cohesion and direction.)

: *The Dilemma of the Democrats*

The Democratic party too will be seriously affected by the shifting alignments. It has to gain the allegiance of the "new majority," the educated, employed middle class. But it must at the same time hold the allegience of the old power groups, the economic blocs and the ethnic blocs. The attempt to hold the one is likely to alienate the other. It may alienate both—as did the Democratic strategy in the 1965 New York City elections in which the patent attempt to have the "right" old-fashioned ticket: one Jew, one Irish Catholic, one Italian, and so on, only made the younger and better-educated members of those groups cross over and vote Republican in large numbers.

For a good many years to come the Democratic party will, of necessity, feel attracted to yesterday—whether to aging labor leaders, to successful urban political manipulators, or to the successful organizer of such old-line power centers as the Firemen's Protective Association. At the same time the sons of these same people react only negatively to appeals based on these traditional ties. This next generation tries as hard as possible to move out of this environment

—just as John F. Kennedy with his Harvard education, his Boston Brahmin accent, and his artistic and intellectual tastes tried to put the greatest possible distance between himself and his grandfather "Honey Fitz" Fitzgerald, the prototype of old-style boss rule. Kennedy's example shows, however, that the job can be done. He succeeded, though only after his election (and perhaps only after his assassination) in becoming the hero of the core support of the old-line Democratic connection, especially the industrial worker.

In this dilemma the Democratic party will try to focus on what are likely to unify these two groups—and these are the urban issues: the metropolis, health care, and above all, education. By the same token they are likely to play down what will divide these two groups: the old-style economic issues, and foreign affairs.

: *The Future Challenge*

Victory in the long run will not go to the party that does the best job gluing together the shards of yesterday. Victory will go to whoever creates a new national alignment and a new power base, resting not on economic interests but on the "new majority" of the educated professional middle class, and capable of crystallizing the issues that are meaningful to them.

The last time a similar job was done in American politics was after the election of 1896 when Mark Hanna used the economic blocs as his building blocks to erect the structure that is still housing American politics even though the tenant has changed. Today one can barely speculate what these alignments might be and on what they might rest. But it is reasonably clear that they will not rest on the Solid South, on economic blocs, or on ethnic blocs. They will rest on foundations appropriate to the new reality—which probably means such interests as education, science, and so on in domestic politics, and on principles if not on "ideologies" in foreign politics.

The conclusion: both parties, if not indeed the entire structure of American political alignments, are in crisis. The crisis cannot be resolved by restoring the old order—its pillars, the Solid South, the economic blocs, the white Protestant plurality of rural areas and small towns, are gone.

Whichever party first succeeds in building a new alignment around the "new majority," the young educated members of the employed professional middle class will emerge as the majority party, perhaps for long years to come. But in its present form neither party is yet geared to this task—the Republicans because they are by temperament still far too much a party of farms and small towns, the Democrats because they are still far too much beholden to yesterday's economic interests and ethnic blocs.

There is thus great opportunity for creative party politics—and great need for it. Politicians are needed who can establish the new alignments—politicians who can dramatize the new issues, mobilize the new power centers, and build new, durable alignments.

POLITICS FOR A NEW GENERATION

THE NEW SITUATION

Let me recapitulate the main points made so far.

(1.) Both at home and abroad new realities have been overtaking the traditional issues of American politics.

At home we live in a metropolitan society of big organizations; with an affluent and highly educated though employed middle class as the new majority; with a new federalism replacing steadily the old simplicity of federal-states relations; with new power centers, the military, education, and big business; and with a governmental commitment to scientific and technological change.

Internationally the assumptions of the postwar era are becoming obsolete—in respect to the international economy as well as in respect to international policy. And with the whole world turning into one "global village"—albeit a most unquiet one—our perceptions as well as our role are changing. Increasingly the issues and problems of the world outside project deeply into domestic affairs. The old distinction between domestic matters and foreign affairs will become blurred.

(2.) As a result we face a shift to new issues: away from economic issues to truly political ones: constitutional, moral, esthetic in domestic politics; and toward issues on foreign affairs that are likely sharply to pose the question whether the United States is primarily just another nation-state, albeit the most powerful and most heavily armed one, or whether it is still the "last best hope on earth," the leader of, and exemplar of, a better free-world community. Bipartisanship in foreign affairs is unlikely to last. And both at home and abroad we face the need to move from a pragmatism based on the truisms of yesteryear to new policy based on new thinking and new ideas.

(3.) The pillars of the traditional alignments: the Solid South and economic interests can no longer support the American political process. New alignments are needed, built around the new majority, the employed professional middle class. And both parties are threatened—the Republicans because the new population structure threatens to make them into a permanent minority; the Democrats because their majority still rests on yesterday's power centers, especially the economic blocs.

There is thus both need and opportunity for the creative politician who can build new, durable alignments based on the new power structure of American society and focused on the new tasks of American politics.

What this adds up to is a New Political Situation.

THE GENERATION SHIFT

Still, so far we have given an inventory rather than an analysis. Even if correct in every detail, it would still not enable us to anticipate American politics in the years ahead. What matters in politics is far less the specific problems and the answers found to them, but the pattern, the configuration. It is not what issues are debated but what emphasis is given to issues in relation to each other and a scale of political values. It is not so much what laws are being written as what kind of personality can exercise leadership. Measures and policy matter less than the mood and the basic assumptions.

The most important fact with respect to this configuration of tomorrow may well be that the United States—indeed the whole world —is in the midst of a major generation shift.

The outward sign of this is of course that so many of the world's political leaders, from President Johnson to Chairman Mao, are so clearly the last of their line, by age alone. Their formative years were the 1920's and 1930's, but even the postwar era of the 1940's and 1950's is rapidly becoming history.

In terms of age structure of the population, the United States is not a particularly young country today—compared to underdeveloped Latin America, India, or China, where the population explosion triggered by a drastic drop in infant mortality is pushing the average age down to fifteen or so. But compared to its own history and recent experience, the United States is becoming a very young country indeed, with half the population already less than twenty-six years old

—and most of them highly educated and with experiences and expectations that differ markedly from those that still underlie our social, political, and economic policies. The middle generation (thirty to fifty) by contrast is very thin in this country today and bound to get thinner for another decade—the result, of course, of the lean birth years of the thirties.

Power and position are therefore likely to pass fast from people now reaching retirement age—that is, people whose working life began before or during the Great Depression—to people to whom the Depression is at best a dim childhood memory if not to people to whom even World War II is something they read about in high school. President Johnson's young men—his assistants in their early thirties—are only the advance guard of the generation that must get to the top in all important areas of American life very soon: in business and in government, in the universities and in the armed services, and perhaps even in the labor unions.

But this, even more than a shift in chronological age, is a shift in outlook, perception, and formative experience. The world this new generation of Americans considers "normal" is one of long years of advanced education, very high job security, affluence, a world dominated by science and technology. It is also a world of international turmoil and dangers such as would have been unimaginable to their parents at the same age.

Even greater perhaps is the jump in perception. What the new generation takes for granted, the older one has not really learned to see. For the new generation takes for granted (1) the "global village" —that is, the integration of the entire earth through communications into one locus of immediate experience; (2) "man in space"—that is, the reaching out beyond what were considered the human limits of existence; (3) technology, both in respect to doing physical tasks and in respect to making economic problems amenable to systematic, organized, and essentially technical solutions.

This new perception may not have the results most people envisage. But it will have very significant results. The perception of the global village may not, for instance, make us more internationalist. Finding out at firsthand the truth of the old adage that all men are brothers under the skin and that they and their communities are really alike may well lead to a preference for staying near the surface, where men and their societies are remarkably unlike. It may not lead to greater willingness to help others. Indeed it may considerably discourage the old American missionary impulse to do things *for* others without necessarily increasing the desire—also an old American tradition—to do things *with* others.

The perception of the global village is, however, likely to make us stop seeing the outside world through the European glasses (whether that of the German *savant* or the English Fabian) with which the American liberal has always seen the world. The American whose introduction to a foreign culture and society is Japan or Greece is unlikely ever to be a parochial "little European." General de Gaulle is almost certainly right in his belief that the American will become less and less of a "European." But so will the young European himself, though perhaps only with the next generation.

There are even strong indications that the new generation will turn away from the "secularism" of their parents—not to organized religion but to a new "inner-directedness" with the stress on personal values and personal commitment. Most of the "crazy, mixed-up kids" on the campus today will of course grow up into depressingly sane adult conformists—and they are a tiny minority anyhow. But they might signal a shift ahead in values and concerns—a shift toward moral and esthetic values and toward a concern with the person.

These are, however, mere speculations. What one can say with a good deal of assurance is that the generation shift ahead is likely to be also a political shift—a shift in the climate, the mood, the values, the alignments, and the issues of American politics.

Such a shift is bound to be disorderly. It implies a time of transition likely to be characterized by vocal dissent, by sudden sharp landslides burying long-familiar landmarks, by partisanship, and by political passion. It is not likely to be a time of "consensus" and exceedingly unlikely to be a time of political apathy. And foreign affairs promises to be one of the political storm centers.

The election of 1964 clearly marked a watershed in American politics. We now face a period rather similar to that after 1896, if not after 1822—periods that ended an Era of Good Feeling and brought lasting realignment to American politics.

THE GREAT SOCIETY—SUBSTANCE AND RHETORIC

In its concerns, President Johnson's Great Society clearly addresses itself to the new realities and to tomorrow's issues. Its mainly domestic themes are the metropolis, education, health care, and the esthetics of an industrial society—not to mention its basic morality. In his most significant speech to date, the speech on the Negro in America given at Howard University last summer, the President clearly put ethics into the center of his politics.

The Johnson administration also has begun work on some of the constitutional problems. This, by the way, is one area where it continues what President Kennedy began. The "White House conferences"—on education, for instance, or on the natural environment— at least remove the planning of the new federalism from the inner office and subject it to public exposure. And the new subordination of the military to civilian control, however much it may be due to the personality and forcefulness of one particular Secretary of Defense, was clearly, from the beginning, presidential policy as well.

Even in international affairs—where neither the Kennedy nor the Johnson administration has been bold or innovative—new thinking may have begun, if only because of the realities of Southeast Asia.

But in its rhetoric the Great Society is old and addresses itself to yesterday.

"Consensus," as President Johnson uses that term, means in effect bringing *all* of yesterday's power groups (and especially all economic interests) together behind one policy for today's problems. In particular, of course, it means bringing in the one economic interest that has hitherto not joined up with the other economic interests in a common economic policy—the business interest.

In practical politics consensus unites all who accept the accomplished facts of yesterday and excludes only the irreconcilables who still want to repeal history.

The effectiveness of this approach, at least so far, cannot be denied. It has enabled the Johnson administration to get more done than any administration in living memory. It has above all enabled the Johnson administration to get more of the *new* tasks done. I doubt that this country—or any other—has ever seen greater skill or more purpose than the President exhibits when he uses the near-unanimity of the country on the problems of yesterday to advance new solutions to the problems of today. Perhaps the one thing wrong with the President's effective use of consensus to solve problems and respond to challenges *before* they can become issues, is that it is done so skillfully that many do not fully appreciate the extraordinary performance.

There probably is no other way to get done what Mr. Johnson

gets done—the experience of his predecessor would indicate this. Mr. Kennedy, too, was a man of the transition period. But he reversed the balance between substance and rhetoric. In his actions he was primarily concerned with clearing up and finishing the tasks of yesterday; and his politics was clearly based on the New Deal alignments. But his rhetoric—his "style"—was that of a new generation. Yet he had to fight every inch of the way and accomplished, essentially, very little. This cannot be blamed on Congress: President Johnson had the same Congress during his first year and got out of it all of the legislation it had refused President Kennedy. President Johnson, in other words, may have had to smother dissent to get any action whatever.

There are great dangers, however, in the politics of consensus and they are likely to grow with time.

The first danger is clearly that of losing the young: the "new majority" of the educated professional middle class.

There is little doubt, I believe, that the President is no hero to this group. Indeed there is little doubt that this is the one group in which Mr. Goldwater in 1964 found a great deal of response. This (as has been said before) is in terms of the *old* issues a very conservative group if only because these are not emotional matters to them, not "articles of faith," not even meaningful slogans. Yesterday's "liberal" rhetoric is bound to bore them. That they have much interest in the program of the extreme right is very doubtful. But at least the Goldwaterites talked "principles."

Quite apart from personality—and Mr. Johnson, unlike his predecessor, is so clearly not one of the new generation and not really "sophisticated"—Mr. Johnson is in danger of being totally misunderstood by the "new majority." They are likely to miss the policy in his actions completely, and to mistake it for a clever publicity gimmick; they are likely to hear cleverness where they expect conviction.

How long it will remain prudent to risk losing the young by not talking policy and thereby alienating the old power group is thus a fundamental question for Mr. Johnson. But will he still be able to get through to the young if he waits—maybe it is already too late. Does he indeed understand, even after all those years in Congress, that it is conflict that creates political excitement, generates support, and mobilizes hitherto uncommitted political energies?

Another real danger is that consensus which smothers dissent also smothers discussion and understanding. This is particularly dangerous in foreign policy today, precisely because we may have to execute rather startling shifts fast. The public is totally unprepared for such an eventuality. And the public has been kept intentionally in the dark, whether the reason for this is Mr. Johnson's dislike of criticism or his fear that discussion of his policies might restrict his freedom of action. Very few people in this country even understand that we have committed ourselves to a major new task—that of the containment of China. Fewer still realize the great challenges to our traditional military, diplomatic, and economic policy that lie ahead in Europe. The reason why this is so dangerous is of course that there is grave risk of a violent and irrational reaction should anything go wrong—and something surely will in so complex and dangerous a world.

But the greatest weaknesses of the politics of consensus are in their restrictions on presidential leadership both in respect to formulating policy and in respect to building the new political alignments.

The new thinking is not being done. Mr. Johnson may expect new policies to grow out of his actions. He may be right. But in politics deeds do not necessarily speak louder than words. And the words are not being said. That Mr. Johnson is capable of saying them—forcefully, indeed movingly—he showed in his Howard University speech. But despite (perhaps because of?) his constant public exposure, Mr. Johnson clearly refrains from formulating a new political point of view, a new political idea, a new political direction. And he may thereby misjudge the country and the times. There seem to me to be an expectation in the land, a sense of foreboding beneath all the prosperity, a receptivity to seriousness that are not being satisfied. Both at home and in the world there is, however, need to reformulate and to reaffirm America's role and meaning.

The politics of consensus also make it difficult, if not impossible, for the President to be the political master builder, the designer of the new alignments and the modeler of the new—or at least the changed—configuration of forces, perceptions, and ideas which the new realities at home and abroad demand. He is perforce so busy making the old configuration serve a little longer that he does not seem to have any spare time to work on creating a new one.

This is not said in criticism. In fact, it would be hard to imagine what else President Johnson could have done—and there is no doubt that what he is doing is being done with consummate skill. But still it seems likely that the question whether the Great Society is indeed a destination for the American people and their march through history or a mere whistle-stop which later generations will shrug off will be

decided by Mr. Johnson's ability to become the master builder of tomorrow despite the need to preserve, indeed to perpetuate, yesterday.

That the Johnson administration is a transition is clear. But is it
going to be seen as a transition *from* the old, or as a transition *to* the
new?

The theme of this essay was a simple one: We are in midstream,
already so far away from the bank on which we embarked that we can
barely see it in the distance, and still so far from the other bank that
we cannot make it out at all. We can expect turbulence, confusion,
and misdirection on the way across. To be somewhat less poetical, we
can expect a period of dissension and turmoil in American politics—
perhaps with foreign affairs the storm center and the fundamental
issue around which major power groups organize themselves for the
conquest and exercise of power, and the major point of cleavage between them. It is not going to be a time of consensus or of philosophical resignation. It is going to be a time of strife and passion. Those
critics of America who, in the fine tradition of European condescen-
sion toward the "barbarians" on this continent, have recently com-
mented on our politics as being "middle-aged" (after all those years
of telling us how "immature" we were) are in for quite a surprise, I
would guess.

It is likely to be an exciting time—but a dangerous one as well.
One can only hope that it will also be a time of intelligence, of responsibility, of courage—and of leadership of the highest order.

Chapter 8

Reflections on Great Societies

FRANK E. MANUEL

Over two thousand three hundred and fifty years ago an Athenian aristocrat and philosopher undertook a long, arduous journey to Syracuse, Greece, for the purpose of achieving "some marvelous overhauling" in that city-state in conformity with his already-published paradigm of an ideal society. The fundamental proposition to which he was committed is set forth in what became known as his Seventh Epistle, in a passage paraphrasing his own previous writing: "Wherefore the classes of mankind will have no cessation from evils until either the class of those who are right and true philosophers attains political supremacy, or else the class of those who hold power in the States becomes, by some dispensation of heaven, really philosophic."

The tragic failure of his mission, thrice repeated, should serve to discourage any would-be philosopher with the hope of contributing significantly to the establishment of an ideal republic. It is surely not of Platonic justice that you would have me write, and though the senses of Dionysius have become acute with new technological devices and capable of receiving messages at incredible distances, I am under no illusion that men of power are likely to be converted to philosophy.

Without Plato's absolute before my mind's eye, I am nonetheless prepared to discuss various ideals of great societies in the past and possible ideals for the future, not excluding the fleeting company of the present. For while in a gloomy mood I might repeat Plato's reflection that "all the states which now exist . . . one and all they are badly governed," I have come to learn that some are immeasurably worse than others.

I do of course conceive of the Great Society as more of a wish than a fulfilled present reality, more of a hope than a fixed prospect. One of the ways in which I can examine our contemporary American civilization in historical perspective is by blurring the line between present and future and at the same time sharpening the line which separates us from the ideals and values of societies, once deemed great, that have passed away. This is both an un-Burkean and an un-Marxian exercise, entirely unbecoming to a historian. But perhaps we can the better define ourselves dialectically, by contrasting our visions with those that other societies, now dead, once lived by and that can no longer move us. For past history has set certain limits on the possible—and unless you are as obsessively committed to the cyclical conception of the world as the Stoic Chrysippus, the future *must* be different. My attempt will be a brash twentieth-century American undertaking, alien in spirit to the traditional form of self-examination in Western society that stressed, as a matter of course, the links with the past and that could understand the present only in terms of the generally recognized virtues and hallowed precepts of the Judeo-Christian and Greco-Roman societies.

Whitehead once said: "A traveler who has lost his way should not ask, 'Where am I?' What he really wants to know is, 'Where are the other places?' He has got his own body, but he has lost *them*." If there is understandable bewilderment about our present position, may not some consideration of "them," of the other places in time, not as ancestors, which they doubtless are, but as "other," help to clarify what we are, how very different we have become and are becoming every day.

My approach will be direct. I have selected a number of attributes of great societies of the past, and will try to see which, if any of them at all, could fit the Great Society. By attributes I mean qualities that great societies assigned to themselves as well as those that later reflective historians and philosophers foisted upon them. They have not always been the same.

Some periods of Western history have been peculiarly self-conscious about their own greatness—for example, Periclean Athens, Augustan Rome, Florence of the Renaissance, Elizabethan England, the age of Louis XIV, the epoch of the French Revolution. The epithet "Great Society" which has been adopted by our President is, in its original form at least, not one of the noteworthy expressions of Christian humility. Despite the fact that the term was clearly meant to evoke an ideal image and not to label a current state of affairs, the notion is abroad that at some future date it might well serve as an appropriate chapter heading in a history book on this administration.

ATTRIBUTES OF GREAT SOCIETIES

Great societies have been praised for their military prowess, lawful orderliness and security, devotion to beauty, absolute commitment to a principle of religious transcendence, the prevalence of a warm communal feeling, their size, power, and grandeur, their opportunities for sensate or spiritual happiness, their harmony and justice, peacefulness, egalitarianism, freedom, duration in time, constancy and changelessness, their pursuit of excellence. No society with which I am acquainted has arrogated to itself *all* of these attributes, and some appear to be flagrantly contradictory. There is an old European idea, developed rather fully in the eighteenth century by Montesquieu in France and Herder in Germany, that societies, like individuals, have dominant passions. Without subscribing to the full implications of any such facile analogy between individual psychology and the underlying drives of nations, I should like to quote a famous passage from the *Spirit of the Laws* as the guiding text for this essay: "Though all governments have the same general end, which is that of preservation, yet each has another particular object. Increase of dominion was the object of Rome; war, that of Sparta; religion, that of the Jewish laws; commerce, that of Marseilles; public tranquillity, that of the laws of China; navigation, that of the laws of Rhodes; natural liberty, that of the policy of the Savages; in general, the pleasures of the prince, that of despotic states; that of monarchies, the prince's and the kingdom's glory."

Examples of the magnificent virtues that societies of the past have claimed for themselves can readily be collected in any library. Toynbee takes especial delight in the letter presented in 1793 by the philosophical Emperor Chi'en Lung to a British envoy of King George III on the very eve of China's dismemberment. "Our dynasty's majestic virtue," he wrote, "has penetrated into every country under Heaven, and kings of all nations have offered their costly tribute by land and sea. As your Ambassador can see for himself, we possess all things."

Such expressions of what Toynbee calls the egocentric illusion, the belief that one's own living society is the consummation of human history, which he finds rather general among mankind, must fill the philosophical historian with amusement, when they do not arouse in him a superstitious terror that he is witnessing a tragic spectacle of hubris, of sinful arrogance before a downward plunge.

We all remember Scipio's premonition of the fall of Rome as he watched the burning of Carthage, which he had set to the torch. The *Ubi sunt* theme is a stereotype of the medieval chroniclers, and one does not have to take literally every historical analogy in the works of Spengler, Toynbee, and Sorokin to feel one's tongue cleft to its roof in the utterance of the words Great Society. But though I probably believe in the mortality of all societies, I shall proceed to affirm the current potentialities of our Great Society, and, unlike some of the other contributors to this volume, I shall deliver a eulogy of its emerging character.

It should be taken for granted that everything presented here is predicated upon an era free from nuclear catastrophe. Should this assumption prove to be entirely fallacious, I trust that if we meet some day amid fire and brimstone the reader will forbear adding insult to injury by reminding me of my indecent optimism. Moreover, my remarks may not be totally irrelevant to the indefinite postponement or even prevention of the holocaust. If we are truly committed to the greatness of this society in its peculiar virtues, we may conceivably find the strength to crush the serpents who would have us eat of the tree of unreality with its old and rotting fruit—calls to glory—when we might cause a tree of true knowledge and achievement to flower in our midst, perhaps not forever, perhaps not even for a thousand years, but for a while, a precious while. I will not be outdone by any man in my lack of faith. But I am skeptical about prophecies of doom, as well as those of eternal paradise.

The difficulties inherent in any comparative study of the overriding drives of historical societies widely separated in time and place are obvious. What other civilizations meant by a state or a society is often so different from our daily usage that comparisons of this nature are at best impressionistic. The idea of greatness itself has changed radically—not merely the content that might be poured into greatness but the value of the thing in itself.

But then again, this may be one of the last periods when comparisons of this sort are possible. If there is validity to what will be my underlying premise—that the American model of a society presents a spectacle qualitatively different from anything known before in the tempo of its dynamism and changeability—then we, among the last generations with a historical sensibility, can still ask historical questions which in a while will be meaningless and incomprehensible. When and if the divorce from the past in our civilization becomes absolute, as Paul Valéry suggested in an essay on progress back in 1929—a process that has been accelerating at a far greater rate of speed than even he imagined—then archeological comparisons of great societies may perhaps continue, but they will more and more be reduced to objective measurements totally devoid of feeling tone, to the size and quantity and shape of artifacts. History will present to future generations, Valéry prophesied, "strange, almost ununderstandable tales, for nothing in their epoch will have had an example in the past; and nothing of the past will survive into the present. Everything which is not purely physiological in man will have changed, since our ambitions, our politics, our wars, our customs, our arts, are at present subject to the rule of very rapid replacement. They depend more and more closely upon the positive sciences and, thus, less and less on that which was. The *new fact* tends to assume all the importance which tradition and the *historical fact* have hitherto possessed."

The attributes of great societies upon which I mean to concentrate will tend to be expressed in polar terms: we will probe for commitment to traditionalist constancy or relentless innovation, communal cohesiveness or loose individualism, religious transcendence or secular worldliness, ascetic self-denial or expansive gratification, harmonious beauty or esthetic indifference; aristocratic elitism or democratic egalitarianism, warlike aggressiveness or military restraint. My main function, as I see it, is to evoke images of other societies. For some these images may look like handwriting on the wall; for others they may arouse nostalgia or contempt; for me they will be highlighting the extraordinary uniqueness of the present historical moment.

CONSTANCY OR DYNAMISM

Nowhere is the contrast between our present conception of a great society and that of virtually all previous civilizations more striking than in the different attitudes toward constancy and change, toward an immutable, stable order and dynamic novelty. Most societies have been traditionalist to the point of extolling a changeless state of being as the highest good. In the ancient public documents of the Near East, a plea to the gods for an enduring order was the prayer of the king. When Messianism with its foretelling of a great transformation appeared in Judaic and Christian history, its promise of a radical metamorphosis was looked upon with suspicion by the rulers of society as a dangerous and disruptive idea. Even in war and conquest most societies aimed at the establishment of an immutable order. The ideals of Christian life expressed by the medieval scholastics centered around the concept of *ordo,* which implied fixedness in economic and social conditions. The ideal of *manu tenere,* the preservation of an existing governmental form and its maintenance against intruders, the reaffirmation or restoration of this pristine order when it became subject to decay, was ubiquitous in Renaissance political thought. In the midst of the vicissitudes of states and empires, of which the sixteenth-century *politiques* were so acutely conscious, the establishment of a lasting order was the common purpose of men as diverse as Thomas More and Machiavelli, Bodin and Contarini. The widespread sixteenth- and seventeenth-century myth of Venice as the most perfect society of all time was founded upon its supposed duration from the fifth century onward without any alteration whatsoever in its constitution. As late as Montesquieu, the end of society was to preserve the existing laws true to the national spirit. Rousseau's ideal society allows for few changes in the laws once they have been promulgated by the general will. When Edmund Burke wrote his famous defense of eighteenth-century English society, he boasted of England's stability in contrast with the fickleness of revolutionary France. If you want to know how different we have become, listen to Burke's self-appraisal: "Our political system is placed in a just correspondence and symmetry with the order of the world and with the mode of existence decreed to a permanent body composed of transitory parts, wherein, by the disposition of a stupendous wisdom, molding together the great mysterious incorporation of the human race, the whole, at one time, is never old or middle-aged or young, but in a condition of unchangeable constancy. . . ." Carried away by his own rhetorical portrait of unchanging Britain, Burke proclaimed with pride that his countrymen had not "lost the generosity and dignity of thinking of the fourteenth century."

In hundreds of Western European utopias written prior to the latter part of the eighteenth century, the explicit ideal of social life was calm felicity. The mood of the system was sameness, the tonus one of Stoic placidity, without agitation of the passions. One day was to be like the next, except that natural holidays related to the seasons and nuptial rites would punctuate the year with occasional festivals.

If we move halfway across the globe to China and India, we find that the same attributes of constancy were valued above all others by those civilizations. When Ssu-Ma Tsien, the historian of the Han, wishes to praise an imperial regime, he describes its adherence to the Taoist principles of non-action. Peace is an important element in this picture of constancy, but the purpose of peace is to allow for governmental inaction and the continuation of a natural rhythm of sameness in an agricultural society. "In the reign of Emperor Hui and Empress Lii," the Grand Historian concluded, "the common people succeeded in putting behind them the sufferings of the age of the warring states, and rulers and subject alike sought rest in surcease of action. Therefore Emperor Hui sat with folded hands and unruffled garments and Empress Lii, though a woman ruling in the manner of an emperor, conducted the business of government without ever leaving her private chambers, and the world was at peace. Punishments were seldom meted out and evildoers grew rare, while the people applied themselves to the task of farming, and food and clothing became abundant." In Indian society the good rule of life is dharma, that which is established or firm, the steadfast decree, the law, usage, practice, customary observance, or prescribed conduct, the norm of social class in which a well-defined inalterable duty prevails.

In America we are committed to a rule of life so contradictory to that of these civilizations that at moments one seems to be dealing with another human nature. We are enrolled under the banner of Francis Bacon, who gave pithy expression to the new scientific and technological ideal in the *New Atlantis.* "The end of our foundation is the knowledge of causes, and secret motions of things; and the enlarging of the bounds of human empire, to the effecting of all things possible." Short of the fulfillment of a Spenglerian prognostication of which there are as yet no signs—the engineer's flight from the machine for the sake of his soul—a rampantly dynamic industrialism and scientificism seem to be our destiny. Bacon is our prophet, a somewhat corrupt man who occasionally takes bribes, but he confesses the fact to himself and he has a genius for a certain type of reality. We in America have, in addition, become the primary heirs to an eighteenth-century conception embodied in the writings of two of Bacon's French followers, Turgot and Condorcet. For them sameness and repetition, attributes which men had once contemplated with admiration in nature and in societies that mirrored the cosmic order, became evil things in themselves. Constant inconstancy, eternal change and progress, the taming of nature, were for them the only distinctions of mankind. I single out these French theorists and their nineteenth-century followers as true prophets of what has in fact been happening in American civilization because they joined to Bacon's ideal two elements totally absent from his scientific-technological world view. These are egalitarianism and a sense of accelerating speed in change, elements which would have been utterly abhorrent to the Elizabethan aristocrat. Unlike Bacon and Newton, the French *philosophes* also had an idea of the infinitude of scientific knowledge and technical advance that is akin to our own. They are our real spiritual ancestors.

Amid incredible waste, we in America are continuing to pursue the Baconian ideal of power over nature. There are few new industrial and scientific ideas that fail to get an ultimate hearing somewhere—fads, fashions, fakes, and phonies included. This dynamic growth entails an eternal destruction of the old because old knowledge, prized in the traditionalist society, will in and of itself become dead and useless knowledge. The content of our concept of progress has changed from what it was even as recently as the nineteenth century. Progress toward abstract reason, virtue, and moral goodness no longer has any great significance and many of us doubt its validity. We do understand sheer dynamic change at a rate which defies definition in ordinary literate speech. When a popular magazine a few months ago made an effort to describe the transformations of the contemporary American city, it had to resort to such onomatopoeia as "zip" and "zoom."

No society of the past has shown such dynamism, such changeability, and such kaleidoscopic variety of experience. We destroy cities and rebuild them in three decades. No skyscraper standing today can be considered an inviolable monument. We tear up and throw away our clothes; we junk our machines for the slightest damage; our books have become as expendable as newspapers. The book, once revered as a holy object—Jews would not allow a written letter of the alphabet to be discarded—is now tossed away with a shift of lecture topic, as **any** professor who has seen a littered classroom can testify. Even the past has become for us a vast continent for novelty-seeking. When we conduct historical explorations we are no longer looking to the past as the support of an existing order, its validation in some profound respect, the way Israelite history is conceived in the Bible. We should not be deceived as to the meaning of the proliferation of contemporary historical research. This is merely another form of innovation. We will make a new history every ten years, and thus the past itself is rendered dynamic. Our scientific progress—to turn to our greatest achievement—has become *indéfini* in Condorcet's sense: it is now so immeasurable that you have to climb to a higher level before you can even fantasy what might be in prospect next.

Let me again refer, by way of contrast, to that ideal of social order which dominated the Western mind for more than two thousand years, the Platonic model of justice and harmony. Whether one takes Plato's ideal from the *Republic* or from the *Laws,* he comes out with the same result with respect to the idea of change. His guardians would oust anyone who introduced a new tune or a new dance. The slightest modification would bring down upon the culprit Deuteronomic chastisement. The perfect order can only repeat itself or be destroyed. If Plato appeared today, even the most hidebound conservatives among us would cover him with ridicule.

The momentum of our society is its unique character and we must accommodate ourselves to it. The problems this entails are obvious. How can we live with these explosive concepts of knowledge and power when we are aware of their destructive potentialities? At the moment, many intellectuals have a bad conscience about this power. In the past two decades of the atomic age we have been showing some of the same anxieties as did the nineteenth-century romantics in the face of those minor transformations of the technological landscape that were once grandiloquently labeled the Industrial Revolution. On the other hand, there are American scientists who assure us that only we, of all contemporary societies, have in actuality embarked—and just embarked—upon the great scientific revolution.

In this area, growing self-revelation, even on a superficial level, is a good, lest we recoil before the unknown instead of trying to understand and control it. We have yet to tame ourselves emotionally, so that we can use the instruments of science and technology without fear of their catastrophic effect and without dread that we are toying with the fire of the gods. These new powers, which we try to transform into innocent, familiar, harmless things by sometimes calling them "hardware," are rather recent extensions of our bodies and it will require the passage of time before we are reasonably comfortable with the seven-league boots and magical forces.

There has been nothing comparable to the *internal* dynamism of American society in the twentieth century—and my emphasis is upon the word "internal." There are numerous historical examples of extensive geographic conquest in a brief period—Alexander and Genghis Khan, the Arabs of the seventh century and the Spaniards of the sixteenth, the unification by war of the Andean civilization, and the drive of the Toltecs in Central America. But while our own growth has had its imperialist moments of horizontal extension and we are still enticed by such adventures, in our time the development has been largely within. Our thrust has been vertical. Our energies and aggressions have for the most part been expended upon objects within our midst. The fateful question now is: "Can this same momentum be continued?" And from my vantage point, which deliberately shuts out daily or annual political crises, I see us vacillating.

One type of decision would involve total commitment to the building of a technical-scientific civilization and spreading its benefits as fast as possible to our own people directly, to others indirectly. In this respect everyone is going our way despite verbal noises to the contrary. Even when the voice is the voice of Marx, the technical organization and the artifacts have followed American patterns. It is not less but more science and technology that we should embrace and promote. And by this I do not mean only the physical sciences, where we have been most successful. The whole range of human behavior lies open before us, for probing with a wide variety of methods. Every time a form of knowledge gets into a rut of orthodoxy, like some of our historical and philological sciences, we should try something new. The geographic spread of our universities, the diversity and overlapping of our government agencies, the variety and multiplicity of our private research organizations, despite or perhaps because of the chaos of scientific inquiries, hold a promise of continuous development. Stereotypes may emerge, but the curiosity about novelty seems at least equally strong. In all fields there is a pompous bureaucracy of knowledge, but as long as it does not become hidebound and there is choice and mobility, the dynamism need not be decelerated. If foundations, universities, government agencies, and industries are on the lookout for what is new, even for its own sake, we will not lapse into sameness and we will remain peculiarly ourselves. The Great Society must be prepared to countenance waste. Efficiency can be a grave danger: only those human agencies are most efficient whose purposes are very clearly defined and predetermined, like the Nazi gas chambers. American science and technology should remain flexible and open-ended, and in this respect I need not sidestep the obvious threat of a hypertrophied war science and technology. Thus far, both American universities and American industries have in many instances been willing to encourage creativity irrespective of immediate practical results. If this can continue, we shall be operating in consonance with our historical character, and we may avoid the evils of a mandarin society, a sectarian society, and a warrior society. The role of the individual creative scientist must undergo a transformation. He knows that his discovery will no sooner be published than it will be superseded, and he must feel a certain lack of fulfillment, a certain alienation from the object which he has fashioned. Can we attach his libido to cooperative creative effort without falling into the mire of stifling scientific bureaucracy? This is an open question.

In the often frenetic quest for novelty we necessarily sacrifice the ideals of durability, permanency, and even beauty, which dominated other societies. Perhaps there remains among us some nostalgia for calm felicity, but I cannot help wondering about its authenticity. Santayana once described the restless Dr. Faustus in heaven serving quietly as a teacher for a while, then impatiently throwing his schoolbooks out of the celestial windows and dashing off to some windier place in the clouds. Spengler was right in choosing Faust as the symbolic figure of Western culture, whose dynamic character America has come to embody more than any other sector of the civilization.

COHESION OR LOOSENESS

Great societies of the past often expressed satisfaction with their own cohesiveness, the prevalence among the citizenry of a strong bond of fellow feeling, the warmth of their brotherhood—in a word, their active love for one another.

What happens to these feelings in the fast-moving, sprawling urban agglomerations which are the relentless destiny of our society? That is my next question. Can a society lacking in communal unity be considered great? Of what avail the scientific and technological achievements, if the human beings in these vast urban areas suffer loneliness even though they are well fed and clothed by any historical standards. And by community feeling I do not mean the weak sense of responsibility that manifests itself in sporadic contributions to a community chest or that engages in some charitable activity to drive away boredom. I mean something far stronger.

Ibn Khaldun, the Arab philosopher and historian of the fourteenth century, for example, esteemed fanatical fellow feeling and solidarity, what he called *Assabiya,* above all other qualities of a society. He found it in its most potent form among conquering tribesmen about to overthrow a sedentary urban society that had gone soft and decadent and had lost its own *Assabiya.* Plato's insistence upon absolute unity in the good society is of the same character. It is said by some historians that the citizens of the Greek city-state actually had this *koinōnia,* or community feeling. The dominant self-image of Chinese civilization was that of a society initiated to the discipline of life in the first ages of its existence by wise teachers, with the consequence that perfect social cohesion became the guiding principle. In the Li Yun, the Chinese Golden Age, "a public and common spirit ruled all under the sky." In official orthodox Chinese historiography, there is one recurrent theme—the alternating disintegration and restoration of this unity. The Saint-Simonians of the nineteenth century divided world history into alternating periods which they called organic and critical, and one of the major characteristics of the organic epoch—of which the Middle Ages was for them an example—was the pervasiveness of a feeling of cohesion among the people, in contrast with the isolated, anarchic individualism of the critical epoch. Something of the same sort may even be involved in the responsibility of the Puritan saints for one another's conduct, though in their case the mutual love often assumed rather painful forms. Rousseau is perhaps the greatest modern theorist of this fellow feeling: in the *Social Contract* the ideal society is defined as one in which the individual will and the collective or general will naturally and spontaneously coalesce.

Modern mass movements such as revolutionary nationalism, communism, and fascism are supposed to provide the libidinal satisfactions of cohesiveness and social integration. German sociologists of the late nineteenth century like Tönnies preferred the virtues of what they called *Gemeinschaft* over those of *Gesellschaft.* There has been much talk of alienation in Western society since Hegel resurrected the theological term *Entfremdung* and Marx used it to describe the temper of pre-communist societies—it being understood that with the dawn of communism alienation would automatically disappear. There is something of the French Revolutionary need for *fraternité* in such conceptions. We now talk popularly of the Atlantic community or the academic community. De Gaulle's constitution called France and its overseas territories a *communauté*. President Johnson's notion of consensus appears to border on this idea—rather dangerously, as Hans J. Morgenthau has argued and I would agree. Most of these emotion-laden phrases are used in our society rather artificially, with the hope of calling into being what does not exist by the mere act of naming it.

If we turn to evaluate the possibilities of our society on this polar scale of strong community feeling at one end and isolated individualism without cohesiveness at the other, we shall fortunately find ourselves rather weak on unity and fellow feeling, as great societies of the past and great utopians of the past conceived this emotion.

It was Aristotle who first attacked the promise of Socrates that "the greatest possible unity of the whole polis is the supreme good." But one could go much farther, insisting for our American society upon the original eighteenth-century conception of social life based on individual rights, which stressed security *from* the state as Montesquieu did and praised the great virtue of *secrecy*, which meant privacy, as Hume did. One could glorify pluralism, diversity, and variety; and one could accept alienation from the whole as part of the human condition, to be suffered like mortality without recourse to facile verbal palliatives.

We must face the fact that with the urban agglomerations which the Great Society cannot avoid will come urban anonymity. But there are compensations in the vastly expanded range of human relationships. The urban university will not be a tightly knit group of colleagues, and thank the sprawling city for that. But what is lost in intimacy is won in freedom. The "identity" that can express itself only in professional or racial or age-group terms is no identity at all. It is a mask or a badge on the lapel of a professional convention suit. Love will doubtless be diluted in megalopolis, but it will not be as poisoned as it became in the town where Madame Bovary lived. Community is a contradiction in terms in large units of an overwhelmingly urban civilization. Relationships will not be natural—that is, based on geographical proximity. They will require acts of will. The city of the Great Society is dynamic, eclectic, egalitarian, and above all loose and tolerant, not cohesive.

There is no common heroic ancestry in this society. The hardy farmers of Lexington will be relegated to vague legend. The mothers and fathers of the American Revolution simply will not serve as ancestors for the many different nations and peoples who are today becoming effective members of this society. Some ethnic groups will continue to seek and find their own true fathers and they will cease to live on borrowed family portraits and fake genealogies. In time the dynamism of the society may cause us to forget all the founding fathers. In a way the present administration is more forthright in giving recognition to the new ethnic and racial realities than previous ones have been. President Johnson invites Jews, Italians, Irish, Poles, and Negroes into his administration without the self-consciousness from which Roosevelt—who started the trend—was hardly emancipated.

Growing tolerance of all forms of human life is the inevitable characteristic of our great urban society. One simply cannot be as intolerant in the city, no matter how hard he works at it, as residents are naturally in a rural community. Really open, ethnically tolerant societies have been rare in the past. They have usually been highly restrictive even though metics and slaves were occasionally assimilated. I am here standing on its head the value system inherent in most Germanic philosophy of history, which found the high point of a culture in the period when it was most exclusive, integrated, pure in style, uncomplicated racially or ethnically, untainted by the alien.

Our great urban society is demonstrating far greater powers of absorption than either Alexandria or Rome. As each stratum of immigrants or of the racially ostracized enters the society, it is shaken up with new impressions. Only those obsessed with the Germanic fetish of purity will worry about its mongrel quality. As each ghetto finally sends its sons out—and the process is admittedly far slower and more painful than was once imagined—new colors and tones are added to our existence. The picture of a uniform America is shattered; there is religious and ethnic diversity under government. If we can live with this diversity, our example may yet be the salvation of fragmented African and Asian polities. In praise of the pluralism of what he already called the great society in 1929—on the eve of a collapse from which it recuperated rather amazingly—Walter Lippmann wrote: "There is little doubt that in the great metropolitan centers there exists a disposition to live and to let live, to give and take, to agree and to agree to differ, which is not to be found in simple homogeneous communities. In complex communities life quickly becomes intolerable if men are intolerant. . . . The terrible indictments drawn up in a Mississippi village against the Pope in Rome, the Russian nation, the vices of Paris, and the enormities of New York are in the main quite lyrical. The Pope may never even know what the Mississippi preacher thinks of him and New York continues to go to, but never apparently to reach, hell."

The American urban area which I identify with American society, because the rural space is fast losing all but recreational significance, is an inadequately regulated unit which experiences frequent crises. But it is a much more alive and human social form than the tight-knit, intolerant little town of the nineteenth century that de Tocqueville described. The great American city is likely to continue to be formless, the great university eclectic, the architecture of private and public buildings spectacular rather than beautiful. Spontaneity, ease, freedom of movement, immediacy of emotional response—attributes that some psychological historians have identified with the great aristocratic societies—can be found in the democratic American city. The tempo of life will be fast, the painting gaudy, the music loud and brassy; the noise decibels will reach new heights. And let those who do not like it go back to the beastly, cantankerous New England or Midwestern towns whence they came.

The question now is whether this Great Society can preserve its looseness, its often vulgar eclecticism, its tolerance and skepticism, for these are its great glory. It is one-dimensional only to those who see it that way and refuse to plumb its depths. So far, this is not 1984. Our society is uniform only to the lazy, and the secret persuaders are effective only on the unaware. The libraries of the city are large and free, its sidewalks are thronged with persons, its hospitals open to all-comers, including staphylococci, its public administration anarchic, its private enterprise aggressive. It is more or less equal. Most automobiles look virtually alike and they are equally unsafe and generally operative. One used to talk about the acquisitive society. I have become impressed with its spendthrift quality, which gives it an expansive character even when it gets junk for its money.

To try to do all things possible and to find out about all things possible is one of the rare attributes of this loose-jointed society. I know of nothing so open to new experiences in modern times since France of the Directorate and Weimar Germany, two great creative moments often maligned by priggish historians. These, too, were great societies, and I would like, in passing, to rehabilitate their image along with our own. In variety of artistic and scientific expression there were no holds barred. Knowledge was pursued into hitherto forbidden areas in the newly founded schools of France in 1795 and the artistic and scientific genius of Germany of the 1920's is still a seedbed for our contemporary accomplishments, despite the defamation of the period in the Germanic world. We today in America are in a similar time of imaginative expression. The multiplication of universities in our society has some disadvantages, but the increase in the number of centers with the intoxicating variety of opportunities they afford moves one to praise sheer proliferation. I am not dismayed if vulgar objects win prizes, as long as there are enough rewards to go around and originality is not officially suffocated. I am not in sympathy with Herbert Marcuse's attack on the eclecticism of the American university. This is its grandeur. As we are forced to build urban universities we will abandon the Ivy League model with its unauthentic forms, and transform the university into an intellectual whirlpool where anything can happen.

Without being cohesive and centripetal, our Great Society is nevertheless likely to be relatively orderly, as in the age of the Antonines, of the good Chinese Emperors, and in nineteenth-century Europe. Those who have watched the American megalopolis in crises have been impressed with its capacity to reorganize itself under shock. New York during a power blackout or New York with its major arteries of communication severed has shown extraordinary recuperative powers and a spirit of mutual helpfulness.

One final word about the lack of cohesiveness in American society in contrast with other civilizations. We, too, have ceremonials of cohesion in sports arenas, during the funerals of national heroes, during the filming of dramatic scientific exploits, perhaps in our elections and inaugurations. But I doubt whether they have the potency and intensity of mystical communion that took place between participants and onlookers in dance ceremonials or during human sacrifices in as noble a culture as the Mayan. And maybe that is all to the good—the social bond created among us is looser and more humane.

THE SACRED AND THE PROFANE

This brings me to religion in American culture. Although American society is an offspring of European society and until our own time had remained culturally under the tutelage of the nourishing mother in most expressions of life and thought, the declaration of independence is by now quite complete. If anything, it is the parent who has taken to imitating the rather rambunctious child. In the United States, the secularization of life has advanced farther than in many countries of Western Europe, despite the growing number of formal religious affiliations, which seem to be surpassing population growth. The character of this Great Society is secular to a degree never reached by other great societies, not even in the period of their hypersophistication and decline. The Egyptian, Tigris-Euphrates, Indian, Mayan, Andean civilizations at their zenith were pervaded by a transcendental religious feeling, a sentiment that seems quite feeble in ours, at least in the last half century. This has led some historical commentators to conclude that our society has passed its peak and is probably on the downgrade. But such jeremiads are the consequence of defining the objectives of our society in spiritual terms which may have been of paramount importance in other civilizations but seem to be irrelevant in ours.

The religious establishments in America appear to be essentially political and social institutions whose structure and formal nature may render them useful in binding together groups of men in civility, even in brotherhood, but which cannot foster, convey, or interpret religious emotion as it was known, let us say, in the great moments of Judaism and Christianity. I believe that the current revival of religion is primarily an aspect and manifestation of middle-class prosperity in the land, and this explains its patently dry character, its failure to create either in the word or in the religious object. Our society is rather Roman in matters of religion, which means that it is both tolerant and indifferent. Religion is extrinsic rather than intrinsic to our culture. We are trinitarian in our fashion. There are three formal establishments—Protestant, Catholic, and Jewish—which in public ceremonials enjoy virtual equality. A Greek Orthodox establishment may be in the making, but at the moment it has not yet achieved the same official status as the big three. As long as a vague, inchoate state civil religion known as Americanism is subscribed to, almost any form of worship is countenanced. We are somewhat disturbed only by those who in the eyes of the state seem to have no visible gods—as were the ancient Romans when confronted by the Jews and the Christians of the first centuries.

The Judeo-Greco-Christian chain of traditions once significantly fed the scientific experimental spirit, but its values no longer seem to control the life of this society. Their world was for the most part anti-egalitarian, rather rigid, based on communal love and responsibility. It was negative, or at most forbearing, toward the body and its passions. Nevertheless, these principles have endured for more than two thousand years, and in some form they may continue to be part of our civilization. Our problem is: Can our present psychic drives, if divorced from these traditions, sustain the momentum of our scientific-technological society? Thus far we have combined this scientific-technological civilization with certain Greek concepts of harmony, Roman concepts of restrictive law, order, and power, and Judeo-Christian concepts of justice, mercy, and perhaps love. Science and technology are now becoming values in themselves and seem emancipated from their cultural origins. There are, of course, those who feel that granted a human science of behavior that is developed enough, we shall come around to the Greco-Roman-Judeo-Christian values in some balanced admixture as the best of all possible regimens for men. At the moment the spiritual foundation of our scientific-technological society is one of the great unknowns.

THE PROBLEM OF GRATIFICATION

Conceding that the Great Society is not likely to give birth to major expressions of religious transcendence, we may then ask: How does it measure up on the sensate level? Is it moving to gratify man's desires for food and drink and beauty?

When the tyrants of the sixth century in the Hellenic world, the aristocrats of Magna Graecia, the princes of Pergamon, and the Seleucid kings built monumental cities, outstanding both in esthetic quality and in functional perfection, these cities certainly far surpassed in harmonious beauty anything we seem able to achieve. They were not democratic cities, and with few notable exceptions were meant to reflect the glory of the prince or the aristocracy. The same holds true for the Renaissance city. The aristocratic ideal of Castiglione's Urbino cannot be ours. Leonardo's sketch for a city provided for two architectural planes corresponding to the needs of an upper and a lower class. Our democratic commitment makes their exclusive esthetic ideal virtually impossible. Alberti's conception of beauty was a moral value and his vision implied an eternal order. Beauty and durability were identified. Such lofty moral sensibility will be denied us. Our great urban concentrations seem far too big ever to be harmonious units. To the extent that the city becomes a living landscape it will be as disorganized as nature itself, changing with the vantage point, the moment, and the mood. There may never again be architectural agglomerations comparable to those of the Acropolis, or Florence, or Cambridge, England. Our contemporary monumental structures look alike, and those in New York resemble those in Moscow, London, and, I am told, Peking.

On a lower level, the prospects of gratification are plentiful despite the present realities of mass poverty, which the Great Society aims to eradicate. There is nothing inherent in our situation that excludes an abundance of what Thomas More called "allowable honest pleasures." "To each according to his needs," the second half of the Marxist slogan in the Gotha Program, is a fast-changing concept. Within our own brief lives the definition of minimal needs has been radically transformed and will continue to be altered. I doubt whether we shall ever provide for total freedom from repression, though there is every reason to hope that the traditional chains on instinctual gratification will be loosened. The utopia of a playful rather than a working society seems far off indeed, but the facts are that our museums and theaters and universities can become the popular houses of play which they should be if they are not morgues. In our great urban agglomerations more dancing and feasting and drinking goes on than in Rome. Many are still not invited to the banquet, but more are being asked all the time.

Confucianism, with its emphasis on society as a graded but harmonious organism; the Indian outlook, with its view of the special dharma of each encapsulated social class; the medieval anthropomorphic and organismic conception of society—all have been rejected in the name of a simple egalitarianism which really allows for no rigid class differences. This egalitarianism is naturally suspicious of exclusivity unless it recognizes its immediate utility, and it will not, in the long run, tolerate any significant impediments to equality of opportunity among citizens of the society—which in effect means an equal chance for sensate gratification. Formal differences of rank even now make its members uncomfortable. While most great societies of the past have been elitist and aristocratic, we are irrevocably committed to a democratic society of more or less equals. The only historical analogue I know to what we really are trying to do is Periclean Athens, and it was stained by slavery. The portrait of Athenian de-

mocracy in the famous funeral oration as recounted by Thucydides is
certainly touched up, but *mutatis mutandis* it still has some relevance
to our intentions. "It is true that we are called a democracy," said
Pericles, "for the administration is in the hands of the many and not
of the few. But while the law secures equal justice to all alike in their
private disputes, the claim of excellence is also recognized; and when
a citizen is in any way distinguished, he is preferred to the public
service, not as a matter of privilege, but as a reward of merit. Neither
is poverty a bar, but a man may benefit his country whatever be the
obscurity of his condition. There is no exclusiveness in our public
life, and in our private intercourse we are not suspicious of one another nor angry with our neighbor if he does what he likes." An
American President might have delivered the same eulogy of his fellow countrymen, and if he, too, would be exaggerating somewhat, as
Pericles doubtless did, it would be hyperbole in the same general direction.

MILITARY PROWESS AND OVEREXTENSION

Finally, we come to consider that attribute of societies that has until
recent years always earned them the epithet "great." Sometimes it has
been attached to the names of their rulers. I refer of course to military
grandeur and power. For Plato, prowess in war was the ultimate test
of the perfection of a polity and its system of education. Those who
sought to provoke war among Hellenes or who maltreated prisoners
were condemned, but the heroic virtues were appreciated above all
others. The mythic Athens of the age of the Atlantans had, according
to the *Critias*, withstood the trial and was the perfect society in action.

Military might is relatively easy to measure. It can be done
crudely by counting the square inches of national color on a map. By
this criterion, Persians, Macedonians, Romans, Chinese, Mongols,
Turks, Spaniards, Englishmen, Russians, Germans, among others,
have been great.

But this attribute is a two-legged sword. On the one hand, it has to
be admitted that the organizers of great societies have almost always
been successful warriors; but on the other hand, there is a strong consensus among philosophers of history from the Renaissance on that
the military overextension of societies has ultimately led to their
downfall.

The hubris of overextension was Montesquieu's explanation for the decline and fall of Rome. This theory was already a cornerstone of Jean Bodin's system in the sixteenth century, and has been entertained by men as remote from each other as John Adams and Arnold Toynbee. But then again, as Freud has pointed out, men have learned to love one another in the city by killing others, the outsiders. They have killed for a vast complex of verbal reasons and they have buried their dead in grand ceremonials. War has united men in adventurous enterprise and has provided outlets for their aggressiveness. In most ages wars have been brutal and cruel, but on occasion they have been playful, like dancing exercises. For our Great Society, however, maximal war is no longer possible. We must remain unfulfilled and we must sublimate our aggressiveness in other activities. This creates a difficulty: How can we be dynamic and aggressive internally in science and technology while remaining mere holders of the mark on the outside? We know that if we use our colossal strength, we may invite total annihilation; but will not external passivity be impossible to a society that operates in terms of dynamic power? Plato faced the problem of training his guardians to be gentle to the citizens and ferocious to the enemy, like certain types of dogs. We are now called upon to hold the line with no prospect of victory when the nature of our upbringing has made us incorrigible activists. And yet this is our only way, if we are to continue to build a uniquely great society with the many virtues I have presented. For many centuries the Romans fended off the barbarians without advancing beyond the Rhine-Danube boundary that Augustus had established, and we must train ourselves to a similar operation.

As things stand now, the Great Society is still rather burdened with heroic conceptions that are as antiquated as Achilles. We act as though every insult must be requited a thousandfold. Talk of destiny or mission or honor in the tradition of the duello still seems to dominate policy. Such notions belonged to other great societies; they have no place in ours.

"Let the world be destroyed yet justice must prevail" is a heroic posture. But aristocratic punctilio is contrary to the nature of our middle-class sensate society where injuries are adjudicated. It is told of late nineteenth-century soldier hygienists that they could not endure to see certain primitive African tribes die of fever in the swamps they inhabited, and so they drove the savages at the point of the bayonet to migrate to salubrious plateaus that were taboo. One German expedition, however, unable to force compliance, killed all of the natives in order successfully to fulfill their humane mission.

A great society now must exercise restraint even in the face of provocation, and worry less about its image than the reality of its existence. The peace-loving intent of American foreign policy—which I believe in—is not in question, but its implementation is. Great societies have faced strange enemies before. Perhaps there is something to be learned from the Confucian Emperor Wen. "The emperor made peace with the Hsiung-nu," we are told, "and, when they violated their agreement and invaded and plundered the borders, he ordered the border guards to stick to their posts, but would not send troops into barbarian territory. This was because he hated to bring hardship to the common people."

Aristophanes, the poet of apolitical individualism and peace and good feeling, is in many ways a better guide for the Great Society than Christ or Plato. The age of heroes, like the age of the gods, is dead. It is time that the age of men began.

Chapter 9

🐚 *The Great Society in a Small World—Dampening Reflections from the Dismal Science* KENNETH E. BOULDING

Economics is first and foremost the science of scarcity. This is why it is a dismal science. Its problems arise only if there is not enough to go around. One of its greatest principles, though not necessarily the truest, I have sometimes called the "Duchess's Law," enunciated by the Duchess in *Alice in Wonderland:* "The more there is of yours, the less there is of mine." A variant is Goering's law: "We cannot have both guns and butter." What he actually seems to have said, incidentally, according to the invaluable Bartlett, is that, "Guns will make us powerful; butter will only make us fat."

There is a fundamental conflict which has gone on through almost all of recorded history between the heroic and the economic, between greatness and prudence, between extravagance and sobriety, and between glory and common sense. Economics is the good, gray, rational science. After the charge of the Light Brigade, economics asks the reason why. Byronic frenzy may inspire us to say, "Let joy be unconfined"; the economist says: "You will have to pay for this tomorrow." Even when St. Francis urges us to give and not to count the cost, the economist says that somebody has to count the cost; and when somebody wants a Great Society, the economist says: "Who is going to pay for it?" It is no wonder that the economist is not very popular.

At this point someone is sure to come up and say, "But we have changed all that. Science and technology have produced the age of affluence. Scarcity has been abolished. Let us eat, drink, and be merry; there is plenty for all." Among biology, automation, and systems engineering, we can produce all we need with a fraction of the labor force, and today not even the sky is the limit. There are a good many voices today urging that we can have both guns and butter, "more for everybody and more for me too," and that economics can be put in the ash can.

This view seems to me to involve delusions of grandeur and a totally unwarranted euphoria derived from the careless and poorly sampled observation of a few special cases. It is true, of course, that the Duchess's Law is only a half-truth. Where there is economic development, where the total to be distributed is increasing, then it is possible that the more there is of yours, the more there is of mine too. We can all indulge in the delightful positive-sum game of getting richer together. It is true also that the process of economic development in a very real sense diminishes scarcity, and diminishes the urgency of rational choice. This is the essential point that Galbraith is making in *The Affluent Society,* and qualitatively it is perfectly valid. One of the principal delights of being rich is that we do not have to economize so much—that is, we do not have to devote so much time and attention to the careful balancing of gain against loss at the margin, and what Wordsworth decries as "the lore of nicely calculated less or more."

There is a familiar proposition in economics that the richer we are, the less is the marginal utility of money, and the less significance for our welfare is the expenditure of an extra dollar in any particular line. Using money as a symbol of resources in general, we can expand this proposition to say that the richer we are, the less is the marginal utility of a unit of general resources, and the less it matters, in effect, whether we make mistakes in allocation. For a poor man in a poor society, a mistake in allocation may be fatal; a rich society can afford to be careless and extravagant. Another billion dollars is only two thousandths of the G.N.P., so why not spend it? Furthermore, even though unemployment is now down below 4 per cent, we should be able to get it down to 3 per cent. There is still a good deal of slack in the economy, and by absorbing it we could easily raise the G.N.P. by five or ten billion and in these circumstances practically anything we want to do is virtually costless, it simply comes out of unemployed resources. In a sense World War II was virtually costless to the American consumer. Come on in, everybody, the water's fine!

THE SCIENCE OF SCARCITY

By this time, any economist who defends scarcity looks like a Prohibitionist on a bathing beach. Truth, however, requires me to adopt the garment of gloom, and to start an anti-euphoria society. In the face of the "Scarcity Is Dead" theology which is celebrated with such enthusiasm in certain segments of our society, the economist needs to bring to the attention of the celebrants a few skeletons at their feast.

In the first place, there is no evidence that we are undergoing anything very unusual in the way of technological change and economic developments. If we take, for instance, the indices of output per man-hour calculated by the Department of Labor, we find, for example, that in the last eighteen years the average rate of increase of output per man-hour has been 3.4 per cent per annum for the total private sector, 5.9 per cent in agriculture, and 2.8 per cent in the non-agricultural industries. The only thing that approaches the spectacular is the remarkable increase in agriculture, though even this is only a speeding up of what has been going on for more than a hundred years. In spite of automation, the rate of increase in output per man-hour in non-agricultural industries is not spectacular, and since agriculture is a constantly declining proportion of the total economy, its impact on the total gets smaller all the time. It is, indeed, one of the paradoxes of economic development that the more successful any segment of the economy is in achieving rapid technological progress, the more it is likely to decline as a segment of the total. Hence there is a constant tendency for the more stagnant sectors of the economy, such as government, education, the service trades, and so on, to increase in the proportion which they bear to the total, and, inversely, rapid technological change in one sector of the economy has in it, as it were, the seeds of declining influence.

Furthermore, the American economy is by no means the most rapidly developing in the world. It is indeed quite a long way down the list. Direct productivity measures are not easy to come by for comparative purposes, but in cases where the proportion of total resources employed is approximately constant, the rise in the gross national product per head is a good first approximation measure of the rate of technical change. On this score, the record of the United States in the last twenty years is by no means impressive. In the 1950's there were forty-five countries that had a higher rate of economic development than the United States. This figure is a little unfair, because the

1950's were to some extent a period of stagnation for the United States and of unusually rapid development in other countries, and the record of the 1960's will unquestionably look rather different. Nevertheless, in the last twenty years, some countries, notably Japan, West Germany, and some other European countries on both sides of the Iron Curtain, have achieved rates of development which are unprecedented in human history. A sustained rate of development of 8 per cent per annum per capita, as in the case of Japan, for instance, represents a new phenomenon in human history. It is almost a quantum jump from anything which has happened before. In the period before World War II, no country sustained a rate of increase in per capita G.N.P. of more than about 2.3 per cent. The difference between 2.3 per cent and 8 per cent may be dramatically illustrated by pointing out that under conditions of what might be called successful prewar development, the children are twice as rich as the parents; per capita income approximately doubles every generation. At 8 per cent per annum, the children are six times as rich as the parents. Whether this can be kept up for more than a generation is of course a question. It is true also that both Japanese and West German rates of development reflect the recovery of defeated and destroyed societies which, however, preserved their essential knowledge structure. They represent also an abnormal proportion of the G.N.P. devoted to investment, and hence cannot wholly be attributed to a high rate of technological change.

Even when we have made all these downward adjustments, however, the fact remains that we seem to be in the presence of a new phenomenon which is associated in my mind with what might be called the second phase of the impact of the scientific revolution on economic life.

The first phase was the period from, shall we say, 1860, to World War II, in which we began to get the science-based industries such as electrical engineering, chemical engineering, the nuclear industry, and so on. Before 1860 the impact of science on the economy was very small. The so-called Industrial Revolution of the eighteenth century was in fact the tag-end of the long process of developing folk technology of the Middle Ages.

Now I think we can identify a second phase of the impact of science on economic life which is reflected in very widespread scientific technologies in a great many sectors: in agriculture, in virtually all forms of industry, in organization and information processing, and so on. It is this second phase of the impact of science on economic life that produces these 8 per cent per annum rates of growth, whereas 2–3 per cent per annum was characteristic of the first phase.

By this criterion, the United States is still in the first phase, and is in a very real sense a backward country; or should we say more politely, a developing country of the second rank, in spite of the fact that we are by reason of our past growth and history still, by far, the richest country in the world. If present trends continue, however, we will not remain in this relatively advanced position for very long. I have calculated what I call the "overtake dates," based on the countries' performance in the 1950's; that is, at what dates would various countries overtake the United States in real G.N.P. per capita, if the growth of all countries continued to be what it was in the 1950's (see Note 1). In the 1960's, of course, the picture looks rather different. Rates of economic growth in the United States have increased, mainly, however, because we have been absorbing unemployed resources, and not because our rate of technological progress has increased. Rates of growth in many other countries, especially in the socialist camp, have declined, perhaps because of certain horizons which socialist organizations tend to impose, especially in agriculture. The table of overtake dates,[1] therefore, was obsolete as soon as it was calculated. Nevertheless, it represents a certain possibility which cannot be ignored, and certainly any blithe and unthinking optimism about the future of economic development in the United States would be quite unjustified.

THE MONONUCLEOSIS OF THE AMERICAN ECONOMY

What are the reasons behind what I have sometimes called the mononucleosis of the American economy, a condition in which we are not sick enough to go to bed but in which nobody can pretend that we are operating in perfect health? Part of it unquestionably is the result of fiscal and financial timidity, and our unwillingness or ineptitude in pursuing a full-employment policy. Certainly no European country would have tolerated the levels of unemployment which the United States has tolerated in the last twenty years. Part of this arises from an almost paranoid fear of inflation on the part of the Federal Reserve and financial institutions. Another part arises from an equally paranoid fear of government deficits on the part of Congress. Thanks to the extraordinary success of the tax cut in 1964, we may now have learned a little better and be entering a somewhat new era. It is still early, however, to be wholly optimistic, and the fact that so many Americans seem to attribute the long prosperity to the war in Vietnam is a bad sign. We have certainly done better than we did in the 1930's. The Council of Economic Advisers and the Joint Economic Committee have exerted fairly persistent pressure toward economic policies for high levels of employment, and they must be credited with at least a modest success. Nevertheless, the best that can be said about economic policy in the last twenty years is that we could have done worse. The level of unemployment which we have tolerated has probably prevented a more rapid spread of technical improvements. The fact that it has been concentrated so heavily in two segments of the population, the Negroes on the one hand and young people on the other, is enough to offset much that has been done in these twenty years toward the integration of both youth and the Negro into the larger society. In 1965, for instance, when unemployment rates for all workers were only 4.6 per cent, the rate was 13.6 per cent for young people between fourteen and nineteen, 8.3 per cent for non-whites, and only 2.4 per cent for married men. The fact that unemployment is so unevenly distributed, therefore, makes it a much more serious problem than it seems from the over-all figures.

One should not, of course, overlook the genuine accomplishments of the American economy in this period. In the last generation we have approximately doubled per capita real income, and this increase has been quite widely distributed. The real wages of the employed have almost doubled; the proportion of national income going to labor has actually shown some increase; and the record of the twenty years after World War II is unquestionably much superior to the record of the twenty years after World War I, which was a total failure. However, the fact that we could have done worse, perhaps much worse, should not blind us to the fact that we also could have done better. The record should inspire neither despair and self-hatred nor smugness and self-congratulation. We should at the same time be glad that we have done as well as we did and ashamed that we didn't do better.

At least of equal importance with fiscal conservatism in explaining the sluggish performance of the American economy is the absorption of the whole American society in international political and military competition, its neurotic determination to be the only great power, and the consequent absorption of a large proportion of our total effort by the war industry, or what might be called the space-military complex. The rise of the war industry has been far and away the greatest internal change in American society in the last generation. In the 1930's it was barely 1 per cent of the gross national product. Today it is between 9 and 10 per cent, and if the Vietnam war continues to escalate, it will almost certainly go beyond 10 per cent. This change exceeds by whole orders of magnitude any other change in the system. The only other proportional change in the last generation which anywhere approaches it is the decline in agriculture. Furthermore, from the point of view of growth and development, the 10 per cent of the G.N.P. which is absorbed by the war industry greatly understates its impact. Seymour Melman has estimated that some 60 per cent of the total research and development effort is channeled into the space-military operation. Melman's claim that the technological development of the civilian sector of the economy has been severely and adversely affected by this absorption of what might be called the growth resource by the space-military complex is to be taken very seriously.[2] It is one of the astonishing facts of our times that there has been no comprehensive economic study of the distribution and impact of technological change in detail over the economy as a whole. The many instances which Melman cites of depletion and of relative technological stagnation in our society (for example, in railroad, shipbuilding, machine tools, civilian electronics, and in education and health—the list is frighteningly large) are of course selective, and can be offset to some extent by reports of spectacular technical change in other selected cases, e.g., due to automation. Nevertheless, the evidence for widespread technological malaise in the American economy is not to be dismissed. The most obvious explanation is the absorption of such an enormous proportion of our intellectual, research, engineering, and growth resources by the relatively sterile activities of the space-military complex.

It may be argued, of course, that those activities are not as sterile as I have accused them of being, and that there are in fact considerable spillovers from the space-military industry into the civilian economy. In the early days this may have had some truth to it. Certainly, for instance, we would not have had the jets as early as we did if it had not been for the enormous research resources devoted to the military industry. It is becoming increasingly apparent, however, that those spillovers are declining, mainly because the space-military complex is now at least a whole technological generation ahead of the civilian economy as a result of the enormous resources that have been put into it. There are very great difficulties involved in the transfer of technology between two societies, or even between two parts of the same society, where one is more than a technological generation ahead of the other. We see this problem in its extreme form in the difficulty of translating Western agricultural techniques into forms which have any use for the poor countries of Asia and Africa. The two technologies speak such totally different languages that they cannot communicate at all. There may be a few side transfers from one to the other, as, for instance, in the use of pesticides, but often these attempts to transfer from a high technology to a low technology are more disruptive of the low technology than they are helpful. We have seen many examples of this in different parts of the world.

The same phenomenon is now becoming apparent between the space-military complex within the United States and the civilian economy. While there may be long-run technological payoffs on earth for all this elaborateness of space and rocketry, miniaturization, and so on, the payoffs do not seem to be for this generation. A recent study of the Denver Research Institute, for instance, suggested that the spillover effects from the space-military operation in Colorado into the civilian economy were very small. Melman, again, has given a number of instances in which there has been complete failure to make this transfer.

The end result of all this enormous resource devoted to the space-military complex may be the self-subsistent household or grounded space capsule, resting comfortably on earth, but getting all its power from solar batteries, all its food from algae on the roof, and all its information from predigested tapes. This seems a long way off and I am not sure I want it even if we can get it.

THE COSTS OF GREATNESS

In considering the impact of "greatness" on the American economy, we must take into account not merely the direct alternative costs for economic development and human welfare of the space-military complex, high as these are; we must also take into account the possible discounted costs of deterrence as an international system, particularly when deterrence itself is threatened by greatness in the sense of a Napoleonic desire to impose our will and our way of life on all the peoples of the world. Even if we suppose that the international system operates by pure deterrence, or balance of terror, it can be shown that this has a fairly high negative present value. A system of deterrence is a system of mutual threat and counter-threat, summed up by the mutual posture: "If you do something nasty to me, I will do something nasty to you." In the case of the United States and the Soviet Union, and eventually other potential nuclear powers, the "something nasty" is very large indeed. It could involve the loss of more than half of the total population, and perhaps considerably more than half of the total capital. We do not really know much about the full consequences of a large-scale nuclear exchange. It is certain, however, that it would alter the whole ecological system of the earth very adversely from the point of view of man's welfare, and the probability that the disaster might prove to be irretrievable in view of its ecological consequences is at least an uncomfortably high number. In a system of deterrence, however, the probability that the threats will be carried out *must* be above some "noticeable" minimum. Otherwise the credibility of the threats falls to zero, and since the stability of the system depends on the credibility of the threats being above a certain threshold, it is clear that if the probability of the threats being carried out falls below a certain point, the whole system collapses. Either it simply ceases to organize human behavior—that is, the bluff is called—or in an attempt to restore credibility, the threats are actually carried out. There is, of course, no empirical method of estimating the probability of nuclear disaster in any one year. In the light of the previous history of the international system, however, in which systems of deterrence have rarely lasted more than twenty-five years, it would seem not unreasonable to put this probability at something between 1 and 5 per cent per annum. Even if we take the lower of these figures, this cumulates rather alarmingly in a hundred years. Thus the probability of its not coming off in a hundred years is $(99/100)^{100}$, which is 0.36. So that the probability of disaster in any hundred years' period under this system is 0.64—two in three! If the chance is 5 per cent per annum, of course, the chance of disaster even in twenty years is 0.64, and in one hundred years is .994! In making any estimate of the cost of the Great Society, therefore, assuming that the Great Society implied a rather grand Napoleonic military posture, we should calculate the present value of the possible loss from nuclear warfare and subtract this from the gross national product. In spite of the fact that there is no empirical method of estimating these probabilities and any figures can be only illustrative, it is clear that this deduction from the real value of the G.N.P. could easily be very large, even on the order of magnitude of the G.N.P. itself. If the disaster is really irretrievable, then even the smallest chance of it reduces the real value of the G.N.P. to zero, or, rather, reduces the capital value in terms of human welfare of the United States itself as an organization to zero. Consequently, in any decent world the United States would be bankrupted and dissolved. It is quite possible, therefore, that the real cost of the Great Society is so high as to make its net value zero or even negative.

Economists are notoriously interested in the long run. They have a habit, indeed, of regarding themselves as the trustees for posterity. I may be excused, therefore, as an economist, for looking beyond the immediate political and economic exigencies of the present day and asking, what does the Great Society mean in the longer perspective of human history? I have elsewhere expanded on the idea[3] that the present period in human history represents an extraordinary transition, what I have sometimes called the Third Great Transition, from the age of civilization which began with the urban revolution of 3000 B.C. to something which is qualitatively different and which I now call the Developed Society. The Developed Society, of course, is the kind of world that will result from the process of development as we see it going on today. It is very important, therefore, to ask of any particular political program what is its contribution toward this great transition. Is it going to make it more dangerous or less dangerous? Will it speed it up or slow it down? Or will it even prevent it altogether? I am not arguing, of course, that the Developed Society will be a stagnant perfection. I do argue, however, that the evolutionary process throughout its whole vast span of time has been characterized by short periods of very rapid change followed by rather long periods of slow change, and one sees this also in human history. We have already gone through two transition periods of very rapid change. One from the paleolithic to the neolithic, the other from the neolithic to civilization. The present period is entirely comparable to these and of even greater magnitude. If we are interested in development, therefore, it is quite legitimate to ask what the developed society looks like, even though we are not going to be able to spell it out in detail, and even though the developed society itself will undergo a continuous change and transformation, albeit, one suspects, at a somewhat slower rate than we are having now.

THE SPACESHIP ECONOMY

The present transition is characterized by, and indeed largely caused by, a mutation in the process of growth of human knowledge which we call science. We are still very much in the middle of this process. In fact, it is doubtful whether we have yet reached the middle, and it seems probable that the next fifty years will see a rate of change at least equal to what we have seen in the last century, perhaps even greater. Certainly, the impact of the biological sciences on the condition of man and the nature of his social system is going to be as spectacular as the impact of physics and chemistry, and we have hardly seen the beginning of this. Some people tend to view the transition as a prospect of absolutely unlimited expansion. This tends to be the communist view, with the deification of man and what seems to me a naïve faith in his absolutely unlimited powers.

I take a somewhat more restricted and pessimistic view myself: that the real significance of this transition is that it represents a change from an open society characterized by a through-put of material (with ores and fossil fuels as inputs and pollutable reservoirs as recipients of outputs), to a closed society in the material sense, in which there are no longer any mines or pollutable reservoirs, and in which therefore all material has to be recycled. This is what I have called the "spaceship earth," since a spaceship, especially if it has to go on long voyages, will have to be a miniature of a closed system of this kind. In a spaceship, clearly there are no mines and no sewers. Everything has to be recycled; man has to find a place in the middle of this cycle. The spaceship earth simply repeats this on a larger scale. Up until the present transition, man has always lived from the point of view of his own inner image of himself and his environment, on a great plane. There has always been somewhere to go, mountains or oceans to cross, new sources of supply to exploit, and new geographical worlds to conquer. Today the great plane has become a sphere, and the spherical closed nature of man's physical environment is becoming increasingly a part of his image. When we look at the earth from space, we realize very closely what a small, closed, crowded spaceship it is. National boundaries are virtually invisible even from a jet, and nobody has the nerve to claim national sovereignty beyond the atmosphere.

The consequences of this transition from the great plane to the closed sphere are profound in all spheres of life. In economics, this represents a transition from what I have called the "cowboy economy" of exploitation and pollution to the "space man economy" which is characterized by extreme conservation. Whether the desperate necessity of conservation will produce conservatism is an interesting problem. It is certainly not beyond the bounds of possibility that one of the things we will need to conserve is change itself, and the ability to change. In the spaceship economy, consumption is no longer a virtue but a vice; and a mounting G.N.P. will be regarded with horror. Human welfare will clearly be seen to depend not on the through-put of the society—that is, not on the amount it can produce and consume—but on the richness and variety of its capital stock, including, of course, the human capital. Consequently, anything which will conserve consumption and enable us to maintain a larger and more elaborate capital stock with smaller production would be regarded as desirable. Great stress would have to be placed on durability, both of things and of people. We may find, indeed, that the spaceship economy is not feasible without a substantial extension of human life, as George Bernard Shaw suggested in *Back to Methuselah*. I have discussed elsewhere[4] the appalling short-run consequences of cracking the aging barrier and extending human life beyond the Biblical allotted span. Nevertheless, if the spaceship earth is to be tolerable at all, it may well be that the consumption of human knowledge which takes place by the frightful toll of aging and death at the average age of seventy will be more than the resources of a depleted planet can cope with. We may end up, indeed, with a society not unlike the extraordinary vision of Godwin:

The whole will be a people of men, and not of children. Generation will not succeed generation, or truth have, in a certain degree, to recommence her career every thirty years. . . . There will be no war, no crimes, no administration of justice, as it is called, and no government. Besides this, there will be neither disease, anguish, melancholy, nor resentment. Every man will seek, with ineffable ardour, the good of all.[5]

What seemed absurd utopianism in 1793 may not seem absurd at all by 2500, for this may be the only way of life left open to the depleted earth.

A spaceship society does not preclude, I think, a certain affluence, in the sense that man will be able to maintain a physical state and environment which will involve good health, creative activity, beautiful surroundings, love and joy, art, the pursuit of the life of the spirit, and so on. This affluence, however, will have to be combined with a curious parsimony. Far from scarcity's disappearing, it will be the most dominant aspect of the society. Every grain of sand will have to be treasured, and the waste and profligacy of our own day will seem so horrible that our descendants will hardly be able to bear to think about us, for we will appear as monsters in their eyes.

RHETORIC AND REALITY

How far, then, does the Great Society assist in making this transition? It is hard to avoid giving it some rather bad marks. Greatness is a totally inappropriate moral attitude for a spaceship society, which has to be, above all things, modest. Greatness is all right on the great plains or on the great plane. It is wholly inappropriate to a tiny, fragile sphere. A spaceship cannot afford cowboys. It probably cannot even afford horses, and it certainly cannot afford men on horseback. It looks like a tea ceremony, not a parade ground. The slightest touch of grandiosity could ruin it. It involves conservation, coexistence, extreme care in conflict resolution, and, above all, no rocking of the boat. The careless expansionism which is characteristic of the idea of greatness is not merely inappropriate, it is a deep threat to the system.

It may be that I am being profoundly unfair, that I am confusing rhetoric with reality, and that my attack on the concept of greatness, which I fear and despise, is an attack only on political rhetoric, a rhetoric which is not to be taken seriously. Certainly the present administration should not be damned merely for its rhetoric, it should be judged also by its acts. My own rhetoric is that of the modest society, as I put it in speeches these days: "a little society where little people can have a little fun." Still, you may say, are not many of the acts of the present administration consistent with this? Is there not the anti-poverty program, the Peace Corps, Medicare, the new interest in the reform of cities, pollution control, civil rights, and so on? I am prepared to give credit here and without grudging. The anti-poverty program is a token, but it also represents a real social invention which may have large consequences for the future in the whole idea that the poor should organize themselves. The Peace Corps is likewise a token, but it is perhaps a symbol of better things to come, and returned Peace Corps members will unquestionably be a force for the enlivening and purification of American life. Medicare is a last act of a long drama of social security, and is at least designed to meet a real need. Possibly the new Department of Housing and Urban Development can act as a long-run force to undo some of the damage that has been done by public housing and urban renewal, which has been a ruthless destroyer of communities and, by and large, an instrument to inconvenience the poor with the object of restoring the central city to the middle classes.

I try to be fair, I even feel a desire to be helpful, yet I find myself seized with an uncontrollable revulsion which reduces me to a state of complete political incapacitation. At this point I cannot help being personal, and what follows has no pretensions to science, nor even to philosophy. Something about the senseless cruelty of the war in Vietnam and the attitude of self-righteous grandiosity which is implied has produced in me a political revulsion so deep that I have called into question the whole political movement of the last forty years, and I now perceive it as a gigantic piece of overlearning and mislearning. I belong to a generation which was traumatized by three great episodes: World War I, the Great Depression, and World War II. If graded, the world social system to which I belong clearly deserves a failing mark. On the other hand, my dissatisfaction with western liberalism does not drive me into the socialist camp, for what I see over there I like even less. I see there revolutionary sentimentality, oblivious of the fact that most revolutions have cost two generations of growth. I see miserable corruption of the arts; an appalling centralization of power; enormous and costly mistakes in social planning, such as the First Collectivization in the Soviet Union and the Great Leap Forward in China. I see sentimental imperialism, in the case of both the Soviet Union and China—there is no reason why Lithuania, Uzbekistan, Tibet, and so on should not be at least as independent as Poland or Rumania—and I see also an obsolete ideology corrupting the sciences as well as the arts and oppressing the free spirit of man. Where, then, do we go? To what standard do we repair? There seems to be nothing but sleazy national flags and obsolete slogans.

AN ALLIANCE OF RIGHT AND LEFT

In this vast political and spiritual desert one looks for cases, where the springs of alienation can perhaps water new political mutations. One looks, perhaps for an uneasy alliance of right and left, producing hybrid vigor. The trouble with the center is that it is enormously powerful, for it can move either way, just as the present administration holds down the Right with its foreign policy and the Left with its domestic policy. The dissidents of both Right and Left are helpless and powerless, unless they can join to form a new center. A very critical question today, therefore, is whether the political spectrum is a line or a circle, and whether a new constellation is conceivable in which the learning process, of which the center is almost incapable because of its very success, can go on at the edges and unite to form a new center. This sounds almost absurd. Nevertheless, the political crisis of the world is so deep, the present system so untenable and outrageous, that the time may be ripening for a profound dialectical shift. Ordinarily I am not much impressed by dialectics, having much more faith in the long, slow, continuous changes which produce growth and knowledge and development. Yet, there are times when certain regroupings occur and are fruitful. This may be one of them.

It is far too early to try to spell out a program for the Right-Left, especially since if this comes off at all, there will have to be some hard bargaining. Each side will have to sacrifice something, and it is not altogether clear what will be sacrificed. Nevertheless, one might outline some tentative principles upon which such a bargain might be made:

1. A rediscovery of individualism, or what might, to get the best of all possible worlds, be called social individualism, as a political and social objective. This means stress on variety, peculiarity, even eccentricity; on the freedom to develop innumerable small subcultures; on the richness and variety of human potentiality. The enemies of this are conformity, consensus, compulsory chapel, the draft, monopolistic public education, the corporate image, and everything that tries to force people into too few molds. Granted that there must be molds, let's have a lot of them.

2. If social individualism is the objective, we must have a fairly sophisticated view as to how to get it. Freedom does not just happen, it has to be organized. Freedom is not anarchy, but neither does government necessarily produce it. The problem of how to organize so-

cial life in order to maximize freedom is a good operations-research type of problem, the solution to which, however, is by no means easy. In searching for the solution, some things must be borne in mind.

(a.) The market and the price system are enormously useful devices for the reconciliation of personal freedom with social control. I have illustrated this in my "green stamp plan" for population control, whereby every person receives by right of being an individual a license to have the socially desirable average number of children. Then a market is established in these licenses or fractions thereof, so that the philoprogenitive can buy them from those who do not wish to have children. Wide individual freedom is assured in a highly sensitive area, and yet over-all social control can be established, which is absolutely necessary in the spaceship earth. Political democracy and the legal system must be looked at as essentially generating and distributing processes for information and knowledge, and they must eventually be integrated with the broadening knowledge and methodology of the social sciences. There must be room here for social inventions yet to come, at the same time that traditional values are cherished. One speculates about limited world government, an antitrust law for nations, the breakup of the larger nations into smaller states to give something like perfect competition, the political legitimation of international business, and all sorts of problems which cannot be dealt with here.

(b.) There must be some doctrine about the dynamics of the transition from the great to the "modest" society. Revolution is out, since this just creates and reinforces greatness, pomposity, corruption of taste, and is likely to establish tyrannies. If revolution is out, however, we need to have an image of a dynamic by which legitimacy is gradually withdrawn from the old system and is acquired by the new, to the point where eventually the old system becomes merely a show and cannot cause any trouble. I am convinced that the dynamics of legitimacy is the key to this whole problem. The trouble is that I don't know anything about the dynamics of legitimacy.

Are there any signs in the above of the alliance of Right and Left to which I have referred? There are strong signs of social individualism on the Left. The "New Left" in the United States is far more individualistic than the old, much more concerned with freedom, with personality, really more anarchist than socialist, and it has at least a different set of illusions from its fathers. Even in the socialist countries, especially in Yugoslavia and Poland, one can see a movement toward social individualism. One sees this, for instance, in the revolt of the artists, one sees it in the extraordinary reawakening of interest in the market. Yugoslav economists come through all the time preaching Adam Smith and the virtues of the market, though none will go so far as to recommend a stock exchange. It may be that the collapse of empires and the doubling of the number of nations in the last twenty years is again a symptom of something very important—— the realization that national greatness is too expensive and that the people of a modest nation have a much better time, or at least a better chance in the long run of a better time.

In social policy one even finds curious alliances, for instance, on the principle of a guaranteed annual income or a negative income tax as a substitute for welfare, social security, and the whole impertinent apparatus of parental government. Furthermore, the rise of the peace movement, feeble as it is, in both the socialist and the liberal nationalist world, is again a symptom of a deep longing, of a profound dissatisfaction with the world as it is, even if at the moment it seems pitifully weak.

I am prepared therefore to detect an oasis, fed perhaps by two different springs. If their flow can be increased, the desert may yet turn into a garden.

•NOTES

1.   OVERTAKE DATES

	Per Capita G.N.P., 1957 $U.S.	Rate of Growth, 1950–1960	Year in Which Country Overtakes U.S. in Per Capita G.N.P.
United States	2577	1.6%	—
West Germany	927	6.5	1979
Switzerland	1428	3.7	1986
Japan	306	8.0	1992
Italy	516	5.2	1999
France	943	3.5	2011
Netherlands	836	3.6	2014
Sweden	1380	2.6	2020
Norway	1130	2.6	2040
Denmark	1057	2.6	2047
Belgium	1196	2.3	2069
United Kingdom	1189	2.2	2086
Canada	1947	1.2	Never

SOURCES: Bruce M. Russett, *World Handbook of Political and Social Indicators* (New Haven: Yale University Press, 1964), p. 155; Angus Maddison, *Economic Growth in the West* (New York: Twentieth Century Fund, 1964), p. 30.

2. Seymour Melman, *Our Depleted Society* (New York: Holt, Rinehart, and Winston, 1965).

3. K. E. Boulding, *The Meaning of the Twentieth Century* (New York: Harper & Row, 1964).

4. K. E. Boulding, "The Menace of Methuselah: Possible Consequences of Increased Life Expectancy," *Journal of the Washington Academy of Sciences*, LV, No. 7 (October 1965), 171–179.

5. William Godwin, *Enquiry Concerning Political Justice* (1793).

Chapter 10

🐚 *Science in the Great Society*

DON K. PRICE

Anyone who proposes to talk about the relationship of two things, especially such abstract things as science and the Great Society, will find it helpful to know something about at least one of them. To this end, it was hoped that my collaborators in this volume would agree on what the Great Society is, so I would be informed. But alas, no matter how powerful President Johnson's magic may be in producing a consensus among congressmen, it is clear that his spell has not worked on this particular group of scholars. Since my colleagues do not agree on a definition of the Great Society, I shall have to produce my own, or go without one.

If a definition of the Great Society means a systematic statement of its purpose and goals, I think I must get along without it. This is not altogether because I am too lazy or timid to propose one. It is even more because I believe that it is a good thing that, over the past several centuries, we have shifted from the traditional philosophy to the experimental sciences as the main method of getting the knowledge we need to guide political action. Consequently we think less in terms of defining our ideal ends or purposes, and more in terms of putting together the results of our experiments in as workable a fashion as possible. And so, I believe that science serves society best not merely by helping to carry out purposes that have been predetermined by politics, but by helping to discover new goals for the politician, and—perhaps even more important—by helping to determine the nature of the processes by which goals are discovered and determined. In short, it seems to me that it is useful to think of science not as a tool of politics, but as an important part of politics.

This way of looking at the problem obviously makes it impossible to continue the conventional administrative view that, in governmental affairs, the scientist should simply do what politicians or administrators tell him to do. But it does not mean that the scientist is to be a new kind of philosopher-king, or even that there is no difference between his role and that of the politician. It only requires us to work out a more sophisticated theory of the role of science and scientists in a free political system. How should we approach this problem in the light of our hopes for the Great Society?

While I do not propose to define the Great Society, it is useful to start by appreciating its general flavor. I am less inclined than some of my colleagues to judge it as either a statement of academic philosophy or as a systematic political theory, which we could credit or blame for the state of the world today. It is a slogan summing up a political attitude that I generally share. It obviously contains a large dose of sympathy with the common man, and impatience with the privileges of those who have exploited or oppressed him. It has some traces of American populism, with the breeziness and breadth of the old Southwest. If we were to be pedantic and try to trace its earliest origins, we might even go back much earlier—to the fourteenth century, when, Trevelyan tells us, the agitators of the Peasants' Rebellion "came bearing, not general exhortations, but a particular command from 'the Great Society,' as they called the union of the lower classes which they were attempting to form." [1]

But it should clearly be seen in a different context, for the Great Society, as President Johnson has talked about it, certainly has no trace of class warfare in it. Its strongest element seems to me to be a staunch confidence in a distinctively Western idea that has come to seem naïve to many intellectuals in the mid-twentieth century: the idea of progress. As Yen Fu, one of the leaders of the Chinese revolution against the traditional philosophy and toward a scientific approach to society, remarked in the late nineteenth century, "The Chinese think of the process of nature and of human affairs in terms of a cycle of order and disorder, prosperity and decay. The Westerners make their ultimate principle of learning and political action the idea that the possibilities of daily progress are inexhaustible, that prosperity once achieved will not decline, and that order will not fall back to disorder." [2]

This was the Western view of progress—progress pushed ahead by a union of science with social purpose—as seen from the outside by a traditional Oriental country almost a century ago. Since that time this vision of progress has completed its transformation of European civilization, revolutionized Russia, and served as a beacon for the developing countries of Asia and Africa. It is obvious that science and technology are essential elements in this great series of revolutions. It is by no means obvious whether or not they influence those revolutions toward freedom or tyranny. Nor can we know whether the ultimate outcome of our so-called progress will be a utopia of peace and plenty, or the destruction of civilization in a nuclear holocaust, or (as I hopefully think more probable) some new way of carrying on the difficult and quarrelsome compromises by which men maintain their political existence. But mankind has learned how to use technology to enlarge its opportunities for good and for evil, by advancing its material progress. And the Great Society has embraced with enthusiasm the idea of furthering such progress by the advancement of science and education. Accordingly, we shall do well to pay particular attention to the relation of science to the development of our own political habits and institutions.

THE GREAT SOCIETY: POPULISM PLUS AN ESTABLISHMENT

We may as well start with the most conspicuously political phenomenon of science in the Great Society, in the vulgar sense of the word "political." President Johnson, in the 1964 election, had a large and aggressive organization of scientists and engineers campaigning for him. Earlier presidents, of course, had had groups of academic supporters, and Franklin Roosevelt, in particular, had commanded conspicuous groups of followers in the major universities. But those who were most conspicuous in the Roosevelt Brain Trust (and later among the Kennedy advisers) were not natural scientists, and they were sometimes thought of as more of a handicap than a help in the business of competing for votes. At that time, the typical politician still held to the myth that the average voter distrusted and disliked the egghead, and the official leadership of the scientific and academic communities was still predominantly inclined to distrust politics generally and to share the political views of the upper classes in whichever metropolitan centers they happened to live. For, as everyone knew, the American voter was not interested in basic science or higher education, and in the West and South he was especially inclined to dislike anyone who had been given an impractical education in a center of intellectual snobbery, and to dislike even more the pretensions of the intellectual or professional elites and any influence that they might claim on the policies of the nation. Our populist tradition was, in short, intolerant of theoretical learning and the financial establishment that supported it. I recall with affection a backwoods Oklahoma politician in the depths of the Depression, who refused to let me interview him because he had learned that my political research was supported by money from the Rockefeller Foundation.

In the era of Bryan and McKinley, many conservatives made the mistake of thinking that the agrarian populists were economic radicals who were against private property. What the populists really wanted was not to abolish property, but to get some for themselves. Rural economic radicalism became much less important after cheap farm credit and soil conservation and crop controls—and after the agricultural scientists, in the years 1940 to 1960, doubled the grain output per acre on the better farms of the country.

Something like the same change has now taken place in the political attitude toward science. We began to give federal support to universities—private as well as state universities—as a matter of wartime expediency, under the guise of contracts for particular weapons systems. For a generation our scientists have been frightened by the thought that, once the backwoods politicians caught on to the fact that a lot of money was really going into basic research and education in our major universities, they would want to stop it. And now we have a President from a teachers' college in Texas who has continued to expand his budget for basic research while cutting down on funds for the engineering aspects of space and atomic energy—and who has brought into the most influential position in his Cabinet with respect to education and science a man from the Carnegie Corporation of New York who is an unabashed advocate of maintaining the highest standards of education and scientific excellence in the best universities in the country. All the President has asked for the Great Society is that a lot of other institutions, in all parts of the country, be brought up to something like the same high standards of excellence, and that federal money be distributed accordingly. The Great Society may have its roots in the populist tradition, but populism now is to have its own establishments. The complaint among academic conservatives, we may well expect, will be that the man in the White House wants to share the wealth of the intellectuals and may even get around to making every man a professor.

It is clear, moreover, that the Great Society is committed not merely to using the resources of government to support science but to calling on science to help attain the objectives of government. When President Johnson appeals for a massive attack on disease, on the pollution of our air and water, and on the degradation of our urban environment—indeed, as he goes on to propose that we plan to control the weather—it is clear that he and his lieutenants intend to mobilize the nation's science and technology in those campaigns. And never before has a President so sweepingly proposed to apply the methods of science to the improvement of the management of government departments. The operations researchers, having conquered the generals and the admirals in the pitched battles of the Pentagon, are now being sent off, under the banner of cost effectiveness, on an even more difficult and protracted mission: to track down the guerrillas in the jungles of the civilian bureaus and to eliminate insurgency among them and their covert allies in the congressional committees.

We must not, of course, give President Johnson either the praise or the blame for all these developments, which were well on their way before his inauguration. But when he embraces and extends them— he, as the first President from a Southern backwoods constituency since his namesake a century ago—it is an obvious sign that we have passed a turning point in our political history. In the days of Jefferson and John Quincy Adams, the more popular of our parties was conspicuous for its support of science and for its enlistment of men of science into public affairs. The Jacksonian revolution was significant not merely for what it did to the civil service and the banking system but for what it did to the political role of scientific intellectuals. It drove them out of politics, and for more than a century the scientific leadership of the country turned naturally to private universities and private donors to protect themselves against political interference— and in the process generally allied themselves with the conservative leadership of urban and industrial America. Now we have swung back again, and anyone who is eager to maintain a reasonable balance between our two major political parties may have reason to worry that we seem today to be putting all our eggheads in one basket. At least, one might have been distressed a couple of years ago, before the egghead vote began to split—as the egghead vote always does—because of the intellectual's characteristic discomfort when he finds himself associated with the common or majority opinion.

UTOPIA DESOCIALIZED

Science has clearly become a part of our political system, and scientists have joined the other pressure groups in political action. This phenomenon tempts us to worry about the possibility that science may become an arm of dictatorship. After all, from Bacon's *New Atlantis* to modern science fiction, the utopian dream of a civilization in which science is the dominant influence never seems to be one that would tolerate a great deal of political difference of opinion or leave room for a free political contest for power. And the actual nature of political systems whose ideologies are most ostentatiously based on science—namely, the professedly Marxist systems—give some cause for the same concern.

We have plenty of problems, but this is not one of them. Or so I am strongly inclined to believe when I consider either the practical institutional ways in which science has been influencing the Great Society, or the ways in which the basic theory of science seems to be influencing the political thought of the United States.

Arthur Bentley's most useful insight, it seems to me, was one that cut through the legalistic view of the political system, and saw that institutions and groups that we conventionally consider private are just as effectively a part of the process of government as are legislatures and bureaucrats and party leaders. This insight has been confirmed by what has been happening first in the major scientific and technological programs of government since the beginning of World War II, and next in the major new social programs of the Great Society. No one seemed to be very surprised when, on the model of the wartime research programs, the postwar atomic energy and space programs were built on a system that was not an extended bureaucracy but a network of contracts with private institutions. And then later it apparently seemed entirely natural when the federal poverty program began to be administered not by direct federal agents, not even by grants to the states or the municipalities, but by contracts in city after city with specially created private corporations. And hardly anyone noticed when California, being concerned about some of the older and grubbier problems of government—problems like garbage disposal, urban transportation, and criminal law enforcement—contracted with aerospace industries to help plan what the state and municipal agencies should do in these traditional fields. Theoretical political scientists in the philosophical tradition used to ridicule professors of public administration by saying that they were the types who counted the manholes in the sewers. Now the theorists are punished for their snobbery: they are in turn being snubbed by the types who count manholes, or anything else, with the help of mathematical methods that the theorists cannot understand and computing machinery that they cannot afford. Even though I am an old public administrator, my sympathy for the underdog is now leading me to rise to the defense of the political theorist.

And as any theorist observes the ways in which the new methods of science are being brought to bear on our old problems, he should not fail to note this point: science can be used either to serve the purposes of centralized authority or to help decentralize it. On this great issue of politics, science as such is neutral. But American scientists are obviously not. My favorite example has to do with my old home territory of Appalachia. The Systems Development Corporation, one of our foremost institutions for encouraging the application of the behavioral and informational sciences—especially the more advanced information processing systems—to various areas of public concern, undertook to help the Department of Commerce set up its Appalachian redevelopment program. It did not see its objective as that of creating a single authoritative agency or program; it defined it instead as one of helping the Appalachian Regional Commission work out the details of its "interface with federal, state and local governmental jurisdictions and agencies." It is this kind of decentralized effort for which I am sure President Johnson was searching when he called for new concepts of creative federalism in a society that is being tied ever more tightly together by the new power of modern technology.

If scientists are throwing their influence in the direction of decentralizing, rather than centralizing, power, one might ask whether this is only a matter of tradition or whether, in some fundamental sense, their ideas about science give them a bias in the direction of political freedom. On the side of tradition, one might argue that the notions of freedom of thought to which their university traditions have trained them were the product not so much of the scientific as of a particular religious set of beliefs. But even so, it seems clear that the idea of science that has been most influential in the United States is not one that proposes to make a single system of scientific thought the basis for a political philosophy. And it seems equally clear that recent developments in the basic sciences themselves—in both their theory and their forms of institutional support—are making it even less likely that any authoritarian ideology can be built on modern scientific ideas. In short, it seems to me as a layman that the trends of thought in modern science are strengthening the basis of our traditional preference for a free and pluralistic social system rather than undermining it.

The difference of opinion on this question is the great gulf in political thought in the modern world. A decade ago, I quite accidentally turned up in Warsaw at the same time that the International Philosophical Association was for the first time bringing together the most eminent philosophers of the West with those of the communist East. As a rank outsider, I was smuggled into the meeting by a friend. And I shall never forget how the communist Chinese delegates, graduates of a major American university, threw a monkey wrench into the intellectual gears of the meeting when they announced at the outset that the three leading social scientists of the twentieth century were Lenin, Stalin, and Mao Tse-tung, who had stated for all time the theoretical basis for philosophy, the natural sciences, and politics, all rolled into one—the perfect guide for an ordered society.

It is tempting, of course, to dismiss this kind of idea, and to say that political dictatorship invents such an ideology to justify its own purposes. But it seems to me that the opposite is nearer the truth: an authoritarian way of thought brings a dictatorship into being. You can find the intellectual roots of Lenin's system in a revolutionary thinker like Chernyshevsky, who avowedly based his political thought on scientism—the idea of Feuerbach that philosophy should be wholly replaced by the natural sciences.[3] Or you can find the roots of Mao in Yen Fu's belief that Western science was not merely useful for its practical applications, but as a basis for the ordering of human society, especially if mixed judiciously with the traditionally monistic philosophy of the Tao.[4]

It seems to me a most interesting coincidence that American liberals and radicals turned away from the idea of reforming the nation by a progressively more centralized system soon after the period in the development of science in which the neat unity of the old mechanistic physics began to break up. In the late nineteenth century, it must have seemed plausible to the Marxists that their materialist theory of politics could be married to the notion of a single system of scientific thought. For were not the positivists, following Comte, proving that the methods of the physical sciences were being extended to the biological, and would soon be able to conquer the social sciences? But today, it seems to laymen like myself that, since the scientific revolution of relativity, indeterminacy, and the quantum theory, the philosophic outlook of physicists has become much less clear and certain, much less confident and united, than it must have seemed to laymen a few generations ago. And while biologists are just as eager as ever to base their knowledge of living organisms on what physics and chemistry can reveal as to the molecular foundation of living matter, they are obviously divided with respect to the possible extent of determining and predicting organic behavior, and even with respect to the extent to which they should base their research strategy on a "reductionist" approach. From its own point of view, Marxism was lucky in growing up in an era of simple faith in the authority of science.

But I do not really believe that differences in political thought are mainly accounted for by this kind of change in the philosophy of science. One reason is that the philosophy of science has not changed in any fundamental way: it still, of course, seeks to explain and predict material phenomena by understanding the basic nature of matter and by correlating material events. The difference of opinion regarding the political function of science, moreover, did not develop as a result of the twentieth-century scientific revolution. It was already in existence at a much earlier stage of scientific thought. For example, Jefferson, even though confident that science was the natural source of political revolution, refused to accept the theory of some of the French scientists who would have made their deterministic beliefs into a substitute for religion and ethics. Or for a later example, T. H. Huxley, whom we tend to remember as the scientist who was always at war with the bishops over evolution, attacked Comte's positivism for disregarding freedom in human nature and in society. Huxley, even though he was eager to see society organized on a new and scientific basis, drew a sharp distinction between his ideas and Comte's. For Comte, he said, wanted to make scientists into a "new priesthood," and to have them govern by a political system that amounted to "Catholicism *minus* Christianity." [5] Huxley himself saw freedom of choice and ethical responsibility as the essential bases for progress in science itself, just as he assumed them as the foundations of a free political system. It was not the last time that a natural scientist was to be less ambitious than a social scientist for the assumption of political authority by the scientific method and the scientific community.

TECHNOLOGICAL PURPOSE AND THE PUBLIC INTEREST

But if the typical American scientist is not interested in uniting his science to any general ideology or any general political purpose, he has been deeply interested in uniting it to some particular political purpose. Scientists in academic institutions have greatly strengthened the basic research programs of the United States during the last generation and have gone far toward persuading politicians that science is worth supporting for the sake of the advancement of knowledge. Nevertheless, nine-tenths of what laymen call "science" in America today is applied research and technological development, supported by government or business for the practical benefits that it will bring to society, or to some segment of society. Of the remaining part that is labeled "basic research," four-fifths, if not nine-tenths, is supported by business corporations or government agencies which expect it to contribute, in the long run, to their practical purposes. Even the National Science Foundation itself, which comes the closest to getting funds for the support of basic research for its own sake, occasionally finds that congressmen support its budget because they see a long-run connection between the advancement of basic knowledge and concrete political objectives like national security or industrial wealth.

Many scientists feel that they are trapped by their new source of wealth. Fundamental science—the work of men whose main motive is to advance knowledge and understanding—is supported largely by funds granted in the hope of advancing some particular policy or purpose. Scientists may therefore fear that their new dependence on politicians may some day subject them to political control.

Now obviously this is a danger, in theory. In practice, I do not consider it a clear and present danger, since we have several protections against it. One protection is the system by which universities are governed; the better state universities have proved that dependence on public funds does not inevitably lead to political interference with the freedom of research. Another protection is the variety of the sources of funds; as long as scientists and universities can shop around among various donors, their free bargaining position is considerably enhanced. Given these protections, the small minority of scientists who are interested in—and capable of—doing work of the most original and fundamental nature are probably freer today in the United States to pursue their own interests than they ever were. If a danger arises, the scientific community is now better organized than ever, more alert to the problem, and in a stronger position to present its case to the public. There is no doubt about the potential danger, but at least we are on our guard.

But the new relation of science to politics has created another danger—one that is more subtle and that we are less prepared to deal with. This is the danger, not to science, but to politics. Our traditional system of political responsibility was based on the assumption that elected politicians would first determine our purposes—that is, enact or proclaim our policies—and then use science and technology as tools by which such purposes would be served and such policies administered. Under such a system, the narrow purposes of the specialist would be kept subordinated to the general interests of the citizen: the citizen as voter could hold accountable his elected political leaders, and they in turn could coordinate and direct the work of the scientists and technological specialists. Underlying the procedures of this system, of course, were philosophical and educational assumptions: the philosophical assumption was that men should deduce their right actions from a permanent system of values, and the educational assumption was that the ruling politicians should have an education designed to inculcate those values.

This pattern obviously did not fit a country that, in response to ideas such as those of Franklin and Jefferson, had abolished established churches and set up land-grant colleges. Yet as students of politics, or as political reformers, we are still tempted by it and still inclined to think that we could restore the supremacy of humane values over impersonal technology, and restore the control of the elected representative over specialized bureaucrats, if by some electronic magic we could only give Congress instantaneous and complete access to all facts. This kind of notion reduces a difficult problem—the problem of relating our technology to our ethical and political purposes—to a simple problem, one of defeating a conspiracy within the executive branch to escape congressional control. As most people who work in the executive office of the President soon learn, however, the President himself is in just as much difficulty as the Congress; the new policies that technology has enabled the executive departments to adopt are not simply deductions from the President's wishes or additions to his power.

Quite aside from what we have been learning from experience with technological programs, we have been learning in administration and economics a number of useful lessons about the way in which policies and plans are developed within a government. The process is not one that simply deduces means from a predetermined end. As the economists have learned even in more or less socialized states, the authority that goes with government ownership does not make it possible or desirable to eliminate competition or to control all transactions in conformity with a predetermined plan; the plan itself must respond to the actions and experience of subordinate units. As students of management have learned, planning cannot be separated completely from responsibility for operations; the day-to-day decisions help to revise old plans of action and determine new ones, and effective administration requires initiative from the bottom as well as from the top.

What has happened in the sciences and technology is only the most powerful special case in this general lesson. The military services learned that the most important function of science was not to develop new weapons required by the generals and admirals; on the contrary, the innovations independently initiated by scientists and engineers became the basis of new strategy and the key to the roles and missions of the services. This made it desirable not merely to hire engineers to do particular jobs, but to establish alliances with scientific institutions, subsidizing their independent work. The A.E.C. and N.A.S.A. got the key point: if you wish to push ahead in a new field of action, you must not only pay for applied work directed toward what you know you want to do; you must also enlist in your cause a share of the best scientists in relevant fields, knowing that what they do may in the middle-range future bring about major changes in your own policies.

When I say "A.E.C." and "N.A.S.A.," I am of course personifying programs in the traditional way. A new Arthur Bentley would probably say, with more accuracy, not the A.E.C. but "The American Institute of Physics plus the Atomic Industrial Forum plus the Joint Committee on Atomic Energy"; and not N.A.S.A., but "the two congressional space committees, plus the aerospace industry, plus the electronics engineers and astronomers and computer specialists of America." These would be incomplete descriptions of the clusters of power involved—if I read Bentley correctly, he would have called them "cross-sectional activities"—but they serve to illustrate the point. Quite obviously our political leaders did not first decide to go to the moon and then instruct scientists and engineers to find out how to get there, but instead our politicians are committed to go there as a result of technological initiatives that produced a political consensus. And from the point of view of a system of political responsibility, this clearly is not a problem of the collapse of Congress in the face of Executive dictatorship; it was Senator Lyndon B. Johnson who got the process rolling while President Eisenhower was still trying to keep us from getting involved in an expensive space race.

So we should not be surprised to see the strategy which is now being used in various major fields of policy. If you want to get something done in a policy field, you get a group of research institutions allied with a congressional committee and an executive agency, preferably with the support of an enthusiastic economic pressure group. Oceanography, metropolitan transportation, air pollution, supersonic air transport, water resources, and Medicare are fields in which the technical experts and congressional leaders are now trying to create new government policy commitments more or less on the A.E.C. and N.A.S.A. models. This is not socialism in the traditional sense of government ownership; indeed, whenever the government now finds that it is doing something itself directly, it is tempted to look for ways to contract it out, or to offer to insure private institutions against loss on condition that they take the function over. Like a speculator on the stock market, it is not interested in full ownership; it buys its policies on margin, so to speak. Or, like an investment banker, it controls without ownership by underwriting the risky ventures. Any high-minded Fabian socialist, to say nothing of a stodgy old-fashioned Marxist, would look on what the United States is now doing as an irresponsible kind of bucket-shop socialism.

It is a system that has the great merits of flexibility and dynamism. It has its dangers, too, especially with respect to our system of political responsibility. But the dangers are not those that come from the encroachment on the functions of the Congress of a disciplined bureaucracy, controlled by a powerful presidency. As a nation, we have got accustomed to the fact that the old slogans of either socialism or free enterprise are irrelevant to our main issues today; we have pretty well learned the main lesson of our mixed economy. But we have not learned the corresponding lesson of our mixed political sys-

tem—a system in which the main problem of balance is not one between the President and Congress, but between the desires and beliefs
of politicians, on the one hand, and the constraints and imperative
impulses of science and technology, on the other. It is hard for us to
see the problem this way because of our habit of personifying both
the presidency and the Congress. We give the President credit, or
blame, for all the policy impulses that are manifested in the executive
branch, even those which he would wish to stop if anyone would only
tell him about them, and if he only had time to control the detailed
actions of his subordinates; and we attribute to Congress as a whole
the frustrations of any individual member who would like to control
a particular policy but cannot get the attention or support of a majority of his colleagues for the purpose.

The problem of political responsibility that is most acute in this
system is not how to find ways to give particular congressional committees more control over the Executive. It is how to give Congress
control over the several policies of its own committees. And the solution to that problem, if it is ever found at all, will surely include a
stronger demand from the Congress as a whole that the President exercise more effective political control over the myriad policies that
well up from the technological interests of the competing bureaus and
agencies that are supposed to report to him.

THE SOCIAL SCIENCES AND POLITICAL PURPOSES

The problem of political responsibility hardly exists at all in the
mind of anyone interested only in a particular technological purpose.
If you are obsessed with the development of supersonic transport, you
are likely to be impatient with the ideas of those who want to reduce
the nuisance of noise in metropolitan areas. If you are obsessed with
the need to increase the production of grain to feed a starving world,
you are not likely to give much weight to the views of those who are
worried about the dangers of pesticides to trout or quail. But a sense
of general responsibility is forced on anyone whose position requires
him to think about the ways in which various technological initiatives
come into conflict with each other, or with more general popular sen-
timents.

This happens both to politicians like the President whose responsibilities are general in nature and to those scientists who are called on to advise at levels in the hierarchy where generalizing decisions must be made. It also happens whenever any member of a committee of Congress chooses to look at problems from the general point of view and to ask for scientific advice accordingly.

For example, the Committee on Science and Astronautics of the House of Representatives has undertaken from time to time to stand aside from its main jurisdictional preoccupation with astronautics and to look at the more general issues arising from the impact of science on policy. When it called in an assorted group of scientists for such a general discussion earlier this year, the program covered everything from the effect on employment in Pittsburgh of new inventions in plastics to the threats posed to mankind by the danger of either too much political control over genetic processes in the United States or too little in India. And whenever any especially difficult issue would arise in the discussion, a congressman would ask some physicist or chemist or biologist for an answer, and he would reply, "But that is a problem for the social scientists."

Now everyone knows that in the caste system of the sciences, chemists and biologists rank a little below physicists, and the social sciences are only just moving up out of an untouchable status. So this willingness to call on the social sciences might seem a touching mark of esteem and affection. But I remembered Dorothy Parker's advice to the girl who had just been told that *he* loved her, and that he had

Never loved another one—
Lady, lady, better run.

If the social sciences hope to consolidate the degree of respectability as objective sciences that they have gradually been winning—if they wish to continue, as one physicist put it, to creep into the National Academy of Sciences—they had better run whenever they are asked by congressmen to answer the more difficult questions of contemporary social policy.

Dorothy Parker probably hoped, and certainly expected, that her counsel of prudence and conventionality would be ignored. And as for my own advice, so do I. Yet since I am not a poet, the form of prose discourse requires me to spell out, rather prosily, a couple of reasons why this counsel of prudence should not be merely overlooked —why, if the social sciences are to permit themselves to be seduced, they should know what they are getting into. The first reason is political; the second is scientific.

The political reason is that the social sciences do not know who will support them if they yield to this seduction. A generation or two ago, the answer to this question would have been easy. It was the liberals or the radicals who wanted to develop the social sciences so as to give government the ability, as it grew in scope and importance, to solve its problems in the public interest. Even though most reputable social scientists wanted to be objective and nonpartisan, their natural affinity was with the left. For they saw the main ills of society as the results of the selfishness of private interests, and the obvious remedy was to enable government to take action in the public interest. This was plausible as long as private business was opposing the increase in the scope of government action, and the underprivileged radicals were advocating it. But the world has changed: government now looks—through Arthur Bentley's spectacles—less like the embodiment of the natural law or general will and more like a conglomeration of special interests; private business is the operating partner in most government programs and likes the resulting combination of more money and less risk; organized labor looks less like a league of the oppressed and more like another powerful pressure group; and the radicals—at least the most conspicuous contemporary types—no longer have a formula for saving the world, but have evidently decided that it is not worth saving, especially by any processes that involve rational and organized effort. So obviously it is more prudent for social scientists to avoid tackling the big problems on which men disagree fundamentally with respect to values and purposes, and to take on assignments of a limited and instrumental nature in fields in which the big combinations of money and technology are producing the most novel and interesting special problems that can be handled by objective techniques.

But the social sciences have a more scientific reason for avoiding the big political and social issues. Only if they do so can they continue to pursue their development along lines that they consider truly scientific. The test of what is thought of as scientific, of course, includes two criteria: first, a science must try to understand phenomena not in terms of purpose or moral significance, but in more objective and less value-ridden terms; and second, it should try to concentrate on those aspects of any problem that can be measured and stated in quantitative terms.

Even within these limits, of course, the social sciences can find much to do that will have an important influence on major issues. In many subtle ways, our political system can act only on information that is available to it, and it is led in the directions that the information guideposts suggest. Where would our economic policy be today if the whole battery of economic data and techniques had not been built up, beginning with the work of the Department of Commerce on national income accounts in the 1920's—work that was first supported by grants from the Carnegie Corporation in one of the more far-sighted of its pilot projects—and continuing on to the more sophisticated economic indicators of the present time? Today, as the federal government sees its responsibility for social problems that run far beyond the scope of economic science, we doubtless need a more sophisticated set of measurements of social problems and of the effectiveness of policies that may be adopted to deal with them. Elsewhere in this volume Bell and Gross have made the case for more adequate "social indicators," and I need do no more in this essay than say that I share in the hope for their development.

As social scientists try to establish their status as objective and quantitative scientists, and concentrate more and more on methodological problems of a limited nature, they may be enhancing their actual influence but they are sure to seem more and more conservative in their influence on politics. This may be a matter of appearances only; after all, a man can believe firmly in a deterministic system and still have pronounced prejudices and a lively determination to change the nature of the system. The histories of Islam, of Calvinism, and of Marxism suggest that the most redoubtable efforts are exerted by those who believe in fate or predestination or some fixed law of history and are sure that they are cooperating with it. Even Arthur Bentley saw no incongruity in mixing his efforts to develop a rigorously scientific approach with an affirmation of faith in international peace—a faith which has, of course, been shabbily treated by subsequent history. As social scientists come to believe that they cannot mix their methodology and their policy views without damaging their status as scientists, they tend to seem much more neutral or conservative in their politics than their predecessors of a generation or two ago.

By contrast, the physical and biological scientists are under no such inhibitions. It has come to be accepted as an act of virtue whenever they manifest an interest not merely in science and technology but in their effects on the society or the political system. And there is surprisingly little complaint that such political activity jeopardizes their status as objective scientists.

The usual explanation for this difference is that the natural sciences are more mature, more fully developed than the social sciences, in the sense that they command a more exact body of data and a more highly generalized body of concepts. Obviously, in a conventional sense, physics differs from sociology or political science in some such way. But as Huxley noted nearly a century ago, social phenomena, so far as they can be dealt with scientifically, are just as materialistic and mathematical in theory as physics or astronomy—and the difference in degree is not the fundamental difference. The main distinction, it seems to me, is not in the nature of the sciences as such. If intelligent beings from another galaxy could study the earth without any idea of ever becoming involved in human affairs, they could be as scientific about the earth's economics or sociology as about its meteorology or geology.

The important difference between the sciences (or so it seems to one political scientist) is a political one. An economist is like a chemist in having a stake in the outcome of his research, in the sense that each can gain wealth or power by his knowledge. But the economist is unlike the chemist in that he can also influence the whole nature of the system that he studies by the power or wealth he may be able to command: that seems to me the essential difference between the chairman of the Council of Economic Advisers and the chairman of the Atomic Energy Commission. In the physical sciences it may be true that the observer cannot stand apart from his data to quite the extent believed in the nineteenth century; in some esoteric experiments, his own processes of observation may influence the data that he observes, no matter how hard he tries to avoid doing so. But the physical scientist is not involved with his data in the sense that, within the scope of his science, he has both the desire and the ability to influence the way his data behave. But the economist or sociologist or political scientist is so involved—whether he knows it or not— either as one who has entered the arena of public action as an operator or an adviser to operators, or as one who confines himself to purely objective and quantitative calculations in a spirit of academic detachment, which is itself a form of commitment to a particular theory regarding the duty of the scholar in society. In short, all social scientists are condemned by the nature of their subjects to work in fields where it is especially hard to establish their objectivity and their status as true scientists.

All social scientists, that is, except me. Like all of them, I consider myself the uniquely detached and objective observer. In that capacity I am obliged to sum up my observations regarding the status of social science today: if it wishes to be prudent, and to establish its scientific status, it should concentrate on methodology and avoid the big issues.

Having done my duty as a scientist, I am free to shift to a normative role and conclude by giving advice, both direct advice and advice disguised as predictions. And this advice is quite the opposite of my counsel of prudence. It goes counter to the prevailing academic fashions, which are pushing the social sciences entirely in the direction of the methods of the natural sciences, and are pushing administrators to convert themselves into operations researchers or systems analysts.

The main point, of course, is that wherever science touches on action—wherever research is related to political decisions—the facts alone are never a sufficient guide. This is (I trust the distinction is obvious) not to deny that one should decide only after knowing the facts as fully and clearly as possible, and not to deny that science provides indispensable methods, ever growing in power and discrimination, for understanding those facts. But the methods of systems analysis work only within the broad constraints of policy judgments and assumptions and purposes, and if the systems analyst is given a manageable assignment, the responsible political authority must still fit his system into a larger framework. How voters visualize that larger framework is, I suppose, a pedantic way to define the people's vision of the Great Society.

In dealing with that larger framework, we need both the understanding of the scholar and the skill of the practitioner.

As for the role of scholarship, the social sciences now have a special opportunity. In relation to government, they are caught in the middle: the National Science Foundation proposes to support those parts of the social sciences that look most scientific in their method, and the others are free to turn to the new Foundation for the Arts and Humanities. This split is not a new one: the social science Research Council has always had its scientific wing embraced by the National Research Council and its historical and philosophical wing by the American Council of Learned Societies. But this position is one of promise as well as difficulty. Social scientists should simply accept the fact that their interests inevitably include problems that will respond to objective and mathematical methods of analysis, along with others that can be dealt with only synthetically, with guidance from a sense of historical or philosophical or moral purpose. If they do, they will be able to deal with the big as well as the little issues of the day. If they can train themselves to be restrained and discriminating in their judgments, so that they can tell when they are being relatively precise and objective in their methods, and when they are guided by other types of thought, they may find their work more generally acceptable and less likely to be identified with one or another political interest. But we had better not expect such perfection in the predictable future. The layman will, sooner or later, get used to the fact that economists and sociologists, as well as physicists and chemists, can have political differences of opinion even in the fields in which their own scientific skills are involved.

As for the practitioners, it is clear that the American politician is not eager to have a closed corps of bureaucrats separating him from the scientific and technical specialists whose work is continuously shaping the future of our policy. The role of administration, as a function which helps synthesize the output of the specialists into material the top politicians can use, will surely continue to grow in importance, but not to become identified with any corporate personnel system or with any set type of educational preparation. It is a generalizing or synthesizing function for which scientific training alone is not a sufficient preparation. But natural scientists, social scientists, and men of all sorts of education and experience are likely to learn it. The competition of various disciplines and professions for pre-eminence in this governmental function will be one of the most important and interesting phenomena of the American political system within the next generation.

Administration is not a job for a club of amateurs; it will require a mixture of men who together can understand and command a wide range of professional skills. And it is not a job for those with no interest in policy objectives; it requires (as Paul Appleby long since taught us) men who are aware of the political and power significance of what they do. But if it is not a job for the neutral amateur, neither is it one for the zealot or the committed partisan. A measure of detachment, of temperamental objectivity, has an advantage in this role that goes beyond mere survival value. This type of objectivity comes from a kind of social tradition or corporate value system, not from a rigorously quantitative method: the men who come closest to exemplifying it in the upper ranges of public administration are those trained in the least scientific of the professions—the law.

We are fully committed, in the Great Society, to supporting the sciences both for their own sake and for the practical benefits that they can bring us. They have become a positive force, with an initiative of their own, in our political system. How they will redefine our conception of the public interest and the purposes of civilization, and whether their forces can be kept under the control of responsible constitutional processes, will be a crucial question, through the next generation or two, for both the scholar and the politician. In the Great Society, they are going to be obliged to be partners whether they like it or not.

•NOTES

1. G. M. Trevelyan, *England in the Age of Wycliffe* (London: Longmans, Green, 1915), p. 199.

2. Benjamin Schwartz, *In Search of Wealth and Power* (Cambridge, Mass.: Belknap Press of Harvard University, 1964), p. 44.

3. Adam B. Ulam, *The Bolsheviks* (New York: Macmillan, 1965), p. 58.

4. Schwartz, *op. cit.,* pp. 37, 78.

5. T. H. Huxley, "The Scientific Aspects of Positivism," in *Lay Sermons, Addresses, and Reviews* (New York: Appleton, 1871).

Chapter 11

The Politics of the Impossible— Art and Society   ALVIN TOFFLER

THE NEED FOR RATIONAL ART POLICIES

As America accelerates its thrust toward superindustrialism, strange new problems will erupt into the arena of politics. Among these, none will be more awkward than the dilemmas relating to cultural policy. Such problems will frustrate even the most astute political leaders and administrators, for in no field are the issues cloudier, the verbiage thicker, the data thinner, and the whole basis for rational decision making more doubtful. Politics may be the art of the possible; art may turn out to be the politics of the impossible.

The emergence of art as an important political concern in the United States has already begun. Behind much of the oratory about the Great Society lies an assumption that the nation must aspire to artistic greatness and that government must, in some manner, help bring this about. Presidential statements are increasingly peppered with references to art, beauty, and the quality of life. Whether such remarks are inspired by altruism or, as some have suggested, by shrewd politics on the part of a President unpopular among Eastern intellectuals, is quite unimportant. What matters—what is propelling art into politics—is that controversial phenomenon known as the "culture explosion."

Since the end of World War II broad sectors of the American public have noticeably shifted their attitude toward the arts. Part of a generalized concern with the texture of life, the new attitude is re-

flected in rising attendance at theaters, museums, and concert halls.
Sales of books, records, and other cultural goods and services are
mounting. Handsome new cultural centers are cropping up in city
after city, and amateur participation in music, painting, theater, and
dance is increasing. By 1965 this wave of interest had grown so strong
that the term "culture boom" was part of the nation's everyday vo-
cabulary, and Congress, after years of dawdling, enacted legislation
creating a National Foundation on the Arts and Humanities to channel federal funds into the arts.

It is by no means surprising, therefore, that a "culture lobby" has
begun to take form across the nation. This lobby, composed of arts
organizations, foundations, fund raisers, patrons, businessmen, and
ordinary culture consumers, will in the future make itself felt not
merely at local and state levels but on the national scene as well. It
will form temporary alliances with other interest groups—with education, with conservationists, with non-profit organizations such as
hospitals and research centers, with professional societies, and others.
It will adopt novel methods to attract public attention and support,
and, occasionally, to harass its foes. As time goes by, its demands will
increase in number, complexity, and scale.

At present neither the lobby nor the rapidly expanding "industry" it represents has anything like a national program. Indeed, little
effort has been made anywhere to define cultural goals for the nation,
except in the most rhetorical terms. The result is that pragmatic policy makers, at whatever level, have no systematic frame of reference
against which to evaluate a welter of proposals for the support of the
arts.

The policy maker, moreover, confronts two special problems in
dealing with the arts. First, communication is difficult because the
cultural community and its representatives are accustomed to discourse in annoyingly imprecise language. Second, and more important,
attempts to measure, quantify, or even to approach ordinary problems rationally are frequently resented. (The fact that planning, organization, and management in cultural institutions have been, until
now, extremely haphazard is not unrelated to the widespread belief
that art, at its core, is non- or anti-rational.)

It is not necessary here to debate the relationship of reason to art,
for there is an indispensable distinction to be drawn between creating
a work of art and creating the social arrangements necessary to the
support of art. The artist must know his medium. Those who wish to

modify social arrangements must know their medium, too. But their medium is society itself. And whether the artist works rationally or not, those charged with the organization of social institutions are unquestionably more effective when they employ rational means than when they fail to do so.

In this essay, therefore, I shall attempt to apply rational method to the design of cultural goals. I shall use the terms "culture" and "the arts" to refer, more or less loosely, to what others prefer to call the fine arts or high culture. Thus, I will include under these terms painting, sculpture, music, drama, dance, literature, and the art film. Although a perfectly legitimate case might be made for extending the definition to include such activities as industrial design, city planning, or handicrafts, for the purposes of this discussion it will be useful to use the narrower definition.

This essay is, in one sense, an exercise. The method to be employed in arriving at cultural goals will strike those accustomed to policy making in other fields as hopelessly naïve and simplistic. To many in the arts, on the other hand, it will appear mechanistic and "overscientific." I am not prepared to defend the method against these charges, but rather to suggest that it is a first primitive attempt to raise the process of decision making in the arts above the level of total subjectivity. I would argue that, with all its defects, it is superior to the way in which most cultural policy issues are now decided.

Those who read the essay hoping to find in it a comprehensive list of objectives, a neat, ten-point policy guide to the arts, will also be disappointed. For the result of this exercise is nothing more than three proposals, highly tentative and in no sense all-inclusive. The goals I propose represent only a few points on an otherwise blank sheet of paper. They need to be supplemented with ten or twenty additional items.

Nevertheless, application of rational method to the problem of cultural policy yields novel insights. It leads, I think the reader will agree, to some surprising and controversial proposals. Thus, it is not my hope that the goals proposed here will be adopted widely and easily, but rather that they—and especially the method used in arriving at them—will serve as the basis for fresh and fruitful debate about the whole untidy business of cultural policy and policy making.

In any field, at any given moment, the policy maker must operate from a hierarchy of values, tacit or stated. His highest order values may be handed down by higher authority, they may be prescribed by the constitution of his organization, or he may be free to specify them himself. One may take issue with these high order values, and they may, of course, change from time to time. Once given, however, they provide the criteria needed to measure the relevance of any proposal. And only if these high order values are clear, is it possible for the policy maker to assess alternatives rationally.

The first step in the design of rational policies is the clarification of high order values. Here, therefore, are the criteria I shall apply in measuring the relevance of the arts:

Diversity. I start from the simple assumption that people are different. Although there is a substratum of biological needs and drives that are apparently universal within the species, once these are met there is no visible limit to the psychological differences among men. Throughout history man has struggled to fulfill his basic biological needs, and societies have been organized primarily around this objective. Today for the first time it is possible to shift the emphasis of social policy from the fulfillment of immediate food, clothing, and shelter needs to the provision of arrangements that make possible maximum psychological fulfillment. If this is roughly true, then we need to create a society of great diversity. We want, I believe, to order a society in which there are very many ecological niches for many different types of human beings.

Democracy. The existence of a multiplicity of niches—whether we call them life-styles, roles, or by some other name—is of value to the individual only if he is able to move freely among them. In the relatively undifferentiated societies of the past, the number of roles and life-styles open to the individual were quite limited. Moreover, individuals were frozen into their niches by political and social barriers. If we want people to have the opportunity to "find themselves," we need a society in which movement from one niche to another is minimally obstructed by political restrictions, racial bigotry, snobbery, and so on. In short, I place high value on a highly differentiated social system characterized by easy mobility and fluidity.

Adaptability. In a period of sharply accelerating scientific and technological change, both the structure of niches and the needs of individuals undergo frequent and radical alteration. The existence of a large repertory of life-styles to choose from, and even the relative freedom to move from one to another, is of little help to the individual who is ignorant of their existence. Shifting from one to another, as the acceleration of change in society compels one to do, is always in some respects difficult. This difficulty can be minimized if the society's information system is geared for the job. Thus, the more varied the niches and the configurations they form, the more up-to-date information the individual needs about their requirements and their potential benefits. The more he knows, the better he can choose among the alternatives confronting him. That which fosters adaptability in a period of high-speed social change is good.

I shall not attempt to justify these value judgments any further. Anyone setting out to design cultural policies can begin with quite a different list. But these reflect my biases, and I believe they provide useful touchstones for measuring the relevance of the arts to modern society.

Regardless of the particular high order values any policy maker begins with, once they are established, he must ask himself whether or not the arts can foster his ends. Indeed, do the arts have anything at all to do with his purposes? What purposes do they serve? What, if anything, justifies their very existence?

It is easy to justify jobs, agricultural production, housing units, or hospital beds. It is even possible nowadays to justify education in terms that an economist or traditional planner can understand—i.e., as investment. But how does one justify the allocation of social resources for music, drama, dance, or poetry? What benefits are supposed to derive from the costs? Once one begins to search for answers to such questions, he runs squarely up against the rhetoric of ignorance.

Several years ago, in connection with the building of the John F. Kennedy Cultural Center in Washington, a survey was conducted among many of the nation's leading artists, critics, patrons, and foundation executives.[1] They were asked, among other things, to discuss the meaning or purpose of the arts. Their answers formed a depressing pastiche of confusing, contradictory, philosophically meaningless, and unverified assertions.

We were told that "our character flows from our creative arts," and that "the arts help us to understand and to love each other." The arts, it was explained, "make life more tolerable," or "provide adventures of the spirit," or "show us ourselves in our purest form." "They are interrelated with man's profound awareness." They "can make one feel a moment of truth." They "lead to more complete lives," and they "provide the spirit of creativity without which no country has achieved major importance."

One respondent, a museum official, declared that Los Angeles has "the number one crime rate, drug addict rate, a very high divorce rate, a very high juvenile delinquency rate, and it is not accidental that Los Angeles has not had great libraries, great operas, great art centers." Build art centers, libraries, and opera houses, he clearly implied, and it becomes possible to lower police protection costs, control addiction, reduce delinquency, and bolster the family.

Once in a while a single statement gathers up many different clichés about the arts. One such classic is attributable to composer William Schuman, president of Lincoln Center, according to whom "Art is a form of revelation. It touches the spirit and engages the intellect. Art is a civilizing experience." [2]

Just exactly what is revealed by art, Mr. Schuman doesn't tell us. When he says that art "touches the spirit," he employs a hackneyed figure of speech that has to be squeezed very hard to yield any meaningful content at all. Art "engages the intellect"? Certainly some art does. But so might a mathematical analysis of the operations of a pharmaceutical factory. Art a "civilizing experience"? Perhaps. Yet many a Nazi may have enjoyed the music of Wagner while signing the orders that condemned innocent children to the death ovens. What evidence is there to support Congreve's belief that "music hath charms to sooth the savage breast"?

Mr. Schuman and others are driven to such rhetoric, it should be noted, not by any lack of intelligence but by a lack of knowledge, and their remarks reflect not a personal but a general condition of ignorance. Just as intelligent men could believe that the earth was flat because no one knew any better, so can intelligent men today believe all kinds of tripe about the arts. If they are to be faulted, it is only for uncritically accepting hypotheses as fact.

Faced with this situation, how does a practical policy maker make sensible choices between alternatives, how does he even know whether or not the arts are relevant to his purposes?

THE SOCIAL FUNCTIONS OF THE ARTS

If we cut through the rhetoric, we find that most of the clichés quoted above are, in reality, guesses about how the arts function in society. They are hypotheses, and once recognized as such, they become useful in the policy making process. Despite their muddiness, it is possible to sort them out, to classify them, and to rephrase them in terms more useful, or at least more familiar, to the policy maker.

When we do this, we emerge not with a large number of messy and overlapping assertions, but with six basic hypotheses about the role played by art in society. The policy maker, confronted by any hypothesis about a social process, must make two separate and distinct decisions regarding it. He must first decide whether it is, or is not, relevant to his high order values. Once having eliminated from consideration all hypotheses deemed irrelevant, he must then assign some degree of validity to each of the others. A hypothesis may be relevant; but it may also be false. The decision maker needs to know this. It is sometimes difficult to determine, but he must do the best he can with the available data to reach a sound decision on this issue. Later I shall discuss some of the problems involved in determining relevance and validity. For the moment, however, let us proceed with an examination of the six basic hypotheses that are distillable from art rhetoric.

We begin by asking what does art "do"? What impact does it have on individuals or on society? Translating from the rhetoric, we can restate the answers to these questions in hypothetical form. I shall thus present each of the six basic hypotheses; make my own judgment as to its relevance to the high order values set out above; then evaluate its validity. Each hypothesis will be judged either "relevant" or "irrelevant." The validity of each will be termed either "probable," "uncertain," or "improbable."

1. ART AS SOCIAL LUBRICANT

This is the hypothesis that art provides a safe way for us to release antisocial passions. It assumes that vicarious participation in antisocial behavior through literature or the theater, for example, serves as an emotional cathartic, purging us of the need to behave in an antisocial way. This idea can be traced directly to Freud and, with modifications, all the way back to Aristotle. It is relied on heavily by critics who defend violence in art on the ground that it does not provoke, but rather squelches, violent behavior in real life. This is one basis for the widely held belief that art makes us better. By helping us to discharge tensions arising from the conflict between irrational drives and the constraints of society, it lubricates the social order.

Not everyone, of course, subscribes to this belief. Censors, for example, persist in the conviction that reading sexy books makes people sexy, rather than the reverse. Nonetheless, statements to the effect that the arts "civilize" us are often based on art-as-social-lubricant reasoning.

Similarly, the various descriptions of art as "self-expression" usually boil down to the idea that man has a need for communication that is inadequately met by society, thus generating frustration, which in turn is released through artistic expression. This is merely one of many variations on the same theme. Art is seen as having therapeutic value for both the individual and society.

If the Art-as-Social-Lubricant hypothesis is correct, then art deserves social support for the same reasons as psychiatry and mental health programs generally.

Is this hypothesis relevant, however, to the three high order values of diversity, democracy, and adaptability? I would argue that it is relevant to only two of these criteria—democracy and adaptability. My reasoning runs as follows: If it is true that the arts provide a vehicle for the harmless discharge of potentially harmful passions, then it may be said that the arts bolster law and order, both essential to democracy. It can also be said that, by providing a safety valve for potentially dangerous impulses, they free the individual to cope more rationally with the problems of change and adaptation.

Given relevance, however, we still need to decide whether the hypothesis is valid. Is it *true* that art encourages a harmless discharge of potentially dangerous impulses, or that it releases frustrations through self-expression? Psychologists tell us there is evidence on both sides of the first question. While some people seem to release frustrations through vicarious experience, others react in quite a different way. Thus, for some, exposure to brutality in art is an encouragement to brutality in real life. The evidence is, however, so thin and contradictory that the validity of the argument must be judged "uncertain."

Similarly, the frequently voiced theory that people need more and more outlets for self-expression may or may not be credible. Communication in our society is increasingly one-way—i.e., it moves from the mass media to individuals who have no opportunity to respond directly. It may well be true that there is some optimum ratio of received to transmitted messages. If so, any channel that helps maintain the optimum ratio would be socially beneficial. I know of no solid evidence, however, that would confirm or disprove this view either.

On balance, therefore, I conclude that the Art-as-Social-Lubricant hypothesis is relevant, but of uncertain validity.

2. ART AS EDUCATION

This hypothesis claims that art is socially useful because it instructs us about the nature of the universe and, more specifically, about society, itself. Thus, the verbal arts, for example, may show us how others live. The typist learns from a novel how the suburban matron lives, the banker has an opportunity, through drama, to observe a biologist or a boxer at work. The arts thus hold up for examination alternative modes of sexual behavior, status striving, family organization, conflict, conflict resolution, and so on. They permit us to study the everyday consequences of actions based on values different from our own, and compare them with the consequences of our own value systems. The verbal arts may thus be seen as a gold mine of sociological and historical data. The same might be said of representational painting and sculpture, although the argument loses much of its force with respect to music, dance, and non-representational visual art.

One variant of the Art-as-Education theme assumes its importance as a specially significant source of psychological knowledge. Statements of the type "the arts show us ourselves in the purest form" or "they are interrelated with man's profound awareness" make this assumption. All statements of the type "the arts make a vast contribution to the minds of men" or "the arts teach us to cope with life" can thus be traced ultimately to the Art-as-Education hypothesis.

There is one additional variation of the same theme: the idea that the artist is "ahead of his time" and hence in possession of important knowledge denied to the rest of us. The belief that the artist is a good prognosticator is, not surprisingly, very popular among artists, but it is accepted uncritically by others, too. Marshall McLuhan, for example, writes that "The artist picks up the message of cultural and technological challenge decades before its transforming impact occurs." [3] There is an equally convincing argument to be made for the case that the artist is chronically behind his time, but this is an unpopular idea. At any rate, the artist-as-prognosticator differs from the artist-as-knowledge-bearer only in that he is a specialist in a certain kind of knowledge.

If the second hypothesis is true, then art merits social support for the same reasons as research and education.

I would take the position that the Art-as-Education hypothesis is, indeed, relevant to all three criteria. Democracy, as we ordinarily use the term, implies that the citizen has some influence over political events that affect him. His ability to make his influence felt is related to his knowledge about the way in which society works, and education theoretically helps him gain this knowledge. To the degree that the arts give insight into the workings of society, they can be said to further democracy.

With respect to adaptability, the relevance of the arts is, I think, more direct. The hypothesis asserts that artistic presentations—plays, novels, films, and so on—permit an individual to "try on" various possible roles or styles of behavior before actually adopting or rejecting them. He is able to do so without injuring himself, as he might if he experimented with them in real life. The arts may thus alert him to role possibilities and consequences the existence of which he may not have sensed. In this way, the arts can be said to be part of the information system of society that helps people adapt to rapid change. This, in turn, encourages diversity in society. For these reasons, I shall consider the second hypothesis, Art-as-Education, as relevant to diversity, democracy and adaptability.

Moreover, the Art-as-Education hypothesis impresses me as coming close to the truth. I am strongly convinced that people *do* learn from the arts. From the verbal arts they learn not only facts but also that niches other than their own exist in the great ecology of society. I would go so far as to argue that even the non-verbal arts "teach," in that the artist, by presenting colors, sounds, or movements outside the range of ordinary everyday experience, calls attention to them, thus widening the individual's conception of the alternatives available to him. I am not at all convinced that artists are good prognosticators. But they are, I believe, good at suggesting alternatives, something our educational system, in its accent on specialism, does not do well. For these reasons, I term it "probable" that the Art-as-Education hypothesis is valid.

3. ART AS MYSTICAL EXPERIENCE

This hypothesis holds that art arouses a certain unusual state of being in the individual. The artist, either through his own resources or through "divine inspiration," generates a condition in his audience that presumably cannot be stimulated in other, more mundane ways. He supposedly bypasses the ordinary processes of communication and touches off an essentially indescribable experience in the audience member.

Most statements that art "is a form of revelation" or that the arts "make one feel a moment of truth" or that they "touch the spirit" usually imply this hypothesis. There is a tacit assumption that the state of being triggered by art is in some sense desirable.

Another way of formulating this point of view—in less ethereal terminology—is to suggest that art is capable of engendering certain rare psychological, and ultimately, biochemical states in the individual, and that these states are highly prized by those who have them. These states are sometimes referred to as the "esthetic response."

If the third hypothesis is correct, then the arts deserve support for some of the same reasons as religion.

The case for relevance here is thin, however. I personally reject the term "mystical experience" as unnecessarily obscurantist. But even if, as suggested, the hypothesis is reformulated into the simple statement that the arts are capable of arousing highly unusual and pleasurable states, then it still requires a considerable stretch of logic to show that this advances diversity, democracy, or adaptability. I shall therefore regard it as irrelevant, and, having made this arbitrary, and no doubt disputable, decision, I need not estimate its validity.

4. ART AS INTEGRATIVE MECHANISM

According to this hypothesis, art is important to society because it somehow helps hold it together. In Herbert Read's words, "It is the artist's business to make the group aware of its unity, its community. He can do this because he, more than other men, has access to the common unconsciousness, to the collective instincts which underlie the brittle surface of convention and normality." [4] This same theme is voiced by Ernst Fischer, who says, "Evidently man wants to be more than just himself. . . . He is not satisfied with being a separate individual. . . . He wants to refer to something that is more than 'I,' something outside himself and yet essential to himself . . . to unite his 'I' in art with a communal existence; to make his individuality *social*." [5]

This notion that art serves to unite man goes back to anthropological and archeological research into the magic and ritual of prehistoric times. It rests on the assumption that the arts transmit group values to the individual. In effect, it regards art as highly complex, affect-laden propaganda for the norms of the group.

If the fourth hypothesis is true, and the arts serve to integrate man into his society, then the arts merit support for the same reasons that society sponsors national holidays, national monuments, national Olympic teams, flags, and patriotic symbolism generally, if for no other reason.

Whether or not the hypothesis is true, it is clearly relevant to the high order value of diversity. Diversity implies toleration of many different scales of value within the same society. If the arts propagandized only for the accepted or central values of the society, they would tend to reduce diversity.

But do they operate this way? Is the assertion that art integrates man into society valid, and, if so, how?

The simple idea that art integrates the individual into his society may have been adequate at one time. Today, however, the process is far more complicated than Read and Fischer imply. Modern society, unlike primitive society, is not a monolithic structure, but a conglomerate, an awesomely complex organization of subcultures (and sub-subcultures) each with its own hierarchy of values. The values of any subculture overlap and conflict with the values of other subcultures. Some values, however, are so widely shared that they cut through many subcultures and may be regarded, for all practical purposes, as society-wide.

By examining the shifting patterns of overlap among subcultural value hierarchies, we can deduce the society-wide or "core" values. We can then rank subcultures according to the degree to which their values coincide with or differ from these core values.[6] For example, we can speak of a Negro subculture in the United States that shares many values of the society, but which at key points clashes with the core values. At some distance from the center of society there is a value perimeter. Those subcultures (or, for that matter, individuals) whose values conflict most with the central values of the larger society fall beyond this perimeter and may be regarded as "outsiders."

When we speak of art, therefore, as an integrative mechanism, we must always ask, integration into what? To the degree that the arts propagate only the core values of society, they may be said to integrate individuals into the total society. But much art reflects and propagandizes for the values of subcultures rather than those of the larger society. Indeed, few works of art nowadays reach the majority of the population of any modern society. Instead, most art works reach homogeneous slices of the public. Even when a novel is read all over the country, or a play is seen in city after city, it attracts—it selects out from the population—only certain types of people. Culture consumption, therefore, is increasingly specialized, and artists, consciously or otherwise, produce work for differentiated "markets," aiming their works at specific subcultures. Thus, there is an entire body of underground art produced specifically for a homosexual audience. When a play or a novel or any other work of art reflecting the values of this subculture turns up in the marketplace, word gets around through the subculture's grapevine and the art work "pulls" a highly selective audience out of the total population. Similarly, there is art aimed directly at L.S.D. users. There is art directed more broadly at the educated urban middle-class consumer. There is art produced only for an esoteric intellectual audience. And there are many varieties of art and what might be termed sub-art aimed at teenagers, Negroes, and other social groups.

Whether or not a work of art helps integrate an individual into the larger or core society, or merely into a subculture is, therefore, dependent upon the particular values propagated by it. The issue is still further complicated by the fact that when people are free to select the art they want, they tend, on the whole, to choose novels, plays, or poems that confirm their already existing values. To the degree that these are the values of one or another subculture, the experience merely reinforces the individual's allegiance to the group.

However, many people are not firmly committed to the values of any definite subculture. They may be in mid-passage between one subculture and another; they may be vacillating in the social space that exists between subcultures; they may be in the process of shedding or taking on a subculture's values; they may even be busy creating a totally new subculture. Moreover, with the exception of blatant propaganda, most art works transmit, not a single clear message about a single value, but complex statements about many different values. Often the normative content of the art work is self-contradictory. As a result, the experience generated by a work of art in an individual may lead to doubt and dissonance rather than to an affirmation of a clearly defined hierarchy of values.

Given these complexities, therefore, can we consider the fourth hypothesis to be valid? The answer is yes—if we change its wording. If, instead of saying that art *is* an integrative mechanism, we say merely that it *can be* an integrative mechanism, we come much closer to the truth. Thus, having reformulated the hypothesis in these terms, we may assign the hypothesis a validity rating of "probably."

5. ART AS POLICY REVIEW

This hypothesis asserts that art is valuable to society because it functions as a critic of the status quo. The notion that the artist must stand apart from his society and criticize it has been especially popular since the rise of the romantic bohemian. It is widely held today. "The poet must be an anarchist," argues Herbert Read. "He has no other choice. He may temporize with liberalism, with democratic socialism, with state socialism," but, in the end, he must always maintain a position of disaffection.[7]

Criticism of the social order may be individualistic, anarchistic, and negative, or it can be organized and positive, in the sense that it systematically advocates alternatives. Today, Western literature, art, and drama tend to be highly critical of rationalism, science, technology, and contemporary industrialism generally. As a rule, they are intensely negative, holding out little in the way of social alternatives. But whether the artist is wholly negative, or constructive, his criticism, *per se,* is deemed valuable.[8]

Putting this hypothesis into political science terminology, it might be said that the artist is a particularly useful citizen because he serves a judicial function, continuously reviewing policies of society at both the macro- and micro-level. (When I say "the policies of society," I mean this in the broadest possible sense, so that a dramatist who comments on marriage or on sex is as much a policy reviewer as one who comments on racial bigotry or militarism. Nor do the comments have to be explicit or even intentional. Any work of literature or drama, any film, and many paintings and sculptures carry implicit criticism of the status quo.) The wider the freedom of the artist, the better he is able to provide a necessary review of social policies.

If the fifth hypothesis is correct, therefore, it follows that a democratic society must allocate resources for the support of the arts for the same reason that it provides the wherewithal for a free press and a loyal opposition. And if art serves the purpose of policy review, as stated by the fifth hypothesis, then it is directly relevant to the democracy criterion.

As for validity, I think that the arts, at least the verbal arts, do function in this way, and that the artist's criticisms or praise of the status quo carry considerable force. I have elsewhere challenged the view that the artist must be "alienated" from or "disaffected" with his society in order to produce valuable work. The artist who expresses and reinforces the core values of his society is quite as much a critic of the status quo as the artist who spews contempt on all he sees around him. Both evaluate the reality they perceive. Both use certain communicative techniques that give their opinions more force than the average man's. The arts are by no means the only, or even the most important, mechanism for the continuous review of social policy, but they tend to focus on issues largely disregarded by the press, opposition political parties, and other evaluative agencies. I thus conclude that the arts perform a very important policy review function and thereby strengthen democracy. Consequently, I rate the validity of the hypothesis as "probable."

6. ART FOR ART'S SAKE

This hypothesis, another favorite among artists and art lovers, holds that art is somehow its own justification and that questions asked about its social purposes are irrelevant at best, and more likely pernicious. Art, they argue, does not and ought not fulfill any social purpose, except, perhaps, by accident.

In its most rarefied and extreme form, the art for art's sake philosophy endows art with a purpose that transcends society and even life itself. It sees society as the tail wagged by the dog of art. In the words of Albert Guérard, "Art for Art's Sake means Art Dominant, Life for the Sake of Art, life subordinated to the service of beauty. . . ." [9]

The idea of remaking society or individual life to fit esthetic criteria is attractive to certain romantics in both art and politics. In its less meretricious forms it merely results in such things as buildings that are inefficient because the architect's esthetic prejudices were allowed to override functional necessities. In its more dangerous form, it results in messianic politics.

The art for art's sake advocate adopts the position that art is good—*a priori*—and that it should not merely be tolerated but supported by society without strings attached. Behind this view, there are, of course, tacit values which imply that art, even when it is "for its own sake," is good for the community at large.

This is an odd position, but it has an exact parallel in the insistence of many scientists that "pure research" should be conducted without reference to possible social utility because somehow, in some unspecified way, it will be to society's advantage.

If the sixth hypothesis is sensible at all—and if one accepts the notion that pure research is non-functional—art has as much right to social support as pure research. On the other hand, given the above set of criteria or values, the final hypothesis, art-for-art's-sake, seems to me to be not relevant to any of my criteria, unless twisted in some manner beyond the meaning I have given to it. If this is so, the validity of the hypothesis need not concern us.

These, then, are the half dozen hypotheses that sneak into nearly all discussions of the arts, usually in the guise of assumptions. They are not mutually exclusive. Nor is the list by any means exhaustive.[10] Nevertheless, even if one limits oneself to the basic six and their variants, it becomes possible to classify perhaps 90 per cent of art rhetoric. Any public official who has to read or listen to a presentation requesting aid to the arts will immediately recognize most of the arguments as fitting into one or another of these categories.

This effort to classify, determine the relevance and assign a validity rating, yields results that can now be summed up by Table 11–1.

Table 11–1. THE LIKELIHOOD THAT ART SERVES SPECIFIED HIGH ORDER VALUES

	VALUES		
Hypotheses	*Diversity*	*Democracy*	*Adaptability*
1. Art as Social Lubricant	Irrelevant	Uncertain	Uncertain
2. Art as Education	Probable	Probable	Probable
3. Art as Mystical Experience	Irrelevant	Irrelevant	Irrelevant
4. Art as Integrative Mechanism (reformulated)	Probable	Irrelevant	Irrelevant
5. Art as Policy Review	Irrelevant	Probable	Irrelevant
6. Art for Art's Sake	Irrelevant	Irrelevant	Irrelevant

The table indicates values to which each hypothesis is deemed relevant or irrelevant. Where judged relevant, validity rating is shown.

RELEVANCE AND VALIDITY

Before going on to draw policy conclusions from this exercise, a word about the procedure itself is in order. It is clear, to put it mildly, that the above table is too tidy and categorical. The conclusions it summarizes are contestable. My statement, for example, that the Art-for-Art's-Sake hypothesis is not relevant to any of the three high order values, is quite debatable. But the procedure, I suggest, elevates the ground of debate.

While it does not, by any means, eliminate subjective bias from cultural policy making, it does provide a basis for reducing that bias. For it rests on statements that are, in principle, empirically verifiable.

If one conceives of the world as a totality, each of its elements related, directly or indirectly, to all others, then it can logically be argued that everything is relevant to everything else. If, however, we define relevance to mean "impact of more than a given strength," the question becomes an empirical one. Similarly, the validity of the various hypotheses can, at least in theory, be subject to empirical verification.

In short, the proposed procedure rests on questions that are not inherently matters of opinion. It rests on propositions that can, and should, be systematically investigated by behavioral scientists. As this research is done, the data base will improve. So, presumably, will the decisions.

Until then, however, the policy maker is compelled to rely almost wholly on opinions as to the relevance or validity of the various propositions. For there is, in this field, an almost complete absence of what in other fields would be regarded as absolutely essential data. While centuries of scholarship have filled libraries with historical studies, philosophical speculations, critical interpretations, and introspection, the actual amount of useful sociological or psychological information about the arts in contemporary society is scant. Our ignorance is stupendous.

In the United States we are only just beginning to accumulate simple descriptive data about the numbers of people who participate in or attend artistic events. We know very little about their characteristics. We have no comprehensive data on the number, type, capacity, and distribution of physical facilities appropriate for artistic activity. We know very little about the degree to which culture consumption is fragmented or overlapping—e.g., the degree to which the same people go to museums as attend ballet performances. And if we know next to nothing about these relatively simple matters, we know even less about the motivations of either the culture consumer or the culture producer. Does art civilize? To my knowledge, we have no data whatever that attempt to correlate the degree of cultural activity in a community with the level of crime, racial bigotry, respect for law, and so on. We know nothing about the correlation (or lack of correlation) between high levels of cultural activity in a community and, say, admissions to mental hospitals. We know virtually nothing about the impact of the arts on sexual behavior, friendship patterns, and individual or community adaptability to change, not to mention the different effects of the various arts taken individually.

It is true that many of these subjects—and one could go on listing them indefinitely—are extremely difficult, if not impossible, to investigate with scientific means at present. We lack both the hardware and the necessary conceptual tools. But across a broad range of questions our ignorance derives from simple neglect. There are many researchable questions which have simply never attracted the attention of social scientists or of research funding agencies.

Fortunately, this situation is beginning to change. In 1961–62, when I began work on *The Culture Consumers,* the first published attempt to assemble data on the size and character of the cultural audience in the United States, it was difficult to interest reputable social scientists in the subject. The data, patchy today, was far worse, and there were few theoretical concepts ready at hand around which useful research might be organized. Since then, the Rockefeller Brothers Fund has pulled together a great deal of previously scattered materials for a study of the performing arts. The Office of Education has begun to sponsor research. Various cities have engaged management consultants and others to inventory their cultural resources, and the Twentieth Century Fund has financed a study limited to the economics of the professional performing arts. It is to be hoped that this research activity will expand in the years to come, and that, eventually, it will be brought into systematic relationship with research in related fields such as education and mass communications. Yet most of what has been done to date consists of one-shot efforts, mostly incompatible with one another, and there is still no single center, federal, state or local, to which a puzzled policy maker can turn for comprehensive, well-organized data.

This dearth of data does not, however, weaken the case for rational method. Rather, it implies that greater than ordinary attention must be paid to how information is used. No decision maker ever has all the data he needs to make a perfect decision. Rational decision making requires not that the decision maker knows "all" there is to know before making a decision, but rather that he uses what information is available in the most scientific manner. The smaller the data base, the more important the procedure. The procedure sketched here does not supply the missing data. But, if nothing else, it clarifies the questions to which decision makers need answers. It provides a rough framework for rational choice among alternative policies.

Where we lack the data to make well-informed decisions, we can still make sensible efforts to avoid the worst effects of ignorance. Thus it is possible within the framework of the method proposed here to reduce the element of purely individual bias. Confronted by the need to make a decision, an agency need not rely on one man's assessment of relevance and validity. It can convene a panel of artists and social and behavioral scientists to help make the necessary judgments. Even allowing full measure for the well-known faults of committees and advisory panels, such groups can, at a minimum, help the decision maker avoid skewing policies because of a single individual's whim or prejudice.

More important, there are now highly promising techniques available for systematically evaluating and applying expert opinion in fields in which the experts themselves lack "hard data." Not all opinion is equally valuable, and these techniques suggest ways of refining the decision-making process to take advantage of the "best" opinions.[11] The combination of these techniques with the procedure outlined here could, I believe, substantially improve goal-setting in the arts.

Finally, the entire process could—and should—be enriched and further improved by feeding additional values and subvalues in at the top, and many more hypotheses in at the bottom. The degree to which a policy maker can or should refine the process will, of course, depend upon the resources available to him and the importance of the decision under consideration.

Today virtually every important agency of the federal government faces issues that significantly influence, or are influenced by, the arts. The National Foundation on the Arts and Humanities is only the most visibly involved. The State Department, through its cultural exchange program, is a world-wide cultural impresario. The Office of Education concerns itself, among other things, with the place of the arts in the educational curriculum. The Department of Commerce deals with tourism, a phenomenon heavily affected by the arts. In the design of airports, in the presentation of musical and dramatic performances for the armed services, in the provision of funds for sculpture in housing projects, in labor and manpower policies, the government is inextricably tied up with the future of the arts in American society.

Whether or not the procedures discussed here are adopted, or other, more sophisticated methods are found, something more than sheer, haphazard guesswork is needed. As the scope of cultural programs expands, this need becomes more urgent.

PARALLEL PROFESSIONALISM

It is now possible to design cultural goals that foster our high order values and rely on relevant processes that "probably" do work rather than on irrelevant processes or those deemed "uncertain" or "improbable." We want a society that is richly diverse, that provides a place for highly varied types of people. Can the arts contribute to this? And, if so, how?

I contend that the arts contribute to diversity in society in at least three important ways. First, they tend to generate new subcultures within the society or to help embryonic ones take shape. Thus a cult and eventually a subculture may spring up around the novels of Camus or Kerouac. Timothy Leary, in proselytizing for a new religion based on L.S.D., consciously uses art to develop a symbolism that will recruit followers and provide them with their own language. The Art-as-Integrative-Mechanism hypothesis suggests that, as new subcultures arise, based on new professions, new leisure-time patterns or political-ideological groupings, the power of art will be enlisted to attract converts, formulate values, and, as suggested earlier, integrate members into them.

Second, the arts provide a key method by which individuals differentiate themselves from their neighbors. Although any number of people may have the same automobile, the same dress, or the same cookie-cutter house in the suburbs, although no one's refrigerator is *sui generis*, it is possible to own a painting or work of sculpture that is one of a kind, a defiant assertion of the individual's one-and-onliness. This is especially true if the art is self-made. Two neighbors may both own copies of the same recording of *Don Giovanni*, but no two will have precisely the same record library. People use other media for differentiating themselves, but the arts make possible extremely subtle and refined variations.

Finally, by educating individuals to the existence of ways of life other than their own, and helping them adapt to change, as suggested by the second hypothesis, the arts permit an increase in diversity that might not otherwise be possible.

Richness and variation in the arts thus contribute to the richness and variation in society. Diversity of cultural output, in short, tends to encourage and reinforce diversity in society. This being so, I believe we can and should pursue quite specific policies to promote increasing diversity of cultural output.

If we examine the professional institutions in the culture industry in the United States today, we are immediately struck by their division into a profit sector and a nonprofit sector. Professional producing organizations in the profit sector are wholly dependent upon the sale of their goods or services in the open marketplace. Thus a Broadway play producer survives only if he is able to sell enough tickets at the box office to cover his costs and make a profit. All this income is sales income.

Professional institutions in the nonprofit sector, by contrast, are only partially, if at all, dependent upon the marketplace. They may or may not sell their goods and services—some museums, for example, charge no admission, thus, in effect, giving their services away free. But even if they do sell their wares at the box office, their sales income is seldom enough to cover all the costs of production. They balance their books by soliciting contributions from individual patrons, from foundations, corporations, and public agencies. Such institutions, in other words, must supplement sales income with public or private patronage.

This economic distinction between the two sectors has significant social and artistic consequences. Patronage, for example, frees the recipient from the pressure of the box office. This means a freedom to soar beyond the immediate limits of popular taste. In an institution, the higher the percentage of patronage income as against income earned at the ticket window, the freer it is to present programs that are esoteric, experimental, perhaps even offensive to the public. This freedom is essential to the continuing development of art. In short, patronage makes it possible for the artist or the institution to lead, rather than merely reflect, public taste.

The marketplace, in turn, also has artistic consequences. Its chief fault is that it compels the artist to court a wide public. This may not be good for him, as an individual, or for his art. The market mechanism is limited, by and large, to the production or distribution of the safe and sane. One need only look at the Broadway theater, which is wholly dependent upon the box office, and which receives no patronage, to see the limitations of that system.

But the commercial system has a balancing advantage. For the freedom made possible by patronage sometimes leads to an artistic *cul de sac*. Subjectivism carried to the point of incomprehensibility, triviality masked by rhetoric, obscurity for obscurity's sake, preciousness— these are some of the dangers of an art that is divorced from the public. And whatever its other faults, the market system does not permit such a divorce to occur.

We need an art that ranges richly from the easily accessible to the difficult, from the seemingly simple to the clearly complex. The market system is well equipped to provide the accessible. It keeps the artist in close touch with the public. It thus serves as an anchor, discouraging him from flying off into rarefied regions of solipsism.

What all this strongly points up is that diversity in the economic arrangements for the support of culture tends to encourage diversity in the cultural product itself. This is not to say that diverse economic arrangements themselves create diversity in art. They are only one of many factors that influence the kind of cultural goods and services a society produces. But the existence of alternate, perhaps even partially competing, systems fosters cultural pluralism and openness in a society.

Imagine the changes, for example, if the United States lacked university-subsidized presses and were totally dependent upon commercial publishing. Many of the most important works of humanistic scholarship, much of our poetry, many of our literary magazines, would not exist. The market alone could not justify their publication. On the other hand, the United States would have a narrow and lopsided literary life indeed if it depended solely upon patronage-supported publishing by universities. The jargon, the literary and scholarly incest, the obscurantism and ineptness that characterize much of the output of the university presses today would be the rule.

The presence of parallel systems of publishing makes for a diverse and balanced harvest of books each year, the profit sector of the industry by and large taking care of the obvious, gross needs of society, the subsidized sector filling in the gaps and crevices by performing specialized functions that the marketplace alone cannot support.

What all this suggests is a novel theory about the proper structure of a culture industry in a modern democracy. We might call it the Theory of Parallel Support. It holds that in each branch of the culture industry a conscious effort should be made to encourage the existence of both a profit and a nonprofit sector. Moreover, further diversity can be achieved within the nonprofit sector itself by varying widely the degree of dependence upon subsidy among the institutions in this sector.

This is more easily understood if we visualize each branch of the culture industry as a spectrum. (See Table 11–2.) This spectrum is divided by a vertical line down the middle. To the left of the center line is the commercial or profit sector. Each of the institutions in this sector is a business, operating within the framework of the market economy. To the right of the center line lies the nonprofit or subsidized sector. Within this sector there is wide differentiation among the institutions. Immediately to the right of the center line, for example, is a hypothetical institution that manages to earn fully 95 per cent of its income from the sale of tickets or services to the public. It requires patronage to make up only 5 per cent of its annual budget. At the extreme right is an institution that earns zero per cent of its income. It offers its wares free to the public and depends upon patronage to provide 100 per cent of its money. Between these two extremes are many institutions reflecting intermediate degrees of dependence on subsidy.

Table 11–2. THEORY OF PARALLEL SUPPORT:
MODEL FOR A BRANCH OF THE CULTURE INDUSTRY

A	B	C	D	A	B	C	D
100% income earned	100% income earned	100% income earned	100% income earned	95% income earned	60% income earned	10% income earned	0% income earned
Profit sector: a variety of business establishments directly responsive to popular taste.				*Non-profit sector:* varying degrees of dependence upon patronage; varying responsiveness to popular taste.			

By structuring a culture industry along these lines, we take maximum advantage of the power of economic organization to contribute to diversity in culture output. We make the economic structure work toward, rather than against, our high order value of diversity.

Of course, the two sectors need not be airtight compartments. In reality, they can and often should crisscross and interpenetrate. A nonprofit institution can be a subsidiary of a profit-making organization and can receive grants and other forms of patronage; a nonprofit institution can, if it so desires, create a profit-making subsidiary. Both these and other organizational permutations are familiar in the research industry, for example. The central point is that, by manipulating structure, it is possible to encourage diversification of output.

This is **not** the place for a detailed description of the present structure of the culture industry. I have written about it elsewhere.[12] It is enough to point out that we are a long way from having well-developed parallel production systems. Across the board in the United States, we can discern a general movement toward a better balance than has existed until now. But in a number of fields, as the summary below will show, the profit/nonprofit relationship is still highly unbalanced, to the detriment of our cultural output. The overall situation can be capsuled in the following way:

Book Publishing
> Balanced; small but energetic nonprofit sector supplements large and successful profit sector.

Record Manufacture
> Unbalanced; virtually no nonprofit sector. Almost total reliance on market economics restricts publication of contemporary music, particularly that of living American composers.

Radio
> Unbalanced; within profit sector a substantial group of FM stations now broadcast classical music and cultural programs; nonprofit sector, devoted exclusively to high quality cultural, educational programming, extremely undeveloped.

Television
> Unbalanced; nonprofit educational sector very small and weak. Cultural content (apart from purely educational or instructional) limited.

Professional Theater
> Unbalanced. Until recently almost all professional theater was in the profit sector (Broadway); in recent years professional resident companies, organized on a nonprofit basis, have begun to multiply, improving balance. But nonprofit sector still undeveloped.

Professional Orchestra, Opera, Dance
> Unbalanced. In all these fields, professional work is almost all organized on nonprofit basis. There is *no* profit-making professional, permanent orchestra, opera company.

Visual Arts
> Unbalanced. Virtually all art museums are nonprofit. This is being slightly offset by a rapid proliferation of art galleries and salesrooms organized on a for-profit basis.

I have not attempted in this essay to describe the diversity of structure *within* the nonprofit sector, but only the relationship of one sector to another. It should also be noted that amateur activity in every field is almost all nonprofit. (Very little profit-motivated entrepreneurial skill has been devoted to the organization of amateur activities in the arts, although we can expect that it will be.) Moreover, since this essay concerns itself with goals rather than with their implementation, I have made no effort to discuss the conditions that have led to and now perpetuate the present lack of balance in the culture industry. There are many seemingly insuperable obstacles to overcome if the sharp imbalances of today are to be righted.

Nevertheless, I believe that a rough balance *can* be achieved, and I will, therefore, without further elaboration, put forth as a long-range cultural objective the development of more or less balanced and parallel systems of cultural production in the United States. Policy makers, whether in government, foundations, corporations, or in cultural institutions, can measure proposals, at least in part, by whether or not they contribute toward that goal.[13] If we succeed in achieving parallel systems of cultural production, we shall have done much to promote diversity in society generally.

THE ALIGNMENT OF AMATEURISM

The development of parallel systems of production in the professional field should be matched by a strong, positive policy toward amateurism in the arts. The acceleration of technological and scientific progress sends shock waves through society. This penetrates into the life of individuals in the form of a succession of demands. They are compelled to cope with novel issues, strange new role configurations, and a field of constantly shifting expectations. They are forced to adopt and then rapidly discard life styles. They must be prepared to move from niche to niche in society.

I have argued that art can help them to do this. To the degree that the Art-as-Education hypothesis holds true, the arts serve to inform people about the possibilities and the changing requirements thrown up by a churning, innovating society.

I have suggested that, in its simplest form, art informs the individual about alternate modes of behavior by picturing them for him —that the banker has an opportunity, through watching a play or reading a novel, to "try on" the role of biologist or boxer, to test it vicariously against his own value hierarchy and, thereby, form a clearer picture of the alternatives presented to him by society. I would now like to argue that what is true when the individual reads, or listens, or otherwise attends to a work of art, is at least as true, if not more so, when he himself attempts to create or interpret a work of art.

It is easy to see this in the case of, say, the faithful young wife who tries on the role of town hussy in a performance by a church theater group. It is less obvious with respect to other forms of art, but the principle is the same. In the process of constructing a play, writing a poem, or painting a picture, the individual explores possibilities outside the range of ordinary daily experience. This exploratory process is, I believe, highly useful to the individual when the time comes to choose new behavior patterns.

Moreover, amateur participation in the arts has a special value for those individuals who, as a consequence of repeated failure in other fields, suffer from a lack of the self-esteem necessary to active participation in the society. This is particularly true of the disadvantaged.

Whereas in other fields the ability to cope with, or master, the environment frequently depends on a high level of education, it is possible for uneducated individuals, especially if they have talent, to perform well as amateur painters, musicians, actors, or dancers. All that we have learned about education tells us that success breeds success, that the individual who feels competent at something is more likely to try something new than the individual who has been defeated again and again by a complex environment. Participation in amateur art activity, thus, can give many people, adults as well as children, a taste of success that may be critically useful in helping them to learn and adapt.

I would, therefore, argue that amateur participation in the arts should be widely encouraged by public policy makers interested in cushioning the impact of change.

Thus, just as I would argue for programs that bring the professional arts to those segments of the population not now a part of the culture public, so I would urge the need for many and varied amateur art activities in which they can actively participate.

The conscious expansion of amateur art activity in the United States as a matter of public policy will, however, face two criticisms. The first comes from professional artists who regard amateurs as a threat to their earning power and prestige. Many musicians and painters complain bitterly about the rise of the amateur. The second criticism comes from those who view amateurism as a threat to standards of excellence in the arts. They are appalled by the acres of bad amateur paintings hung in supermarket galleries, by the low quality of amateur performances in theaters and concert halls. The growing ubiquity of amateur-produced work, they claim, leads to a generalized acceptance of the mediocre.

Both these criticisms flow, I believe, from a mistaken conception of the function of amateurism with respect to the culture industry. The relationship of amateurism to professionalism is, and ought to be, a matter of concern. But it is a serious error to conceive of these two sectors of the culture industry as being necessarily in conflict. There are ways of organizing them so as to make the two sectors mutually reinforcing rather than antagonistic.

Thus, the existence of sand-lot baseball and minor leagues does not threaten the major league ballplayer; nor does it lower respect for professional excellence. Indeed, there is ample evidence in athletics generally, in chess, and in other fields, that properly organized amateur activities can greatly strengthen professionalism and raise standards significantly.[14]

The real question then becomes not how to contain or restrict amateurism, but rather how to encourage it and how to build links between the two sectors. For example, it is possible to conceive of the professional cultural institutions of a city banding together to organize amateur activity where it does not yet exist or to improve it where it does. A museum can literally send organizers into the neighborhoods and the schools to start art clubs and studios for amateurs; an orchestra can send out staff to build ensembles; a ballet company can work with local dance schools.

Today, with the exception of very limited activity by some museums, few professional cultural institutions regard it as part of their responsibility to organize amateurs. They fear that contact with the amateur movement will arouse the contempt of critics or will suggest to the public that their own offerings are somehow less than first class. Moreover, orchestras, opera companies, and similar organizations are too underfinanced and understaffed to take on this responsibility, even if they so desired. Yet the amorphous amateur movement now springing up around the country, if properly organized, could vastly increase the audience, and even the funds, available to professional institutions. At the same time, professional institutions could, through their influence, develop programming for amateur groups that would help raise the level of sophistication and appreciation among the amateurs. Far from downgrading respect for excellence, such activities could help develop a more critical and educated audience.

Thus, I would argue that a third major cultural goal in our society should be the rapid expansion and proper organization of amateurism. Among the comfort classes, amateurism is already strongly on the rise. It will not, however, grow among the disadvantaged populations unless we take specific steps to see that it does. Moreover, it will require conscious policies to help swing the amateur movement and the professional arts into fruitful alignment. We need not less, but more, and much better organized amateurism. In a rapidly changing society moving toward greater leisure time, nothing could be more appropriate from a long-range point of view.

THE EXTENSION OF DEMOCRACY

Diversifying the output of the professional arts, strengthening amateurism, and bringing the two into sympathetic alignment would serve the values of diversity and adaptability. But still another goal flows from the above analysis. For if there are imbalances in artistic production, those in the field of culture consumption are even more noticeable.

The rise of public interest in the arts since the end of World War II did not merely increase the over-all size of the audience, it also transformed its composition. Museums, theaters, and concert halls were once filled largely by high-income, old-stock families, with a handful of bohemians thrown in. Today, the rich and the bohemian remain, but the majority of culture consumers are middle-class Americans. In aggregate, the new audience is far more representative of the total population than the prewar audience was. Yet the process of democratization has gone so far, and no further. There are still tens of millions of Americans, particularly among racial minorities and the poor, who never make contact at all with the arts.

Having argued the case for diversity, it is important to note that while we may want a highly variegated society, there are certain kinds of variety we don't want. By common consent, we do not want homicidal maniacs. We do not want lepers. Nor do we want people frozen into their social niches, merely to preserve diversity. In short, we don't want to maintain poverty and ignorance coercively for the sake of the quaintness or diversity they add to modern society. The value of diversity is conditioned by the value of democracy and the freedom of choice it implies.

Today racial discrimination and poverty effectively freeze millions of Americans into niches they do not necessarily wish to occupy. I believe the arts can help unfreeze the position of our disadvantaged minorities, thus fostering the high order value, democracy.

As the central society grows more wealthy, more educated, more sophisticated about the outside world, more capable of coping with high level abstractions, and more interested in esthetic phenomena, those groups locked outside the central society because of poverty or bias become more and more sharply cut off from the mainstream. They develop ways of perceiving and evaluating events that differ more and more significantly from the ways of the larger society. A psychic chasm cleaves the society.

This means that poverty and the related problems of racial discrimination cannot be solved by economic means alone. Nor will they be solved by vocational training or retraining programs alone, nor even by broader educational programs of a traditional nature. While the attack on poverty must obviously include economic, political, social, and educational components, it is increasingly clear that efforts to bring millions of disadvantaged individuals *into* the central society will fail unless a conscious effort is also made to alter their values and their ways of perceiving society and themselves.

For example, Margaret Mead has pointed out that high-rise housing projects are towns, in and of themselves. It should not surprise anyone, she notes, that a certain amount of crime occurs in the corridors of these buildings, just as it occurs in the streets of more conventional towns. Such projects tend to perpetuate slum behavior, she argues, because no effort is made to teach newcomers how to live under the new conditions. She suggests that we might consider establishing reception centers where new arrivals might be taught new habits.[15]

This kind of education is not just formal. It is not classroom education. It involves teaching people not merely facts, but new ways of evaluating facts, new ways of communicating their needs, new ways of using not only words but non-verbal communication, gestures and facial expressions, and new conceptions of time and space. It entails presenting a whole range of alternate behavior possibilities to people who have led narrow and squalid lives. It means calling their attention to different life styles, roles, and values. And, if the Art-as-Education hypothesis is correct, these are precisely the things that art does best.

I am not suggesting that a crew of playwrights be assembled to prepare little "educational" playlets for training purposes, because, by and large, art produced to order for such purposes turns out to be tepid, thin, and lacking in exactly the emotional power that good art has. But I am suggesting that a tremendous body of art work already exists that serves to transmit insights and values that would help integrate individuals and subcultures now outside the perimeter of society into the central society itself. Indeed, most of the plays and musicals shown on our stages, most of the opera, dance, and visual art now being enjoyed by comfort-class culture consumers fall into this category.

Yet the culture explosion we are now witnessing in the United States is strictly a white middle- and upper-class affair. What little audience research has been done to date tells us that Negroes, the unemployed, and even employed blue-collar workers form only an infinitesimal part of the culture public.[16]

I should like to suggest therefore, that one part of the over-all attack on poverty and discrimination should be cultural—that one major goal of our society should be to bring art into the lives of millions now virtually untouched by the culture explosion. The process of education through art, I contend, can complement efforts to educate in more orthodox ways. Skillfully employed, it will get at precisely those behavior patterns and values that classroom teaching copes with badly or ignores. Through art it will be possible to hold up for emulation styles of life and value hierarchies that, in the end, must be adopted by the disadvantaged, if they are ever to become part of an increasingly affluent and complex super-industrial society.[17]

But making our disadvantaged population part of the culture boom, bringing them within reach of the artist, so to speak, requires a several-sided effort. Partly, it is a matter of distribution. Many imaginative programs can be designed to bring art, music, dance, and drama into the housing projects, into slum schools, into cabarets, churches, union halls, and other public places. For example, Joseph Papp's New York Shakespeare Festival has mounted *A Midsummer Night's Dream* in Harlem and Bedford Stuyvesant. Such efforts are merely primitive examples of what might be done along these lines. At the same time, appropriate patronage or subsidy programs can see to it that admission price is no obstacle. Right now, price *is* a serious problem. For all practical purposes, the Broadway theater, the Metropolitan Opera, and major symphony or ballet associations charge prices which bar poor people.

There are other problems. For example, the entire social setting in which art is presented to the public is a hangover from the days when art was an aristocratic luxury. Musicians in white tie and tails, the sale of subscription tickets, even the hours at which performances or exhibitions are held, reflect the assumption that the culture consumer is monied and leisured. How many plays or concerts are given in the morning? Can a night-shift worker ever attend? The entire culture industry is oriented away from the poor, even when well-intentioned efforts are made to attract them.

Then there is the blatant fact of segregation. While Negro performers are welcome in some branches of the culture industry, in others they are so rare as to suggest a pattern of exclusion. The history of jazz in the United States proves, if proof is needed, that many Negroes are superb musicians. Yet there are scarcely any Negroes to be found in American symphony orchestras.

Any program to bring millions of disadvantaged Americans into contact with cultural activity must fail if they are looked upon purely as "recipients" rather than as participants, but the expansion of amateurism implies widespread opportunities for individual and group participation. For the moment, it merely needs to be emphasized that the arts must, and can, become a field in which anyone who excels, regardless of origin, can find an appropriate place.

Such a program, I argue, would not merely help us cure the disease of poverty but would, at the same time, stimulate the arts. It would do this in at least three ways. First, it would provide additional employment opportunities for artists, many of whom, even in the midst of the culture boom, find it difficult to earn a full-time living from art. Second, it would have a refreshing effect even on established and successful artists by bringing them into contact with new kinds of audiences. Many performers, for example, are invigorated by the experience of confronting something other than a manicured middle-class audience. Facing a fresh audience compels the artist to re-examine his craft and to develop his skills. And third, such a program would be helpful to the artist by giving him a sense of social purpose,

the feeling of participating directly in a worthy and humane enterprise.

For all these reasons, therefore, I would put forward as another
goal for a Great Society the extension of the postwar culture boom to
those sectors of the public still untouched by it. Democracy, I argue,
needs the arts. And the arts are in need of further democratization.

TOWARD THE POSSIBLE

Parallel systems of cultural production to encourage diversity of artistic output; expansion and proper organization of amateurism; and
extension of the culture explosion to reach disadvantaged populations—these, then, are three of the cultural goals that flow from the
high order values of diversity, democracy, and adaptability. All are
based on social processes whose validity is deemed to be probable
rather than improbable or uncertain. They are intended as examples
of goal-setting by more or less rational methods. But, taken together,
they do not add up to a comprehensive set of goals for the arts in our
society.

It is clear, in fact, that we have touched on only a few issues.
From the same set of high order values, many other goals could be
extracted. We might, for example, formulate a goal having to do with
the degree of freedom to be accorded the artist in society. If the artist
is to serve the function of policy review, what limits, if any, should be
placed on his freedom of expression? Similarly, we might devise a goal
statement about the role of criticism as a kind of cybernetic mechanism for calling the artist's attention to social policies that need review.

Other goals might be explored, too. Should it be a goal of national policy to produce art that will "be better than" the art of other
nations—and if so, how is it to be judged? Should it be a goal to
produce a distinctively American art?

The discussion, moreover, brushes only lightly across the issue of
excellence in the arts. Indeed, what is implied here, though not developed, is the notion that excellence itself must have a purpose; that it
is not an end in itself, but that, on the contrary, it can only be judged
in terms of explicit high order values.

The method proposed here also raises questions about the degree
to which the arts should be consciously used for social ends. There

are, of course, many who assume the position that any attempt to use art must, in the end, degrade it. Before rushing to judgment on this issue, however, it pays to remember that from the very beginning art has been exploited for essentially nonesthetic purposes. The cave artist drew to ensure a good hunt, and the Church regarded investment in the artists of the Renaissance as a direct expenditure on propaganda. This did not, apparently, rule out the possibility of producing art that would last beyond its own time.

Is there not, however, a danger that the conscious use of art to foster social ends might lead to totalitarian control and the support of dull, lifeless "agitprop" art of the kind familiar to those who have toured Russian museums?

Unless one is prepared to proclaim ignorance a virtue, the answer is plain. It is not the willingness to use reason that is the danger. The danger lies rather in our *unwillingness* to apply conscious intelligence to our problems. The danger is not that the arts will be controlled— for they are controlled today, in the sense that they are enmeshed in a web of mutual dependencies. The danger is that we will feed the wrong values in at the top, or that we will examine so few hypotheses and conceive of art so narrowly, that we assign it *simple* purposes. That is why the goals proposed here must be regarded as only a small part of a far more complex whole. The danger, in short, lies not in rational method, but in its inadequate use.

In a pluralistic society, with many centers of power and many different kinds of institutions responsible for policy making, the best safeguard for freedom is openness and competition at the value-specifying stage. If every policy maker began with the same set of high order values, and the same set of data about the hypotheses, we might have cause for fear. So long, however, as the society is pluralistic in structure, we can be reasonably certain that different policy makers will specify different high order values, and that the arts will therefore reflect, as they should in our society, multiple purposes and complex objectives. Rationality is not synonymous with either simplicity or intolerance. We may argue all we want about the purposes of art; the clash will be healthy. What is unhealthy is any effort to remove art from the sphere of rational debate.

In the years to come, as the arts become more deeply rooted in American life, as policy makers gain experience in confronting cultural issues, and as government advances toward what might be called "the qualitative society," we shall develop ways of making the politics of the impossible possible. If this essay has contributed toward that end, it will have served its own purpose well.

• NOTES

1. "National Cultural Center, Part III: America's Cultural Needs—Interview Excerpts," prepared by G. A. Brakely and Co., New York, October, 1960. Quotes taken from "Excerpts from Interviews," pp. 1–12.

2. William Schuman, quoted in a speech by James N. Stevens, Secretary of Inland Steel-Ryerson Foundation, June 23, 1962.

3. Marshall McLuhan, *Understanding Media: The Extensions of Man* (New York: McGraw-Hill, 1965), p. 65.

4. Herbert Read, *To Hell with Culture and Other Essays on Art and Society* (New York: Schocken Books, 1963), p. 4

5. Ernst Fischer, *The Necessity of Art* (Baltimore: Penguin Books, 1963), p. 8.

6. The truth, of course, is more complex. In measuring the position of individuals and subcultures, it is not merely the distribution of values that matters but the varying intensities with which they are held, the standards used by value holders to determine whether the value has been attained, and many other criteria. An excellent discussion of the complexities, and a contribution to the methodology of value change measurement, is to be found in "The Dynamics of Value Change," an unpublished paper by Nicholas Rescher, Department of Philosophy, University of Pittsburgh.

7. Read, *op. cit.*, p. 9.

8. In communist countries, this hypothesis is formulated differently. The function of the artist is seen as extending beyond mere criticism. Prevailing orthodoxy insists that the artist, to fulfill his proper function, must be an active agent of social change. Within the range of permissible opinion, and within the canons of socialist realism, the artist is expected to judge reality and to change it in the direction indicated by political authority. Since Stalin's death, there have been periodic contractions and relaxations of political control over the arts in the communist countries, but the belief that the artist must change society, rather than merely comment on it, remains unshaken.

9. Albert Guérard, *Art for Art's Sake* (New York: Schocken Books, 1963), p. xiii.

10. No list of hypotheses can ever be complete because it is possible to assert anything about anything. Not wishing to encumber the reader, I have limited myself to those hypotheses most frequently voiced. For those who may have a more specialized interest, however, I would like to call attention to four others, at least two of which seem to me to be quite testable by scientific means. I would thus continue the list in the following manner:

7. *Art as Sensitizer.* This hypothesis holds that the arts make one more sensitive to sensory stimuli. For example, it is argued that repeated exposure to the array of color in a museum makes the viewer more sophisticated and more subtly discriminative with respect to color perception. It seems to me not too difficult to devise a number of before-and-after experiments that would confirm or disconfirm such contentions.

8. *Art as Creativity Generator.* It is often argued that the arts infuse society with creativity. If we take this to mean that they encourage innovation and imagination, this, too, ought to be testable. For example, if we began with a sample of executives or scientists, we could ask their associates to classify them according to whether or not they are considered to be "imaginative" or "creative" in their work. It would then be interesting to learn whether those rated as

"creative" had had more instruction in or exposure to music or art than those in the "non-creative" group. We assume that teaching art and music in the schools encourages creativity. Does it? And if there is any relationship, is it causal?

9. Art as Social Indicator. Art is said to reflect the values and interests of society. To the degree that it does, it can be exploited as a diagnostic tool by those interested in social trends. Would it be possible to design some kind of index based on themes or other characteristics of art works that would be useful in making predictions about future "states of the system"?

10. Art as Needed Novelty. Too much or too little novelty in life can impair the successful functioning of the human organism. Novelty is an important element in much art—e.g., the unusual juxtaposition of words in poetry, or of hitherto unassociated sounds in music. Each work of art has a different degree of novelty. The individual who puts an "old favorite" on his phonograph may be looking for a little of the unexpected, but not too much. The painting is loved that "always seems to have something new" in it. Effective functioning in daily life depends upon a mix of routine and non-routine activity. Art with high novelty content can be regarded as a means of adjusting the level of novelty in the environment. Thus, art can be said to add dash or verve to the lives of those who are otherwise locked in a routinized existence.

11. The Delphi technique developed by Helmer and Gordon suggests ways for systematizing and quantifying the opinions of experts in fields in which hard data are scarce. The method can be used as a predictive tool; it can also be adapted for use in policy setting. See Olaf Helmar, *Social Technology* (New York: Basic Books, 1966).

12. Alvin Toffler, *The Culture Consumers* (Baltimore: Penguin Books, 1965). See Chs. 10, 11, and 12.

13. This is a goal, moreover, which lends itself to measurement. It is possible to measure statistically the degree of diversity in the cultural infrastructure. It is, therefore, possible to measure progress toward or away from this goal. Moreover, it is possible to measure the degree of diversity not merely of the economic structure of the culture industry, but even of the industry's output. It would be possible, for example, to log the types of productions staged by theaters all over America; the types of music played by symphony orchestras; the types of paintings or sculptures exhibited by galleries and museums, etc. There are already several crude annual surveys of orchestral performances broken down by national origin of composer and by date of composition. These show the degree to which contemporary music, or American music, is part of orchestral programming in the United States. Organizations such as Broadcast Music, Inc., and ASCAP log the types of music broadcast or performed in order to collect royalties for composers. It would be possible to set up a representative sample of cultural institutions and monitor their output regularly. In short, diversity, whether of economic organization or of cultural output, is a measurable phenomenon. If we set diversity as a goal, we can know whether or not we are achieving it.

14. For a more detailed discussion of the ways in which amateurism can support professionalism and excellence, see Toffler, *op. cit.,* pp. 247–250.

15. Margaret Mead, quoted in an article by Richard Lewis in the Chicago *Sun-Times,* November 2, 1966.

16. See Toffler, *op. cit.,* Ch. 3.

17. Final resolution of the poverty problem requires not merely that we change the values of Negroes and poor people, but that the core values of the society itself be altered. The arts can contribute to this end, as well, but this is a far more complicated problem and requires separate treatment.

Chapter 12

Arthur F. Bentley—Fashioner of Social Tools   SIDNEY RATNER

This volume on the Great Society grapples with the major aspects and problems of President Lyndon Johnson's program. The complexities of both the domestic and international scene are so great that we need all the aid we can get from seminal thinkers. Among these is Arthur F. Bentley, a man of such varied achievements and interests that no one scholarly group may claim him exclusively as its own. To political scientists, he is the author of the classic work on pressure groups, *The Process of Government* (1908). To sociologists and psychologists, he is the formulator of a sociological relativism and a social behaviorism embodied in two probing volumes, *Relativity in Man and Society* (1926) and *Behavior, Knowledge, Fact* (1935). To semanticists and mathematicians, he is known for a pioneering, suggestive study, *Linguistic Analysis of Mathematics* (1932). To philosophers, he is a penetrating writer on scientific method and the theory of knowledge, the author of *Inquiry into Inquiries* (1954) and the co-author, with John Dewey, of *Knowing and the Known* (1949). To historians, he is a writer of a pioneer study on the agrarian West, "The Condition of the Western Farmer as Illustrated by the Economic History of a Nebraska Township" (1893).

Bentley's range and profundity of analysis cannot be exemplified by any single essay or volume. It is necessary to study the whole compass of his work. Like Aristotle and Hobbes, he is also a controversial figure. To some, he represents an embodiment of hard-boiled empiricism, radicalism, and skepticism about democracy and the general welfare. Those anxious for world revolution at any cost see him as a champion of the *status quo* because they believe he exalted social equilibrium in order to preserve the existing balance of social classes. But to most behavioral scientists, Bentley's name signifies a major breakthrough in our understanding of politics, society, and the nature of scientific method. This conflict in opinion about Bentley reflects the conflict among different social groups in America, both about the past of American society and the possible future courses it may take. The consensus that President Johnson seeks as the basis for his Great Society invites us to examine the contribution Bentley made to an understanding of social processes. As we study his life, we shall see how he fashioned tools that had a cutting edge both for the problems of his day and for those we face today. A book he wrote in 1920, *Makers, Users, and Masters,* when published, will throw light on the parallel problems arising from the economic power structure in the United States in two notable presidencies: Woodrow Wilson's and Lyndon B. Johnson's.

MULTIDISCIPLINARY BEGINNINGS

Arthur F. Bentley, the eldest son of a small-town banker, was born on October 16, 1870, in Freeport, Illinois. The United States was going through the throes of reconstructing the South and transforming a predominantly rural society into a predominantly urban, industrial society. Bentley went to school in Freeport and was graduated from high school in Grand Island, Nebraska, at the early age of fourteen. After a brief period of study at York College in Nebraska and the University of Denver, he worked for three years as a bank clerk and then entered, at the age of twenty, Johns Hopkins University. There he majored in economics and succeeded in doing the three-year college program in two years. He received an excellent training in economics, history, and political science as well as in philosophy and psychology.

At Hopkins, the professors who undoubtedly influenced him most were two visiting lecturers in economics, John Bates Clark, then at Smith College, and Simon Nelson Patten of Pennsylvania. Richard T. Ely, an authority on European socialism and a critic of unscrupulous business methods, had attracted Bentley to Hopkins through his unorthodox reputation. Unfortunately, Ely went to Wisconsin after

Bentley's first year. Yet Bentley read Ely's writings from that time on and was influenced by him intellectually, even though he had had no personal contact with him. After receiving his A.B. degree, Bentley wrote an excellent essay, "The Condition of the Western Farmer as Illustrated by the Economic History of a Nebraska Township." Published in 1893 in the *Johns Hopkins University Studies in Historical and Political Science,* this monograph revealed his compassion for the struggling American farmer as well as his ability to write objectively and incisively on the problems of the farmer.

Following another year's graduate work in economics and sociology at Johns Hopkins, Bentley went to Germany to study at the universities of Berlin and Freiburg im Breisgau. This transatlantic experience contributed significantly to his intellectual and emotional development.[1] At Berlin Bentley gained views of political economy and the social sciences different from those he had received from laissez-faire economists in America. He learned from Adolf Wagner and Gustav Schmoller why German economists were in favor of supporting state measures for social and economic reform. Wagner stressed the importance of historical relativity through his famous distinction between the historico-legal and the "economic" categories of institutions, forms of behavior, and processes. Schmoller won Bentley's approval for the idea of developing economics on an inductive basis from detailed historical, descriptive studies instead of following the English and Austrian *a priori* hypothetical-deductive model. Bentley eventually concluded that Schmoller did not adequately develop the economic principles or theories needed by economists.

Georg Simmel, however, was the teacher at Berlin who gave the greatest impetus to Bentley's development as an original social thinker. Bentley later characterized Simmel as "the keenest and most searching investigator society has yet had." [2] Bentley was especially impressed by Simmel's analysis of the groups which cross one another in a thousand directions in the social mass, and at whose intersections "personality" and individuality are to be found. Simmel also advanced the thesis that two groups cannot even have a conflict except with some common ground to stand on (culturally as well as physically). Bentley derived much later from Simmel's great treatise *Soziologie,* published in 1908, the insight that in the *Geisteswissenschaften* the "philosophical foundations" are usually much weaker than the scientific structure supposedly built on them.

In June 1894, after one liberating year in Germany, Bentley won a $500 fellowship in economics from Johns Hopkins and decided to accept it. That summer he visited France and England before returning to America. He admired Paris and London, but was horrified by the human misery he discovered in the slums of London.

After returning to Hopkins as a graduate fellow in economics, Bentley worked hard at fulfilling his obligations as a candidate for the doctorate. He read everything he could find on economics and sociology in English, French, and German. He recalled being primarily interested in the problem: What are the components of economic theory? He was dissatisfied with the explanations then offered by all the schools of economics. But he was not able, then or later, to develop in detail his own theory of economic behavior as a phase of the social processes. Instead he wrote an essay, "Units of Investigation in the Social Sciences," which was accepted as a doctoral thesis.[3] In this study Bentley stressed the human mind as a central point in the study of all social phenomena. He soon came, however, to disregard the mentalistic views presented in this thesis.

In June 1895, Bentley received the Ph.D. degree at Johns Hopkins for his work in economics, philosophy, and jurisprudence. He was fortunate in obtaining a position as a docent (lecturer) in sociology at the University of Chicago for the following academic year. But he ran into disaster when he attempted to discuss French and German systems of sociology with about five students. They and he soon agreed to discontinue their meetings. Bentley had become a superb research scholar, but evidently he was not gifted as a teacher. Nevertheless, his position at the University of Chicago gave him a chance to extend his readings in French and German sociology and in the fields of logic and the philosophy of science. Bentley was impressed by Emile Durkheim's analysis, in *De la division du travail social* (1893), of the complex organic unity of an advanced society in which the numerous differences of personal ability, interest, and training are utilized.

An even greater influence on Bentley was John Dewey, chairman of the Chicago Philosophy Department and already the rising star in American philosophy. Dewey was then formulating the basic ideas of the experimental logic and evolutionary naturalism for which he was to become world famous. Bentley attended Dewey's seminars on the Theory of Logic and the Logic of Ethics. In the first seminar, Bentley was especially struck by Dewey's statement that the individual mind or self *is not* an existing thing by itself. Bentley later put this idea as follows: The "individual" formulation can be developed out of the "social" formulation much more vividly and completely than the purportedly "social" can be developed out of the "individual." [4]

GOVERNMENT AS GROUP ACTIVITIES

After a year at the University of Chicago, Bentley left the academic world for a career in journalism. He worked first as a reporter, then (after 1903) as an editorial writer on the Chicago *Times-Herald* and the *Record-Herald*. This experience was the best thing that could have happened to a young intellectual like Bentley, better even than going to a Center for Advanced Study in the Behavioral Sciences! He was brought up against the harsh facts of life as he investigated at firsthand the political, social, and economic activities of that turbulent industrial and transportation center, with all its dramatic contrasts in wealth and poverty, virtue and iniquity. Heroic figures such as Eugene V. Debs, John P. Altgeld, and Jane Addams had to work for the welfare of the working classes against the ruthless and often brutal opposition of many leading businessmen. Here Thorstein Veblen initially got the inspiration for his subtle yet scathing critiques of the American business enterprise.

While earning his livelihood as a newspaper reporter and editorial writer, Bentley carried through the massive and demanding research and writing which resulted in his magnum opus, *The Process of Government*. Ironically enough, he confessed: "My interest in politics is not primary, but derived from my interest in the economic life. . . . I hope from this point of view ultimately to gain a better understanding of the economic life than I have succeeded in gaining hitherto" (p. 210).

Nevertheless, from 1896 until the book's publication in 1908, Bentley was absorbed in studying the stream of political facts that constantly came across his newspaper desk.[5] These facts were about "man-acting." The rich raw material that he accumulated on the role of diverse interest groups in the Chicago City Council and in the Illinois State Legislature spurred him to develop a general theory of social pressures for all phases of government in the United States and the rest of the world. The first sketch and outline of his volume was written in 1905–06 and has an inscription to "Ludwig Gumplowicz, John Dewey, Walt Whitman, Georg Simmel, and the many other joint makers of this book." The Finis reads: "To Any Reader—I am no more the slave of this book than are you."

The original preface read: "Politics in the older sense meant statecraft. In the current sense in America, it means business of acquiring rulership in a titular democracy. In the not far distant future it will mean the activity of the people, who are now sovereign, but not their own rulers, in exercising their sovereignty as rule. In that fact lies the justification of the title, 'Practical Politics,' as applied to the discussions which compose this volume." Bentley experimented with several alternative titles: in December 1905, "The Control of Government: The United States at the opening of the Twentieth Century"; in January 1906, "The Forces of Government & Their Control: A Study of U. S. of America at opening of 20th Century"; finally he hit on this solution: "Why not simply the Process of Gov't., instead of Forces of Gov't. & Their Control—'Forces' are always metaphysical: I am positive—or try to be."

Bentley's concern about social welfare was also expressed in the following manuscript notes for his book:

Scheme: Abandon private ethical ideas. Trust to will of people. Cultivate knowledge, free play for expression of popular will. These are all that democracy requires—not "high personal virtue."

It is not poor private morals, but popular ignorance of state facts, greed of individuals and popular ignorance of harmfulness of this greed that makes our present government rotten. As to nature of social ethics needed, compare union class ethics (labor).

"Plan of Work." "Our gov't."—or "self-governing" Society must be treated under two aspects: (1) personal, (2) policy-making administering. Under (1) will be included how the persons use the policies in their trade. Under (2) How the policies work themselves out thro' the persons. . . .

These seem the best aspects for envisaging the complicated business.

In the past two decades, *The Process of Government* has come to be recognized as one of the outstanding classics in political science. But when it was first published, and for almost thirty years thereafter, it was not widely appreciated. Only a few scholars such as Charles Beard, Peter Odegard, Pendleton Herring, and Karl Llewellyn initially recognized its importance. The "rediscovery" of Bentley's work on a large scale dates from the early 1950's, when Stephen Bailey, Bertram Gross, Earl Latham, David Truman, the present writer, and others first brought Bentley's ideas to a wide public.

The Process of Government has a one-line preface: "This book is an attempt to fashion a tool." Bentley sought a method for understanding the processes of social life. He took the processes of government as his main focus or starting point. The first part of his book is devoted to demonstrating that feelings and faculties, ideas and ideals, including the "social-will," are not separate substantial entities or "things" in or behind society. He did not deny the existence of the feelings, thoughts, and ideals which political, legal, and social theorists such as Herbert Spencer, Rudolph von Jhering, and Albert V. Dicey invoked as social causes or forces. But Bentley rejected the separation of these feelings, ideas, and ideals from social activities as a valid scientific procedure.

Bentley's own revolutionary advance over the "dead political science" of his time is to be found in the last two-thirds of his book. The raw materials of government, he asserted, cannot be found in the law books, in the proceedings of constitutional conventions, in the addresses and essays on tyranny or democracy, or in the "character of the people," in their specific "feelings" or "thoughts," in their "hearts" or "minds." "The raw material can be found only in the actually performed legislating-administrating-adjudicating activities of the nation, and the streams and kinds of activity that gather among the people and rush into these spheres" (p. 180).

After developing his theory of group interests and activities, Bentley examined some cardinal problems of political science: public opinion and leadership, individual endowment and race type, government, law, classifications of governments, and the separation of government agencies. Each subject received incisive analysis and illuminating illustrations from a wide range of countries and historical periods. Among the notable contributions made by Bentley was his repudiation of any simple, rigid classification of social groups.

The major contribution of Bentley, however, is to be found in his positive theory of group interests and activities. Pragmatism had taught: "A thing is what it does." Bentley characterized the term "group" as "a certain portion of the men of a society, taken, however, not as a physical mass cut off from other masses of men, but as a mass activity, which does not preclude the men who participate in it from participating likewise in many other group activities" (p. 211). In other words, a group is a way of action in which many men participate. To him "group" and "group activity" are inseparable in existence though distinguishable in analysis through emphasis on one phase: the *set* or *aggregate* of men, or on the other phase: the *action* of that set of men.

Similarly, "group" and "group interest" are conjoined phases of one process: "so many men bound together in or along the path of a certain activity." Bentley assumed the existence of a goal or a set of goals for each group, but stressed the "going" or "action" as the observable phenomenon. He postulated that there is no group without its interest. "An interest . . . is the equivalent of a group. We may also speak of an interest group or of a group interest. . . . The group and the interest are not separate" (p. 211). Sometimes Bentley emphasized the interest phase, sometimes the group phase, but he never pushed them apart. He spurned as non-scientific the question whether the interest is responsible for the group, or the group for the existence of the interest. "What we actually find in this world, what we can *observe* and *study*, is *interested* men, nothing more and nothing else" (p. 212, my italics).

"Interest" then is operationally defined as *what* a set of men engaged in a joint activity is *interested* in. The social scientist must study each group's own verbally expressed valuation of itself, its activities and objectives, yet he must primarily rely upon what he can observe of that group's line or course of action. If there is a discrepancy between the profession and the conduct of the group, he must give priority to the conduct as against the verbalization. His own valuation of what he thinks is the group's "interest" may supplement, but should not replace, his objective description of the group's goal-directed behavior.

It is important to elucidate here that the same human being who participates in one joint activity with other human beings usually participates in other shared activities with other people. A man, for example, may be a member of a church, a labor union, a consumers' cooperative, a local, state, and national party. These groups will have varying memberships and sometimes may have conflicting interests. With each new activity directed toward a new goal, a new group emerges. A person achieves individuality first by choosing the various groups with which he will act and then deciding, when group conflicts occur, which group loyalty or interest he will give priority to. The individual achieves a rounded life only through multiple group membership. Each group develops another phase of his personality.[6] I have made this analysis of the relation of the individual to diverse groups so explicit because Bentley's text is not so clear as it should be on this point.

Though each group has a certain individuality through its distinctive activities and interests, no group can be described, defined, or valued except in relation to other groups. All group activities are interconnected in a social system, and "get their appearance of individuality by being abstracted from the system; they brace each other up, hold each other together, move forward by their interaction, and in general, are in a state of continuous pressure upon one another" (p. 218).

Each group activity rests in a great sea of social life and is carried on against a "habit background," a set of "rules of the game" that the society has established and lives by. Different societies have different "habit backgrounds," "rules of the game," or socially sanctioned ways of resolving conflicts. What may be customary in one society—for example, Spain, Argentina, or Iran—is not customary in England, Sweden, or the United States. Hence, the "habit background" of each society must be established by careful observation of the conditions under which the different groups in that society operate at the time that they are studied. No reliance can be placed upon "traditions" that may be dead or upon a desired "social whole," "social welfare," or "national interest" that is not embodied in the "habit background" (pp. 218–22).

Bentley has been criticized by Robert MacIver[7] and Leo Weinstein[8] for failing to recognize that the logic of democracy requires a conception of a national unity and welfare superior to the play of special interests. Bentley, however, contended that the whole logic of democracy rests on the postulate that opportunities be provided for competition between opposing group views of the national unity and common welfare.[9] Moreover, he pointed out that when different groups act according to common "habit backgrounds" or "rules of the game," e.g., relying on free elections and the ballot box rather than the suppression of their opponents and the use of bullets, such action means that these "rules of the game" (or moral values) are more important than the particular programs on which they differ. The champions of the civil rights movement, for example, have met resistance by Southern opponents of Negro equality, but these white Southerners have submitted to decisions handed down by the United States Supreme Court. Hotheads still try to circumvent these decisions and even resort to sporadic violence. Nevertheless, no secession by the South from the United States has been attempted, and submission to Federal troops and officials has taken place when the national government has intervened. In other words, the civil rights part of the Great

Society program has gone forward because the inculcated respect for the Constitution, the Supreme Court, and the presidency are superior to the white Southerners' sectional and racial feelings and interests.[10]

Bentley repudiated Marx's theory of the class struggle because Marx had made his classes "too hard and fast," and had overemphasized the economic basis of social groups in too crude a form (pp. 467–468). Bentley also criticized the varied group theories of leading European sociologists as too rigid for "the limitless criss-cross of the groups." He found it useful to distinguish discussion, organization and political groups from the "underlying" geographic, ethnic, property-owning, and occupational groups. But he was free of the tendency to regard social groups or classes as fixed entities. Unlike Marx or Charles Beard, he saw as many classes as there are problems that scientists are interested in exploring in terms of the different interests that human beings pursue through varied group activities. Bentley was a champion of a fluid, flexible group pluralism and a foe of rigid, *a priori* social dogmatism and determinism.

The subject of leadership in politics and government in recent decades has received increased attention owing to the important role played by Hitler in Germany, Stalin in Russia, Churchill in England, and Franklin D. Roosevelt in the United States. Many historians have come to share with Carlyle his belief in great men as major forces in history. Against this tendency to isolate and to exalt historic figures from their social milieu, Bentley spoke out emphatically. Leadership, he explained, is no mere affair of a self-sufficient leader. "The great phenomena of leadership are phenomena of groups differentiated for the purpose of leading other groups." One specialized political or governmental group leads other political or governmental groups in these phases of their activity. Within this sphere of activity in the United States, for instance, occur the decisions and actions of different local, state, and national leaders. Each leader, however, needs to win the support of his group and is as much influenced by it as it is by him. Each national leader could initiate policies but only when backed by powerful interest groups.[11] Franklin D. Roosevelt was the spearhead for the Democratic party leadership groups, each representing different pressure groups. Similarly, Churchill was the spokesman for his World War II coalition government supporters in the British Conservative party and the British Labour party.

At the present time, Lyndon B. Johnson is proposing various domestic and foreign programs designed to create full employment and to raise the quality of living for the great majority of people within the United States. Yet skilled and forceful a political leader as he is, he requires advisers and shock troops from different economic, ethnic, and cultural groups throughout the nation: labor, business, agriculture; white, Negro, Indian; English, West European, East European, Asiatic; Protestant, Catholic, Jew, agnostic, atheist. When Congress does not respond adequately to any of these groups, they usually make demands on the President that he tries to realize in the policies he and his supporters formulate. These groups, then, need him as their spokesman and as their vehicle for getting action. Nevertheless, President Johnson needs their support if he is to realize any of the projects he advances, either at their suggestion or on his own initiative with a view to satisfying them. This relationship of mutual dependence can be seen in fields ranging from foreign policy and national defense to farm, labor, housing, education, and social security programs. The presidency has one man at the top of the governmental leadership groups. But a number of close personal advisers and cabinet officials, e.g., Acheson, McNamara, Rusk, are next to the man at the very apex of the pyramid. Below them is a powerful hierarchy of party and government officials to carry out the orders that come from above. Members of this underlying bureaucracy, however, often suggest to their superiors ideas that are taken up and then presented as coming from the topmost leader. Of course, he has a national responsibility that his subordinates do not bear directly, but do share in varying degrees, according to the rank of their importance.

The insights that Bentley displayed in his study of group interests and governmental leadership can be matched by his analyses of the legislative process, the legal system, political parties, and representative government. Among his achievements in writing *The Process of Government* we should not scant his fashioning a new tool, *process analysis,* based on the examples he drew from his study of group activities. His masterful dismissal of such causal "spooks" as instinct and ideology, and his concentration on the sequences and complex interrelations of men's actions should have alerted political scientists to the central role that "process" played in his thinking. But it is only within the last few years that the word has gone out that "Bentley" means "social change and continuity" or "process," as well as "group." [12] He stressed political "log-rolling," the "adjustment of interests," and "social equilibrium" as phases of change within relatively stable societies. But he was hospitable to social reform and even to revolution, where the proper organs for peaceful change did not or do not exist.[13]

VARIETIES OF PROGRESS IN MAN-SOCIETY

After the publication of *The Process of Government,* Bentley continued in his newspaper work until 1911, when he decided to quit Chicago and the newspaper world. From then on he made Paoli, Indiana, the center of his activities. During World War I he supported the American war effort and helped to organize the state of Indiana for the American Red Cross. With the return of peace Bentley became intensely interested in the cooperatives sponsored by the Non-Partisan League in North Dakota and made a personal investigation of their "radical" activities. In 1920 he wrote an exciting book of some 100,000 words or more on the American business and political scene, entitled *Makers, Users, and Masters.* Unfortunately, the volume was turned down by several publishers and Bentley allowed the manuscript to remain unpublished. The book, however, is valuable for revealing Bentley's social philosophy and his reform program. Since this unknown work is so important, I shall return to it later for detailed discussion.

During the early 1920's, the era of Babbitt, Coolidge, and the postwar boom, Bentley concentrated on a reformulation of his ideas about a science of society. Some time before the outbreak of World War I he had sought to develop, in partial cooperation with a physicist, a technical terminology for the kinds of social phenomena he treated in *The Process of Government.* After the verification and triumph of Einstein's theory of relativity in 1919, Bentley regarded this earlier attempt as antiquated. By 1924 he had written a volume that he felt justified publication. It was not so thoroughly reconstructive of social theory as he desired, but it carried the critical preliminaries as far as possible, given the existing stage of the social sciences.

Relativity in Man and Society reveals Bentley in a new stage of his development as a toolmaker in the social sciences. In the spirit of Hobbes at the time of Galileo, Bentley argued that Einstein's revolutionary theories and methods radically affected the social sciences. Sociologists should discard the absolute space and time of Newton and use instead Einstein's method of viewing space and time as dimensions or integral phases of the events they studied. They needed to introduce their own observational position in space-time and society as an essential factor in their reports on social events.

After reviewing various social theories, Bentley presented a new frame of reference for sociological investigation. He coined the term "man-society" to replace the old dichotomy between the individual and society and to designate the proper subject matter of sociology. Each social fact or situation should be understood as a "cross-section of activity" occurring in a group of human beings. This phrase he later replaced by the term "transaction." Men's minds, feelings, and sensations should be seen as phases of men's bodily behavior. No social situation, he affirmed, is ever instantaneously present, but is always within a duration, involving past and future, "involving by the same token full anticipatory and purposive values."

Every statement about social facts and values (e.g., that Negroes are inferior to whites), Bentley explained, needs to be stated relative to the conditions of its origin and use (e.g., statements by Ku Klux Klan members in an effort to retain white supremacy in the South). Sociological frames of reference comparable to those now used by physics can be established for handling social facts. Perhaps the key statement of Bentley's position on the meaning of social relativism is the following passage:

No social fact [or situation] may be taken in terms of its own description of itself, but every social fact must be taken in terms of its representative values for all other social facts [or situations]. . . .

No value reference may be universalized for an assumed social whole.

No posited individual man, nor any abstraction or personification of him may be used as a measure or standard of value. . . .

The first duty of each of us in investigating [society] is to analyze and bring out clearly to ourselves the social cross-sectional activities [of our class, ethnic group, religion] we ourselves are identified with and representing, not only generally, but in each special piece of work. . . .

What is emphasized around us is no test . . . of what is emphasized or scientifically important in societies *socially remote* from us [my italics]: and social remoteness may coexist with nearness in time and in Euclidean space (pp. 211–212).

In other words, Einstein had shown how it was possible (1) to explain the diversity of physical perspectives and (2) to translate the results obtained by one observer in one coordinate system into the perspective of an observer in another coordinate system. Similarly, American society today is seen very differently by middle-class white Anglo-

Saxon Protestants and socially insecure, culturally deprived immigrants from Puerto Rico or Negroes in the black ghettos of Harlem and Watts. A balanced picture of the United States requires the presentation of the divergent views of our society held by all the different groups in our country. Then we have achieved an approximation to true objectivity.

To some readers, Bentley's plea for making explicit the frames of reference for various social groups made him seem Olympian, far above the social battle, the conflict of classes, churches, nations, and races. Although emotionally concerned about these conflicts, Bentley deliberately sought to be scientifically "neutral" in stating the diversity of group interests on different economic, political, or social questions, e.g., public housing and labor unions. His objectivity in political science was like that of Franz Boas in anthropology when he dealt with the varied behavior patterns and values of primitive and "civilized" peoples.

With Bentley's impartiality went a genuine tolerance for people whose ways of action and standards of value differed from, or even conflicted with, his own. Like Justice Holmes, he had achieved the mark of a civilized man: the ability to question the presuppositions of his group, culture, and age. Bentley's moral relativism was based on an unusually acute sense of how much social scientists still have to learn about human behavior. Much wisdom is required to distinguish between the desire and the desirable, between immediate goods and reasonable goods. Unlike the champions of right-wing or left-wing elites, from Mosca and Pareto to Lenin and Mao Tse-tung, Bentley never believed he had a magic key to the future course of events or the right to prescribe to all of mankind a set of ideal goals. Once, I recall, at a philosophical conference at which Harold Lasswell spoke on the role of political elites, Bentley exclaimed, "What are elites, but sores upon the body politic!"

Yet in *Relativity in Man and Society*, Bentley did take a strong stand on various social issues. He could discern no single line or path of development in history for any human activity: "Not progress, but progresses, is what we find in man-society" (p. 191). This pluralistic approach to progress grew out of his conviction that each social group has its own values. His cultural pluralism, hence, was a means of exposing and counteracting the class, national, or racial arrogance of different groups throughout the world who claim what is "good" for themselves must be good for all other people.

Bentley did identify himself with those groups that took a position against war, "not war absolutely or war forever, but war in the next generation or the next century between the nations as they now exist" (p. 195). He admitted there were profits in war for certain groups, or even for a nation in certain areas. But, he argued, these were profits only in the short run, and the apparent profits were losses in the long run.

The difficulties in the way of achieving world peace he clearly realized were tremendous. But the resistance between social groups might be lessened and overcome by small stages of advance in understanding. Although the world was facing the likelihood of various great conflicts, he did not believe these conflicts were inevitable or irresolvable. "All social life is a resolution of conflicts, provisional always, with new conflicts arising . . . but with new creations succeeding" (p. 199).

Thirteen years later World War II destroyed the hopes of Bentley and others that wisdom and social sympathy would win the race against Nazi Germany and Japan's appeal to force. Bentley, however, was not caught by surprise. He had hoped that cultural pluralism might yield an approximation to "a virile peace," but he confessed this is what we all most despair of "in the hidden parts of our lives, while our values are given us in darkness" (p. 199). Here Bentley seems to say that only as each nation and class agrees to limit its claims to power can peace be established. But he fears that the excesses of nationalism and the class cannot be curbed.

The question arises: Why has *Relativity in Man and Society* been so long overlooked? One reason is that some critics attacked the validity of Bentley's key positions. Pitirim Sorokin unjustly charged that Bentley's sociology was "mechanistic," and was marred by the imperfection of other schools of social physics. Others rejected Bentley's argument about the necessity for basing sociology on non-Euclidean geometry and Einsteinian physics. This proposal was too radical for most sociologists. Yet there is no doubt that Bentley's social relativism contributes to scientific objectivity by making explicit the frame of reference within which observations are made by any one observer.

Some sociologists concurred in Bentley's program for systematized knowledge of the network of human relations. They agreed with his assertion that human behavior is manifest only in cross-sectional activity across varying groups of human beings, e.g., farm, business, and trade union organizations. The overwhelming majority of sociologists, however, contended that the human being who regards himself as a "self" has to be taken as the fulcrum of the sociological lever, as the point of initial and final focus. Bentley's insistence on viewing persons as absorbed in many social groups did not satisfy these critics. Their criticisms prevailed, on the whole, against the praise for Bentley's work by such recognized sociologists as Leopold von Wiese in Germany, G. L. Duprat in Switzerland, George Lundberg in the United States, and the brilliant, anonymous reviewer for the London *Times Literary Supplement.*[14]

After completing in 1924 the manuscript of his *Relativity* book, Bentley tried his hand at reform politics. He became a member of the national Progressive Party committee and was chairman of the Indiana state committee in charge of the campaign for Robert La Follette as President. When Calvin Coolidge, "a Puritan in Babylon," won the election, Bentley turned from politics to the writing of some impressive essays on behaviorism and on the relations of sociology to mathematics. He corresponded or came into personal contact with eminent mathematicians like L. E. J. Brouwer in Holland, Friedrich Waismann in Austria, and P. W. Bridgman at Harvard, and with the semanticist Count Korzybski in New York.

In 1932, Bentley published his *Linguistic Analysis of Mathematics,* a powerful exploration of the nature of meaning and postulate in mathematics and the other sciences. He proposed to resolve various problems in the philosophy of mathematics by clarifying the relations of "ordinary language" to mathematical signs and symbols. He tried to support the efforts of the noted German mathematician, David Hilbert, to exhibit mathematics as a self-sufficient, consistent system.

In moving from the problems of pure mathematics to those of the empirical sciences, Bentley found that his independent judgments on the vital interplay of theory, observation, and experiment in the sciences were supported by the work of John Dewey on experimental logic and of P. W. Bridgman on the logic of modern physics. Bentley concluded that formal logic had to be considered as one valuable element in scientific inquiry, rather than as its *a priori* foundation. His analysis strengthened Dewey's position in his noted treatise, *Logic: The Theory of Inquiry* (1938).

Bentley's next major experiment in toolmaking was in his important critique of social science methodology.[15] After demonstrating the special role of language and communication in human behavior,

Bentley attacked four traditional dichotomies between mind and body, mind and object, man and society, and the biological organism and its environment. He then showed the advantages of viewing individuals and the objects of their perceptions and communications as distinguishable but inseparable aspects of diverse behavioral processes or events. He revolted against the theoretical and social damage created by theories exalting the arbitrary separation of individuals from social groups and of human society from the rest of biological and physical nature. Here Bentley developed ideas that he and Dewey later were to expand and call "the transactional approach."

The philosophical warfare that Bentley carried on against metaphysical dualisms he extended to the hard-and-fast distinctions between the theoretical and the practical, the normative and the descriptive. A rigorous examination of the activities of research workers or theorists in specific space-time frames of reference reveals that all social science research is begun with an anticipation of special goals or consequences. The separation between theory and practice, fact and theory, is tentative and useful up to a point. But when social conflicts become intense, as between capital and labor in the 1929 depression, the wise scientific as well as social policy is for researchers to make explicit their theoretical and value assumptions and the practical import of their studies. Then the class, ethnic, or other biases of supposedly objective observers can be discovered and corrected, or the absence of such bias can win public support for policies that otherwise might be rejected (e.g., deficit-spending in the 1930's as a means of stimulating recovery).

Although *Behavior, Knowledge, Fact* never reached a wide public, it won high praise from leading sociologists and philosophers for its penetrating criticisms and constructive contributions to social science methodology. John Dewey hailed it as a "landmark in more than psychology." He found it of great value in clarifying his ideas on space-time and the relations of logic to psychology for the *Logic* volume he was then engaged in writing.[16]

"TRANSACTIONAL" ANALYSIS

After 1935, for some fourteen years, Bentley published no book, but many important articles. His hope was that his work on the logic and theory of science would benefit future generations, if not the people of his own day. A period of intensified productive activity began with Dewey's suggestion in June 1943 that they do a joint language study. Out of this proposal flowed an unusual co-authorship and a rich correspondence. Bentley's marriage to Imogene Shaw of Indianapolis in May 1946 brought him companionship and encouragement during this period of collaboration with Dewey and throughout the rest of Bentley's life. In 1949 Dewey and Bentley's *Knowing and the Known* was published, just in time to celebrate Dewey's ninetieth birthday and Bentley's seventy-ninth.

The first half of Bentley and Dewey's historic work attacked with verve and great critical severity various errors and linguistic inconsistencies in widely accepted "mentalistic," "realistic," and "positivistic" theories of logic and scientific knowledge. In the constructive portions of the book Dewey and Bentley developed a trial group of terms that would promote cooperation and lessen misunderstanding among philosophers. They sought to help others to see "language, with all its speakings and writings, as man-himself-in-action-dealing-with-things." They rejected the still-fashionable isolation of "real" objects from "mind," of "words" from the speaker, of "knowings" from the "knowns."

They based their repudiation of these and other traditional dualisms on a powerful new tool of social and philosophical inquiry: *transactional analysis.* By means of this procedure they "asserted the right to see together, existentially and durationally, much that is talked about conventionally as if it were composed of irreconcilable separates" (p. 69). In line with this approach, the word "transaction" came to carry two implications: (1) that all parts of a situation (e.g., baseball batter, pitcher, teammates, umpire, fans, rules of the game) enter into it as active participants, and (2) they they owe their special character in the situation to this active participation as elements in one process. They do not appear as already existing entities that can interact with one another without affecting their identity (pp. 103–143).[17]

One example of transaction is the interdependence of our perception and presupposition about any event, object, or person, e.g., whether we see something as near or far, straight or crooked. Other examples of transaction would be the indispensable linkage between governments and citizens; employers and employees; writers, publishers, and the reading public. Another instance of transaction is the placing of all individual and group activities in their varied physical settings. Farmers, miners, businessmen, industrial workers, clerks, professional people: doctors, lawyers, teachers, engineers—each has to be seen in his special geographical location and environment. The separation of history and geography, of the social and the natural sciences, is an artificial one. Life breaks through all the boundary lines of academic disciplines and needs to be studied and presented as a series of transactions between specific biologic organisms and the rest of nature.

But valuable as the transactional approach is, I believe that when the need arises to stress the moral value or historical significance of individual choice and action, e.g., in a dictatorship, a non-transactional approach is justifiable. Too rigid an adherence to the "transaction" formulation could liquidate the special qualities of individuality. Although some readers have inferred that the transactional approach must be mechanistically applied, or interpreted, this is not supported by a careful reading of Dewey and Bentley.

Knowing and the Known provided the stimulus or reinforcement for important creative research in several significant fields. The transactional approach, for example, has been put to use in biology, physics, political science, psychology, and sociology. Leaders in this work have been Adelbert Ames, Jr., Ludwig von Bertalanffy, Niels Bohr, P. W. Bridgman, Hadley Cantril, Theodosius Dobzhansky, Bertram Gross, and George Lundberg, not to mention Dewey and Bentley.

After the critical acclaim given to *Knowing and the Known,* Bentley settled down at the age of seventy-nine to rounding out his ideas on language, logic, and scientific inquiry. These essays and various other seminal papers of Bentley's were collected and published in 1954 in *Inquiry into Inquiries.*[18] In May 1957, shortly before Bentley died, P. W. Bridgman and other noted thinkers sent him a volume of essays in his honor: *Life, Language, Law.*[19] Seven years later the Rutgers University Press published the philosophic dialogues of John Dewey and Arthur F. Bentley: *A Philosophical Correspondence 1932–1951.*[20] The Syracuse University Great Society Seminar which led to the development of the present volume is additional evidence of the continuing impact of Bentley's work.

MAKERS, USERS, AND MASTERS

One of the hoped-for joys of the historian is the discovery of evidence or writings that throw new light on a great author. This pleasure was vouchsafed to me when, in the 1950's, I read the manuscript of Bentley's unpublished work, *Profiteering: The Relations of Makers, Users, and Masters in America*. At that time I was able only to mention it briefly in writing a biographical sketch of Bentley.[21] I am glad of the present opportunity to do greater justice to its importance.

In this volume, written in 1920, Bentley discards the pose of the completely detached, emotionally uninvolved observer. A new aspect of Bentley's personality is revealed to his public: the scrupulously careful observer of economic exploitation and waste who is moved by compassion and anger to indict the profiteering captains of business and finance and to propose a vigorous program of political and economic reform.

When we examine closely the text of *Makers, Users, and Masters* (the title I prefer), we discover that Bentley in 1920 feared that the American people were facing a crisis created by excessive claims against the future national income. Alongside the democratic political government had evolved an autocratic industrial government that was based upon closely concentrated holdings by very small but extremely powerful groups in industry, trade, and finance.

Bentley's book makes basic distinctions between property and fictitious claims to property, between production and appropriation (the power to obtain wealth or income without labor), between profit and "profiteering" (the power to take rather than to produce), between wealth and "capitalization" (the setting of often fictitious values on shares of stock). Fundamentally he saw the system of big business enterprise which had developed after the Civil War as prospering at the expense of the working classes, the farmers, and the small and medium-sized businessmen.

In seven devastating chapters, Bentley showed how exceptionally high gains in wealth and income had been obtained by the giant firms and trusts. With audacity and skill they had seized strategic positions on the highways between maker and user in industry, trade, credit, land, transportation, and technology. The result had been exorbitant gains for a few obtained through restricted production, unnecessary waste, and high prices. The precise magnitude of these gains

Bentley demonstrated in an impressive statistical chapter on the distribution of wealth and income as well as on the concentration of control of industry and finance in the period 1910–20. He also worked out a path-breaking National Balance Sheet of assets and liabilities several decades before they became widely used. Bertram Gross is now proposing National Social Accounting that goes beyond economic assessment, but is in line with Bentley's objectives.

Bentley's indictment was in keeping with the teachings of such laissez-faire economists as J. B. Clark and of such severe critics of capitalism as Thorstein Veblen. Joseph A. Schumpeter and the revisionist school of American historians would have argued that big business had brought many major benefits to America.[22] Nonetheless, Bentley could make a strong case for both his main position and most of his specific charges.

He also sensed that the economic strain of World War I and the success of the Bolshevik Revolution in Russia had created a new critical situation in America and Europe. During the war the tremendous profits of big business, the huge government war debts, and the severe inroads on civil liberties in Europe and America had imposed burdens upon the working classes that made some consider a revolution against industrial and financial capitalism the only solution. In the United States the autocratic behavior of big business had created the conditions for revolution in the ranks of dissatisfied wage-earners, especially among the I.W.W. Bentley thought that a convulsive proletarian revolution in this country would result in radical destructiveness rather than in the construction of a new social order. He anticipated that big business might react to the prospect of a labor revolution by abandoning political democracy and establishing a right-wing dictatorship.

The middle classes in America, Bentley felt, had to avoid being made a supporter or a victim of either the workers' or the big business revolution. The first task of the middle classes was to realize that big business had put through a revolution in the post-Civil War period when it destroyed laissez-faire competition and began replacing it with monopoly (or oligopoly). In so doing, the industrial oligarchy had also been responsible for driving labor toward revolution.

Hence, the middle classes should set in motion a "counter-revolution" that would be directed at abolishing the "profiteering" system. Bentley urged the formation of more small business and farm enterprises. Forty-five years before the Johnson anti-poverty program, he made the revolutionary proposal that the government should establish a minimum income for all workers. Another major objective of the middle class should be to promote the general welfare through an extensive increase in public buildings and parks and the widest expansion of public education. Here Bentley anticipated J. K. Galbraith's plea in 1958 for developing the public sector of the economy on a scale far greater than ever before envisaged.[23]

Since the two major parties operated during and after World War I as the northern and southern sections of one agency for big business, Bentley suggested that the middle class first rely on nonpartisan pressure groups such as the Municipal Voters League of Chicago, the Non-Partisan League in the Northwest, the consumer movement, the Farm Bureau Federation, the Farmers National Council, the members of the old Progressive Party, the moderate socialists, and the reform groups in the Catholic, Protestant, and Jewish religious organizations. Eventually these middle-class groups might form a National Property Rights Party and compel the consolidation of the Democratic and Republican parties, "making one body as well as one spirit out of the twain."

Although during the 1920's there were some bitter struggles between labor and capital, they did not produce a workers' revolution in the United States. Bentley's anticipation of a major economic crisis was realized, however, by the October 1929 stock crash and the ensuing Great Depression. Franklin D. Roosevelt and his New Deal program fortunately averted the possibility of a *coup d'état* either by labor or big business. Yet the seizure of power by Mussolini in 1922 and by Hitler in January 1933 can be regarded as confirming Bentley's uneasy prognostication of deep trouble ahead in Europe and America.

Bentley's belief that the old major parties might merge and one of them be replaced by a new liberal party was proved false. The Democratic party in 1932 became rejuvenated through new ideas of welfare capitalism, as it had in 1896 after borrowing most of the Populist party's planks. Bentley probably had been excessively discouraged by the defeats that Wilson and the liberal wing of the Democratic party had suffered in Congress between 1917 and 1920, and at the Paris Peace Conference.

The economic reforms Bentley wished to see enacted were realized in varying degrees first by F.D.R.'s New Deal and Truman's Fair Deal, then by Kennedy's New Frontier. Now Johnson's Great

Society program is carrying through even more drastic reforms bene-fiting the underprivileged. One major divergence from Bentley's an-ticipations was the evolution of our economic system into "a system of countervailing power." [24] Big business was not cut down in size, but it was counterbalanced by big labor and big agriculture. Bentley un-doubtedly would have favored a vigorous anti-trust program and large-scale government aid for small business. He would have sympa-thized with those champions of the Great Society who advocate de-centralization and utilization of people on the local level for initiat-ing or administering national welfare programs. His heart would have been in the fostering of producers' and consumers' cooperatives.

Bentley's preference for smaller groups would have been based on his theory that they stood a better chance than very large groups to develop communal feelings. Yet he realized that a powerful central government was necessary to liberate oppressed ethnic groups or ex-ploited workers and farmers from the vested local and state interests. He probably would have proposed that the civil rights movement be broadened and strengthened by a full employment and minimum in-come guarantee program for both Negroes and whites. On the inter-national dimensions of a Great Society, Bentley wrote little. But his personal correspondence justifies the belief that he would have ap-proved the American government's resistance to totalitarian aggres-sion, support for the United Nations, and aid to the underdeveloped areas of the world.

The importance of *Makers, Users, and Masters* to political and social scientists stems in part from its revelation of Bentley as one who demonstrated that he could be both a rigorous social scientist and a citizen. As a citizen, he articulated his own values and worked out an action program for the middle-class and working groups with which he identified himself. His citizenship complemented and rounded out his pursuit of science. This volume is also significant because Bentley called attention to important areas where the welfare of the American people was not safeguarded. The social problems he perceived, and his proposed solutions, we have seen, are still relevant to current efforts to create the Great Society. As we grapple with these problems, we are carrying on the great tradition that Bentley exemplifies: the fusion of science, values, and social action.

•NOTES

1. For Bentley's friendship with Hutchins Hapgood, a fellow American student in Europe, see the letters reprinted in Neith Boyce and Hutchins Hapgood (eds.), *The Story of an American Family* (Chicopee, Mass.: Brown-Murphy, n.d.).

2. Arthur F. Bentley, *Relativity in Man and Society* (New York: Putnam's, 1926), p. 163.

3. *Annals of the American Academy of Political and Social Science,* V (1895), 915–941.

4. For a detailed treatment of Dewey and Bentley's overlapping careers, see my Introduction to Sidney Ratner and Jules Altman (eds.), and James W. Wheeler (associate ed.), *John Dewey and Arthur F. Bentley, A Philosophical Correspondence: 1932–1951* (New Brunswick: Rutgers University Press, 1964). On Bentley's relation to Durkheim and other sociologists, see *Relativity in Man and Society,* pp. 157–178, 296–321.

5. In 1899, Bentley married one of the pioneer women doctors, Anna Harrison, whom he had known as a schoolgirl in Nebraska. She died in 1924. Six years later he married Susan Chipman; their marriage lasted until her death in 1942.

6. See Solomon Asch, *Social Psychology* (New York: Prentice-Hall, 1952), pp. 205–272.

7. *The Web of Government* (New York: Macmillan, 1948), p. 220. For a thoughtful, provocative critique of pressure-group theory, see Mancur Olson, Jr., *The Logic of Collective Action* (Cambridge: Harvard University Press, 1965), pp. 117–167.

8. "The Group Approach: Arthur F. Bentley," Herbert J. Storing (ed.), *Essays in the Scientific Study of Politics* (New York: Holt, Rinehart, and Winston, 1962), pp. 151–224, especially p. 197.

9. Bertram M. Gross, "Book Review: *The Process of Government,*" *American Political Science Review,* XL (1950), 742–748.

10. See Anthony Lewis, *Portrait of a Decade: The Second American Revolution* (New York: Random House, 1964).

11. See Richard E. Neustadt, *Presidential Power: The Politics of Leadership* (New York: Wiley, 1960).

12. See Norman Jacobson, "Causality and Time in Political Process," *American Political Science Review,* LXIII (March 1964), 15–22.

13. A distorted view of Bentley as a justifier of "cynical conservatism" and power politics is to be found in Myron Q. Hale, "The Cosmology of Arthur F. Bentley," *American Political Science Review,* LIV (December 1960), 955–961. His misinterpretations are corrected in part by Jacobson, *op. cit.* See Robert T. Golembiewski, " 'The Group Basis of Politics,' " *American Political Science Review,* LIV (December 1960), 962–971.

14. See Pitirim A. Sorokin, *Contemporary Sociological Theories* (New York: Harper, 1928), pp. 12, 28 n., 620 n., 647 n.; George Lundberg, *Foundations of Sociology* (New York: Macmillan, 1940), *passim;* Leopold von Wiese (and Howard Becker), *Systematic Sociology* (New York: Wiley, 1932), pp. 102–108; London *Times Literary Supplement* (December 16, 1926), No. 1,298, p. 924; C. L. Duprat, "Review," *Revue Internationale de Sociologie,* XXXV (1927), 172–177.

15. *Behavior, Knowledge, Fact* (Bloomington, Ind.: Principia Press, 1935).

16. Dewey and Bentley, *A Philosophical Correspondence: 1932–1951, op. cit.,* pp. 53–69.

17. See Bentley, "The Word 'Transaction,' " *The Humanist,* XVII (1957), 17–24; William H. Ittelson and Hadley Cantril, *Perception: A Transactional Approach* (Garden City, N. Y.: Doubleday, 1959).

18. Sidney Ratner (ed.) (Boston: Beacon Press, 1954).

19. Richard Taylor (ed.) (Yellow Springs, Ohio: Antioch Press, 1957).

20. Sidney Ratner and Jules Altman (eds.), James T. Wheeler (associate ed.), with an Introduction by Sidney Ratner, pp. 3–147.

21. "A. F. Bentley's Inquiries into the Behavioral Sciences," *Life, Language, Law, op. cit.*, pp. 35–36.

22. For a critique of both sides, see Fritz Machlup, *The Political Economy of Monopoly* (Baltimore: Johns Hopkins Press, 1952) and Sidney Ratner (ed.), *New Light on the History of Great American Fortunes* (New York: Augustus Kelly, 1953). On the theory of profit and welfare, see William J. Baumol, *Welfare Economics and the Theory of the State* (2nd ed.; Cambridge, Mass.: Harvard University Press, 1965); Frank H. Knight, *Risk, Uncertainty and Profit* (Boston: Houghton Mifflin, 1921); and Joseph A. Schumpeter, *Business Cycles* (2 vols.; New York: McGraw-Hill, 1939).

23. John Kenneth Galbraith, *The Affluent Society* (Boston: Houghton Mifflin, 1958), pp. 189–211, 233–249.

24. Galbraith, *American Capitalism* (Boston: Houghton Mifflin, 1952); Sidney Ratner, "The Need for a Semantic Revolution in Economic History," *Second International Conference of Economic History* (2 vols.; The Hague: Mouton, 1965), Vol. II, 837–852.

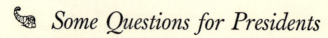 *Some Questions for Presidents*

BERTRAM M. GROSS

> *For your information, let me ask you a question.*
> —Sam Goldwyn

In the face of uncertainty, people and nations may easily lose their bearings. If the center cannot hold, things may fall apart. Since World War II, vast new uncertainties have been created throughout America and its world environment. Old empires have collapsed and new ones have arisen. The industrial revolution that transformed the Western world a century ago is now making itself felt in the two-thirds of the world still mainly agricultural. The highly industrial nations are in the throes of transformation to cybernetic "service societies." Science-based technology—with its computers, worldwide communication networks, information explosions, supersonic and outer-space flight, unbelievable potentialities for saving life and all-too-believable capacities for destroying it—is rendering obsolete many old institutions, beliefs, and concepts. The bipolar world power system of 1945–55 (which replaced the precarious balance of power of previous decades) is being replaced by multicentricity and by interpenetrating, instead of exclusive, spheres of influence. We are now experiencing the painful emergence of a new world society of increasingly interdependent people, organizations and nations. All this means new conflicts at home and abroad, new cultural values, new tensions among and within people, new confusions, new uncertainties, perhaps even a new spiritual malaise. In these circumstances the American presidency has a new role in America and the world.

Over the years, the scope and power of the presidency has steadily grown. The constitution makers gave the President the roles of chief of state, chief executive, commander-in-chief, chief diplomat and chief legislator. Since Jefferson, the President has also become chief of party, since Jackson, voice of the people, since Wilson and Roosevelt, world leader, since Truman, manager of prosperity and the bomb. Since Kennedy's recognition of Negro rights as a moral issue, the President has more clearly than ever had the role of moral leader. The new role of the White House is to provide *a center of creative stability in the midst of turbulent change.*

A weak President cannot live up to this role. By immobility or over-rigidity vis à vis some situations and over-reaction to others, he may contribute to breakdown. A strong President, by combining innovation with stability, can help hold things together. A great President can inspire new confidence among people—even those who oppose him at home and abroad—in their own capability for creative response to unprecedented challenges. In this century Franklin D. Roosevelt, four times elected President of the United States, provided an example of such greatness:

> As great men are reckoned, Franklin Roosevelt was undeniably a great man. His impact on history was enormous. Inspiring the American people and causing them to recapture faith in themselves and in their democracy, he engineered a sweeping social and economic revolution known as the New Deal. He led with magnificent self-assurance, buoyancy, and grace. He intervened successfully and decisively in a global war. He was the chief architect of the United Nations.[1]

But this was a past era.

In 1964 and 1965, with his Great Society programs and their resonant emphasis on the "quality of life," Lyndon Johnson made his first claim to presidential greatness. But by the 1966 mid-term congressional elections, with the expanding Asian war absorbing ever more attention, the administration officially shelved the Great Society slogan. By the summer of 1967, more than 12,000 Americans had been killed in Viet Nam and scores of people met their death in riots at home. With flames and terror rising in the slums of Detroit, Newark and many other cities, many believed that America had become a *sick* society.[2] By 1968, despite the vitality or promise of some continuing Great Society programs, *the Great Society vision—as an energizing political force and a symbol of high aspiration—was dead.*

What will be the new claims to presidential greatness? How can we judge them in terms of their real-life meaning in the lives of people? What are the emerging tests of presidential leadership?

For the information of our Presidents and ourselves, we must ask these questions vigorously. We must put them to presidential candidates, presidential appointees, staff aides, and to the many behind-the-scenes "brain trusters" and unseen or would-be "President makers." In an era of "image making" there is nothing we can do to prevent public relations experts from doing their best at "presidential packaging." But we must also look beneath the tinseled wrapping and assess the contents.

"In the United States, we like to 'rate' a President," writes Richard Neustadt. "We do not wait until a man is dead; we rate him from the moment he takes office." [3] Nor do we wait until a presidential candidate is nominated; we rate him from the moment he is regarded as a possible candidate. We usually rate both Presidents and candidates by "outcomes"—what is happening or may happen to the country. Neustadt suggests that we also rate their personal capacity to influence outcomes—by their skills in persuasion and in achieving a high reputation among government "pro's" as well as the general public.

In this chapter I shall join these two approaches by raising questions bearing on *both* the ability to "get things done" and the nature of the "things." Specifically, I shall suggest that a President be judged —and judge himself—by the extent to which he provides himself, Congress and the country with reliable information on the changing state of the nation and its world environment; contributes to peace among nations; promotes justice at home; helps to improve the quality of American life; and—most important—engenders confidence in his ability to learn from experience. In short, how can a President provide dynamic and stabilizing leadership unless he is—and is seen as—truth teller, peace maker, champion of justice, humanist, and learner?

In discussing these questions I shall be providing some concrete answers to the major questions raised in Chapter 1:

1. Just what is—and should become—the content of the Great Society idea?

2. How can we best measure desired and actual change in any society?

This discussion will be relevant not only to a "just," "creative," "free" or "great" society, but also to other visions of the promised land toward which aspirants to presidential power will inevitably offer to lead us.[4] I shall try to discuss these matters without oversimplifying the enormous complexities of political power and human decision-making at the White House or underestimating a President's dependence on other forces in society.

THE PRESIDENT AS TRUTH TELLER

The President of the United States has long been expected to make some form of accounting—regularly—to the people. His annual State of the Union message is grounded in the Constitution, his Economic and Manpower reports in law, and his press conferences in custom.

By equally hallowed custom, opposition candidates must bluntly challenge (and dissidents in his own party vaguely disparage) the President's credibility. In recent times Franklin Roosevelt, Truman, Eisenhower and Kennedy were all charged with having withheld information from the public. Each was criticized for doing what political necessity, and sometimes national security, has always required—namely, trying to withhold confidential information or protect himself from damaging criticism. By 1968, these charges reached a new high with attacks on the Johnson administration's "credibility gap."

Some of the venom in these attacks stemmed from a sincere but naïve faith in the omniscience of the men in the White House and their cohorts of information gatherers. This myth is partly rooted in the "primitive monistic ideal" that helps adults duplicate childhood experiences of dependence on all-knowing parents.[5] For those who fear drowning in a sea of bewilderment, it provides a straw at which to grasp. The President *really* knows the truth, it is assumed; he should just be more frank.

But does a President—by virtue of his office—really know?

One of the great political quips of all time was Abraham Lincoln's remark that "You can fool *all* the people *some* of the time, *some* of the people *all* of the time—but *not* all the people all of the time." More than a century later, when rapid change has made deception easier, we must grimly add: "We can fool *ourselves* most of the time."

A President, I fear, can do this as well as anyone else. Besides, he has more people avidly eager to help him in the complex processes of self-deception:

powerful bureaucracies, corporations and political factions, each deluging the President with information designed to have him serve as *their* instrument;

a vast statistical establishment steadily grinding out data based on obsolescing concepts and definitions;[6]

an unbalanced array of specialized staff experts (mainly budgeteers, economists and "national security" personnel) refining all this information into bits and pieces that rarely fit together; and

devoted personal advisers trying to protect the President from drowning in the informational deluge by sifting out tidbits to help cope with last month's crisis or the next elections.

Among all these helpers are people with distinguished records of self-deception. Some are merely ostriches, their heads snugly buried in the warm sands of ancient memos and bureaucratic fantasy. The more dangerous ones are the dinosaurs, basking in the memory of former glory, blind to the social or technological changes that have rendered them obsolete, ever willing to carry the President with them as they stumble into the graveyard of history.

The result of all this is an "intelligence gap" that often denies the President indispensable information on where we have been, where we are, and on new happenings just around the corner. To the extent that this is so, it is far more terrifying than the "credibility gap." Incredible though it may seem, it means that the President himself may not have *obtained or absorbed enough information worth sharing with the public.*

Accordingly, we must ask some blunt questions concerning not only the micro-intelligence provided by government agencies but also a President's or candidate's capacity to appreciate the broader changes taking place in American society.

THE INTELLIGENCE GAP

American military history has been punctuated by many dramatic failures in intelligence. In the fall of 1950, while American troops under United Nations flags were moving northward in Korea, American intelligence officers were busy reporting such pearls of wisdom as agricultural production levels in China. What General MacArthur and President Truman apparently did not learn was that masses of Chinese troops were already moving southward. This piece of intelligence seems to have been first acquired on the day when waves of Chinese infantry rolled across the border.

Eight years earlier at Pearl Harbor the intelligence gap consisted of failure to pay attention to available information. Two days before the Japanese attack, three Signal Corps officers in Washington intercepted Japanese code messages indicating "attack on an American installation in the Pacific by one p.m. on December 7, 1941." But their efforts to communicate with high military officials were unsuccessful. The general in charge of the War Plans Division felt that "enemy information of such grave moment would be brought to my attention by the Assistant Chief of Staff, G–2, and not by a Signal Corps officer."[7] Indeed, at Pearl Harbor itself local officers received many warnings relating to the possibility of external attack. But these were screened out by the prevailing military premise concerning the probable Japanese danger: internal sabotage by the large Japanese population in Hawaii.[8]

It would be comfortable to think that such intelligence failures could not possibly exist in domestic affairs. At home, we feel much closer to what's going on—and we don't have to worry so much about the "brass hats" with narrow premises.

Indeed, since World War II, we have been steadily harnessing our data processing potentials to the need for improved, coordinated information.

1. Under the Employment Act of 1946, we have been building up a sophisticated system of improved macro-economic intelligence.

2. In 1963, the annual Economic Reports of the President were supplemented by an annual Manpower Report.

3. In 1965, the President established the new Planning-Programming-Budgeting System to provide better information on the short- and long-range impact of all government programs.

4. In 1966, under criticism for emphasizing *economic* at the expense of *social* information, the President asked the Secretary of Health, Education and Welfare to initiate work on the first of a series of annual Social Reports of the President.[9] Indeed, long-range preparations are already being made to convert our antiquated State of the Union Message into an up-to-date, professionally-grounded and popularly understandable review of the changing state of the nation. A few far-sighted mayors and governors have also begun to plan for annual surveys of the changing state of the city, the metropolis, the state, or the region.[10]

The tragic paradox underlying all this activity is *the paucity of intelligence amidst all this growing abundance of data.*

A simple example may be found in the Federal government's profound lack of preparation—particularly with respect to the prevailing economic premise—for the "urban disorders" in the summer of 1967. Thus, in his January 1967 Economic Report to Congress, President Johnson boasted of great progress in the reduction of unemployment in "major labor markets," that is, metropolitan areas. Three months later, those willing to burrow through the Labor Department's appendix to the President's Manpower Report, could find that in the slum areas of 13 major cities "about 1 out of every 10 workers was unemployed in November 1966 . . ." In 10 of these slums, moreover, the average rate of *subemployment*—the more meaningful measure discussed in Chapter 1[11]—was well over 3 out of 10. If such conditions had existed throughout our metropolitan areas, rather than in the slums alone, the President and his advisers would have declared a national emergency. Since the information related only to the slums—and was counterbalanced by aggregate data of a more pleasant nature—it was not regarded as a serious alarm signal.

One of the sources of countervailing solace was the misleading premise underlying the official view—also published in the January 1967 Economic Report—that "between 1961 and 1965, the number of Americans in poverty declined 5.5 million, and probably fell at least another 1.25 million in 1966." [12] This official "poverty line" approach is based upon a rigid form of statistical absolutism that concentrates on *absolute* figures, studiously avoiding information on *comparative* income and human resentment against perceived inequity. One wonders whether the President's advisers allowed him to see the United States Chamber of Commerce report showing that in comparative terms "the percentage of poor has not declined since 1947." [13] Certainly, such information—together with the "subemployment" estimates—was enough to suggest that our low income slum areas were tinder boxes of rising indignation. Indeed, the indignation was being repeatedly expressed throughout the country—by actions as well as angry words. It was steadily exacerbated not only by the conspicuously rising affluence of the well-to-do but by the higher aspirations of the poor and the jobless nourished by the Administration's resonant anti-poverty slogans, promises, and programs. But how did the Johnson Administration appraise the situation? In July 1967, was President Johnson much better prepared for the "urban disorders" than President Truman had been for the Chinese attack in November 1950?

THE UNPROCLAIMED REVOLUTION

Presidents and presidential candidates usually use the term "revolution" ritualistically. Communist revolutions are to be viewed with alarm, our 1776 Revolution and the "revolution of rising expectations" in underdeveloped nations, with approbation, and the modern technological revolution, with cautious admiration.

Like the industrial revolution that shook up Europe and the world more than a century ago, the social revolution now taking place in America is not proclaimed by any victorious revolutionaries. It is just happening. While the name of the game stays the same, the game and all its rules are changing.

A President cannot know what is happening if he is blinded by the "present-as-culmination" illusion set forth by economist and presidential adviser Walt Rostow.[14] "This is the myth that *we* in the United States *have arrived,* that countries like India and Nigeria are 'transitional' societies close to the take-off point for self-sustained growth." [15] This point of view blinds us to the tremendous changes taking place in the United States, as hammered home in earlier chapters by Robin Williams, Daniel Bell, Peter F. Drucker, and Frank E. Manuel. It obscures the fact that all the highly industrialized countries are moving painfully into the first stages of what Daniel Bell has called "post-industrialism." [16] It totally misses one of the central facts of this century: *the United States is itself a transitional society undergoing a profound and painful social transformation.*

The most obvious aspect of this revolutionary transformation is science-based technology. In "mobiletics"—that is, the movement of information, things, and energy over space—new developments are so rapid that in high technology areas engineers and business leaders act on the principle "If it's in operation, it's obsolete—in comparison with the new developments on the drawing boards." This applies to today's telestar, computers, supersonic airplanes, and electric power grids.

Somewhat less obvious is the unevenness of technological change. In such areas as house construction, city planning, traffic safety, integrated transportation, the prevention of air and water pollution, pedagogy, nutrition, penology, mental illness, and social statistics, our current technologies are unbelievably backward. In these areas, with but a few rare exceptions, current "R and D" (research and development) is pale, poverty-stricken and myopic—particularly in comparison with R and D for "overkill" and outer space technologies. Our economists solemnly define countries like India and Indonesia as *dual economies*—with their combination of agriculturalism and nascent industrialism. But the United States is even more of a *dual society*. One part of us lives in the rapidly-moving world of science-based, post-industrial technology, the other in an underdeveloped realm of human, technological, and scientific backwardness.

Still less obvious are the changes in the structure and performance of American society—changes which have also been taking place at uneven, varying, and in some cases, unprecedented rates. Some of the more important changes are the following:

1. *From the production of goods to the provision of services.* The industrial revolution has always meant higher labor productivity in agriculture and a major shift in employment from agriculture to industry. Similarly, with much higher labor productivity in manufacturing, the post-industrial revolution is bringing about a major shift in employment from goods production to services.

2. *From big organizations to complex macro-systems.* Big Government, Big Industry, and Big Labor have tended to merge into overlapping networks of organizational clusters. These are gigantic, loose and heterogeneous systems such as the banking system, the mass communications system and the "military-space complex."

3. *From white-collar work to extended professionalism.* Far more important than "collar color" is the relentless drive in every field of human employment toward some form of sub-, quasi-, full-, or super-professionalism. This extended professionalism is rooted in galloping specialization, university-based credentialism, and elaborate networks of formal assocations and "invisible colleges."

4. *From Metropolis to Megalopolis.* The larger metropolitan areas are converging into 20 "metropolitan clusters," comprising over 45 percent of the population. Twelve of these clusters—with about 40 percent of the population—are coming together into three huge *megalopolitan* areas on the northeast seaboard, in the Great Lakes region and on the West coast.

5. *From less to more family life.* With more people getting married and at somewhat younger ages, and with married couples living longer, there has been a major extension of family life. Many married couples now face two decades of post-children life together. At all stages, family life has become highly capitalized, with investment in housing, consumer durables and family transportation already far more sizable than capital investment by business.[17]

With each of the above, **growing complexity has brought new** problems of cohesion. People providing intangible services—particularly those of a controversial and ambiguous nature—cannot as readily develop a unifying sense of mission. In macro-systems we find diffused responsibility. The request "Take me to your leader" cannot be answered; no one knows his name. Leadership emanates from the system, not a person. In extended professionalism, we see deeper cultural fragmentation and linguistic barriers creating a new Tower of Babel. We see an undereducated "underclass" not allowed to enter the Tower's ground floor, let alone go higher. Extended family life is pervaded by serious internal cleavages between the nuclear family and kinfolk, between husband and wife, and—above all—between parents and children. In extended urbanism we see the fragmentation of community life and local allegiances, with a decline in the influence of center city party bosses, top managerial elites, and older aristocratic families. Nationally, all these changes in social structure are radically undermining the coalitions that have hitherto provided the power base of the Democratic and Republican parties.

As a result, we suffer internal dislocations, imbalances, and generational gaps more difficult to diagnose than those we so quickly discern in Asian, African, and Latin American nations in the throes of early industrialization. Indeed, relative to the speed of scientific and technological change in the United States, many American ideas, traditions and institutions are more backward and rigid than the caste system in the Indian environment, the therapeutics of the Ubangi medicine men in Africa, or the Catholic clergy in Latin America. Some of the backwardness is found in the narrow provincialism of the affluent and the powerful, some of the rigidity in the hyper-specialization of our scientoids and technopols and the hyper-romanticism of our Radical Right and New Left. Much of our loss of purpose is illustrated by the groping failures of national political leaders to replace the crumbling coalitions of the past with new coalitions geared to the new needs and demands of our nascent post-industrial society.

REVOLUTIONARY ASPIRATIONS

But the greatest change of all—one that underlies all those already referred to—is *an unprecedented rise in human aspirations*. In Asia, the Middle East, Africa, and Latin America, the so-called "revolution of rising expectations" is still confined largely to the minority of educated people; apathy still prevails among the masses. In contrast, the United States—with its relatively high levels of education and wealth—is the true home of the modern revolution of rising expectations.

In 1776, the gentlemen who declared our first revolution proclaimed that governments are constituted to secure to the people of a country such "unalienable rights" as life, liberty, and the pursuit of happiness. As men of the Enlightenment, they were convinced that the wisdom of the philosophers would enable them to direct the course of history toward the unlimited perfectibility of man. Since then, reverence for the eloquent words of the Declaration of Independence has often exceeded any effort to give them new meanings. Faith in philosophic wisdom has declined.

Today, many political leaders find it hard to realize that our undeclared post-industrial revolution has brought into being a new wave of human aspirations for peace at a time when *life* is threatened by nuclear holocaust; justice for those whose *liberty* has been denied by imprisonment in institutionalized inferiority; and a higher quality of life under conditions when the *pursuit of happiness* through material affluence alone may quickly lead to emptiness and loss of purpose.

These new "unalienable rights" of peace, justice, and the quality of life are today supported by a stronger ideology of rational calculation and control. The first principle of this new ideology—which might be called "R-and-D-ology"—is that *"Any* problem can be solved *if* the proper agency provides enough resources for research, development, testing, and evaluation." The details of this new ideology are understood mainly by the technological and technocratic elites, who are rarely known to preoccupy themselves with the rights of man, either old-style or new-style. Faith in the potential of the new ideology is far more widespread. In addition to encouraging a rising aspiration level, it has often led to hopes of "instant progress."

Whether or not the expectations have been realistic, the brutal fact is that many high waves have broken against the hard rocks of war, injustice, sordid materialism and apathy. The denial of "unalienable rights" has meant widespread alienation. The most obvious examples are violence, delinquency, and deviation. The deepest ones are the cynicism of our ablest youth and the still deeper inner despair of their elders in the seats of the mighty.

Is it enough that a President or presidential candidate *know* these things are happening? Should we not expect him also to provide some basis—other than through eloquent words alone—for hope that these rights will be secured. Let us discuss each of these in turn.

THE PRESIDENT AS PEACEMAKER

Throughout the rest of this century our Presidents will act the role of life giver to the American people. This is not merely a matter of more Medicare and Medicaid to pay the bills. It is more a matter of riding the wave of advancing medical technology. With contagious diseases being liquidated, Lyndon Johnson set an example in his campaigns against the degenerative diseases: cancer, heart trouble, and stroke. All future Presidents will offer hope not only for lower infant mortality rates but also for healthier and longer life spans.

But the tragic paradox of our age is that with healthier and longer life seen as an inalienable right, our Presidents have also served in the role of death giver. Truman exploded the first atomic bombs and directed non-atomic operations that brought 25,000 American deaths in Korea. Eisenhower built up our stock piles of atomic over-kill. Kennedy risked a nuclear holocaust in confrontations over Cuba and started the American military build-up in Viet Nam. Johnson took personal responsibility for commanding half a million American men (no longer the "boys" referred to in vulgar political parlance) to risk death in Asia—without legitimating action by either the United Nations or (except for the slender reed of the Tonkin Resolution in 1964) the Congress. The fear of rising death tolls in Viet Nam was often dwarfed by fears of death for almost everyone if our operations on Chinese borders should lead to nuclear retaliation. In the past, Washington, Lincoln, Wilson, and Franklin Roosevelt led all-out wars (by the standard of then-current military technology) on the premise that, in the long run, lives might be saved. Today, the delicate balance of nuclear terror means that presidential use of all-out weapons means a war in which there can be no victors and few, if any, survivors. "Nuclear exchange" is merely a euphemism for *socialized suicide*.

In terms of desirability, the resolution of this paradox is absurdly simple: *our next Presidents must be peacemakers*. In 1952, Dwight Eisenhower was elected to make peace in Korea. He did so without getting us into another war. The first test of future presidential greatness will be the ability to do as well.

But under present and foreseeable conditions, this course of action raises difficult questions. Could not peace in Viet Nam easily be the prelude to dangerous clashes elsewhere—unless followed by presidential action to achieve detente with both China and Russia and, on the basis of such accommodation, strengthen the United Nations as a civilizing force in the world society? Does not action along these lines require liberation of the Presidency—and many important elite groups—from dangerous myths of military power?

POLITICAL SETTLEMENT IN VIET NAM

Just as American historians have developed opposing interpretations on the origins of the Cold War, they will long debate how the United States ever happened to get involved in Viet Nam. Indeed, the question of whom to blame for the vast destruction incurred in the undeclared Viet Nam war will be an unavoidable part of future American politics.

The most crucial question now, however, is "How can the destruction be ended quickly on terms consistent with the most significant, long-run interests of the United States?"

There are two extremist answers: "Immediate and complete withdrawal" and "A military victory that will force the National Liberation Front and their North Viet Nam supporters to desist." Both are wishful thinking. Any United States withdrawal, even if feasible, could be neither immediate nor, over the short-run, complete. A traditional-style victory is no more relevant to the style of combat in Viet Nam than Lyndon Johnson's imagery of "bringing back the coonskin to hang on the wall." Any outcome that could be seriously proclaimed a military victory would be enormously costly not only in the death toll preceding it but the subsequent long-run United States involvement to maintain what had been "won." It could provide a glaring example of how to "win a battle and lose the war." Accordingly, the most immediate test of presidential leadership will be a President's *ability to reach a settlement somewhere between these two extremes.*

The specifics of any international settlement—just as in a domestic controversy—can scarcely be predicted or prescribed in advance. There are probably only four things we can be sure of:

1. The National Liberation Front will play a major role—and will have to be openly recognized by both the United States and any Saigon government.

2. The settlement will be sufficiently ambiguous for each of the parties to interpret it in different ways to various domestic constituencies, with *de facto* understandings over a period of time overshadowing in importance any one-shot written document.

3. After any settlement, militarism, nationalism, and socialism—each with a strong component of anti-Americanism, hidden or open—will long be dominant elements in South Vietnamese politics.

4. Both the settlement and its aftermath in Viet Nam will have major implications for the broader pattern of international conflict and United States foreign policy.

These are the facts of life faced by the American presidency. To handle them creatively requires a remarkable mobilization of energy and skill. At the same time, it requires still greater capacity and vision to put any Viet Nam settlement (once achieved) in proper perspective as merely a minor aspect of a world-wide American strategy for peace.

GREAT POWER ACCOMMODATION

"What after Viet Nam?" Could a Viet Nam settlement be followed by similar, or still more dangerous, conflicts in other areas? in Thailand? in Cuba or elsewhere in Latin America? in Europe? or by a fourth Arab-Israeli war?

At the end of World War II the United States' answer to similar questions tended to be based on the premise of an international Communist conspiracy to take over the world by military expansion. "The central issue" of the crisis of our time was, according to Dean Rusk, "the announced determination to impose a world of coercion upon those not already subject to it. . . . It is posed between the Sino-Soviet empire and all the rest, whether allied or neutral; and it is posed on every continent." [18] The United States response was a policy of containment, military and economic, multilateral and unilateral. This meant the abandonment—at least temporarily—of the earlier policy of Great Power accommodation which President Roosevelt had tried to fashion as the basis of peace after World War II.

Since then, there have been profound changes in the world situation: sharp cleavages among and within the Communist nations (of which the growing Russian-Chinese antagonism is merely the most dramatic), increasing efforts by Communist regimes to raise living standards at home rather than engage in foreign adventures, and the rise of many nationalist (or ultranationalist) regimes embroiled in tangled conflicts with each other. Under these circumstances accommodation *between* the United States and the Soviet Union—rather than mere containment of the Soviet Union *by* the United States—developed as part of United States policy. Because of this accommodation it was possible to settle the war in Laos and remove many African wars from the sphere of Great Power rivalry. More important, with American support in the wings, Russia was able to mediate and settle the war between India and Pakistan, who had been killing one another with weapons originally given them by the United States for the purpose of containing Russia. In short, one of the triumphs of the Johnson administration was its partial extension of the detente with Russia initiated under President Kennedy.

The counterbalancing failure of the Johnson administration has been its failure to move more realistically on accommodation with China as well as the Soviet Union. Indeed, it seems to have indulged in a balancing act reminiscent of small-time ward politics; with every step toward comity with Russia, another act of hostility near or across China's borders. At home, this has served to protect the Johnson administration from the Radical Right's charges that it is "easy on communism." But in this concern with domestic self-protection the Johnson administration has undermined its own policy of comity with the Soviet Union. It may also unwittingly become an instrument of those who would like nothing better than to play off their two rivals, China and the United States, against each other. In any case, the Johnson administration has weakened its position in Europe and the Middle East. Indeed, the grim danger of an all-engulfing flare-up in the Middle East is rooted in the incompleteness of the present Great Power detente—namely, in the probability that *the United States and Russia cannot reach an agreement on the Middle East until the United States has achieved some sort of accommodation in South East Asia.*

In this connection, the issue of China's possible entry into the United Nations has been exaggerated out of all proportions. The much more important issue is United States' recognition of China. The Arab states refusal to recognize the existence of Israel, one of the smallest states in the world, is dwarfed by America's refusal of diplomatic recognition for the most populous country in the world.

A detente between the United States and China, however, does not imply that we should jump toward the other extreme of trying to play off China against Russia. On small things, perhaps; a triadic relationship is usually characterized by shifting 2-to-1 alliances on different issues. But on matters involving the peace of the world, an American President must aim at *triadic comity*. In view of the fact that China will soon have the capacity to deliver nuclear weapons almost anywhere in the world, it is imperative that there be no delay in moving toward such a detente. Inaugural Day in January 1969 will be none too soon for the initiation of this enormously difficult but exceptionally important presidential action.

NEW STRENGTH FOR THE UNITED NATIONS

The League of Nations, despite its fatal weaknesses and America's non-adherence, was Woodrow Wilson's greatest legacy to his country. Franklin Roosevelt's final triumph was the creation—with full American participation—of the United Nations and its network of specialized and regional agencies. It remains for some future American President to achieve greatness for himself and his country by major action to strengthen the United Nations as a force for world peace.

The present weakness of the United Nations is not primarily due to the structural weaknesses of the organization or any possible shortcomings of its complicated secretariat. Nor is it due to the lack of interdependent, reciprocal, or common interests among the many nations of the world. Indeed, the growth of nationalism has been more than counterbalanced by the much more remarkable growth of far-flung, trans-national interests and activities on the part of individuals, organizations, and governments. The *central weakness of the United Nations has been the breakdown of the Great Power accommodation which was properly regarded as the condition for its successful operation.*

With a political settlement in Viet Nam and movement (no matter how tortuous) toward American-Russian-Chinese comity, it will be possible once again to strengthen international collaboration through the United Nations system. The opportunities for vigorous United States leadership are so numerous that future American Presidents will have a large menu from which to choose. For example:

1. New arrangements for the United Nations to have armed forces immediately available for swift deployment to insulate and dampen local conflicts. The excess energies of many national military leaders may well be employed in helping develop such international capacities.

2. An expansion of the United Nation's economic development activities. Unilateral foreign aid by the United States (improperly re-

ferred to as "bilateral") has proved of limited utility. United States contributions will be more effective—and much more appreciated on the receiving end—if channelled through the United Nations. In the last decade United States corporations have made enormous strides in developing multi-national corporations under United States' leadership. Why should not the United Nations devise a legal framework for sponsoring United Nations chartered (or World Bank chartered) development corporations to pioneer in major international enterprises? [19]

3. United Nations action extending the principle of demilitarization—now applied to outer space—to the two-thirds of our planet beyond the boundaries of Nation-States: namely, the high seas and the sea beds. As pointed out by the Commission to Study the Organization of Peace, deep sea exploration and research is already being undertaken in a manner that can create a new upward spiral in the arms race. It is therefore essential that the General Assembly declare that the high seas, like outer space, are "not subject to appropriation by any state." [20]

4. Creation of a United Nations Marine Resources Agency for the conservation, development and equitable sharing of the fishery and mineral resources of the high seas. By the end of the 1970's, it has been estimated, leasing rights alone might bring the United Nations an income of $5 billion a year—about ten times the present budget of the entire United Nations system. Any possible savings to United Nations members would be the least of the benefits. The greatest benefits would be (a.) the promotion of cooperative exploration and development of this planet's greatest reserve of untapped resources and (b.) the additional financial strength provided for our fragile institutions of world order.

All such actions will be enormously difficult. They require a vast mobilization of technical, scientific, managerial, and political skills. They require persistent maneuvering through the labyrinths of intertwined bureaucracies, continuous compromising of conflicting interests, and sustained efforts to tolerate—and partially overcome—the inevitable misunderstandings based on diverse linguistic and cultural backgrounds. Above all, they require a large part of the imagination and dedication that has been wasted through the alienation and disillusionment of younger generations in many countries. Will any American President be able to devise summit conferences that might inspire the mobilization of these lost energies?

FREEDOM FROM MILITARY MYTHS

In one of the most dangerous historical interpretations ever made, historian Thomas A. Bailey suggests that a President can become great only by becoming a war leader:

If the President craves preeminence, he should be 'lucky' enough to get the nation not into just any war but into large-scale war. In general, the bigger the conflict the bigger the President—witness Lincoln, Wilson, and Franklin Roosevelt.

With the escalation of bombing and shooting in South Vietnam, Johnson may enjoy this added advantage as he eagerly seeks an honored place beside Lincoln, Wilson, and Franklin Roosevelt . . . If crisis times make great men, he is well on his way to greatness.[21]

As Bailey himself indicates, the historical analogy is not clear. First of all, one of the greatest of all Presidents was Thomas Jefferson, who was not a war President at all. When confronted by a possible war with England in 1807, he dodged it artfully by a costly export embargo that provided a middle ground between submission and shooting. As an alternative to war, he concentrated his efforts upon the exploration of the Western lands obtained through the Louisiana Purchase and the building of a continental rather than a mere coastal nation.

Indeed, Franklin Roosevelt will probably go down in history as the *last* of the Great Presidents who served as a leader in war. Kennedy's only step in the direction of greatness was his successful escape —despite his eyeball to eyeball confrontation with Khrushchev—from war over the Cuban crisis. The conduct or settlement of war has hitherto provided the occasions for the great summit conferences at Versailles, off the coast of Newfoundland, and at Teheran, Yalta, and Potsdam. There may still be majesty and grandeur in the summit sessions of the future—but only insofar as they serve to prevent war or strengthen the peace.

In the course of trying to prevent war, unfortunately, American Presidents will have to make many decisions concerning the nature, size, and deployment of United States military forces. Still more unfortunately, such decisions can too easily be affected by outworn policy premises that (no matter what their worth in the past) may have declining relevance to the present and future. Among these are the myths of military bases as the protector of American trade, world communism as a military threat, poverty as the cause of war, and greater destructive capacity as all-purpose power.

The doctrine of military expansion as an aid to trade was formally initiated by Secretary of State Seward as far back as 1867. Since then, as Raymond Moley has pointed out,[22] the "GOP mainstream" —supported by many Democrats—has been committed to making the United States a "power" not only in the Pacific but on the mainland of Asia. This was the background for the charges by Senators Robert Taft and Joseph McCarthy that the Truman administration "lost China." It was the background for the feeling that the "power vacuum" provided by the French withdrawal from Viet Nam in 1956 provided an opportunity for American "responsibility." But does modern American business really need this kind of help? May not our military involvement in Southeast Asia have *prevented* a peaceful expansion of trade and industrial development in an area of the world, including mainland China, that could become the largest future market for American enterprise?

The doctrine of world communism as a world-wide military conspiracy developed more as an expression of internal political conflict in the United States than as a sober effort to analyze the nature of Communist successes (and failures) in either Eastern Europe or mainland China. It was developed by the frenetics on the Radical Right— and the foreign influence of Chiang Kai-shek's China Lobby—who tried to pillory Truman, Eisenhower, Marshall, and Acheson for "losing China." It was taken up by many Marshall-Acheson associates (such as Dean Rusk) in a manner that served to protect them against similar vilification. In prettied up form, it helped justify new programs before Congressional committees that seemed willing to approve foreign expenditures only if justified as "anti-communist." As a result, we have a new breed of "communoids" in America. Specializing in paranoid forms of violent reaction to communism, they have a vested interest in the maintenance of communist threats, either real or imaginary.

A more liberal-sounding myth is the doctrine—more frequently associated with the Democratic party—that poverty in pre-industrial nations is the cause of war. Historians may acidly record that this myth was first propagated by rich nations after World War II, when the world was still suffering from the unprecedented devastation of conflict between the more industrialized nations. True, the doctrine has helped rationalize a relatively small flow of non-military economic aid (much of which has been counterbalanced by the "brain drain" and trade restrictions) from the "have" to the "have-not" countries. But it has also helped to obscure the fact that the great stock piles of nuclear bombs capable of destroying life on this planet were being developed by the Haves. The only conflicts threatening to bring these engines of destruction into use have been those among the great world powers. The contention that poverty causes war is like saying pedestrians are the main cause of automobile accidents.

Although poor nations often participate in world-wide conflicts, it has mainly been as victims, pawns, or unwilling allies. When a Serbia, Manchuria, Poland, Korea, Cuba, or Viet Nam serves as a trigger, it is the big powers that hold the gun, put the finger on the trigger, and decide to shoot or not to shoot. This situation is exacerbated not so much by poverty, but by the fact that as the poor nations get more resources, they will be able to acquire more destructive weapons of their own. The rich nations of the world are losing little time in their competitive efforts to help the poor countries move in this direction. As the world's most effective armament salesman, the United States under the Kennedy and Johnson administrations has won leadership in this competition.

The myth of military violence as all-purpose power is rooted in man's long ascent from the jungle. The essence of a nation-state is still regarded as its monopoly over the legitimate use of force. The more force a state can wield, the more it is seen as a "Great Power." In *realpolitik,* of course, it is often useful to exaggerate one's power—as when people talk about America's "awesome" or "unprecedented" military power. It is somewhat less useful for policymakers to become the victims of their own exaggerations. Power is never an "undifferentiated currency." It is merely the ability to produce certain effects under certain circumstances. Under circumstances of spreading inflation of capacities for "second strike" nuclear over-kill, nuclear power declines in use value. The weakness of non-nuclear military power has been dramatized throughout the world by the continuing failure of American and South Viet Nam ground, air, and sea forces to break the resistance of much smaller bands of well-led guerrillas. As former Secretary of Defense McNamara suggested in his 1966 Montreal address, we are entering a period when military force—nuclear or otherwise—has declining relevance to national security.

If hog-tied by the oversimplified doctrines of the past, our future Commanders-in-Chief can scarcely cope effectively with the many war crises that are bound to develop during the remainder of this century. Must not our future Presidents free themselves and their advisers from these outworn myths and develop new doctrines more suitable to the new conditions of a changing world?

THE PRESIDENT AS CHAMPION OF JUSTICE

"Will not injustice," asks Socrates rhetorically in Plato's *Republic,* "when it springs up either among free men or slaves cause them to hate and be at strife with one another, and make them incapable of effective action in common?"

"Not necessarily," we may answer with the benefit of longer hindsight. The discontent created by widespread injustice has been the essential emotional fuel in organized action to seek justice through constitutional or revolutionary means. In the last century modern political systems have responded to such demands in various ways:

in Communist nations, by government ownership of the "means of production" and efforts at centralized planning;

in the Welfare State Nations, by Big Government, and partial socialism often oriented more toward social justice than economic growth; and

in the United States, by the Somewhat Bigger Government and more limited socialism of the Square, New, and Fair Deals, the New Freedom, and the New Frontier.

In varying ways, each nation has responded to the awakening demands of special victims of injustice: ethnic or religious minorities and women.

During the 1963–68 period, Lyndon Johnson sought to become an acknowledged champion of justice by well-publicized activism in three areas: anti-poverty, civil rights, and women's rights. The net result was somehow a vast increase in discontent: openly demonstrated by Negroes and poor people, less openly expressed by women. Indeed, a new era of hatred and strife seems to be opening up—one that, in accordance with the Socratic question, threatens to make us "incapable of effective action in common."

In part, the feelings of discontent arose from the unstable balance between social justice policies at home (designed mainly to please the liberals) and expanding military actions abroad (in response to pressures from the Radical Right). For a while, this reciprocity of domestic reform with foreign military expansion was sustained by a substantial degree of tolerance by liberals for the administration's foreign policies and by reactionaries for its domestic policies. But this tolerance diminished with the expansion of each and by the 1966 mid-term elections the Johnsonian consensus collapsed.

In still greater part, however, the perceptions of domestic injustice stemmed from the nature of social change itself. More people have become newly awakened to injustice or more willing to take the risk of fighting against old evils. Above all, *more people have come to be affected by glaring divergencies between perceived reality and the new ideals and values of post-industrialism.* Under these circumstances future Presidents will have to do much more than offer warmed-up left-overs from past programs. A President cannot serve the cause of justice—let alone build a credible image as its champion—unless he finds *new* policies to meet *new* conditions.

ESCAPE FROM ILLFARE

If the ghost of Joseph McCarthy still haunts our foreign policies, let us not think that domestic policies are free from the infection. The communoid movement of witch-hunting and "redbaiting" is also associated with vituperative, extremist opposition to social measures at home.

With one exception, every nation in the world—including many without the productive capacity to do it—has committed itself to the elementary aim of providing an assured floor below the living standards of its people. In Western Europe, this has been done through welfare state programs which—with American money under the Marshall Plan—were the decisive factors in weakening European communism.

The only country which has failed to make an open commitment to welfare state principles is the one country with enough capacity to make good on them in a truly meaningful manner, the United States. Although the building of a floor was begun (through social security, minimum wages, aid to the needy, policies against mass unemployment, and other New and Fair Deal measures), it was left with gaping holes. With rising prices and greater affluence by the majority, the whole floor has tended to sink into the ground. For millions of Americans the result has been insecurity instead of security—with humiliation added for good measure.

Nonetheless, this rickety, collapsing floor was enough to help the New and Fair Dealers achieve one minor goal: the destruction of the socialist and communist parties as significant forces in domestic politics. Weak to begin with, these fringe parties were soon entangled in the processes of lobbying for improvement of the existing system. Their collapse was a serious loss to the communoid right. This loss was exacerbated by resentment against accompanying increments (minor though they were) in government controls and taxes. The communoid response was to attack as "subversive" of the American system the New and Fair Dealers who, by helping the American system make slow and minor adaptations to change, had successfully subverted the American Left.

In their enthusiasm for vilifying domestic reformers, the communoids and the new Know Nothings have developed a strange "double think" language which is still part of the political atmosphere. By their lexicon of invective, the innovators and intellectuals who wrote the American Constitution and the Bill of Rights would be called "crackpots," Alexander Hamilton a "power-mad bureaucrat," Thomas Jefferson an "egghead," and Abraham Lincoln a "bleeding heart." Still stranger, with "do-gooder" a vituperative term, "good" or the doing of good has been proclaimed "bad." To cap it all, although the Constitution obligates our government to promote and provide for the "general welfare," the terms "welfare" and "welfare state" have been made disreputable.

By the earlier traditions of American political combat, one might have expected the middle-of-the-roaders to defend themselves by a counter-offensive against the "do-badders," "blockheads," and "inhumanists." One might have expected the opponents of "welfare" and the "welfare state" to be forced to defend themselves against being branded the "illfare lobby." Instead, the middle-of-the-roaders became ultra-defensive. Thus, a recent Secretary of Health, Education and Welfare went to tortuous lengths to defend the Kennedy administration against the thought that it was proposing welfare state programs.

This defensive stance was more than semantic. It was embodied in a major retreat from earlier New Deal and Keynesian concepts of removing distributive inequities. The new philosophers of economic growthmanship insisted that everyone would be better off if the "size of the pie" were enlarged—without any change in relative shares. Although this concession helped win a little support for growth programs, it blinded the policymakers themselves to the fact that perception of social injustice is rooted in relative shares, not absolute standards. Still worse, the "economic pie" was defined in terms of income (with practically no attention paid to the distribution of assets and such basic public services as quality education and proper police protection). Little attention was given to the "social pie"—the distribution of status, self-respect, and opportunities for upward mobility, and participation in basic decision-making.

The anti-poverty program has been an important end-run around some of the institutional obstacles to improved social justice. Its major contribution has been to develop new training and educational programs on the periphery of our slow-moving, tradition-encrusted educational system. Their major impact has been to raise the expectations of many poor people. Their major weaknesses lie in the lack of a Federal Government commitment to some of the simplest principles of social justice: useful jobs at decent wages for the sub-employed; training on the job for those not yet qualified; built-in opportunities for advancement associated with continuing education; broader social security coverage, with automatic cost-of-living escalators, and with upward adjustments to reflect our increasing productivity; and aid to the needy (whether through family allowances or a negative income tax) in a form that does not contribute to family breakdown or loss of self-respect.

At the present rate of retarded social progress in the United States, it will be 1984 before we reach welfare state minima comparable to those now provided in most Western European countries. If this is done in terms of present conceptions, our welfare state could be a nightmare. If enlightened presidential leadership helps us escape from illfare, these minima will become like good plumbing is today—relied upon, taken for granted, needing repair from time to time, but hardly the central area in which to "provide for the general welfare" of the American people.

BLACK DIGNITY, WHITE READJUSTMENT

There is probably no area in American life where old doctrines and policies have proved as bankrupt or irrelevant as they have in race relations. Here, where Negro Americans have long been victims of institutionalized injustice, the champions of justice—both white and black—have had growing difficulties in deciding what banners to wave.

For a century American liberals and liberal Presidents conceived of racial justice in terms of formal political equality as promised by the 14th and 15th Amendments to the Constitution. This narrow conception has been made plausible by the sustained denial of Negroes' political rights.

In more recent decades the theme of equality has been embodied in written and unspoken injunctions against special treatment. *"Equal* treatment" has been used as a convenient justification for overlooking differences and denying *"equitable* treatment," the essence of justice. By this standard—to modernize an older axiom of Anatole France—both the rich and the poor are equally free to sleep in rat-ridden ghetto slums. Negro sharecroppers in Mississippi are also free to hire the best Wall Street law firms to represent them in disputes with the "rednecks" at the County Court House. By the same standard, race is not a matter to be dealt with openly in employment applications or government statistics. It is still difficult for public officials—let alone Presidents—to reveal openly the unpleasant facts on unemployment, subemployment, broken families, low educational attainment, poor health, and high crime rates among the Negro population.

From World War II to the Viet Nam war, Negro leaders sought protection for Negroes against certain defined forms of discrimination. With varying degrees of reluctance or enthusiasm, American Presidents supported their demands. But despite all the laws, judicial decisions and administrative actions, the majority of Negro Americans are still caught in a vicious circle of segregated slum housing leading to inferior schooling, subemployment, broken families, and low incomes which lead inevitably back to segregated slums.

For more than a decade American Presidents have been misled by the philistinism of "pie economics." With general economic growth the absolute living standards of Negro Americans have risen in many ways—particularly for the millions who have moved from the South to the North. But this has contributed to greater dissatisfactions than ever before, as easy comparisons are made with the TV-advertised affluence of the white population. More important, there has been a growing polarization into two parts: "an increasingly prosperous and mobile 'middle class' group and—in relative and even absolute terms —a lower class group living under steadily deteriorating conditions." [23]

Racial integration rather than segregation has long been a major liberal objective—even though self-organization on at least a semi-segregated basis has hitherto been the path of every American minority group seeking wider acceptance. By the time it became clear that the Johnson administration could not obtain action on Federal "open housing" legislation, the banner of integration was rolled up and packed away. Whether or not they use the term "Black Power," Negro leaders are now united by the necessity for self-organization, self-respect, and disdain for the white man's double talk.

In previous years "non-violence" was the philosophy behind Negro resistance to the denial of constitutional rights. The aim was to arouse the moral conscience of the white majority against the violent means used by the white extremist minority to deny these rights. The new strategy is one of response to white violence by counter-violence. It is bolstered by the general disposition of the white majority to become actively concerned with justice for Negro Americans only when violent outbreaks threaten their own well-being. It is aimed not merely at constitutional rights, not merely at full and complete entry into American affluence. It is aimed at a breakdown of the entire system of institutionalized inferiority in which Negroes—as pointed out by the British anthropologist, Geoffrey Gorer—"have never been granted completely human status." [24]

Under these new circumstances, Presidential leadership on behalf of racial justice must be based on recognition of three hard facts.

First, despite Negro impatience, redress of centuries' injuries will take a long time. "When potential equality is achieved," Gorer says, "it will need a generation of attention and education before the potentiality can be realized, and skin color can become truly irrelevant." [25] Federal policies must therefore be oriented toward counterbalancing inevitable short-term frustration by providing a visible basis for long-term hope. A 30-year "Reparations program"—similar to the reparations and restitution payments provided by West Germany for the Jews who had suffered under the Nazis—should be considered. Social scientists may be expected to begin an account of the "social costs" of the injuries inflicted upon Negro Americans by those who for over a century have sanctimoniously ignored or violated the protective provisions of the Constitution, Supreme Court decisions, statutes, and religious and moral principles.

Second, during this period of long-delayed self-organization, many new Negro leaders and competitive styles of leadership will emerge. A President can undermine the emerging sense of black dignity if, in the effort to get strategic Negro votes in "swing states," he tries to become a paternalistic white father. He can undermine the older generation of Negro leaders by using them as "favored instruments" and the newer generation by denying them recognition.

Third, America's greatest difficulty during this period will be the painful processes of readjustment on the part of the white majority. *The so-called "white backlash" is White House business.* The white conscience must not only be aroused; it must be improved. Legislative leadership on Negro reparations measures (as well as older civil rights issues) can help. Indeed, it is a pre-condition to any serious change in white attitudes. But it is far from sufficient. Presidential attention must also be paid to the Conservative observation that white attitudes change slowly—by exercising leadership in getting the necessary changes under way more quickly.

FEMALE SELF-FULFILLMENT, MALE READJUSTMENT

"All men are created equal" reads the Declaration of Independence. The clear meaning was, and is, that all people—despite their many differences in heritage, family status, and the conditions of growth after birth—should be protected in the enjoyment of the common rights of man. Any progress we have made since 1776 has come from the redefinition of these rights in terms of the changing needs and interests of people. It has come from greater awareness of the many differences that may impede or promote individual self-fulfillment.

In the case of the Negro minority, it is taking us a long time to get away from the racist idea that the quality of a person is determined by skin color and other obvious ethnic characteristics. It may take longer to realize that genuine (even if temporary) differences *have* been created by the unfavorable social environment to which most Negroes have been subjected.

In the case of the female majority of the population, a genuine awareness of differences and their significance may take still longer. For most of our history, and in most countries, it has long been assumed that biological differences make women inferior to men. In opposition to institutionalized inferiority, feminist leaders have traditionally fought for "women's rights" by denying the significance of biological differences. Progress toward "equality" has led to the emergence of the female as a legal person with right to vote, to get a full education, and to obtain employment outside the home. Female college enrollments and graduates have been slowly rising relative to males'. Female participation in the labor force—particularly among married women—has been steadily growing.

Nonetheless, the present situation is characterized by a double form of injustice. On the one hand, a growing proportion of the more prestigious positions in society are held by men. Thus, between the 1950 and the 1960 Census, there were absolute declines in the number of female self-employed managers, chemists, architects and dentists, and declines (or no changes) in the percentage of women serving as natural and social scientists, college presidents, professors and instructors, lawyers, engineers and technicians. From 1940 to 1964, the number of women on college faculties declined from 28 to 22 percent. The proportion at the higher ranks of prestige declined still more. In 1961, the number of women in the House of Representatives reached 17, its highest point. By 1968, the number had dwindled to 11.

On the other hand, the focusing of attention on employment *outside* the home has tended to aggravate the traditional depreciation of "woman's work" *inside* the home. Despite the growth in the public schools and development of household labor-saving equipment, child care and household management are still difficult and time consuming tasks. They require increasing skill, understanding, and devotion. In a society where monetary income and public prestige are so important, women's tasks are given insufficient recognition in the daily course of events. "Do you work or are you a housewife?" is a typical, insulting question. There is little realization that when a married woman takes a paid job outside the home, she is a "sunlighter"—that is, she is adding a second burden to the unpaid job she must still perform at home.

With higher levels of female education and employment, American women are bound to become increasingly resentful of these multiple inequities. At home, as psychiatrists point out, this resentment can result in excessive female domination of household relations and "male castration." On the job, it may be expressed in apathy or authoritarianism.

The complexities of this situation can no longer be handled by simplistic "equal rights" approaches. The new banner of Federal policy in this area should be *Vive la Différence!* The difference can best be honored by new arrangements and attitudes that offer every woman choices among three fully honored and respected alternatives: full-time concentration on the home, a full-time additional job outside the home, and part-time opportunities as an addition to household activities. The last of these points is critical. We have never provided *enough* part-time jobs to meet the needs of women; those provided have lacked tenure, fringe benefits, status, opportunities for advancement, and ancillary provisions for child care.

Since the battle of the sexes will continue forever (and is probably the most pleasant "moral equivalent of war"), an American President might as well plunge into the fight as a champion of justice for women. To start with, Federal agencies throughout the country should be directed to move toward a growing number of part-time positions —at all levels and with all the perquisites now provided only for full-time positions—for women. Here the major fight will be to attain a readjustment of attitudes on the part of male higher executives. It will not be easy for them to get away from their present premises of female inferiority and to replace "equal treatment" with the various special provisions needed to promote female self-development. With progress in the readjustment process, more men might even learn the strange arithmetic ($3 \times \frac{1}{2} = 2$) of part-time female employment: namely, that the work done by three half-timers will tend to equal that of two full-timers. The more fundamental readjustment—which may take generations—will be to develop new models of masculinity no longer geared to male authoritarianism or female subordination.

THE PRESIDENT AS HUMANIST

Back in 1930, in a little known and less appreciated essay, John Maynard Keynes made the following observations:

> The economic problem, the struggle for subsistence, always has been hitherto the primary, most pressing problem of the human race. If the economic problem is solved, mankind will be deprived of its traditional purpose.

> Will this be a benefit? If one believes at all in the real values of life, the prospect at least opens up the possibility of benefit. Yet I think with dread of the readjustment of the habits and instincts of the ordinary man, bred into him for countless generations, which he may be asked to discard within a few decades . . .[26]

Since World War II, the economic problem of subsistence has largely been solved for the majority of the population in industrialized countries. Indeed, unprecedented numbers have been experiencing unprecedented material affluence.

In part, the readjustment Keynes foresaw has come in the form of higher aspirations pointing toward a new birth of humanism. With security needs being met, more people want to take part in broader realms of decision-making and higher levels of respect, dignity, and power. More people become interested not only in living longer but in longer "activity expectancy," not only in earning a living but in learning to live better, not only in marriage but in love, not only in participation but in beauty, not only in self-respect but in self-fulfillment. People still want more money and more material things—but increasingly to free themselves for the pursuit of what money cannot buy and material things cannot supply.

In part, as Keynes dreaded, many people do seem to have been deprived of their traditional purposes. As suggested earlier, this has often been the result of high aspiration and quick frustration. It may also stem from the increasing mobility, rootlessness, and confusions bred by the transformation to post-industrialism.

The readjustment of political leaders has been particularly tortuous. They have found decreasing political "mileage" in offering more economic security to those who already have it in good measure. They grope for a *new politics of affluence* that may offer something more inspiring than welfare state minima to the well-to-do professionals and semi-professionals of megalopolis, to the increasingly sophisticated younger people who were born after the Great Depression and have never been terrified by the specter of mass unemployment.

In his Great Society slogans and programs President Johnson attempted a giant policy leapfrog. In spirit and content they presented an advanced form of humanism—so far as federal policy is concerned—that might well be described as "Beyond the Welfare State." This was clearly brought out in his early statement that "Millions of Americans have achieved prosperity, and they have found prosperity alone is just not enough. They need a chance to seek knowledge and to touch beauty, to rejoice in achievement and in the closeness of families and communities." [27] The political basis for the many programs that tried to open up these vistas would have been stronger if more people had already achieved economic security, let alone prosperity. As it was, half-hearted humanism had to be combined with a half-hearted anti-poverty program. For a brief period it seemed that President Johnson might perform the miracle of going beyond the welfare state without going through it first—until the escalating inhumanity of the Viet Nam war settled the question.

The paleontologists, it is said, have just discovered the missing link between the apes and civilized man: *us*. In this spirit, Frank E. Manuel in Chapter 8 suggests that "The age of heroes, like the age of the gods, is dead. It is time that the age of men began." In the age of men, government can at last "provide for the general welfare" by helping people in the pursuit of happiness rather than the economic security and material well-being that are the prerequisites of such pursuit. *The new politics of affluence will be a new form of humanism* in which future American Presidents will have to come to grips with the more humanist interests that Lyndon Johnson—no matter how imperfectly—has helped bring to the forefront of national affairs. Among other things, this requires presidential performance in developing meaningful goals for fulfilling employment, for the "City of Man," and for the "newer economics" required to make this possible.

EMPLOYMENT: FULL, FAIR, AND FULFILLING

"Help provide opportunities for every individual to develop his full potentialities." This is now becoming standard language among national leaders—in part because of the advanced rhetoric of the Great Society vision. But rarely do we find a serious presentation of this immensely important idea. Just what is meant by self-fulfillment and self-development? Just what can be done to provide such opportunities without unduly impairing other basic values?

Employment, paid and non-paid, is the first area in which to answer these questions. A person's job is much more than a source of income. It helps determine his or her sense of identity, social status, and opportunities for self-fulfillment. That is why our national goals now include *full* and *fair* employment.

But should we not aim more directly at the quality of jobs as well as their quantity? Should we not set the goal of employment that is *fulfilling* as well as full? In today's world, with automation eliminating dirty and dangerous tasks, work need no longer be a painful burden. It can be—and has already become for many—richly rewarding instead of a punishment for man's sins. The old dividing lines between work, education, and play are beginning to fade. A job can provide continuing opportunities for learning and fun. Moreover, large-scale organizations can be used to enhance these opportunities.

Nevertheless, public and private bureaucracies have inherent tendencies toward routinization, manipulation, and depersonalization.

Too many people may have already become faceless "organization men" or—in Herbert Marcuse's phrase—"one-dimensional men." But for better or worse, large-scale organization is here to stay. What can we do to create conditions—particularly in the public service—under which there will be more "organization individualists"? How can we best utilize the potentialities of computerization and automation to free people from overroutinization and liberate their creative energies?

President Johnson came close to raising these same issues in his question on "recognizing individual excellence and creativity." Our answer—in Chapter 1—touched upon a delicate, and easily ignored, aspect of Presidential leadership: the personal example set by the President in setting the tone for an atmosphere of individuality and creativity throughout the Federal service. We also stressed the importance of vigorous expansion, with public support, of long-starved employment in the arts and humanities. The largest area of expanding employment, let it be added, is in our educational institutions. Here is the most strategic area for improving the quality of employment. Younger generations cannot be very well prepared for self-fulfilling employment in the future by teachers who are themselves ground down by authoritarianism and routinization.

ANTHROPOLIS: THE CITY OF MAN

For old-fashioned city planners, the city is still the City of Things. The things are land, buildings, houses, roads, bridges, and utilities within a bounded area of a given population concentration. They can be portrayed in a pretty map of many colors.

Public administration experts are a trifle more human. For them, a city is the City of Bureaucrats and Politicians: the city government. For economists, it is a City of Markets and Moneyflows.

But the idea of city planning as physical planning alone—or "good government" or economic growth alone—has been riddled with bullets on the streets of Watts, Detroit, and Newark. Burial of the body is less important than a new vision of urban areas that puts people and their social groupings fully into the picture, along with the resources they use. We are still overly wedded to such words as "metropolis" and "megalopolis," which refer mainly to numbers and spatial coverage. Perhaps for a new age we need a new word: Anthropolis, the City of Man.

In scientific terms the City of Man can be envisioned as (1) a spatially-bounded people-resource system composed of a large diversity of people who (2) live, grow, and use physical resources (3) not only as individuals but also as members of families, associations, and formal organizations that (4) have diverse and changing interests of their own and (5) are increasingly moving across and far beyond smaller spatial boundaries and (6) under conditions of post-industrial communication and mobility are beginning to form a Nation-City.[28] The basic criteria of system performance will be found in information on the condition of man and the capacity of institutions and physical environments—natural, man-changed, and man-made—to enhance the quality, style, and grace of life.

The major contribution of presidential leadership will be to rise far above the technical level of bureaucratic specialization, detailed plans, and conditions for Federal aid. Perhaps only a President can launch the vision of cities as *dynamic centers of family growth, culture, elegance, education, science and technology, absorption of immigrants (domestic as well as foreign), and communication with the world*. Perhaps only a President—with his vested interest in getting votes from diverse groups—can encourage *creative localism* and *creative regionalism*. This is the only way to reverse present trends toward urban homogenization and develop anthropolitan areas that are unique and varying Cities of Children, Women, and Men.

A "NEWER ECONOMICS"

Although the essence of a "politics of affluence" is that it goes beyond economics, any trans-economic policies must be firmly grounded on improved knowledge and skill in the allocation of economic resources. As Keynes would have been the first to insist, this demands major departures from the old-time Keynesianism expressed in the obsolete "new economics" of the Kennedy and Johnson Councils of Economic Advisers. Future Presidents will need—and should demand—a "newer economics" that deals creatively with the handling of inflationary pressures, distributive problems at home and abroad, and structural social change.

In its more conservative form the "new" economics provides for liberalization of fiscal and monetary policies to counteract an economic downturn. In its more liberal form the "new" economics favors fiscal and monetary policies that, with less "le Stop-Go" twisting and turning, promote sustained growth without being overly concerned about moderate inflationary developments. The first of these tolerates the human misery of increased unemployment (within bounds) to contain inflation. The second tolerates the injustice of increased inflation (within bounds) to prevent more unemployment. Both of these weaknesses are based on the assumption that, even with demand kept within bounds, no combination of government and private measures could help contain inflationary price and wage increases. This "conventional wisdom" mirrors the political and administrative realities of a past generation. A "newer" economics, as the creative work of people who understand both past and present, should recognize that a healthy economy requires rising, effective demands for private and public goods and services. It should provide a flexible array of new techniques (in addition to the indispensable old faithfuls of fiscal and monetary policy) to restrain and channel these demands.

As already indicated in our discussion of social justice, a "newer" economics must also face up more bravely to the distribution of income, assets, and basic services—all artfully dodged by the oversimplifications of "pie economics." In the age of affluence, let it be added, some of the earlier political terrors of "distributive economics" will unquestionably be diminished. Those who get the larger pieces of pie will probably be less concerned with preserving a previous distribution pattern. Moreover, as Geoffrey Gorer has pointed out, Americans have tended to be more interested in making money than in keeping it.[29] This difference has major implications for future tax policies.

The "new" economics has emphasized the size of the Gross National Product, while giving little attention to its composition. The more imaginative "new" economists have also stressed the inevitability and desirability of a greater proportion of services as contrasted with goods.

But attention must also be paid to other shifts in the economic structure. The employment readjustments created by automation may be minor in comparison with the effects of these other major changes: (1) the replacement or reorganization of major industries through shifts from private automobiles to mass-transport facilities, and from oil-based energy to gas, electric batteries, nuclear power, and other energy sources that may create fewer problems of pollution; (2) the industrial shifts in textiles, glass, pottery, watches, and other sectors that must adjust imaginatively to meet the stiffer competition provided by the lowering of trade barriers and the growing industrialization of previously agricultural countries; (3) the pollution or depletion of basic natural resources; and (4) the tendencies toward the geographical concentration of economic activities in three to five giant megalopoli sprawling across state boundaries. Until recently "locational economics" has been the most backward area in economics. To deal with these emerging problems of the future the "newer" economics must bring space and geography into the very center of its concern.

If this is to be done realistically, economists must join with physical planners, political scientists, and sociologists in a supra-disciplinary analysis of land-resource-people relations. Land-use mapping (and the long-range thinking to which it leads) is too important to be left to the Geological Survey and so-called City Planning departments. It should be developed on a nation-wide basis—with regional working groups in different parts of the country—by a new Land-Use Analysis Division in some Federal department (perhaps in the Bureau of the Census).

Like all public policy issues, of course, none of the above questions is purely economic. They are all closely tied up with political considerations and the values of conflicting groups. This has always been true in economics, a fact that has not prevented economics from becoming the bigwig of social sciences. Nevertheless, a rational handling of these questions demands a new forward surge in economic theory and research (both basic and applied) and major improvements in national economic accounting—as part of the long process of moving from economic to social accounting.

THE PRESIDENT AS LEARNER

No person already qualified to handle the job will ever again be sworn in as President of the United States. The reason is simple:

No possible combination of education, experience, and proved competence can prepare a person in advance for the immense burdens of political leadership which a President must assume under present and coming conditions of unprecedented change in America and the world.

Under these circumstances we can no longer use such simple-minded adages as "A new broom will sweep clean," "Don't change horses in midstream," or "The office makes the man." A new broom may merely sweep more dust under the carpet—without finding out how much is there already. Although we did not change horses in 1944, our "old reliable" died in harness within six months of re-election. Another President may, by re-election time, have exhausted his physical and mental capacities for meeting new challenges. The office has broken many men.

Nor can we rely on presidential "institutions" to compensate for a President's political deficiencies. Although it is true that "the President is many men," the others are primarily *his* men. Most have come in with him and maintain little more than a tenuous footing in the charmed inner circles; almost all will leave when he goes. There are, of course, a growing number of bureaucracies in the presidential office —from the smaller and relatively unstable Council of Economic Advisers and Office of Science and Technology to such huge but partially uncontrollable bureaucracies as the Bureau of the Budget and the Central Intelligence Agency. The old idea that these staff agencies are "extensions of the President's personality" has long since become a cruel joke; if they were, the President could be committed for schizophrenia. Although they include large numbers of people with remarkable political skills (even new "technipols" from economics and the natural sciences), these skills are inevitably used to build the power and prestige of new elite networks. In the very process of helping the President, they may quickly overburden him or distort his vision, weaken other lines of communication, and undermine his effectiveness, *unless he learns how to manage them.*

The brutal fact is that as a member of a species that has not yet risen above trial and error learning, a President must learn many things from mistakes that may bring misery, even death, to others. We must rate Presidents and candidates by their proven capacity for learning—quickly and with the lowest social costs—how to handle managerial tasks far more terrifying than anything they faced before. Such capacity was shown by Harry Truman between 1945, when he walked into the White House unprepared, and 1948, when he became President in his own right. Whatever halo surrounds the memory of John F. Kennedy derives largely from his demonstration of capacity to learn from his own mistakes. The widespread confidence Lyndon Johnson achieved from 1963 to 1966 stemmed from his successes in making the difficult adjustment from the narrowness of Texan politics to the broader vistas of national politics. Since then, was his decline in popularity really due mainly to any lack of photogenic appeal on television, less-than-elegant manners, or wheeling-dealing techniques?

Could it not have been associated with an incomplete learning of national politics and an even slower rate of learning in the international arena?

If, in a world of turbulent change, the White House is to become a center of creative stability, future Presidents will not be able to rely on established traditions of presidential leadership. They will have to develop new strategies of statemanship geared to the new realities of power and human aspiration. This process of learning and readjustment will not be an easy or painless one—nor one that the men in the White House can accomplish entirely by themselves.

THE ART OF THE IMPROBABLE

Politics, the old-timers keep telling us, is the "art of the possible."

This phrase reminds us that what is most desirable may be completely impossible. Feasibility—despite the accompanying postponement, compromises and "muddling through"—must also be sought. A President must be concerned, as Neustadt puts it, with some "balance of political, managerial, psychological, and personal feasibilities." This requires presidential expertise in the arts of persuasion and bargaining (to supplement the great limitations of direct command) and of winning public prestige and a "professional" reputation in government circles.[30] A President must learn how to encourage, communicate with, cajole, and utilize the growing ranks of experts and professionals in the "technostructure" of government, industry, and academia. He must learn how to keep up with the changing patterns of power in the Federal bureaucracy, Congress, business, and other institutions. He must learn how to exploit the mass media without over-exposure. He must develop a sense of timing—particularly of blending strategic retreats on one front with surprise advances on others. He must develop the ability to cope with—if not exploit—continuing conflicts and recurring crises. To meet the vilification that seems to go with even a low degree of presidential effectiveness, a President must develop—in Thomas A. Bailey's phrase—"not only the stamina of a bull moose but the hide of a rhinocerus." [31] Without these skills—to use the old metaphor of the political leader as a man riding a tiger—he will not be able to stay on the tiger's back. Indeed, we Americans, not liking to be ridden, try to consume our political leaders while they are still in the saddle. A President's survival as something more than a titular head-clerk depends upon all such arts of the possible.

But the possible covers a broad spectrum from the inevitable to the impossible. The lesser artists specialize on the easier feasibilities, occasionally rising to heights of imaginative deception by taking credit for having ushered in the inevitable. "The masters of the political process are those who from time to time transcend the limits of imme-diate feasibility and shape sequences of events previously regarded as highly improbable." [32]

While presidential tasks are staggeringly diverse, the more impor-tant ones require a master's touch. There are no magic short-cuts to quick and easy feasibility for presidential efforts to get (or give) a credible picture of what is happening, escape the horrors of war, avoid new forms of injustice, devise a viable politics of affluence, or learn quickly enough from experience. Each of these tasks requires painful processes of institutional and personal adjustment. Every significant move will encounter apathy and resistance. Every forward step will give rise to unforeseen conflicts, new problems, and new uncertainties. *In toto,* these and other presidential tasks come perilously close to the realm of *impossibility.* Let us hope they are merely improbable.

In a world of confusing change, progress requires much more than what Friedrich Engels called "the recognition of necessity." It will de-pend, rather, on the reconstruction of necessity. Any President's role in this reconstruction will depend on his ability to go beyond exper-tise in the art of the possible and achieve wisdom in the *art of the improbable.*

SYNERGIC STATEMANSHIP

During the middle third of the 20th century some progress was made in discovering the weaknesses inherent in over-concentrated power. It is now known that tightly-centralized organizations built on the myth that "power flows down from the top," can no longer cope with the complexities of large-scale operations, changing technology, and en-vironmental uncertainties. Old-style "I am the Law" management is being replaced by new style guidance of a vast grid of interacting components with their own sources of self-generating power. The greater the capacity and initiative of the components, the greater the power of the system as a whole. Mary Follett called this "power with," as contrasted with "power over." A. H. Maslow has called it "syn-ergy." [33] Herman Kahn has pointed out that the "synergistic" fitting together of autonomous parts into new wholes is the essence of im-probable technological advance.[34]

The same period, however, has witnessed the growth of a liberal, reformist philosophy calling for greater personal power and authority in the hands of the President. This philosophy stemmed from memories of the Senate's traumatic rejection of Woodrow Wilson's initiatives in world affairs. It was based on the realities of party irresponsibility, the fragmentation of executive agencies under the onslaught of external pressure groups, and more than twenty years of a massive Congressional logjam on progressive legislation. Thus most public administration experts have called for vastly greater discretion and more hierarchical controls (including a more rationalized presidential budgeting system) in the hands of the President. Many political scientists have advocated more party responsibility or even "party government." In his "Presidential Power," which rose above superficial or irrelevant gadgets, Neustadt frankly urged that a President "must make the most of power for himself." [35]

Other forces in society also press toward the advancing concentration of presidential power and authority. Many conservatives who favor presidential weakness in domestic affairs want untrammelled presidential freedom to conduct military operations abroad. Many staff agencies regard additional presidential discretion as an ideal façade to screen the enlargement of their own power. People numbed by complexity and confusion can escape personal responsibility by "passing the buck" to the President.

The result of all this is the profoundly dangerous idea—widely subscribed to at all levels of government, including the White House —that any increase in a President's power means a decline in the power of others. A President is seen as strong if Congress is weak, if his major appointees are pliable instruments, and if there are no major contenders for political leadership in his cabinet or party. On the other hand, if Congress takes major initiatives, this *ipso facto* reveals presidential weakness, and so on. When this idea is incorporated in a President's style of behavior, it can lead to the hyper-activity of a Lyndon Johnson from 1963 to 1968. Its mirror image is little better, leading to the hyper-passivity of a Dwight Eisenhower during the greater part of eight years in office. Either approach leads to a decline in strategic guidance and in the creative capacities of other components in the American system.

We need, instead, *new concepts of "synergic statesmanship" by which a President's strength or greatness is a function of the initiative and self-developing power of other individuals and groups in the society.* The major elements of such a presidential style cannot be borrowed automatically from the simpler models of synergic guidance at the level of a single business or governmental complex. Nor could they possibly be prefabricated by academic theorists. Rather, they must be designed creatively in response to the opportunities and constraints of current and imminent crises.

In general terms, however, the emergence of presidential leadership in synergic terms will mean a larger proportion of presidential attention to grand strategy and its tactical implications. This means more presidential activity in:

1. *Coalition building.* At a time when the loose coalitions that constitute our major political parties are crumbling, new and strange bedfellows must be brought together in the President's party. In addition, the President must also build the *ad hoc* coalitions on major issues that allow him to practice the politics of non- and bi-partisanship.

2. *Institution building.* This means leadership in overcoming institutional rigidities and promoting institutional change inside and outside the government. Major attention is needed to offsetting the "military-industrial complex" by building what Lyle M. Spencer, head of an IBM subsidiary, has called the "social-industrial complex."

3. *Indirect guidance.* In suggesting national goals, a President can help articulate and integrate underlying human interests. By providing objective information on the state of the nation, he can facilitate constructive interaction. By personal example, he can exert a profound influence on the values and leadership styles of others. With imaginative use of these indirect modes of guidance, the need for more direct interventions may be reduced and their effectiveness —when needed—very considerably enhanced.

THE PRESIDENT'S TEACHERS

The improbable arts of synergic statesmanship can scarcely be developed unless Presidents receive many kinds of help.

At the one extreme is the help he may directly solicit. This includes a large part of his staff assistance and external support.

At the other extreme is the help he may get from history—from strange conjunctures of domestic and foreign circumstance, from crises ideally suited to his special talents.

The most important help probably lies between these two extremes. It includes the unsolicited challenges from "No Men" in his inner circle who refuse to behave like "Yes Men" and accept a President's first thoughts as a sacred directive. It includes the initiatives of countless leaders and institutions.

Much of this help must flow through the complicated channels of executive and legislative decision-making. Some of it must be widely publicized. A good example of the latter was the 1963 television speech in which James Baldwin gave President Kennedy a public lecture on legislative leadership. Within a week or so, having learned his lesson, Kennedy at last presented his civil rights program to the public as a moral issue.

It is, indeed, fortunate that our universities include thousands of people willing to serve as the teachers of Presidents. Recognizing this potentiality, most Presidents will coddle, not kill, the goose that lays the golden eggheads. Unfortunately, the trouble with academic brains —and with any brain trust—is the ease with which they concentrate on "stable knowledge," elaborating fixed assumptions that are not to be questioned. As Amitai Etzioni has forcefully pointed out, decision-making elites tend to discourage the production of "transforming knowledge" that questions the prevailing framework. "The more the ability to transform this basic framework is reduced, the lower the capacity for societal transformation." [36]

If Presidents must learn, so must their would-be teachers. This principle, of course, applies to the whole gamut of individuals interested in influencing the presidency. But it has particular relevance to those who are committed to the discovery and communication of the truth. Each in his own way—from the ultra-positivist scientist to the detached artist or crusading journalist—has a role to play in the synergic processes of social learning and creative adaptation to confusing change.

Such "mental renewal" is needed on many fronts—in our homes, our factories, and our offices, as well as our schools. The hard-nosed businessman should be able to think seriously about justice and beauty, and "doing good." Builders should be concerned with the catalytic effects of physical layout on social relations.

The toughest physical planner or highway engineer and the sharpest-eyed systems-analyzing budgeteer should be able to talk and think about love and politics. The most serious social planner and toughest civil rights or anti-poverty warrior should be able to talk and think about land acquisition, building codes, and mass transport programs. Let us hope that the "Know Nothings" on the extreme right and left will be able to learn just a little more. Let us even hope that the "Know-It-Alls" of academia or government, unlearning some of their narrow or conventional knowledge, may learn more rapidly the extent of their ignorance.

Mental renewal can probably best be attained by some form of "getting where the action is," not from withdrawal. In this mood, let me adapt to a land less green than England the perorational words of William Blake:

> *We shall not cease from mental fight*
> *Nor let the swords rest in our hands*
> *'Til we have built Jerusalem*
> *Throughout these rich and mighty lands . . .*

True progress is not a gift from scientists and Presidents, actual or would-be. In the words of Arthur F. Bentley[37] it can come only from the endless processes of social conflict and adaptation, and will continuously emerge, along with some retrogression, "not as progress but as progresses."

•NOTES

1. Thomas A. Bailey, *Presidential Greatness* (New York: Appleton-Century-Crofts, 1966), p. 320.

2. Senator J. W. Fulbright, "The Great Society Is a Sick Society," *The New York Times*, magazine section, August 20, 1967.

3. Richard E. Neustadt, *Presidential Power* (New York: Wiley, 1966), p. 1.

4. The use of the term "society" underscores the shift of attention from mainly economic to broader social or cultural considerations. In addition to the kinds of societies already called for, we may confidently expect efforts to use such adjectives as the following (in alphabetical order): active, beautiful, civilized, decent, good, human, humane, just, loving, modest, new, peaceful, responsible, sane, wise, and young. But before all such adjectival variants could be tried the noun itself will undoubtedly be worn out and new slogan styles will be invented. In time, the past shift (from an implicit orientation to *economy* to an explicit focussing on *society*) is bound to be followed by a broader focus on the *world community*.

5. Victor A. Thompson, *Modern Organization* (New York: Knopf, 1961), pp. 10, 95.

6. See particularly the discussion of social change and concept obsolescence in Bertram M. Gross and Michael Springer, "New Goals for Social Information," *Social Goals and Indicators for American Society*, Volume II, *The Annals* (September 1967), pp. 213–214.

7. Roberta Wohlstetter, *Pearl Harbor: Warning and Decision* (Stanford: Stanford University Press, 1962), pp. 310–312.

8. Wohlstetter, *op. cit.*, p. 393.

9. The background on this development is reviewed in Bertram M. Gross and Michael Springer, "A New Orientation in American Government," *Social Goals and Indicators for American Society*, Volume I, *The Annals* (May 1967).

10. Reference to this development is made in the conclusion of Barry Gottehrer's "Urban Conditions: New York City" in *Social Goals and Indicators for American Society*, Volume I, 158.

11. The concept of "sub-employment" is defined in Note 3 to Chapter 1 of this volume, p. 31.

12. The Economic Report of the President, January 1967, p. 4.

13. S. M. Miller et al., "Poverty, Inequality and Conflict," *Social Goals and Indicators for American Society*, Volume II, 19–23. The information on the percentage of families with less than half the median income is taken from Victor R. Fuchs, "Toward a Theory of Poverty," *The Concept of Poverty* (Washington, D. C.: Chamber of Commerce of the United States, 1965).

14. Walt W. Rostow, *The Stages of Economic Growth* (Cambridge, England: Cambridge University Press, 1960).

15. Bertram M. Gross, "The City of Man: A Social Systems Reckoning," in William R. Ewald, Jr., ed., *Environment for Man* (Bloomington: University of Indiana Press, 1967), p. 137.

16. Daniel Bell, "The Post-Industrial Society," in Eli Ginzburg, ed., *Technology and Social Change* (New York: Columbia University Press, 1964).

17. The present ratio of annual capital formation by households to business capital formation is about 7 to 5.

18. Dean Rusk, *Winds of Freedom* (Boston: Beacon, 1962), p. 16.

19. The rationale for doing this was set forth some time ago by Sigmund Timberg in "The Corporation as a Technique of International Administration," *University of Chicago Law Review*, Volume 19 (1952), pp. 739–758.

20. Seventeenth Report of the Commission to Study the Organization of Peace, *New Dimensions for the United Nations*, pp. 36–41.

21. Bailey, *op. cit.*, p. 335.

22. Raymond Moley, "The GOP Mainstream," *Newsweek*, November 13, 1967.

23. Daniel P. Moynihan, "Urban Conditions: General," *Social Goals and Indicators for American Society*, Volume I, pp. 159–177.

24. Geoffrey Gorer, *The American People* (revised ed.; New York: Norton, 1964), p. 197.

25. Gorer, *op. cit.*, p. 265.

26. John M. Keynes, "Economic Possibilities for Our Grandchildren" (1930), *Essays on Persuasion* (New York: Norton, 1963), pp. 366–367.

27. Lyndon B. Johnson, Madison Square Garden address, October 31, 1964.

28. A more ample formulation of this approach is found in the discussion of "Urban Areas as Open System Clusters," Gross, *op. cit.*

29. Gorer, *op. cit.*, p. 176.

30. Neustadt, *op. cit., passim.*

31. Bailey, *op. cit.*, p. 253.

32. Bertram M. Gross, "Political Process," *Encyclopedia of the Social Sciences* (New York: Macmillan, 1968).

33. A. H. Maslow (with Larry P. Gross), "Synergy in Society and Individual," *Journal of Individual Psychology*, XX (1964), 153–164. The idea of synergy was first developed by sociologist Lester Ward.

34. Herman Kahn and Anthony J. Wiener, *The Year 2000* (New York: Macmillan, 1967), p. 67.

35. Neustadt, *op. cit.*, p. 181.

36. Amitai Etzioni, "Toward a Theory of Societal Guidance," *American Journal of Sociology*, LXXIII, No. 2 (September 1967), 173–187. This theme is elaborated in the same author's *The Active Society: A Theory of Societal and Political Processes* (New York: Free Press, 1968).

37. Arthur F. Bentley, *Relativity in Man and Society* (New York: Putnam, 1926).

Index